THE GUINNESS BOOK OF
DECISIVE BATTLES

THE GUINNESS BOOK OF

DECISIVE BATTLES

GEOFFREY REGAN

GUINNESS PUBLISHING

To Claire Oulton, with thanks

Published in Great Britain by Guinness Publishing Ltd.,
33 London Road, Enfield, Middlesex EN2 6DJ

'GUINNESS' is a registered trademark of Guinness Publishing Ltd.

First published 1992

ISBN 0–85112–520–4

British Library Cataloguing-in-Publication Data:
A catalogue record for this book is available from the British
Library.

Designed by Cathy Shilling

Maps by Lovell Johns Ltd.

Typeset by Ace Filmsetting Ltd., Frome, Somerset

Printed and bound in Great Britain by The Bath Press, Bath

Picture acknowledgements

The publishers would like to thank the following for permission to
reproduce the pictures in this book, which are individually credited
by the abbreviations listed below:

AAAC	Ancient Art and Architecture Collection
AKG	Archiv für Kunst und Geschichte
BAL	Bridgeman Art Library
CV	Collection Viollet
GAMMA	Gamma (Paris)
HDC	Hulton Deutsch Collection
IPA	Interfoto-Pressebild-Agentur
ME	Mary Evans Picture Library
PN	Peter Newark's Military/Historical Pictures
RC	Royal Collection; reproduced by gracious permission of Her Majesty the Queen

Contents

Contents

Introduction

I believe the early Victorian writer Sir Edward Creasey was the first historian to collect a series of 'decisive battles' – 15 in his case – though even in classical times writers were well aware that certain battles had been of far greater significance than others. In Creasey's words, 'There are some battles . . . which claim our attention, independently of the moral worth of the combatants, on account of their enduring importance, and by reason of the practical influence on our own social and political condition, which we can trace up to the results of those engagements. They have for us an abiding and actual interest, both while we investigate the chain of causes and effects, by which they have helped to make us what we are; and also while we speculate on what we probably should have been, if any one of those battles had come to a different termination.'

While the eternal 'ifs' of history are one of the subject's most interesting sidelines, they involve speculation of a kind that is professionally invalid for a serious historian. Moreover, Creasey displays a Victorian's belief that what happened in the past was merely a staging post on the way to the perfection of his present. This approach makes for bad history in that it studies historical events not within the periods in which they occurred, but in terms of the importance that they had for the present age. In this way Creasey could see the triumph of Aetius and the Visigothic king Theodoric over Attila's barbarian hordes at Châlons in 451 as a triumph for Christianity and Western civilization – for which read Victorian England – over the pagan and Asiatic threat from the east. In fact, both Aetius and Theodoric were acting from purely selfish motives, and it is reasonable to assume that neither was thinking of a Victorian gentleman sitting sunning himself on the lawns of a university and tracing his and his country's good fortune to the squabbling of barbarian warlords, who were really concerned more with plunder than anything else. Nor can I agree with the magisterial 18th-century historian Edward Gibbon when he claims that without a Frankish chief's victory over some Muslim raiders in 732 at Tours, 'the interpretation of the Koran would now be taught in the schools of Oxford, and her pupils might demonstrate to a circumcised people the sanctity and truth of the revelation of Mahomet'.

In my choice of decisive battles I have been guided not by what effect they have had on the present but by how they decided the outcome of struggles between forces within a historical period. These forces could be nation-states as at Orléans or Austerlitz; religious groupings as at Yarmuk, Hattin or Breitenfeld; factions within a state as at Marston Moor or Gettysburg; or racial and colonial struggles as at Tenochtitlán, Plassey and Dien Bien Phu. Yet even here similarities are misleading and conclusions valid only within the period in which the battle took place. The dangers for the historian of claiming too much for his choices are obvious. Long-term consequences are scarcely ever present in the minds of the participants of a battle, however decisive it might be. Harold Godwinson at Hastings was fighting for his life and crown, not for the future of an England he would never see. And Hastings as a battle was decisive because it brought to a deadly conclusion the struggle for the crown of England between two men. Yet the historian is entitled to claim more than the mere fact that the Norman William succeeded and the Saxon Harold failed. This was the immediate result of the fight and the short-term consequence was an imposition of Norman rule in England. Yet few historians would stop there. Without Hastings the social and constitutional reforms of the Norman kings could not have taken place in early medieval England. It is not invalid, therefore, to move from the short-term consequence to the medium term, provided that we are moving out from the event rather than backwards from the effect and explaining it through manufacturing the cause, as Gibbon was doing by exaggerating the importance of a battle at Tours to explain an 18th- or 19th-century phenomenon.

Many of my choices will arouse little controversy: Salamis, Gaugamela, Hastings, Manzikert, Waterloo and so on, but others may not be so generally well-known: Pyrrhus' defeat at Beneventum, for instance, or the battles at Yarmuk, Ain Jalut, Tannenburg, Rocroi and Königgrätz. In each case I have tried to justify my choice and to explain in what way each battle was decisive within its period. I have cautiously moved forward to examine medium- and long-term consequences without, I hope, falling into the same error that I feel distorted Creasey's original selection. Obviously some battles have been omitted that appear in other selections. I find no place for Marathon, whose effects have, I fear, been much exaggerated by generations of Classical scholars. Marathon settled nothing. It certainly did not prevent the Persians returning to attack Greece ten years later. Only after Salamis – and Plataea – were the Greeks able to feel sure of their freedom from Persian power. Nor do I consider the defeat of Hannibal's brother Hasdrubal at the River Metaurus in 207 BC the equal of Scipio's victory over the master himself at Zama. The effect of seeing his brother's head catapulted into his camp was no doubt disturbing for Hannibal, but it did not put an end to the Carthaginian threat; only the defeat of Hannibal's own army could do that. And so one could go on. The importance of Châlons rests in Creasey's over-fertile imagination, while Tours was merely an opportunity for Gibbon to demonstrate his irrational contempt for the Byzantines. For Gibbon nothing that Leo the Isaurian could do at Constantinople could match the achievement of the tall, axe-wielding Frankish warriors.

The choice of battles has been mine and the reader is entitled to weigh my evidence in the balance and find me wanting if he or she chooses. As in so many other fields, 'choice' is contentious, and to claim that the battles discussed in these pages comprise the fifty *most* decisive battles in history is more than I dare to suggest. I would like to conclude by thanking Ian Crofton of Guinness Publishing for his help with this book. His assistance has been invaluable.

The Battle of Salamis 480 BC

The ascendancy of Europe over Asia and the legacy of Greek civilization are just two of the building blocks of the modern world that are taken for granted by today's Europeans. Yet there was a time when the existence of an independent Greece – even of Europe itself – had to be fought for against the overwhelming might of the Persian Empire of the 5th century BC. Victory at Marathon in 490 BC, followed ten years later by the decisive naval encounter of Salamis and the land battle at Plataea, not only ensured the independence of Greece, but allowed Greek civilization to reach its brilliant apogee later in the century. Even more than that, the naval victory at Salamis opened the way for Alexander the Great to reverse the process by which successive kings of Persia had invaded Greece, allowing him to conquer Persia and spread Greek civilization throughout the known world.

After the failure of the Persian king Darius's invasion of Greece in 490 BC, his son Xerxes laboured long and hard to make sure that the Persians did not fail a second time. While Xerxes assembled huge military and naval forces, the Athenian leader Themistocles persuaded the citizens of Athens to strengthen their fleet in anticipation of a renewed struggle. Themistocles was, in the words of Herodotus,

a man who exhibited the most indubitable signs of genius; indeed, in this particular he has a claim on our admiration quite extraordinary and unparalleled. By his own native capacity, alike unformed and unsupplemented by study, he was at once the best judge in those sudden crises that admit of little or no deliberation, and the best prophet of the future, even to its most distant possibilities.

In other words, Themistocles was a man with strategic vision, rightly seeing that the success or failure of any Persian invasion would depend on Xerxes' capacity to keep his vast army supplied by sea. If the Greeks could only defeat the Persian fleet then the whole great army of Asia would be helplessly exposed.

In 480 BC Xerxes began to move his army into Europe across a bridge of boats spanning the Hellespont (the strait between the Aegean and the Sea of Marmara) – an engineering miracle for that time. The Greeks had ample warning of his coming, but many seemed paralysed by fear. The Delphic Oracle warned the Athenians, 'Wretches why sit you here ? Fly, fly to the ends of creation.' This singularly depressing prophecy might have persuaded weaker men to give up the struggle altogether, but the Athenians, not content with the Oracle's answer, asked again. This time the oracle spoke of safety in 'wooden walls' – perhaps the triremes that

Greek soldier and Persian in combat. PN

9

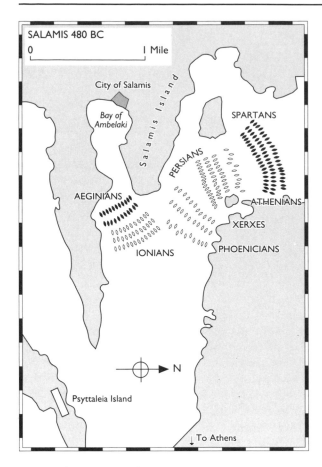

Attention now shifted to the sea, where the decisive encounter would take place – for without defeating the Greek navy the Persians could never feel secure in their conquests. The massive Persian fleet, estimated by Herodotus at 1200 vessels – mostly triremes 100 feet in length and narrow in the beam – had already suffered losses in a storm off Cape Sepias, so that perhaps a third of their number had been wrecked or driven aground. But it was still a mighty armada, which had drawn on the strength of many sea-going peoples. Prominent among these was Artemesia of Helicarnassus, an Amazon of a woman who commanded some of the strongest ships in the Persian fleet. She won the undying hatred of the Greeks by capturing one of their galleys and hanging the captain over the prow with his throat cut, so that his blood could flow into the sea as a libation. The Spartans, outraged at her behaviour, put a price on her head – which no one ever collected.

The allied Greek fleet, with more soldiers aboard than sailors, was ostensibly under the command of the grizzled Spartan general, Eurybiades. Of 366 triremes under his command, 89 were Spartan, 97 came from the Greek islands of the Cyclades, and 180 were new Athenian vessels under the command of Themistocles. At a council of war the Greeks were again divided as to whether to fight at Salamis or withdraw south. Themistocles addressed Eurybiades, the commander-in-chief with these words:

With thee it rests, O Eurybiades! to save Greece, if thou wilt only hearken unto me, and give the enemy battle here, rather than yield to the advice of those among us, who would have the fleet withdraw to the Isthmus. Hear now, I beseech thee, and judge between the two courses. At the Isthmus thou wilt fight in the open sea, which is greatly to our disadvantage... If, on the other hand, thou doest as I advise, these are the advantages which thou wilt secure: in the first place, as we shall fight in the narrow sea with a few ships against many, if the war follows the common course, we shall gain a great victory, for to fight in a narrow space is favourable to us – in an open sea, to them . . .

Themistocles got his way – but only just. Now he had to convince the Persians to come out and fight. He used the ruse of sending deserters to Xerxes with a story that the Greeks had lost heart and were preparing to retreat. As a result, on 22 September, the Persian fleet, in a crescent formation, approached the island of Psyttaleia, behind which the Greek fleet was waiting, between Salamis and Heracleion. Xerxes and his vast entourage established themselves on the slopes of Mount Ægaleos and prepared to watch the battle. Their

were at that moment being constructed all along the coast of Attica. Themistocles next made the brave decision to abandon Athens to the invader and evacuate his people to the nearby island of Salamis as a temporary refuge. The people complained, but the majority agreed to be ferried to the island and housed in primitive huts made of straw and branches. Meanwhile, an Athenian summons had gone out to all the Greeks to assemble their ships at the Straits of Salamis, near the port of Piraeus. Here, according to Themistocles, the Persian fleet should be given battle; but there were many Greek leaders who disagreed with him, pressing for a retreat south to the Peloponnese.

The Spartans, tied by a military tradition that discouraged the sort of novel ideas proposed by Themistocles, sent Leonidas and 300 hoplites (heavily armed infantrymen) to hold the pass at Thermopylae against the tidal wave of Persian power. Incredibly Leonidas and his 300 Spartans held Xerxes in check until a traitor betrayed a secret path to the Persians; this allowed them to fall on the Spartans from the rear and slay them to the last man. It was a heroic – but pointless – sacrifice: the Persians marched on, overunning Athens and burning the Acropolis. Themistocles' decision to evacuate the city had been justified.

camp, with its brightly coloured carpets, luxurious furniture and purple and gold silks hanging from tents shaped more like palaces, stood out brilliantly against the green slopes of the hillside and the cobalt blue sky. In front of Xerxes' tent a great golden throne had been set up, behind which stood slaves with fans, and the nobles who held the royal sword and cup. Sloping away towards the water were the 10,000 'Immortals', Xerxes' royal guard, with plaited hair and beards and ornate tunics of floral and geometric shapes, and lining the shore as if watching a sporting event were the uncountable numbers of the Persian army.

The Greek triremes were being watched by their own people on Salamis. For them it was no sporting event, it was a choice between victory and perpetual slavery under a foreign conqueror. And every Greek soldier and oarsman aboard the galleys felt the same. They bent their backs not as the slaves did aboard the Persian galleys because of the lash, but as free men determined to defend their freedom with their lives. In the van of the Greek fleet were their best ships, filled with heavily armed hoplites, wearing helmets, body armour and carrying great round shields. It was these men who, with sword

Salamis involved more men and more ships than any other naval battle of the ancient world. ME

THE ATHENIAN TRIREME

Beam: 12 ft, 18 ft outrigger
Oar length: 15 ft
Draught: 4 ft
Crew: 170 rowers (62 upper, 54 middle, 54 lower); between 10–30 hoplites; 4 archers; 15 deckhands; flautist to keep time; and the captain (trierarch).

The rowers were not slaves but trained oarsmen, who would fight in a battle. The hoplites were heavily armed professional soldiers. Leather screens protected the rowers from arrows during a battle. The trireme was so heavily armed and crewed that it could not carry provisions and needed to return to base each evening for food and water. This dependence on a home base hampered long-range operations unless supply ships accompanied the fleet, as during the Athenian expedition to Syracuse.

and javelin, would bear the brunt of the fight against the more lightly armed Persian marines.

On the left of the Persian fleet as it advanced was the Phoenician squadron, manned by elite mariners, men who roved the length and breadth of the Mediterranean and even the seas beyond. On the right were the ships from the Greek cities of Ionia, allies of the Persians from Miletus, Samothrace and Ephesus. In the centre of the Persian line were the ships from Asia Minor, filled with Babylonian and Median archers. Against them came the Greek galleys, with the Athenians on the right, the Spartans on the left, and the ships from the Cyclades in the centre. As the Persians drew into sight the Greeks took up the strains of their battle hymn, the Pæan.

As the fleets dashed together all manoeuvring ceased and a vast melee ensued. Hundreds of galleys locked together, providing a platform for the thousands of soldiers to fight hand-to-hand. But the bronze beaks of the Athenian galleys were still ripping into Persian hulls and Themistocles drove on and on, punching a hole through the Phoenicians who faced him. Here was the crux of the fight: Athenian hoplites against Phoenician sailors. Away from shore, with room to manoeuvre, the result could not have been in doubt, but Themistocles crowded his opponents and the well-armed Athenian infantry did the rest. The Persians had misjudged their opponents. By grappling they had given every advantage to the superbly skilled Greek footsoldiers, better by far in close fighting than the Persians. Only their fellow Greeks from Iona fought on equal terms, though for the most part their heart was not in the fight. A notable exception occurred when a Greek galley rammed a ship from Samothrace; before she sank, her crew leaped aboard the attacker and took it over by main force.

As the tide turned against the Persians the rear vessels in the melee tried to disengage, but as they did so they were hit in flank by a small squadron of 30 Aeginian galleys that had been concealed in the bay of Ambelaki. The effect was devastating and panic ran through the massed ranks of the Persian triremes. Showing no mercy the Greeks drove the Persian crews overboard and, as there were few swimmers among them, their losses were enormous. The Persian-held island of Psyttaleia was assaulted by Aristides and his Athenian hoplites and the entire garrison massacred. Defeat was now turning into disaster for the Persians. The Athenian dramatist Æschylus fought at Salamis and lived to record the terror and triumph of that day in his tragedy *The Persians*.

Xerxes, shaken by the terrible fight on the sea in front of his throne, and with the screams of his men on Psyttaleia ringing in his ears, lost his nerve. Handing over command to his satrap Mardonius, he ordered a return to the Hellespont. Like Napoleon's retreat from Moscow, Xerxes' return from Salamis was accompanied by every conceivable disaster. Disease and famine thinned the ranks of his once great army, and the wind had so battered his bridge of boats that the army had to wait for the remnants of the fleet to return to ferry them over the Hellespont. The army he had left under Mardonius was crushed the following year by a united Greek army at Plataea.

The Greek triumph at Salamis destroyed Persian naval domination of the Aegean. Never again could Persia sustain a large army in Greece, and thus threaten Greek independence. In the following century, Greece – united under the Macedonian hegemony of Alexander the Great – was to turn the tables on the Persian Empire, culminating in Alexander's victory at Gaugamela.

The Athenian Expedition to Syracuse 415–413 BC

The Athenian expedition to Syracuse during the Peloponnesian War – the terrible internecine struggle between Athens and Sparta and their respective allies (458–404 BC) – was one of the greatest naval operations of the Greek world. Ostensibly it was undertaken to support a military ally – Segesta, a small city in the northwest of the island of Sicily – but its real purpose was to conquer the whole island (which comprised a number of independent Greek colonies) as a prelude to even greater territorial expansion in the western Mediterranean. It was to be the first step in Athens' 'Grand Design', aimed at expanding at the expense of Carthage, whose colonies extended from North Africa to southern Spain and Etruria in central Italy. If successful, Athens would have turned the Mediterranean into her own ocean centuries before the Romans accomplished it. Yet it was an unwarranted strategic gamble on the part of Athens, based on an inadequate knowledge of the size and geography of Sicily, and could only have succeeded if the Athenians had been able to rely on substantial military aid and money from Sicilian cities hostile to Syracuse. If such help was not forthcoming, and if Syracuse gained help from Athens' enemy Sparta, then the expedition would be a failure.

The expedition that sailed in July 415 BC was commanded by three ill-assorted generals. The richest and, at 60, the oldest of them was Nicias, an experienced officer, but one plagued by nephritis, a serious disease of the kidneys, which made him tire easily and shirk decisions. His wide business contacts gave him connections in high places in Syracuse, and this, it was hoped, might enable him to secure an easy victory through the collusion of fifth columnists in the city. With Nicias sailed the 'heroic Lamarchus', an elderly soldier who had given Athens good service in his younger days. With none of Nicias' wealth or contacts his voice counted for less in decision-making, yet he was 'still a firebrand . . . and adventurous in battle'. The third commander was twenty years younger than his colleagues and one of the most brilliant if flawed Athenians of his age. Alcibiades had been the ward of the great Pericles and the friend of Socrates, but he was also a monstrous egotist and though at 38 somewhat thicker in the waist and fuller in the face than in his youth, he was still Athens' acknowledged *enfant terrible*. Alcibiades made friends and enemies

Bronze figure of a Greek warrior in hoplite armour dating from the 5th century BC. PN

with equal facility, and some of the latter were prepared to see the entire expedition fail as a way of striking him down. In any case, he was embarking with the fleet with an accusation of blasphemy hanging over him. He had stood trial for allegedly profaning the Eleusian Mysteries at his house. The accusation, potentially a capital offence, had been suspended pending his return from Sicily.

Athens had already stretched its military resources to their limits in fifteen years of warfare, and for this expedition she needed to hire large numbers of mercenaries to support her own hoplites. In fact, just 1500 of the 9000 front line soldiers were Athenian, the rest coming from allied states like Argos, Mantinea, Arcadia, Rhodes and Crete. The army amounted to a total of 27,810 fighting men and the navy to 15,250 sailors, oarsmen and marines.

The Athenians had expected to gain support from the Greek cities in the toe of Italy but received a shock when none of them – not even Athens' allied city Rhegium – would offer aid or even allow the fleet to enter harbour, preferring to remain neutral in the struggle ahead. Frustrated at this setback, Nicias wanted to return to Athens, but Alcibiades insisted that the fleet should travel around the coast of Sicily, calling on city after city to support the Athenian cause. He gained some success, for example acquiring a naval base at Catania, but more significantly his actions gave the

---

Retreating from Syracuse, some 18,000 Athenians were massacred on the banks of a muddy stream called the Assinarus. ME

Syracusans warning that the Athenians were going to attack and allowed them time to prepare their defences and contact their allies.

A major blow to the Athenian cause was struck when the Athenian state galley, the *Salaminia,* arrived in Sicily with warrants for the return of Alcibiades and some of his colleagues to answer charges of impiety – he was accused of knocking the faces and phalluses off the statues of Hermes that stood at street corners in Athens. It was a trumped up charge but Alcibiades was unwilling to face trial – and possible execution – in Athens, where he had too many enemies. As he said, 'When my life's at stake, I wouldn't trust my own mother to vote for an acquittal.' On the journey back to Athens Alcibiades made his escape and fled to Sparta. Tried *in absentia* he was found guilty and sentenced to death. On hearing the verdict, Alcibiades retorted, 'I'll show them I'm still alive.' He promised the Spartans, 'that he would render them services greater than all the harm he had done them, when he was their enemy'. And he was as good as his word.

Throughout 414 BC the Athenians blockaded

Syracuse, certain that victory was imminent. However, by settling for a prolonged siege the numerically superior Athenians were allowing the Syracusans to dictate the conduct of the war. While Lamarchus favoured direct assaults he was forced to submit to Nicias' 'over-cautious and hesitant tactics'. Nicias was simply waiting for Syracuse to surrender, confident that his fifth column in the city would achieve victory for him without the need to fight. But he was wrong. In Sparta, Alcibiades had persuaded the government to send aid to Syracuse in the person of an able general named Gylippus, with a small fleet of 14 galleys. How the Athenians must have regretted the time they had wasted. Now the struggle became one of survival. So slack was the Athenian blockade of the harbour that Gylippus with his flotilla was able to slip in undetected. The Spartan immediately set about revitalizing the Syracusans, giving them the will to win that had been lacking since the Athenian fleet had first arrived. But he had come not a moment too soon. A radical group – perhaps in the pay of Nicias – had won over the Syracusans to the idea of surrender. Gylippus soon put a stop to that. He immediately completed the counter-walls that the defenders had been building to prevent Nicias ringing the city with siege walls. The addition of Spartan and Corinthian ships to the Syracusan fleet meant that the Athenians were in danger of losing their supremacy at sea. And to compound Athenian woes, Lamarchus was unnecessarily killed in a skirmish and Nicias – now suffering severely from his nephritis – was left in sole command.

Gylippus had an unpleasant and cold personality even for a Spartan – for the Spartans were a people who cultivated a harsh austerity. But what he lacked in generosity and sophistication he more than made up for in military skill and determination. He soon came to understand the limitations of the Syracusan soldiers and did not make the mistake of expecting of them what he would of Spartans. After one setback he called his men together and apologized for his mistakes. The fault had been his not theirs, he told them. While Gylippus worked busily to turn raw recruits into trained soldiers, and the city's motley array of ships into a fleet strong enough to match the Athenians, Nicias became even more indecisive. Having placed all his hopes on a negotiated surrender, the Athenian commander seemed to collapse when this plan failed. He sent messages back to Athens asking to be relieved, but his request was denied. He explained that the fleet was deteriorating day by day, and was in desperate need of an overhaul, while the soldiers deserted or succumbed to disease. Athens must send a new

expedition – at least the size of the first one – or be prepared to evacuate her troops. Nicias won no sympathy in Athens: had he returned he would probably have faced execution for his failure. Yet his poor health made him unfit for active service. When the Athenians grasped the nettle and prepared a new expedition, they sent their best general – Demosthenes – surely a match for Gylippus.

But even the arrival of Demosthenes with fresh troops and ships did not relieve the depression in the Athenian camp. In order to enforce the siege the Athenians had to set up their tents on low-lying swampy ground, where they were prone to fever and sickness. Nicias himself was virtually confined to his bed and by the summer of 413 BC the Athenians were clearly in trouble. Demosthenes decided to gamble on an all-out night attack by the full Athenian force of nearly 40,000 men, including 9500 elite hoplites, to capture the Syracusan counter-wall. Planning to make use of moonlight, the attackers found that the harvest moon was inadequate to help them find their way across the rocky ground. With the moon behind them they cast long shadows ahead of them, concealing bushes, rocks and undergrowth. The moonlight even glinted from the enemy's shields and spears and blinded the attackers. It was a fiasco. The Syracusans fought on the defensive, meeting the Athenians with an unbroken shieldwall, while the attackers stumbled

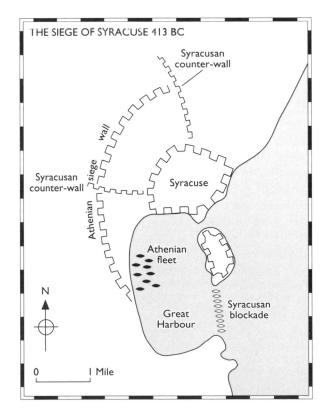

THE SIEGE OF SYRACUSE 413 BC

Syracusan counter-wall

siege wall

Syracusan counter-wall

Athenian siege wall

Syracuse

Athenian fleet

Great Harbour

Syracusan blockade

N

0   1 Mile

and fell, fought with each other, and finally fled in headlong retreat. In this single attack Demosthenes lost 2000 men killed and many more injured. He now saw that there was no chance of success and that the only option was to raise the siege and retreat while they still could. Yet the sickly Nicias persuaded him to delay the evacuation, believing that the Syracusans would still force the Spartans to surrender the city to him. This was wishful thinking. Another month passed, during which more Spartan reinforcements arrived on the island. Demosthenes pressed Nicias for an immediate withdrawal. The Athenian camp resounded to the cries of delirious men screaming in the throes of malaria and dysentery, while others raised the angry chant of 'Take us home'. At last a date was set for the evacuation – 27 August – but as fate would have it a lunar eclipse occurred on the night chosen, 'a supernatural portent and a warning from the gods that fearful calamities were at hand'. Nicias, we are told by the historian Thucydides, was a great believer in omens and superstitions and decided that there was no option now but to honour the fates and wait the 'thrice nine days prescribed by the soothsayers'.

The Syracusans drove home their advantage. Gylippus had transformed their fighting ships by introducing Corinthian-style rams and by strengthening the bows with extra planking to allow head-on ramming. He was eager to prevent the Athenians from evacuating their camp by seizing control of the harbour. But to achieve this he needed supremacy at sea. The Syracusans tried a ploy to force the Athenian ships to leave their naval stockade. A Syracusan boy rowed a small boat over to the Athenian stockade and began to call out abuse at a trireme commander, who responded by chasing him out to sea. Several Syracusan vessels now rowed to the boy's rescue, while the Athenians sent other galleys to support their first trireme. By a process of escalation a full-fleet battle ensued between 76 Syracusan and 84 Athenian galleys. Gylippus was totally vindicated: 25 Athenian ships were sunk or captured, and Athenian supremacy at sea was broken. To the horror of Demosthenes, Gylippus now blocked the mouth of the harbour with a line of triremes and merchant ships chained together, cutting off the Athenians' last escape route by sea.

The dreadful retreat by land began on 11 September. Some 40,000 men – assembled in two huge hollow squares, one commanded by Nicias, the other by Demosthenes – began the march towards the city of Catania. But the Syracusans and their allies were waiting for them and hunted them through the countryside, keeping them away from any water. Eventually, when the thirst–crazed Athenians broke ranks and struggled towards the muddy stream of Assinarus, the Syracusans closed in and began massacring them until the water was red from blood and heaving like the sea from the death struggles of the doomed Athenians. It was the most terrible slaughter in Greek history – probably 18,000 men died in the river and along its banks. So terrible was the scene that Nicias rode up to Gylippus and threw himself at his feet, begging him to stop. Few Athenians – less than 1000 of the entire force – escaped to reach Catania. The rest were slaughtered by the relentless Syracusans, or taken to end their days working in the stone quarries, each man branded on the forehead like a dumb beast. Thucydides writes that 'no single suffering to be apprehended by men thrust into such a place was spared them'.

The fate of Demosthenes and Nicias was particularly atrocious. Having surrendered to Gylippus on a promise of their lives, they were tortured and executed by the Syracusans, who no longer listened to their Spartan commander. The bodies of the two generals were thrown naked outside the city gates 'as a public spectacle'. Nothing more clearly illustrated the failure of the Athenians than the sight of dogs ripping at the corpses of men who had left Athens rich in honour, wealth and years only to end as offal for scavengers.

The disaster at Syracuse marked a collapse in the fortunes of Athens, and in the next eight years she suffered defeat after defeat, culminating in the Spartan victory at Aegospotami in 405 BC, which concluded the Peloponnesian War. It was the end of Athenian military hegemony in the Greek world, and marked the failure of the Greeks to establish their dominion over the states of the western Mediterranean. Had Athens succeeded in conquering Sicily, and extending her influence into central Italy and North Africa, it is inconceivable that the Romans would have emerged as the dominant force in the Mediterranean in the 3rd century BC.

The Battle of Gaugamela 331 BC

Whether Alexander the Great burned the great Persian capital of Persepolis in 331 BC as retaliation for Persian depredations in Greece in the days of Marathon and Salamis, or in a drunken fit at the prompting of a prostitute, we will never know. But the event had symbolic importance: the Greeks had ended the threat from the east and would now carry their civilization and culture throughout the Middle East and to the gates of India. Alexander's crushing victory at Gaugamela gave birth to the Hellenistic Age, in which east and west were brought together in commerce and culture, a process completed under the Roman Empire.

Inheriting a powerful army from his father – Philip of Macedon – as well as a united Greece, Alexander took up his father's mission of war against the national enemy – Persia. In spring 334 BC he crossed into Asia at the head of a veteran Macedonian and allied Greek army of 40,000 infantry and 7000 cavalry. Although in the Persians he would face the greatest military power on earth, Alexander was confident in the quality of his troops and in his own revolutionary tactics. Victories at the River Granicus, Tyre and Issus confirmed his

opinion, and within three years he was ready to deal with Darius, the Persian emperor, once and for all. By September 331 BC he had located Darius and his huge army north of the River Tigris, near the great plain of Gaugamela.

The size of the Persian army is impossible to estimate, as contemporaries were so overwhelmed by its teeming numbers that they resorted to figures far beyond the capacity of any ancient logistical system to support. Some details are precise, for example Darius had 200 scythe-wheeled chariots and 15 elephants; but others, such as claims that he had 40,000 cavalry and 1 million infantry, are at the best dubious, and at the worst fantastical. Nevertheless, troops came from throughout Darius's widespread empire, and Alexander's army was clearly outnumbered by perhaps four or five to one. From Scythia, Sogdiana and Bactria, south of the Aral Sea, the Satrap Bessus brought heavily armoured cataphtacts, both rider and horse encased in lamellar armour; from Parthia, Media and Mesopotamia Darius's best general, Mazeus, brought horse archers, while from the furthest east of the empire came Indians, Afghans and Arachosians under Satibazarnes. But the whole was far less than the sum of its parts. Only the presence of Darius himself tied together these disparate peoples; should he fall in battle or flee, then the whole mighty force might simply disintegrate as their focus disappeared.

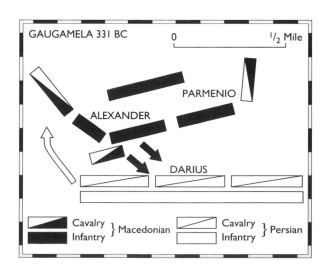

Darius had waited months for this moment. He would at last be able to fight Alexander on ground that he had prepared: near Gaugamela, a small village alongside the River Bumodus and not far from the ruins of ancient Nineveh, lay a vast plain, especially flattened to provide prime conditions for his chariots and masses of cavalry. This was where the decisive battle would be fought.

Hearing of the arrival of the Persian army Alexander made camp, leaving behind all his prisoners, baggage and pack animals in the care of camp followers. Next he advanced in battle formation onto a treeless ridge, where he could look out across the vast plain to where the Persians were encamped. Rejecting Parmenio's suggestion for a night attack to offset the Macedonian inferiority in numbers, Alexander allowed his army to rest, and retired to his tent to sleep. The Persians, fearing that he would attack them by night, spent a long, exhausting vigil at battle stations, without food or rest.

Alexander had taken immense care over his order of battle, reinforcing his central Macedonian phalanx with a rear phalanx, made up of mercenaries and Greek allied troops. If Darius's vast force succeeded in outflanking his army and attacking the rear, these men would simply about-face and present the Persians with an impenetrable defence. On his left – the defensive wing – Alexander placed Parmenio, with Thracian and Thessalian cavalry, while he led the right himself, with his Companion cavalry. It was with this strong right wing that he expected to make the decisive breakthrough when the time came.

At dawn Alexander rose and dressed in his ceremonial armour, before praying to Father Zeus. His men were delighted to see his prayer answered immediately, for an eagle was observed flying in the direction of the Persians – a certain portent of victory. The Macedonians now marched down onto the plain, and it soon became apparent that the Persian battle-front was so long that it would outflank them on both sides. Alexander, aware of the risk of encirclement, ordered his right wing to begin a general move to the right, forcing the Scythian and Bactrian cavalry opposite him to move to their left, until both the Macedonians and their enemies were separated from the centres of their armies. But Alexander was confident in the capacity of his phalanx commanders to operate independently and was feinting a flank attack in the hope that the Persian army would crack open as he pulled its left wing further and further from the centre; if this happened, he planned to strike with his cavalry at the point where the break occurred.

Darius, meanwhile, was furious to see Alexander's manoeuvre as it took the Macedonians away from the flat ground that had been specially prepared for his chariots. Hoping to pin down their right wing Darius launched swarms of cavalry against Alexander, throwing up clouds of choking dust, and a full-scale cavalry battle ensued. The heavily armoured Scythians inflicted heavy casualties on the Greeks, but Alexander knew that even at this early stage of the battle the crisis had arrived and he spared no efforts in repelling Bessus, pouring in every trooper he had and mixing his javelin-men and archers with the cavalry. As the battle swayed back and forth Darius launched his chariots, but they proved wholly ineffective. The Agrianian light infantry and javelin men easily dodged the clumsy vehicles, killing the drivers, and sometimes leaping onto the backs of the running horses and cutting the reins. Those chariots that were allowed to pass through to the rear unharmed were destroyed there by the hypaspists (light infantry).

With his left-wing cavalry falling back, Darius detached a large force of Persian cavalry from his centre, leaving a gap of the kind Alexander had been trying to create. Showing a masterly appreciation of the situation Alexander recognized that the decisive moment was at hand, and sent for his favourite horse, Bucephalus – now 24 years of age – who was being held by a groom for the climactic charge.

Rallying his Companion cavalry and mounted on Bucephalus, Alexander charged leftwards, straight for the gap and for Darius himself. Simultaneously the central Macedonian phalanx advanced, closing in on the gap their king had created. Soon the Persian centre began to break up. Darius did not stay to face his brilliant enemy, easily identified by his golden armour, and fled the field, as he had at Issus two years earlier. The Persians had now lost the battle in the centre and on the right, where Aretes' Peaonian cavalry had finally driven Bessus' milling hordes off the field. 'So thick a cloud of dust was raised by the mighty mass of fugitives', wrote Diodorus, 'that nothing could be clearly distinguished and thus the Macedonians lost the track of Darius. The noise of the shouting and the cracking of whips served as guides to the pursuers.'

However, matters had taken a different turn on the left, where Parmenio's wing was breached by Indian cavalry, who, instead of engaging the Macedonians in the rear, kept riding to Alexander's camp – some five miles away – and there engaged the camp-followers and Thracian troops who had been

---

Alexander (left) leads his cavalry against Darius (centre) at the battle of Issus (333 BC) in this reconstruction of the famous mosaic at Pompeii. After this defeat the Persians had one last chance – at Gaugamela. PN

THE GREEK PHALANX

The phalanx was not a Greek invention – similar formations had been used by the Assyrians and Egyptians – but it was brought to perfection in the ancient world by Philip of Macedon, building on the model developed by Epaminondas of Thebes. The Macedonian phalanx – used by Alexander in all his battles – comprised 64 *syntagma* (battalions), each of 256 men. Each *syntagma* could be 8 or 16 deep, and its phalangists were armed with the *sarissa* (a long pike some 20 feet long). The front five rows held their *sarissas* horizontally to form an impenetrable hedge of spears, while the centre and rear ranks held their pikes vertically to protect against arrows and missiles falling from above.

left to defend it. But Alexander had allowed for such a breakthrough and the reserve phalanx moved at high speed back to their camp, defeating the enemy cavalry in the process. Parmenio had sent messengers with requests for help to Alexander, who now turned his Companion cavalry and led them across the great plain to shatter Mazaeus's horsemen. News that their leader had left the field so dispirited the Persians that most of them lost heart and fled, with Alexander's cavalry pursuing them relentlessly, even beyond the River Lycus. Darius's camp was taken – as at Issus – though the Persian emperor escaped his pursuers.

It had been a victory for inspired generalship and discipline over mere numbers. Casualties on the Macedonian side were not light, but those suffered by the Persians must have been enormous, for thousands died in the retreat. In victory, Alexander showed magnanimity worthy of his name. He pursued Darius, but more in sorrow than in anger, and when the tragic emperor's body was found, Alexander's anger against his murderer, Bessus, was genuine. Alexander now became 'King of Kings' – on the one hand successor to Darius and on the other, the avenger of the Greeks – a dual role he played with supreme authority.

The battle of Gaugamela was Alexander's greatest victory and its consequences for the ancient world were incalculable. In the words of one historian, 'The previous barriers between East and West were removed, and in the next generation thousands of Greek traders and artisans entered the new world, to seek their fortunes in the new Greek cities, which shot up out of the ground like mushrooms. In this way the two previously detached circles came more and more to coincide and form a single economic circle; and when the western Mediterranean was attracted into the orbit of the great revolution that occurred in the East, there was finally created a world commerce, which embraced the whole inhabited world.'

The Battle of Beneventum 275 BC

In her attempts to become supreme in Italy in the 4th and 3rd centuries BC, Rome faced strong opposition from the Greek cities in the south, particularly Tarentum. When the Romans tried to conquer these cities the Greeks called in support from Pyrrhus, king of Epirus, a state in northern Greece, just 100 miles away across the Adriatic. Pyrrhus – nicknamed the 'Eagle' – was a first cousin of Alexander the Great and the foremost general of his age. His invasion of Italy in 280 BC brought about a decisive clash between the dominant Greek military system and the rising power of Rome. His motives for intervening in Italian affairs are significant. According to Plutarch, Pyrrhus admitted, 'The Romans once conquered, there is neither barbarian nor Greek city there which is a match for us, but we shall at once possess all Italy.' Indeed, Pyrrhus was beginning in the west the kind of campaign of conquest that his cousin Alexander had conducted so successfully in the east, and was planning for the west at the time of his early death. After Italy, Pyrrhus intended to conquer Sicily, Libya, Carthage and Spain.

Pyrrhus sailed from Epirus with an elite army of 20 elephants, 3000 cavalry, 20,000 infantry and 2500 archers and slingmen. He was naturally expecting to receive substantial reinforcements from the Tarentines, as well as from Italian states hostile to Rome, but it was on his Greek troops – particularly the phalangists – that the main burden of fighting would fall. If these should suffer severe losses against the Romans, it would prove difficult to replace them. On his arrival in Italy – after a dreadful storm that scattered his fleet – Pyrrhus heard that a large Roman army was advancing on him. Surprised and impressed by the military discipline of the 'barbarians', as he called the Romans, he attacked them at Heraclea and defeated them after a terrible struggle. Only the panic in the Roman ranks caused by his elephants, each carrying a fighting tower housing archers and pikemen, won him the day. Roman losses of 7000 could be set against Epirot losses of 4000, but it was an expensive victory.

With his local reputation enhanced by the battle, Pyrrhus occupied the Roman camp and received promises of support from some of Rome's enemies, including the Lucanians and Samnites. He next marched up the east coast of Italy, hoping to dictate terms of peace to the Romans, but he had underestimated his enemy. Instead of peace negotiators, a new Roman army under the Consuls Fabricius and Quintus Aemilius confronted him at Asculum. Here Pyrrhus was forced to fight in conditions less suited to his elephants and phalanx, and in a two-

WAR ELEPHANTS

Elephants were widely used in ancient Persian and Indian warfare, and although Alexander the Great found ways of dealing with the threat they posed, he was impressed by the potential of the beasts. His successors – the Diadochi – combined elephants with the phalanx to form a dominant tactic in the warfare of the 3rd century BC. The elephants generally carried a wooden tower from which a pikeman and at least one archer were able to fight, while the beast's driver – almost always an Indian – also fought with javelin or bow. King Pyrrhus of Epirus – Alexander the Great's cousin – used elephants to strike terror into the Romans, notably their cavalry, for horses could not bear the smell of elephants. Hannibal also made great use of African elephants during the Second Punic War. But the elephant could be a double-edged weapon, panicking when hearing trumpets or pricked with spears and trampling friend and foe indiscriminately. To prevent damage to the elephant the Macedonians often used hoops of leather or metal armour.

Pyrrhus, king of Epirus, whose defeat at Beneventum opened the way to the Roman domination of Italy. PN

day struggle only overcame his enemies with great difficulty. Again the elephants won the day for him but it had been a close-run thing. He himself was wounded in the fighting and his casualties of 3500 against 6000 Romans were again felt most heavily by his elite Greek troops. Losses among his senior officers made this truly a 'Pyrrhic victory'. After the battle Pyrrhus was heard to comment, 'If we are victorious in one more battle against the Romans, we shall be utterly ruined.' He could not replace the veteran troops he was losing in this attritional warfare, whereas the Romans seemed to have limitless manpower on which to draw.

During the next two years Pyrrhus campaigned in Sicily, only returning to the Italian mainland at the urgent news from his allies the Samnites and Tarentines that they were in danger of being completely defeated by the Romans. In 275 Pyrrhus faced two new Roman armies: one, under Cornelius Lentulus, was operating in Lucania; the other, led by Manius Curius, had invaded the territory of the Samnites. Pyrrhus divided his own army, sending a force to block Lentulus, while he dealt with Manius Curius himself. His scouts encountered the Romans near Maleventum – significantly later renamed Beneventum by the Romans. The two armies were of almost equal strength at 40,000, though Pyrrhus was now using an increasing number of Italian replacements for his Greek veterans.

Pyrrhus decided to try to take the enemy in the rear. His plan involved a difficult night march that would enable his troops to fall on the Roman camp at the first light of dawn. He selected an elite corps of warriors to make the march, through a forest and up a steep slope to command a ridge. Before ordering the troops to set off, Pyrrhus had an unpleasant experience in which he dreamed that all his teeth fell out and his mouth was filled with blood. Being superstitious, Pyrrhus believed the dream was an augury of disaster and tried to cancel the orders for the night march. But his generals told him that it was much too late to alter the plan and the march went ahead.

The Epirot troops set off into the darkness, taking the best elephants with them, and guided by men with torches, for the night was intensely dark. Unfortunately they had miscalculated the distance involved and all the torches went out before they emerged from the forest. The result was that they were lost amongst the trees and undergrowth and only found their way to the ridge once it was light enough to do so. But in the dawn light they were easily spotted by the Romans, who attacked them and put them to flight.

Manius Curius now turned on Pyrrhus's main

army, driving back one of the wings. But like Alexander at Gaugamela, Pyrrhus personally turned the tide, leading a charge with his Thessalian cavalry that drove the Romans back within their palisaded camp. However, the Romans had learned from their earlier defeats at Heraclea and Asculum. The reserves within their camp now poured out, firing a storm of arrows, spiked objects and heated missiles onto the Greek elephants, which began to panic. One young elephant, maddened by spear points and fiery torches thrust into its face, rushed about the field seeking its mother and crashed into Pyrrhus's phalanx, breaking its cohesion so that the Roman legionaries were able to come to close quarters with the pikemen, whose clumsy weapons made them easy victims for the Roman short swords.

Pyrrhus's army reeled back in chaos and for the first time the 'Eagle' tasted bitter defeat. With just 8000 infantry and 1000 cavalry left to him, he knew that his invasion of Italy had failed and withdrew to Epirus. The Roman victory at Beneventum was to have consequences for both Italy and Greece, consequences that only Pyrrhus realized at the time. He warned his fellow Greek rulers that if the Romans were not stopped in Italy it would not be long before they tried to extend their sovereignty into Greece itself. But Pyrrhus's words went unheeded, and Greece was to make no more effort to maintain the supremacy in the eastern Mediterranean that had been established for her by Alexander the Great. The way was now open for Rome to complete her domination of Italy before setting up 'the universal dominion of Rome'.

The Battle of Zama 202 BC

Zama

Carthaginians
Commander:	Hannibal
Left wing:	3000 Numidian cavalry
Centre:	Hannibal and Mago with 36,000 infantry and 80 elephants
Right wing:	2000 Carthaginian cavalry

Romans
Commander:	Scipio
Left wing:	Laelius with 2000 Roman cavalry
Centre:	Scipio with 29,000 infantry
Right wing:	Masinissa with 4600 Numidian cavalry

The struggle between Rome and Carthage for the control of the Mediterranean – predicted by King Pyrrhus of Epirus in 275 BC – raged for much of the 3rd century BC. Roman successes in the First Punic War, which ended in 241 BC, had cost the Carthaginians control of Sicily and Sardinia. Nevertheless, Carthaginian power in Spain remained strong, and it was from there that the great Carthaginian general Hannibal launched the Second Punic War in 218 BC. For some 16 years Hannibal campaigned in Italy, inflicting on Rome some of the most tremendous defeats in her history. At Trebbia, Lake Trasimene and most notably at Cannae, where as many as 60–70,000 Romans may have died, Hannibal's superiority over Roman generals was demonstrated time and time again. But the resilience of the Romans and their apparently bottomless supply of manpower allowed them to absorb such defeats and hit back against lesser Carthaginian generals. And when, in 207 BC, Hasdrubal tried to join his brother Hannibal with reinforcements, he was defeated by the Consul Nero and his head catapulted into Hannibal's camp. This great Roman victory at the River Metaurus was enough to confine Hannibal, outnumbered and short of supplies, to the toe of Italy.

In Spain the Roman armies were led by a brilliant young general of just 24, Publius Cornelius Scipio. By 205 BC Scipio had cleared the Carthaginians from Spain and had negotiated an alliance with two Numidian chieftains, Syphax and Masinissa. The following year he invaded Africa with an army of 26,000 legionaries and 2000 cavalry, clearly expecting to raise substantial numbers of horsemen from his Numidian allies. Masinissa joined Scipio straight away, but Syphax broke his agreement and decided to side with Hannibal.

In 203 BC Scipio won a series of victories over Carthaginian forces near Utica and the Carthaginians had no option now but to recall their best general – Hannibal – from Italy to defend the homeland. The two great generals – the best that either side had produced in 70 years of warfare – would now fight the decisive battle of the entire conflict. According to Appian, they both understood how high the stakes were. Hannibal apparently declared that 'the battle would decide the fate of Carthage and all Africa', while Scipio admitted that 'there was no safe refuge for his men if they were vanquished'.

In October 202 BC, the two armies met at Draa el Metnan, not far from the Zama ridge. Hannibal fielded 36,000 infantry and 4000 cavalry against Scipio's 29,000 legionaries and 6000 horse, many of them Numidians under Masinissa. Hannibal also used as many as 80 elephants, but some of these were untrained and did more harm than good.

Scipio's army was arrayed in three lines as usual: in the front line were the *hastati*, armed with sword, javelin and shield; in the second line were the *principes*, heavily armoured infantry; while in the third line were the *triarii*, the picked veterans and Scipio's best troops. Because of the threat from Hannibal's elephants, Scipio arranged the *maniples* (companies of 120 infantrymen) in widely dispersed columns so that the crazed animals could rush harmlessly to the rear of the army, being speared on both flanks as they ran. His Roman cavalry – 1500 strong under Laelius – took the left wing, but his 4500 Numidian horsemen under Masinissa were given pride of place on the right, opposite Hannibal's Numidians.

Hannibal's army required expert handling as it was composed of partly veteran and partly inexperienced troops, as well as men of many different nationalities and languages. But Hannibal had more experience than anyone at getting the best out of such disparate resources, and the 10,000 veterans he had brought back from Italy were as sound as any troops on the field. In front of his first line Hannibal placed his elephants, more in hope than expectation. These were not the same experienced beasts he had taken into Italy so many years before, and he could not trust them to do much more than disorder the Roman lines. Behind them were the Ligurian and Gallic mercenaries as well as Balearic slingmen and Moorish spearmen. The second line of Libyans and Carthaginians had been recently recruited but were at least fighting on their home ground. The third line – Hannibal's veteran Bruttians – were kept some 200 yards behind the second line, in case Scipio's cavalry should manage to turn his flanks and attack the rear of the army.

At the start of the battle the Romans, experienced by now at irritating elephants, made such a terrible noise with trumpets and horns that the animals charged all over the place, wrecking Hannibal's left-wing cavalry, which was promptly charged by Masinissa and driven off the field in headlong flight. Other elephants charged relatively harmlessly down the corridors between the Roman *maniples*. Seeing the success of Masinissa on the right, Laelius charged the cavalry facing him and achieved similar success. Hannibal's army had now lost both its wings, but would the triumphant Romans and Numidians return? And if so, would they be in time?

The clash of the infantry now took place, the two front lines laying into each other with sword and spear. Soon the Romans were pressing the Gauls and Ligurians back, in many cases with the weight of their heavy embossed shields. Now it was the turn of the Africans to advance and join battle with the triumphant Roman *hastati*. After an hour of

Hannibal's defeat at Zama marked the end of Carthage as a major power. Even his elephants did Hannibal more harm than good. Contrary to this 18th-century depiction (centre background), war elephants carried no more than three or four men. ME

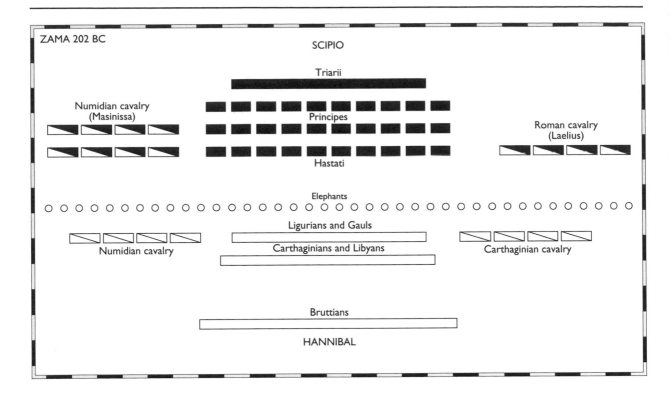

ZAMA 202 BC

SCIPIO

Triarii

Numidian cavalry (Masinissa)

Principes

Roman cavalry (Laelius)

Hastati

Elephants

Ligurians and Gauls

Numidian cavalry

Carthaginians and Libyans

Carthaginian cavalry

Bruttians

HANNIBAL

hand-to-hand fighting, Scipio recalled his first line and extended his front by pushing the second and third lines onto the flanks until they overlapped Hannibal's army on both wings. Hannibal must have blinked at this. Surely Scipio was not going to try to re-enact Cannae against its master architect? But now the Romans were breaking on the rock of Hannibal's Bruttian veterans and the Carthaginians were gaining the upper hand. Hannibal had deliberately spared these men the tiresome work of the early skirmishes so that they would be fresh for this moment. The Roman *hastati* were at the end of their endurance. But suddenly the Roman horse under Laelius returned – as Hannibal feared they might – and charged into the rear of his veterans. This was the end. He was now virtually surrounded and the

battle became a massacre in which perhaps 20,000 of his men died.

Hannibal fled the field when it was clear that his army was disintegrating. The Senate in Carthage immediately surrendered the city to Scipio, who now added the title 'Africanus' to his name. The Carthaginian empire, founded over 400 years before, was ended. Rome was now dominant in Spain and North Africa, as well as in Sicily, Sardinia and Corsica. The western Mediterranean was clearly a Roman sea. Rome now turned her attention to the control of the eastern Mediterranean and the conquest of the Greeks, who had acted as allies of Carthage. Rome would in time conquer both Macedonia and Greece, and become mistress of the entire Mediterranean world.

The Battle of Actium
31 BC

Actium

Antony and Cleopatra

Right wing:	Antony
Centre:	Marcus Octavius
Left wing:	Sosius
Galleys:	230
Marines:	22,000

Octavian

Right wing:	Octavian
Centre:	Arruntius
Left wing:	Agrippa
Galleys:	400
Marines:	40,000

The civil wars that had rent the Roman Republic since the murder of Julius Caesar in 43 BC ended with the defeat of Mark Antony and the Egyptian queen, Cleopatra, at the naval battle of Actium. The joint rule that had been established by Antony and Octavian, Caesar's heir, after their victory over Caesar's murderers at Philippi in 42 BC, had been brought to an end by 33 BC. Octavian and Antony had become rivals for supremacy: Antony dominant in Egypt and the eastern provinces, Octavian in Rome and the west; the third member of the Triumvirate, Lepidus, was insignificant in comparison. The rivalry of Antony and Octavian came to a head when Antony put aside his wife Octavia, sister of Octavian, and married Cleopatra instead, acknowledging her and her son Caesarion as joint rulers of Egypt and Cyprus, and his own children by Cleopatra as rulers of the Eastern Empire. This was a challenge that could not be ignored by Octavian and in accepting it he knew that he had the support of all the people of Italy. They knew that the coming struggle between the two men was more than a personal one; its outcome would decide whether the imperial city on the Tiber would remain the centre of the Roman world or whether Alexandria or some other Hellenistic city of the east would take its place.

Octavian acted quickly to secure the support of the Senate by seizing Antony's will – which was lodged with the Vestal Virgins and therefore supposedly inviolate – and publicly revealing the contents. Dio relates that he made much of the fact that Antony had asked to be buried alongside Cleopatra in Alexandria, fanning the fears of the Italians that he planned to make Egypt the new centre of the empire. Octavian and his party vilified Cleopatra 'with one of the most terrible outbursts of hatred in history', and so successful was their smear campaign that Antony's friends in Italy were forced into silence and the country spoke as if with one voice in urging Octavian to go to war against Antony and the Egyptian 'sorceress'.

Anticipating war, Antony was assembling his forces in Greece. He had 19 legions – not all at full strength and some recently recruited – amounting to over 70,000 men, with perhaps a further 12,000 cavalry. His fleet, supplemented by Egyptian and Phoenician galleys, amounted to some 450 vessels, many of them larger and more heavily armed than those available to Octavian. During the winter of 32/31 BC Antony's forces encamped at Actium on the coast of Epirus, 40 miles south of Corcyra. But such a large army imposed logistical problems, as

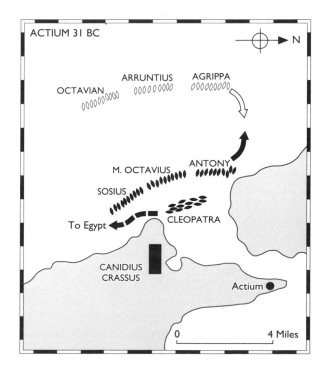

Cleopatra as romantic heroine at Actium. AAAC

fleet at Methone, but when Octavian with eight legions tried to surprise the base at Actium by landing on the coast of Epirus at Fanari, Antony was ready for him and drove him back after a brief encounter. Octavian now established his camp at Mikalitzi, five miles to the north. Yet like knights in a game of chess Octavian and Agrippa were outmanoeuvring the strangely sluggish Antony at every opportunity, cutting off his supply route to Egypt and threatening him with the prospect of starvation or retreat into the barren interior of Greece.

Only now did Antony react – but it was already too late. Shipping a force of cavalry north of Octavian's camp he tried to cut his enemy off from his water supply in the Luro River. The plan might have worked, but part of Antony's force deserted to Octavian and the expedition ended in fiasco. Octavian's grip grew tighter every day and Antony was forced to bring in supplies from the Greek interior over the mountains, using manpower alone. This might serve for a short while but in the long run Antony knew that he faced starvation. In the meantime disease was beginning to ravage his army. As morale plummeted in Antony's camp desertions became a daily affair. Nor was the problem confined to the men alone: one of Antony's senior commanders, Domitius Ahenobarbus, went over to Octavian. Antony responded with honour, sending after him 'all his baggage together with his friends and servants'. His senior officers tried to persuade Antony to withdraw the army into the interior and make a fighting retreat – but Antony knew that he would still face the ever-present spectre of starvation.

In desperation he called a council of war to discuss the remaining options: he could abandon his fleet and withdraw his army to the eastern side of Greece, or he could try to force his way through the naval blockade and leave the army to make its own way to safety. His army commander, Canidius Crassus, argued strongly for a withdrawal into the interior. After all, Octavian had the mastery at sea but on land Antony was the greater general. In a land encounter, Antony's generalship might offset the superior quality of Octavian's Italian legions. But Canidius found an opponent in Cleopatra. She argued that a retreat with a demoralized army was a gamble, particularly if food supplies could not be found, and that the problem of supplies could only be solved by a victory at sea. The fleet would have to break through Agrippa's squadrons and reestablish contact with Egypt. Cleopatra's arguments were conclusive. Yet Antony was not looking for a decisive victory over Agrippa; his fleet was by now

Greece could not keep it supplied indefinitely, and food had to be constantly shipped from Egypt.

Octavian, on the other hand, had no such problems. He prepared his army of 16 legions – 80,000 men, most of them veterans – and a fleet of 400 ships in the south of Italy at the ports of Brundisium and Tarentum. He had already consigned command of the fleet to one of his closest friends, the able Marcus Agrippa, while retaining command of the army for himself.

The aggressive Agrippa took Antony by surprise with a brilliant attack on the Egyptian merchant undermanned and many of his ships unseaworthy. The best he could hope for was to escape to Egypt with as many ships as possible. There he could rebuild his army with the troops – six legions – in Egypt and Syria.

Antony's veteran soldiers were alarmed by his decision to fight at sea instead of on land. Shakespeare in his *Antony and Cleopatra* puts the counter argument in the words of one of his soldiers:

O noble emperor, do not fight by sea;
Trust not to rotten planks. Do you misdoubt
This sword and these my wounds ? Let the Egyptians
And the Phoenicians go a-ducking; we
Have used to conquer standing on the earth,
And fighting foot to foot.

Octavian had no need for spies. The daily haemorrhage of Antony's senior officers to the enemy camp kept him fully informed of his rival's predicament. Even after the council of war, where the decision to break out was discussed, Dellius deserted and briefed Octavian and Agrippa on Antony's latest thoughts.

Without rowers to man all his ships, Antony had no option but to burn many of his transports and slower vessels. The funeral pyres of Antony's fleet were clearly visible to Octavian and spoke volumes for the desperation of his rival. Equipping just 230 galleys, ranging in size from triremes to 'tens' – huge unwieldy monsters with armoured beaks at their prow – Antony knew that his vessels were heavier and larger than Agrippa's but, unfortunately, less numerous – 230 to 400 – and considerably less mobile. In Roman galley warfare size counted for much, particularly in ramming, but Antony's intention was not victory but break-out. His tactics would be built around this basic purpose, and so he ordered his ships to keep their sails aboard, in anticipation of a long journey if the chance came to escape.

On 2 September 31 BC Antony's fleet, consisting of three fighting squadrons (170 vessels) and a fourth – Cleopatra's – of merchant ships carrying the treasure chest and her personal valuables, moved slowly out of Actium, carrying over 20,000 legionary soldiers. The rest of the army – now less than 50,000 strong – remained with Canidius Crassus, lining the hills and watching their fate being decided in the harbour and beyond.

Octavian, fully appraised of Antony's intentions, still feared a fight in the shallow waters of Actium harbour, where his more mobile fleet would be deprived of space. He preferred to allow Antony to sail past unopposed and then be attacked in the open seas. But Agrippa was against this. Antony's ships were carrying sails and if they once got ahead of Octavian's fleet it might be impossible to catch them. Agrippa argued for simplicity: block Antony's escape and force him to come out into deeper water. He would have to come out of the harbour eventually – or starve.

Antony's three battle squadrons slowly crossed the shallow water of the bar and emerged from the harbour, with Cleopatra's squadron – a blaze of colour compared to the Roman ships, with gilded

ROMAN GALLEYS: A DECERE

Length: 145 ft
Beam: 20 ft, 28 ft outrigger
Oar length: 40 ft
Draught: 7 ft
Crew: 572 Rowers; 30 sailors; 250 marines.
Armaments: 2 fighting towers; as many as 6 catapults.

This was the largest type of Roman warship and Antony undoubtedly used some at Actium, where Agrippa concentrated on smaller quinquiremes, which were more manoeuvrable. The decere carried a *harpargo*, a kind of harpoon that could be used to grapple and 'reel in' enemy ships until they were close enough to board. From the fighting towers at bow and stern, archers could fire down onto the decks of enemy ships.

A Roman war galley depicted on a coin honouring Quintus Nasidius, who was sent to relieve Massilia in 49 BC. AAAC

bows, painted superstructure and flags and streamers flying – staying well to the rear and out of range of missiles. Antony himself, with Gellius Publicola, commanded the right wing, which was strengthened by some of the largest of his ships – 'nines' and 'tens'. The weaker centre was commanded by Marcus Octavius, while the left, also strengthened by the most heavily armoured ships, was commanded by Antony's best commander, the admiral Sosius. Clearly Antony planned to try to draw the enemy strength away from the centre and towards the two wings where he and Sosius were to be found. This might open a gap in the middle of Agrippa's fleet for Cleopatra's squadron to sail through and escape. If this should happen, the rest of the fleet could try to disengage and follow the Egyptian queen. It was a sensible strategy, born of realism rather than fear.

Antony's fleet waited just outside the harbour for Agrippa to attack, but Octavian's wily admiral had no intention of being drawn into the shallows and refused the challenge. Until noon the two fleets confronted each other across a mile of windless water. But Antony was waiting for more than just Agrippa, he was waiting for the god of the winds to answer his call. Plutarch notes that just after midday a breeze sprang up from the sea. It was for this that Antony had shipped his sails and the time had now come to grapple his opponents. Antony closed with the enemy left wing, which was commanded by Agrippa in person. As both squadrons moved northwards in an attempt to outflank each other, they broke away from their respective centres, leaving a gap that Cleopatra's squadron, with sails already hoisted, immediately exploited. In Plutarch's words, 'The enemy watched them in amazement as they made use of the breeze to sail away in the direction of the Peloponnese [south].'

Antony had achieved his first objective: Cleopatra and the transports had broken clear. But how could he break off the engagement with Agrippa and follow her? The two Roman fleets were now fully engaged. Grappling hooks hugged ship to ship, providing a platform for the marines and legionary soldiers to fight it out hand-to-hand on the decks. Catapults fired flaming missiles across the sea, igniting ropes and superstructure, before catching on the deck beams and suffocating the rowers below. Oars were splintered by passing vessels, great metal beaks gouged holes below the water line before reversing and allowing in a torrent of water.

Arrows and sling shots fired by men high up on the masts picked off officers on deck, while the smoke of burning ships lay like a shroud across the scene. Antony's heaviest vessels were now each surrounded by two or three of Agrippa's ships, and Octavian's advantage in marines – 40,000 against 20,000 – was beginning to tell. With his own flagship beset on all sides, Antony transferred to a smaller, faster vessel and set off in pursuit of the queen of Egypt. How those of his men felt who witnessed his flight can best be left to the imagination. All around, Romans were fighting and dying in the cause of Mark Antony, and he was abandoning them to their fate. He had obviously chosen to command the right wing as his chances of escape were better on that side. To the south, Sosius and his squadron were doomed; no sea breeze would come to their aid.

With the advantage of their sails, Antony and Cleopatra made their escape from Actium. Antony had salvaged perhaps 70 ships from the wreck, but his army was lost and his reputation, after Actium, severely tainted. His abandonment of the army – which negotiated a surrender with Octavian – lost him all credibility with the Roman people. He had made his choice when he followed the Egyptian sorceress. Cleopatra, however, was jubilant, sailing into Alexandria harbour with her ships garlanded with flowers. To her the break-out had been a victory; to Antony it had been not only physical but moral cowardice. Octavian and his forces were not long in following them to Egypt. What followed provided material for the final part of Shakespeare's tragedy: the suicide of Mark Antony, a great Roman, and the death by snakebite of the beautiful Cleopatra, who scorned to return to Rome as an exhibit in Octavian's triumph.

Actium was an unheroic battle, but its consequences were great. Octavian's victory put a stop to years of civil war, and ended the power struggle between east and west within the Roman world, ensuring that Rome would remain at the centre, and that there would be no cultural shift to Alexandria. Octavian looted the treasures of Egypt and returned to Rome as undisputed master. With the end of the Triumvirate, he showed that there could be no return to a republic. Within three years he had been voted the title 'Augustus' by the Senate, and became sole ruler of of the Roman world. In that sense, Actium saw the birth of the Roman Empire.

The Battle of the Teutoburger Wald AD 9

Drusus and then Drusus' brother Tiberius campaigned successfully in western Germany. There were setbacks, as when the Cherusci revolted in 1 BC, but Roman pressure was relentless and when Tiberius handed over command to Publius Quintilius Varus in AD 6, he had every reason to think that the main task had been achieved: the German tribes were pacified. But he was wrong. The German tribes respected strength; instead they were given weakness and stupidity. The appointment of Varus was a terrible mistake. He had previously been governor of Syria and 'was more accustomed to the

Some decisive battles, like those at Hastings or Waterloo, have consequences that are immediate and irreversible. They are recognized as decisive by contemporaries. Other battles are seen to have been decisive by later commentators, while at the time their effects, though severe, were not regarded as irreversible. Such a battle was the defeat of three Roman legions led by Quintilius Varus in the Teutoburger Wald in AD 9.

The Roman conquest of Gaul by Julius Caesar had succeeded in pacifying the warlike Celtic peoples and spreading among them the benefits of Roman civilization. However, on the northern frontier of the Roman Empire – to the east of the River Rhine and to the north of the River Danube – the land was occupied by Germanic tribes, fierce but crude fighters who lived a primitive, nomadic existence. As Gaul grew richer and more settled, it became an increasingly attractive target for German raiders, and this worried the Romans, who had come to value secure frontiers above all else. Could they afford to leave the German tribes outside the Roman system? The Emperor Augustus concluded that although the river-frontier of the Rhine and Danube was formidable, the German problem would be an ever-present one unless the Romans attempted a pacification of the tribes and pushed the frontier 250 miles eastwards to the River Elbe. This was a dramatic decision, but one based on sound strategy. After all, the security of Gaul would be guaranteed if potential German invaders were forced back so far from the Rhine.

From 15 BC until AD 6, first Augustus' stepson

German tribesmen of the 1st century AD, as pictured by J. Gehrts in 1907. PN

leisure of the camp than to actual service in war'. He
was related to the Emperor Augustus and was
something of a court appointment, lacking the drive
necessary to govern the German tribes. He made
the cardinal error of treating the Germans as if they
were slaves of Rome and as passive in character as
the more sophisticated and Romanized Syrians. He
extracted scarce gold from the Germans as payment
in taxes, and relaxed the discipline of the legions,
neglecting training and manoeuvres. According to
Velleius Paterculus, 'when placed in charge of the
army in Germany, he entertained a notion that the
Germans were a people who were men only in limbs
and voice, and that they, who could not be subdued
by the sword, could be soothed by the law'.

The full strength of the Roman army in Germany
was five legions – two stationed at Mogontiacum
(Mainz) and three at Aliso (Haltern). In view of the
apparent peacefulness of the tribes the Romans had
let their guard slip. Instead of being kept on
constant alert, the legions were used in civil building
projects, felling trees, building bridges and roads,
with their wives and families around them.

In September of the year 9, the calm was broken
by reports of minor tribal risings. On his way to
winter camp at Minden, Varus decided to pass
through the troubled area – between the rivers Ems
and Weser in northwest Germany – and restore
order. Regarding the rising as no more than a
localized disturbance he took no precautions to
place his troops on a war footing, and foolishly
allowed families to travel with the troops. In fact,
Varus was marching into a trap planned by Arminius,
son of Sigimer, leader of the Cherusci, a 'frantic
spirit' who nursed a fanatical hatred of the Romans,
although on the surface remaining friendly with
them. Arminius had seen service in the Roman army
in Pannonia and Illyricum and had been granted
Roman citizenship. Part of his motivation for the
revolt seems to have been personal. His uncle
Segestes, a favourite of Varus, had denied Arminius
his daughter Thusnelda, forcing the young couple
to elope together. The hostility between uncle and
nephew had smouldered even after the elopement

and Arminius was determined to strike at his uncle and the Romans at the same time

Arminius concluded that 'no one succumbs to an ambush as easily as the commander who feels completely secure', and he engineered a minor rising so that Varus would have to investigate it by marching first through the friendly territory of the Cherusci. Once the Roman columns had penetrated deep into the forest they would be attacked by Arminius' German hordes. The plan for the ambush was revealed to Varus by Arminius' uncle, but the Roman commander, knowing the bad feeling between the two, neglected to investigate the accusation.

In the early autumn, Varus set out with three legions – XVIIth, XVIIIth, and XIXth – and a long column of baggage wagons and camp followers. Surprisingly he was accompanied by Arminius and an escort of Cherusci, probably to settle any fears the Romans may have felt about his loyalty. All went well until suddenly, deep in the Teutoburger Forest, Arminius and his Germans disappeared. Then news came from the head of the column that small groups of soldiers had been attacked. Amongst the swamps and treacherous paths of the forest Varus was now facing an emergency. To add to his problems a sudden storm turned all the paths into quagmires and the high wind broke off branches from the oak trees, which crashed down startlingly among the troops. Probably the darkness and atmosphere of gloom served to depress the Romans even more.

Suddenly the Cherusci and their allies struck along nearly the whole length of the column, hurling javelins into the Roman ranks. With the legionaries unable to deploy, the fight became a chaotic hand-to-hand struggle in which superior Roman tactics could not be used. Having repulsed the first German waves, Varus built a fortified camp and burned his wagons since they were now useless in the soggy conditions. The Romans battled on against constant attacks the next day, but in driving

Some years after the battle, a Roman force under Germanicus came upon the remains of the slaughtered legions. Some had been crucified, others boiled alive or burned in wicker cages. PN

rain their bowmen found their weapons almost useless and the legionary shields becoming sodden and too heavy to carry. The Roman auxiliaries – many of them German – now deserted and Arminius, scenting victory, closed in for the kill. Afraid of being taken alive Varus and his senior officers killed themselves, while a few contingents of cavalry under Vala Numonis managed to hack their way free. Two of the legions lost their eagles and the vast mass of the Roman column – perhaps 20,000 soldiers, women and children – were either slaughtered in the forest or taken alive to be sacrificed in the sacred oak-groves to the German gods. The horrifying remains of these sacrifices – some crucified, others boiled alive or burned in wicker cages – were later found by Germanicus, grandson of the Emperor Augustus, and even years later turned the stomachs of the toughest of his Roman soldiers. Tacitus writes of limbs of horses and men, skulls and other bones, nailed upon the trunks of oak trees. The terrible carnage in the Teutoburger Forest is commemorated even today in the placenames nearby: 'das Winnefeld' (the field of victory); 'die Knochenbahn' (lane of bones); 'die Knockenleke' (bone-brook); 'der Mordkessel' (the kettle of slaughter).

In Rome the portents were ominous. The temple of Mars was struck by lightning, while 'a statue of Victory that was in the province of Germany, and faced the enemy's territory, turned about to face Italy'. When Augustus heard the news of the disaster he panicked, expecting at any moment to see Germans marching through the Forum. Suetonius writes that from the time he was brought the news Augustus was often heard to say, 'Quintilius Varus, give me back my legions.' Later Romans, more accustomed to disasters, would take such defeats more rationally. It was not long before Germanicus was back on the Rhine punishing the tribes for what they had done. But things had changed. Through the careless stupidity of Quintilius Varus Rome's prestige north of the Rhine could never be restored completely, and the Rhine remained the northern frontier of the empire – and an insecure frontier at that.

Arminius' victory was for long celebrated by German schoolchildren as the first great victory of the German nation. While Gaul became thoroughly Romanized, and Britain at least partially so, most of Germany remained free of Roman influence. Had Varus not suffered defeat, and had Augustus not lost confidence in his plan to push the German frontier to the River Elbe, an entirely different Germany would have developed. There would have been no Anglo-Saxon raids on Roman Britain – and thus no England. And would Rome have succumbed to waves of German invaders in the 4th and 5th centuries if the Germans had experienced Roman government and civilization for as long as the inhabitants of Gaul? The consequences are so enormous that the mind struggles to encompass them.

The Battle of Adrianople
378

Adrianople

Romans
Commander: Emperor Valens
Numbers: 10,000 cavalry, 30,000 legionaries
                        and auxiliaries

Goths
Commanders: Fridigern, Alatheus, Saphrax
Numbers: 20,000 Gothic and Alan cavalry,
                        50,000 Gothic infantry

Decisive battles can be decisive in many ways. Never in Roman history was a battle more decisive than that at Cannae in 216 BC. A huge Roman army was virtually exterminated by Hannibal's Carthaginians, some reports speaking of 60–70,000 dead. Yet the consequences of Cannae, apart from the creation of innumerable widows and orphans, was not so severe that Rome could not make a complete recovery. Fourteen years later at Zama Hannibal was decisively defeated and the power of Carthage extinguished for all time. Purely military victories, therefore, rarely have long-term repercussions. And yet just occasionally, as at Adrianople or Crécy, it is the military consequences that are significant. At Adrianople, in 378, the legionary system of Rome, which had served her so well for five or six centuries, was shown to be outdated. The hardfighting legionary – conqueror of Pyrrhus and Hannibal – who had carried the Roman eagles from Spain to Persia, and from the North Sea to the Nile, was no match for the mailed horseman who was sweeping into Europe from the Steppes of Russia and the vast plains of Asia in the 4th and 5th centuries. The traditional Roman army was dead and Rome faced the stark choice: adapt or die. Unable to defeat the incoming hordes Rome tried to absorb them. For a while it worked – until the barbarian leaders realized that they did not need to serve Rome's rulers any more; instead they became Rome's rulers themselves.

Climatic changes affecting their pastures may account for the movement of the Huing-Nu people from northern China and Mongolia in the early years of the Christian era. At first, this movement – that was eventually to affect the lives of millions of people in Europe and Asia – happened so gradually that its progress was almost imperceptible. However, by the 4th century the westward march of the Huing-Nu – the people we now know as the Huns – was building up pressure on the nomadic tribes of the Asian steppes. In 370 the Huns drove the Alans from their lands in southern Russia, and the Alans in turn clashed with a Germanic people, the Goths, living to their west. While the main body of Goths was driven westwards under their chiefs Alatheus and Saphrax, a group of Christianized Goths, under Fridigern, living on the borders of the Roman Empire, begged the emperor Valens to be allowed to cross the Danube and live under Roman protection. Valens saw the opportunity of recruiting Goths into his army and so welcomed Fridigern's people. However, the Roman administrators Lupicinus and Maximus treated the Goths so badly on their arrival, taxing them heavily, taking their children as hostages and prostituting their wives,

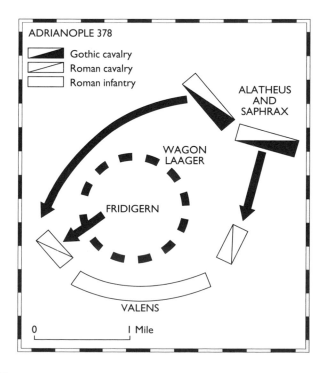

ADRIANOPLE 378

Gothic cavalry
Roman cavalry
Roman infantry

ALATHEUS
AND
SAPHRAX

WAGON
LAAGER

FRIDIGERN

VALENS

0   1 Mile

Romans fighting barbarians; from a Roman sarcophagus, 3rd century AD. PN

that Fridigern immediately revolted and helped the Goths of Alatheus and Saphrax to cross the Danube on rafts. Lupicinus clumsily tried to have the Gothic leaders assassinated at a feast; the Goths responded by wiping out a Roman army at Marcianopolis, equipping themselves with the weapons of the dead Romans.

Fridigern now led the Goths towards Adrianople in Thrace, but, without siege weapons, he could make no impression on its walls. The emperor Valens, who was at that time on campaign in Persia, sent a message to his co-emperor in Rome, his nephew Gratian, asking for help against the Goths. He also sent a force under an able commander named Sebastianus to strengthen the garrison at Adrianople, while he assembled the army of the Eastern Empire to follow him.

Having received a promise from Gratian that a western army was marching directly to his aid, Valens would have been well advised to wait. But he held the Goths in contempt, and, encouraged by the sycophants who surrounded him to believe that Gratian might rob him of some of the glory, he decided to fight the Goths as soon as he had found them. In the sweltering heat of a midsummer day, Valens located the Goths about eight miles from Adrianople on 9 August 378. Like many of the steppe peoples the Goths fought from behind a wagon-laager, flinging every kind of missile on the enemy as they attacked. But although they had large bodies of infantry, who fought with swords and shields, pikes and the throwing axe (*francisca*), their greatest strength was in their armoured cavalry. And as Valens advanced towards the Gothic laager he seems not to have noticed that there was no sign of the Gothic cavalry, who were away foraging.

The Roman army – 40,000 strong, including cavalry – was already exhausted and straggling as it reached the laager, with the right-wing cavalry leading the way, the massed legions in the centre and the left wing cavalry in the rear. Fridigern tried to play for time, sending ambassadors to the emperor asking for peace, while he sent horsemen riding pell-mell to call back his cavalry. The Romans had begun to surround the laager prior to an attack when suddenly an undisciplined group of Iberian auxiliaries opened fire on the Goths and a general exchange of missiles took place. From the high ground on the right of the Roman army masses of armoured horsemen now began to appear under Alatheus and Saphrax. Seeing the situation on the plain, a horde of Alans – allied to the Goths – charged down the slopes 'like a thunderbolt' and crashed into the right wing of the Roman cavalry, who caved in and were utterly defeated. Thousands upon thousands of Gothic horsemen came pouring behind them, taking the Romans in flank and rear and compacting them against the wagon laager. The Romans scarcely had time to react, and only a few squadrons of the left-wing cavalry managed to escape before the whole Roman army was surrounded. According to Ammianus Marcellianus:

The different companies became so huddled together that hardly anyone could pull out his sword or draw back his arm, and because of clouds of dust the heavens could no longer be seen, and echoed with frightful cries. Hence the arrows whirling death from every side always found their mark with fatal effect, since they could not be seen beforehand nor guarded against.

With the massed Roman legions helpless, Fridigern launched his infantry – perhaps 50,000 men – from within the laager, and the tempo of the killing increased. Unable to move, the Romans just suffered and died, most casualties unable to fall because of the press. Hundreds suffocated or were trampled, while the rest endured until their luck ran out and a missile struck them on the head or in the face. It had ceased to be a battle; it was a massacre. Probably 30,000 Romans died on that plain, including Valens himself, Sebastianus and 35 tribunes.

This defeat was far more serious than that at Cannae, which it resembled. According to one historian, 'The Empire rocked to its foundations. Sheer panic fell upon all that bore the name of Rome. The power and glory of the Empire seemed stamped into the dust by the barbarian hordes.' As Sir Charles Oman has pointed out:

Such was the battle of Adrianople, the first great victory won by that heavy cavalry which had now shown its ability to supplant the heavy infantry of Rome as the ruling power of war . . . The Goth found that his stout

THE STEPPE NOMADS

The Huns were a nomadic Mongol people often associated with the Huing-Nu. They inhabited the barren steppes of Central Asia and their movement westward in the first three centuries of the Christian era unsettled many peoples, including the Gepids, Alans and Heruls, driving them onto the lands of numerous Gothic tribes who inhabited the area to the north of the Danube. The Huns were entirely dependent on their herds of animals for food and clothing. Superb horsemen, they learned to ride their small shaggy ponies almost before they learned to walk. Their main weapon was the composite bow from which they fired bone-pointed arrows. They added terror to their armoury by slashing their cheeks when young. The Huns were only the first of a wave of nomadic steppe horsemen who terrorized the civilized areas of Europe for the next 600 years; to follow were the Avars, Bulgars, Magyars, Khazars, Mongols, and, finally, Turks.

lance and his good steed would carry him through the serried ranks of the Imperial infantry. He had become the arbiter of war, the lineal ancestor of all the knights of the Middle Ages, the inaugurator of that ascendancy of the horseman which was to endure for a thousand years.

Not until the English longbowmen cut down the heavy cavalry of France at Crécy in 1346 was the lesson of Adrianople to fade.

The Battle of Taginae
552

Taginae

Byzantines
Commander: Narses
Left wing: Valerian
Right wing: John the Glutton
Numbers: 20,000, including 8000 Herul and
             Lombard mercenaries

Goths
Commander: Totila
Numbers: Unknown

The collapse of Roman power in the West in the late 5th century led to the fragmentation of the old empire and the creation of a number of new states, among them the Ostrogothic kingdom in Italy, established by Theodoric. For a while it seemed that the Goths would breathe new life into the moribund Roman state, helping to maintain elements of Roman civilization and combining them with the teachings of the Christian scholar Arius. However, the Eastern emperor Justin I outlawed the Arian heresy in 523 and threatened the whole of Italy with a crusade to suppress Arianism there. Ever since the loss of the Western Empire it had been the dream of successive Eastern emperors to reconquer the lost lands in the West. None of them took this more seriously than Justinian the Great, born of peasant stock, who was elevated to the imperial purple in 527. Justinian was convinced that he was divinely ordained to restore the Western Empire, as well as to suppress the Arian heresy. To achieve these aims he would need to overthrow the Gothic kingdom in Italy.

During his long reign he employed two great generals in Italy: Belisarius and Narses. Narses was a court eunuch of advanced years, small but cunning, and absolutely loyal to the emperor. Unlike a younger man, who might have been concerned with concepts such as honour and fame, Narses was far too old and cynical to care what people thought of him. He was a tough disciplinarian, a fine strategist and a ruthless opponent. Aged 74 at the time of the battle of Taginae, he had lost none of his faculties and directed his troops with a sure and steady hand.

For twenty years the armies of the Byzantine Empire – for that is how the Eastern Empire was increasingly described – fought the Goths throughout Italy, burning towns and cities, wrecking the economic structure of the country, turning it into a virtual desert. By 552 Justinian so hated the name of the Goths that his campaign was beginning to turn into genocide. The army Narses commanded in that year had few Roman elements, consisting almost entirely of barbarian mercenaries. Against the Christian Goths he fielded Persians, Heruls, Gepids, Huns and the ferocious Lombards. It was as if history was playing tricks and that Attila the Hun now rode under the imperial eagle. Narses knew that all that kept these men together was the love of loot; they had come to Italy not to liberate but to pillage. The old eunuch was wise enough to keep 'exceedingly large amounts of money' with him in case the loot dried up. His mercenaries would willingly change sides if the pickings were better.

The Gothic king, Totila, was a champion horseman with a sense of honour more suited to an Arthurian knight. On hearing of the Byzantine army, he left Rome and advanced to the village of Taginae, a mere 13 miles from where Narses was camped. The eunuch sent heralds to the Gothic king demanding his surrender as his cause was hopeless, but Totila returned his defiance. A decision was reached to fight at Taginae. Narses showed remarkable tactical skill in the lay-out of his forces. In the centre of his line Narses dismounted his 8000 Herul and Lombard mercenaries and formed a massive phalanx with them and his other barbarian allies. Perhaps he thought he could rely more on their loyalty if they were locked in the centre of the battle and hemmed in by both wings. On left and right he located his Roman cavalry, which he commanded himself, with the assistance of Valerian and John the Glutton. The novel aspect of his

Opposite: The bodyguard of the Emperor Justinian; from the 5th-century mosaics at S. Vitale, Ravenna. PN

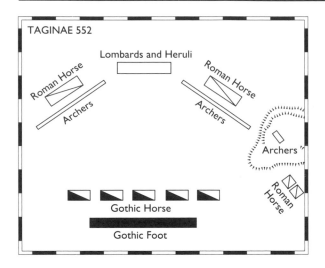

TAGINAE 552

Lombards and Heruli

Roman Horse

Roman Horse

Archers

Archers

Archers

Roman Horse

Gothic Horse

Gothic Foot

preparation was the way that both the cavalry and the 4000 foot archers split between the two wings were set at an angle and protected by pointed stakes, so that an enemy attacking the dismounted phalanx in the centre would be hit by a cross-fire of arrows as they charged down the middle of the field. The eunuch's keen eye also picked out a strategic hill overlooking his position on the left, and he occupied this with 50 archers, as well as placing a further force of 1000 cavalry in hiding behind the hill to spring a trap once the mass of Gothic cavalry had engaged the main part of the Byzantine force.

It was all too scientific for Totila, who was what in a later age would be called a *beau sabreur*. While Narses waited patiently for the Goths to attack, Totila entertained the troops on both sides by an amazing display of horsemanship, resplendent in his golden armour. In fact, Totila had a good reason for his display; he was waiting for Teias to reach the field with 2000 reinforcements before beginning the battle. In the event, once Teias had arrived, Totila changed into the armour of a private soldier and joined the ranks of the Gothic cavalry. As was usual with the Goths, the infantry were placed at some distance behind the horsemen and rarely reached the enemy except to despatch the wounded or help in a pursuit. The Goths relied entirely on the momentum of their cavalry to break the enemy line. If, as happened at Taginae, the enemy front line held, then they had no other tactic than to repeat the charge over and over again.

Some time after midday the Gothic cavalry began their attack, charging straight towards the Byzantine phalanx, ignoring the foot archers on both sides. The result was predictable. The Gothic flanks were peppered with arrows, while the centre recoiled from the bristling mass of pikes and spears. The scene was chaotic. With the Byzantines standing resolutely behind their pikes and stakes the Goths impaled themselves on the phalanx, while the horses stopped dead, throwing their riders forward to their deaths. The Goths could find no way through and all the while the Byzantine archers took a steady toll of their lives. Before the Gothic infantry could come to close quarters, Narses sprang his trap and the 1000 Byzantine horsemen hidden behind the hill charged out and hit them on their unguarded flank, rolling up their line and driving them off the field.

Procopius speaks of 6000 Gothic dead, including many Byzantine deserters from armies Justinian had sent to Italy in previous years. Totila was wounded on the battlefield and died in a peasant's hut nearby. Narses pursued the beaten Goths with a grim determination, occupying the city of Rome and finally killing Teias, whom the remaining Goths had taken as their king. The extermination of the Goths followed, until in an agreement at Monte Lettere the pitifully few survivors were allowed to leave Italy in peace and settle in another barbarian kingdom.

The Byzantine victory was absolute, and by 554 Justinian had achieved in Italy what he had set out to do over 20 years before. Hundreds of thousands of people had died and Italy had been ruined in the process, but the land was Byzantine and Arianism had been wiped out with the last of the Goths. According to one modern scholar, 'The largest towns, such as Naples, Milan and especially Rome, were almost devoid of inhabitants, the depopulated country was uncultivated and the large Italian proprietors were repaid for their devotion to Byzantium and their hostility to Totila by total ruin.'

Byzantine rule lasted just 14 years before an invasion of Lombards under Alboin swept it away. Instead of a powerful and virile Gothic state that might have fought off the barbarians, Italy had no resistance to offer. Rome became a backwater, and the victories of Justinian a disaster for the Christians of the West.

The Battle of Yarmuk 636

Yarmuk

Byzantines
Commanders: Theodore Trithurius and Vahan
Numbers: 50,000, including 10,000
              Ghassanid Arabs

Arabs
Commander: Khalid ibn-al Walid
Numbers: 25,000

In February 638 the caliph Omar rode into Jerusalem and was conducted by the Christian patriarch Sophronius to the site of the Temple of Solomon. Here Omar stood alone for a while gazing outwards and upwards. From here, it was believed, Omar's friend Mohammed had ascended into heaven, and this spot would become one of the holiest places in all Islam – the Dome of the Rock. As the caliph stood, bareheaded and in a tattered robe, the patriarch's resolution left him and in despair he said, 'Behold, the Abomination of Desolation, spoken of by the Prophet Daniel, that standeth in the Holy Place.' At this moment – one of history's most momentous – the guardianship of Jerusalem, holy city to three great world religions, was changing hands.

Yet just nine years before there had been another visitor to Jerusalem, one who had come not in humble tattered robes but in the most glorious garments, the purples and golds of a Byzantine emperor. Heraclius, after one of the greatest military campaigns in history, had shattered the Persian Sassanid Empire and regained the True Cross taken by the Persians in their sack of Jerusalem in 615. Now, in 629, personally carrying the Cross along the Via Dolorosa, Heraclius returned the relic to the Patriarch Zacharias, confirming the Holy City as once again part of the Roman world. No one who witnessed the emperor's triumphant progress that day could have imagined that within a few years the whole edifice of imperial government in Palestine and Syria would collapse in the face of attacks by tribesmen from Arabia, followers of a new faith

propounded by the Prophet Mohammed.

Traditional views of early Arab conquests can be very misleading. The victories of a rabble of desert nomads over powerful military states like the Byzantines and the Persians seemed inexplicable. To medieval Christians it seemed to be the work of Satan himself. Yet the truth was very different. Mohammed had not preached world conquest, nor encouraged his followers to spread the faith by fire and sword; the 'people of the Book' – Christians and Jews – were never to be converted by force. For the tribes of Arabia Islam was not the motive for their expansion; instead it acted as a cement to unite them. The early Arabs were conquerors, inspired by the desire to loot richer communities, to seize food and pasture from areas more fertile than their lands, which were undergoing climatic changes by the 7th century, and were gradually drying up. For the Arabs the lands of the Fertile Crescent – Palestine, Syria, Iraq and Iran – presented an irresistible lure. These men of the desert rode in the name of Allah, but it was not converts they sought but booty.

Coincidentally, at the same time as the climate of Arabia underwent a change, the powerful states that controlled the 'fertile crescent' – Byzantium and Sassanid Persia – were involved in a dramatic fight to the finish – a conclusion to over 600 years of Romano-Persian warfare. The emperor Heraclius's decisive victory at Nineveh in 627 had overthrown the Sassanid king Chosroes II and plunged Persia into anarchy, making her an easy target for any invader. And though the Byzantines had emerged victorious from this terrible struggle, they had been militarily weakened by a decade of intense fighting. In addition, the Byzantine hold on the Semitic populations of Syria and Palestine – who were Monophysite Christians – had been weakened by the imposition of unacceptable religious dogma and excessive taxation. When the time came for Heraclius to call on these people to stand up to the Arabs and their new faith, he found that most of them welcomed the invaders and fought with them against their former masters. Most seriously this affected the Christian Arabs of the Ghassanid tribe, who for many years had provided a buffer between the nomads of the desert and the civilized areas of

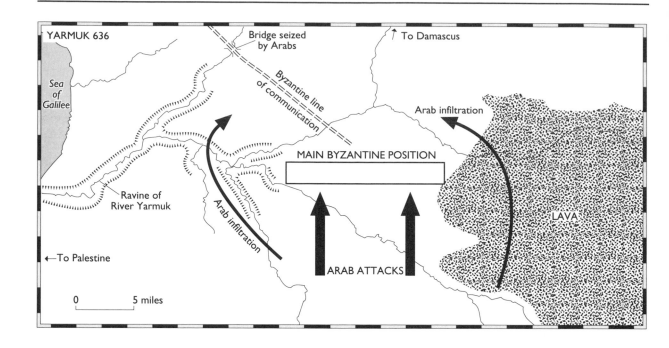

Palestine. These Arabs had formed an important part of all Byzantine armies in the war against Persia, but when facing their Semitic brothers of the desert their loyalties were strained. In this sense, it was not the influence of an aggressive Islamic faith that contributed to the Arab conquests of the 7th century, but the intolerance between Christians of different churches and the feelings of racial affinity among the Arab peoples of the Near East. The Arab victory at Yarmuk in 636 was a victory for the Arab people rather than the Muslim faith. Inferior in numbers, weapons and military training, it was only in morale and in leadership that their superiority lay.

In 633 about 10,000 Arab warriors left the Hijaz in search of plunder; two columns led by Yazid ibn Abi Sufyan headed northwards towards Transjordan, while a third took the coast road towards Palestine. They met little resistance before linking up in February 634 in southern Palestine, where they defeated a small Byzantine force. Reinforcements led by Sergius the Patrician were rushed from Caesarea and fought two battles against the Arabs near Gaza and at Wadi 'Araba, south of the Dead Sea, but they were badly cut up and their general killed. From his headquarters in northern Syria, at Homs, Heraclius was deeply disturbed by the news of these Arab successes. He was exhausted and prematurely old from his tremendous exertions of the previous decade, but he stirred himself to raise a new army, which was to be commanded by his brother Theodore. However, at this juncture a startling new figure entered the lists, a figure whose influence can hardly be exaggerated. The caliph

Abu-Bakr sent his most brilliant general, Khalid ibn-al Walid, to bolster his forces in Palestine. Khalid's impact was electrifying; he managed to weld the disparate Arab groups into a unified fighting force in time to inflict a tremendous defeat on the Byzantines at the battle of Ajnadain on 30 July 634. It had been possible to explain previous Arab victories as isolated occurrences, but the defeat and flight of the emperor's brother with an army of perhaps 60,000 men was an epoch-making event.

Khalid's victory – he was named 'Sword of God' after the battle – established Arab rule in the whole of Palestine and opened the floodgates to thousands of immigrants from Arabia. Yet Khalid knew that he had won just the first battle in a war and that the Byzantines would not sacrifice these lands without a far greater effort. He pushed his forces northwards into Syria, defeating the Armenian general Vahan in two battles at Fihl and Marj as-Suffar early in 635. His target was Damascus, which he reached in March and which surrendered to him after a six-month blockade. By the end of 635 the whole of Syria and Palestine, apart from the small Christian enclaves of Jerusalem, Caesarea and some coastal cities, were in Arab hands.

Heraclius, meanwhile, had scraped together another army, the strongest yet, with which he hoped to turn the tide in Syria. Under the command of Theodore Trithurius and the Armenian general Vahan, the powerful Byzantine force – which in addition to troops from the Anatolian theme (military district) included large contingents of

Armenian heavy cavalry and Christian Arabs – moved into Syria and occupied the Deraa Gap, near the River Yarmuk, south of the Sea of Galilee. In order to maintain freedom of movement, Khalid evacuated Damascus and retreated south, taking up a position facing the Byzantines near the Yarmuk, but with his back to the desert. Although outnumbered two to one – 25,000 Arabs to probably 50,000 Byzantines – numbers tell us little. The Arabs were unified by both religion and purpose, and were commanded by a military genius. Large parts of the Byzantine force were mercenaries, and the Armenian and Ghassanid contingents hated the Byzantines almost as much – if not more – than they did their Muslim enemies. The scene was set for a battle that would decide the fate of the region for centuries to come.

While the Byzantines held the Deraa Gap it was impossible for the Arabs to pass in any numbers through the rock-strewn lava beds of Jebel Hauran to the east, or through the sheer gorges of the Yarmuk or Wadi al-Ruqqad to the west. For four months Theodore Trithurios held his enemy at bay. But during this time Arabs had been infiltrating the lava beds singly or in small groups, cutting off stragglers and supplies, and interfering with Byzantine communications. What started as mere irritants became, over a period of four months, a running sore in the body of the Byzantine force, sapping morale and exacerbating the divisions between Greeks, Armenians and Christian Arabs. In fact, the greatest danger facing Theodore was not so much the Muslim army but the disloyalty of his own men. At one stage mutiny among the Armenian contingent saw Vahan elected as commander-in-chief in Theodore's place. As time passed his numbers diminished from desertion and the effects of disease and climate, while Khalid received constant reinforcements from Medina.

On 20 August 636, Khalid decided that time had worked long enough as his ally; and at this crucial juncture the desert came to his aid. A strong, hot wind blew up a sandstorm, which swept dust and sand into the faces of the Byzantine troops, reducing visibility to a few yards. Out of this sandstorm swept Bedouin lancers and Arab swordsmen, enjoying conditions that were as normal to them as they were horrifying to the Greeks and Armenians. The Byzantines, accustomed to fighting in units under the commands of particular officers bearing standards or pennants, had no chance against the hordes of desert riders, fighting individually, as was their custom. In the blinding storm, many of the Byzantines were crouching down with their heads covered and were bowled over by their Arab assailants. At the first clash of arms the Christian Arabs in the Byzantine ranks deserted to the Muslims en masse and even joined the battle against their erstwhile allies. Arab women, ululating and screaming encouragement to the warriors, rode in and out of the battle. Abu Sofian's fierce wife Hind – who had been in earlier battles and cut out and chewed the liver of her victims – was in the front line of the fighting, shouting to the men to cut off the arms of the uncircumcised. As the Byzantines panicked and fled they found to their horror that the Arabs had seized the only bridge over the Wadi al-Ruqqad, so cutting off their retreat. Thousands of fleeing men died in the river gorges. With both Theodore and Vahan killed in the fighting there was now no resistance or organized withdrawal, and the battle ended in the virtual extermination of the whole Byzantine force.

Heraclius was at Antioch when news reached him that Theodore Trithurius was dead and his entire army destroyed at Yarmuk. After a lifetime of struggling against overwhelming odds he must have known bitter despair to see all his efforts brought to nothing. Convinced that God had deserted him the old emperor sadly returned to Constantinople. The Holy Land was lost and Jerusalem with it. Syria was gone. Egypt and North Africa would soon follow. The battle of Yarmuk had determined that these would become Arab lands, which they still are today. Few if any battles in history have matched Yarmuk in their consequences.

The Siege of Constantinople 718

It is rare – perhaps unique – for a single weapon to determine the course of history. A case can be made for the English longbow, but a far better one exists for the Greek fire of the Byzantines, which helped the Eastern Roman Empire to maintain itself against countless enemies for a thousand years after the fall of Rome. This inflammable substance, often fired from siphons in the bows of Byzantine warships, had a secret recipe, though probably the 10th-century writer, Marcus Graecus, came close when he gave its ingredients as: 'pure sulphur, tartar, sarcocolla, pitch, dissolved nitre, petroleum and pine resin', which were all boiled together. The problem for its victims was that it ignited on contact with water – and could only be extinguished by sand or urine. At the siege of Constantinople in 717-18, it may be that its use against the Saracens saved the city and the whole of Europe.

Since the 660s the Arabs had made a number of attempts to capture Constantinople, it having become the goal of Muslim leaders to remove this bastion of Christianity. In August 717 the Saracen general Maslama invaded Anatolia and advanced into Thrace, collecting the harvest there and piling up corn so high it could be seen from the walls of Constantinople. At this moment of great peril the Byzantine state was fortunate in its ruler. After Theodosius III had chosen to enter a monastery, he was succeeded by one of the empire's best warrior-emperors, Leo III, known as the 'Isaurian'. Leo worked tirelessly to fill the granaries and arsenals of Constantinople, trusting to its powerful walls to repel the Arab assault. Leo knew that a blockade by the Arab navy was far more likely to force the city

to surrender than any land assault. He therefore looked to his navy to save the city.

After having failed to take the city by assault, Maslama settled down to a prolonged siege, ringing Constantinople with his 80,000 troops, while the Arab admiral Suleiman, with perhaps 1800 vessels, began a blockade. Half the Arab fleet patrolled to the north of Galata, cutting off supplies coming through the Bosphorus from the Black Sea, while the rest prevented aid coming from the Aegean. The city's main harbour, the Golden Horn, was protected by a vast chain, which the Byzantines lowered to allow ships to pass through or raised to guard against intruders. Within the Golden Horn Leo had assembled his fleet of dromons (galleys) and took the Arab squadron patrolling near Galata completely by surprise with a devastating attack. With the Arab ships in confusion Leo's warships rammed into them, pouring Greek fire onto their decks and consuming many of them in fireballs. So terrifying and sudden was Leo's strike that he was able to order a withdrawal behind the chain before the rest of the Arab ships could come to the aid of their stricken comrades.

Leo had won a psychological victory that stood him in good stead throughout the siege, for the Greek fire had so terrified the Arab crews that their navy was unable to maintain an effective blockade. As the harsh winter weather set in the Arab morale plummeted in their ill-prepared camps around the city. Snow lay thick on the ground and the Arab tents were quite inadequate to protect people more accustomed to deserts than the icy plains of Europe. Maslama's men, it is reported, were reduced to eating all the camp animals and even 'cakes of dead men's flesh, mixed with their own excrement and baked'. But Arab resources seemed limitless. In spite of heavy losses from disease and exposure, the Arabs were reinforced in the spring of 718 by a new fleet from Egypt and a reserve army under Merdasan. Yet Leo was not deterred and, again using the opportunity to lower the chain and make a sudden attack on the Arab fleet, he caught them by surprise a second time, inflicting a terrible defeat on them and leaving hundreds of flaming wrecks littering the Sea of Marmara. Not content with this, Leo used his

newly won naval supremacy to ferry troops to the Asiatic shore, where he ambushed a large Arab force and killed Merdasan.

But final salvation was at hand from an unexpected source. A large Bulgar army under Tervel was persuaded – or bribed – by Leo to join him against the Arabs. Tervel – no great friend of the Byzantines, but a Christian who would fight for his faith – attacked Maslama near Adrianople and killed some 22,000 of the Muslims in a great battle there. As if this was not enough, Leo circulated rumours in the Arab camp that vast armies of Franks were coming to the help of the city. On 15 August 718, the Arabs abandoned their 12-month siege and withdrew, having suffered a catastrophic defeat in men and ships. The numbers given by chroniclers are too fantastic to be taken seriously. But Leo followed up his victory by driving the Arabs out of Anatolia and establishing a firm limit to Muslim expansion.

Historians, led by Gibbon, have not been slow to acclaim the victory of Leo the Isaurian. The tide of Arab expansion that had begun at Yarmuk in 636 and that had witnessed the Muslim occupation of Persia, Egypt, Syria, the whole North African coast and even Spain, had broken on the walls of the 'Queen of Cities' and was in retreat. If Constantinople had fallen in 718 it would have opened the way for an Arab advance into Europe at a time when there was no power in the West capable of resisting it. Had the Eastern Empire fallen then rather than 700 years later the whole development of Western Europe might well have taken a different direction: it is doubtful if Western Christianity would have survived, or if the modern states of France, Germany and Italy would have developed at all. In the words of a Russian historian, 'It is justly claimed that by his successful resistance Leo saved not only the Byzantine Empire and the eastern Christian world, but all of Western European civilization.'

The Battle of Lechfeld
955

Lechfeld

Germans
Commander: Otto I of Saxony
Numbers: 8000 heavy cavalry

Magyars
Commander: Bulchru
Numbers: 30,000 cavalry

In the 9th and 10th centuries the Christian kingdoms of the Franks were under constant threat from Vikings and Arabs. Yet for a period in the early 10th century the embryonic German state was imperilled by an even more terrible danger, recalling that of Attila the Hun in the 5th century: fierce Magyar tribes from western Asia were flooding into the area of the middle-Danube and raiding deep into Saxony and Bavaria. For the Germans the year 955 has rightly been called their *annus mirabilis*; King Otto I's victory at Lechfeld ended forever the threat from the Magyars – the ancestors of today's Hungarians – and paved the way for the creation of the powerful German state of the Middle Ages.

In the summer of 955 a huge Magyar army – described by contemporary chroniclers as numbering 100,000 horsemen, though probably only a third that size – poured into Bavaria and laid waste wide areas to the south and east of the River Lech, burning churches and massacring villagers. On 8 August they laid siege to the cathedral city of Augsburg. Bishop Ulrich aroused the people to defend their city and joined Count Dietpold and his knights in a desperate struggle to hold the gates long enough for the inhabitants to build up the ramparts. As the men laboured in the intense midsummer heat, the women prayed in the cathedral for deliverance from the heathens. The Magyars moved up siege engines and towers, and it seemed only a matter of time before the city fell. But then news reached them that the German king, Otto I, was approaching with a great army of mounted warriors. As the Germans clashed with the Magyar pickets, the main bulk of the invaders drew off from Augsburg and crossed to the right bank of the nearby River Lech, hoping to find the ground there to their advantage, for fighting as horse-archers in the tradition of the Parthians, Avars and Huns they feared to be impeded by woods or broken ground.

On first hearing of the Magyar raid into Bavaria, Otto had wasted no time in setting forth from Saxony with his feudal knights, picking up contingents of soldiers on the way. Reaching the Danube he was joined by Duke Conrad, one of the bravest German warriors, and a strong force of Bavarian and Swabian heavy cavalry, encased in mailed coats and armed with swords and spears. With them came contingents of Franconian infantry, carrying kite-shaped shields of wood and leather, and armed with swords, spears or throwing axes. Otto also had with him garishly dressed but poorly equipped Slavonic troops from Bohemia under their prince, Boleslav. At the last moment, Count Dietpold rode out to join him with the knights of Augsburg. Otto divided

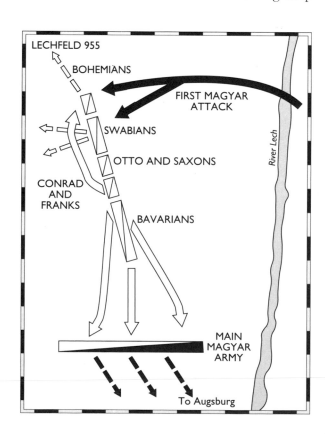

his army into eight corps of 1000 men each, with the great standard of St Michael carried at the head of the host, and the holy lance (reputed to be the one that had pierced the side of Jesus on the Cross) in his own hand.

Originally Asiatic nomads, the Magyars fought almost entirely with the composite bow, relying on the speed and the manoeuvrability of their ponies to avoid the shattering impact of the Western European knights. Some of them carried small round wicker shields and fought with sword and axe, when the situation demanded it, but their prime tactic was to harry the enemy from long range. Individual warriors still had their faces scarred from birth to terrify their enemies, as was common among the Turkic and Mongol peoples of the Steppes. Leading their army rode Bulchru, splendidly apparelled, with feathered helm and carrying a circular shield embossed with silver, and at the head of each division of their army the Magyars carried standards of horse or yak tails, dyed in fantastic colours.

At dawn on 10 August the Germans rose and prepared for battle, having fasted the previous day.

Men who had recently been enemies swore peace and mutual help to each other, pledging to live or die together in defence of their land and religion. When everything was ready, Otto ordered an advance to the banks of the Lech, placing the least reliable of his warriors – the Bohemians – in the rear, in charge of the camp. His Bavarian cavalry was given the place of honour in the van, as it was their territory that had suffered invasion. Watching Otto divide his army, the Magyars immediately exploited his weak rearguard. While part of their army moved out to confront the German vanguard, a large force of Magyars crossed the river and fell on Otto's camp, taking the Bohemians by surprise and scattering them after a brief struggle. The victorious Magyars now charged the rear of the German army, and with the braying of horns,

Otto I at Lechfeld, as depicted in this painting of 1860 by Michael Ehler. Lechfeld for long played a role in German nationalist mythology as the great victory over the 'Eastern Hordes'. IPA

clashing of cymbals and terrible wolf-like cries of 'Hui, Hui', fell on the Swabian corps and scattered it in a hail of arrows. In this crisis Otto turned to his greatest knight – Duke Conrad – to restore the situation. Conrad's knights swept down upon the Magyars, who by this time were immersed in looting the German baggage. The Magyars, forced to fight at close quarters with the heavily armoured Germans, soon broke and fled. Meanwhile, in the van of the German army, the Bavarian knights wielded their swords to good purpose, cutting down the lightly armoured Magyars. Mounted on heavy horses that towered above the light Magyar ponies, the Germans were more than a match for their opponents, and once it became clear that their ruse had failed and their detached force had been defeated, the Magyars lost heart and fled, firing several volleys over their shoulders at their pursuers before going pell-mell for safety. Many of them floundered and were drowned in the River Lech, while those that did escape were hunted for two days by Otto's eager cavalry. Bulchru himself, and a number of Magyar princes, were captured in the pursuit and were taken to Regensburg, where they were hanged by the ruthless duke of Bavaria. The Magyars, shocked by this apparent breach of military protocol, massacred the German prisoners they still held. The hero of the battle, Duke Conrad, did not live to enjoy the victory he had earned: while loosening his helmet to breathe more easily in the great heat of that summer's day, he was struck in the throat by an arrow.

Otto's victory had brought an end to a period of great uncertainty in Central Europe, and seven years later he was crowned Holy Roman Emperor by Pope John XII. The battle of Lechfeld extinguished the centuries-long cycle of nomadic raids that had brought the region to the brink of economic ruin, and led to a flourishing 10th-century revival in artistic, cultural and religious life in Germany. It was the last time that Steppe nomads were ever to threaten Western Europe.

The Battle of Hastings 1066

Before 1066 England had been a peripheral part of the Scandinavian world, rent by internal divisions and open to devastating Viking attacks. William of Normandy's victory at Hastings changed all that, freeing the country from its northern links and making it an integral part of the richer Western European world. William turned a wealthy but loosely governed state into a unified and powerful realm, built around feudalism and a hereditary monarchy. William's victory was one of the most significant events of the Middle Ages, and Hastings perhaps the most important battle in England's history.

The death of Edward the Confessor in 1066 presented the English with a constitutional crisis. The governing council – the Witan – chose as his successor Harold Godwinson, earl of Wessex, who had effectively been ruling the kingdom for a decade before the king's death. But Harold had no royal blood in his veins and had found it necessary to marry Edith, sister of the northern earls Edwin and Morcar, to assure the support of the house of Aelfgar for his accession. There were other claimants besides Harold, two of whom were prepared to back their claims by force. On the death of Harthacanute, last Danish king of England, the Danish claim had passed by agreement to King Magnus of Norway. In 1066 his successor, Harald Hardrada, was preparing a Norwegian army to attack England and overthrow the usurper, Harold Godwinson. The second foreign claimant was William the Bastard, duke of Normandy, who was distantly related to the Confessor and had apparently been promised the throne by him. This rather tenuous claim had been strengthened when Harold Godwinson, shipwrecked in Normandy, had sworn an oath on holy relics to support William's claim when Edward died. But Harold had always claimed that he was tricked into making the oath and denied the Norman charge that he was an oathbreaker. Nevertheless, the pope declared Harold forsworn and excommunicate, and sent William his banner to show that the expedition to England in 1066 would be a crusade blessed by the Holy Catholic Church.

Harold Godwinson therefore faced a twin threat in the summer of 1066: an attack on the northeast coast by the king of Norway, and an invasion of the south coast by the duke of Normandy. Deciding that the Norman threat was the greater, Harold concentrated his strength in the south, maintaining his fleet between the Isle of Wight and Dover to intercept William's armada, and relying on the earls

Harold Godwinson – Harold II of England – on a contemporary coin. AAAC

HOUSECARLS

Housecarls or Huscarles were the household troops of Danish and Saxon kings and thanes in the 11th century. Introduced to England by King Sweyn Forkbeard in 1016 the housecarl was a mercenary warrior who lived by a severe code of conduct and owed personal allegiance to his lord. By 1066 there were perhaps 3000 royal housecarls in England, and Harold II's brothers, Gyrth and Leofwine, brought some of their own to fight with them at Hastings. The housecarl was a well-drilled and heavily armed fighter. Dressed in a conical helmet and byrnie (or mail shirt), he was trained to use the 5-foot Danish axe left-handed to enable him to strike at his enemy's sword arm. The housecarls comprised an elite force of infantry unmatched in the Christian world, and some of the housecarls who survived the battle of Hastings took service in the Byzantine emperor's Varangian Guard. It is reported that in 1081 a force of English Varangians – almost certainly housecarls – was wiped out at the battle of Dyrrachium in Greece by the Norman, Robert Guiscard. Cut off from the main part of the Byzantine army the housecarls fought back-to-back on a small hill, until overrun by Norman cavalry and archers – a pointless but poignant reminder of their fate at Hastings.

day and ended in a total victory for the invaders. The earls escaped from the bloodbath, but the northern English army had been seriously weakened.

News of the Norwegian invasion was a body blow to Harold Godwinson, still watching the south coast for signs that William of Normandy had put to sea. He faced an agonizing choice: whether to stay in the south and leave the north to be ravaged by the Vikings, or to march north to fight Hardrada and leave the south undefended. Ever the man of action, Harold opted to fight the Vikings, knowing that he could hardly expect to maintain the support of the northern earls if he left their lands to the mercy of a pitiless invader like Hardrada. Assembling his housecarls and those of his brothers Gyrth and Leofwine, and sending messengers north to call out the fyrd of the Midland shires, he began his epic march up the old Roman road of Ermine Street. In one of the greatest forced marches in military history, Harold covered 200 miles or so in six days, surprising Hardrada's troops on either side of the River Derwent at Stamford Bridge and inflicting a stunning defeat on the Vikings. It was the most decisive battle in over 200 years of Anglo-Viking warfare, extinguishing forever the Scandinavian threat to northern England and, further, virtually ending the 'Viking Age'. Both Hardrada and Tostig were slain in the intense hand-to-hand fighting, and the Norwegians who managed to escape only filled 24 ships of the original 300. After the battle Harold entered York in triumph, prepared to rest and feast his exhausted army.

But even while Harold was freeing northern England from the Viking threat, the wind had changed in the south. William's armada set out from St Valery on 28 September to make the short crossing of the Channel, landing at Pevensey Bay in Sussex, having avoided the English fleet, which, as luck would have it, was revictualling in the Thames. On landing, William had fallen on his face in the sand – thought by some a bad omen – but he had leapt to his feet saying that thus he had claimed the soil of England. He immediately began ravaging the surrounding country, which he knew to be part of Harold's own earldom, in the hope of making the English king rush precipitately south. William had read his man well. Though Harold was an admirable war-leader, his headstrong nature played into the hands of the more cunning Norman. Harold had everything to gain from moving steadily down to London, bringing what was left of the northern army with him and giving time for the fyrd from distant shires to assemble. In a matter of weeks Harold could have put together an army perhaps

of Mercia and Northumberland – his brothers-in-law Edwin and Morcar – to defy the Norwegians. For much of August the weather was stormy and the wind did not suit William, assembling his forces on the north coast of France. As well as his own feudal troops, William's army was boosted by adventurers from many parts of France and even Italy, who saw the chance of land and booty in England should the duke succeed.

Harald Hardrada, king of Norway – the greatest Viking of a warlike age – had served in the army of the Byzantine Empire and was a formidable warrior, even though he may not quite have reached the height of seven feet attributed to him by chroniclers. Supported by Tostig, Harold Godwinson's estranged and exiled brother, Hardrada assembled a fleet of 300 ships to launch his attack. Arriving off the Yorkshire coast, the fleet raided Scarborough and then sailed up the River Ouse before disembarking an army of nearly 10,000 Vikings a few miles from York. Edwin and Morcar called out the northern fyrd (militia) and with their own housecarls (household warriors) they fought the Vikings at Gate Fulford on 20 September. The battle raged all three times the size of William's, as well as using his fleet to destroy the Norman ships, on which the duke was dependent for supplies and evacuation in the case of defeat. But Harold was not a man to delay any action and he headed south from York on 1 October, reaching London in six days, leaving Edwin and Morcar's northern army far behind, as well as many of his own housecarls.

Harold stayed in London for just five days, setting out with as few as 5000 men. He collected others as he moved south through the great Andredsweald forest, and when he reached Caldbec Hill another group of fyrdmen were already awaiting him. But it had been another exhausting march over rough tracks, and he had lost many men on the way. Florence of Worcester writes that Harold 'was very sensible that some of the bravest men in England had fallen in the two battles [of Gate Fulford and Stamford Bridge] and that one half of his troops were not yet assembled'. He was certainly outnumbered by William's 6–8000 Normans at this stage, but knew that he would gain reinforcements on the morrow by men drifting in from all quarters. Harold's instinct was for a dawn attack on the Normans, hoping to take them unawares as he had caught Hardrada at Stamford Bridge. But the Norman cavalry pickets reported the English approach to William. In any case, Harold's army was a pale reflection of the one he had taken to York, and he eventually decided that a defence of a position on Senlac Ridge would be the best option.

On 14 October the Normans advanced to Telham Hill, and William had his first glimpse of the English army facing him, stretching across Senlac Ridge for about 800–1000 yards. He could not see Harold but he knew where he would be, standing beneath the great Dragon banner of Wessex and his own personal flag of the Fighting Man – later to be the site of the altar of Battle Abbey. It was a magnificent defensive position, with the English left and centre protected by a steep slope and their right fronted by a marsh, so giving William little option but to attack frontally. The first two ranks of the English army comprised elite housecarls – the best troops in Europe – encased in mail and wielding their fearsome double-handed axes. Behind them, fighting under their thanes (aristocratic commanders), were the serried ranks of the fyrd, some well equipped with helmets, mail and swords, others no more than farm labourers with pitchforks and scythes.

At about 9.30 a.m. William ordered his archers to move into range of the English, and let loose a hail of arrows. However, the housecarls were able to use their shields to give themselves effective protection. As the Norman archers moved even closer to increase the hitting power of their arrows they were met by a hail of English missiles – javelins, throwing axes, arrows and stones – which sent many of them

---

Norman cavalry vainly attacking the shieldwall of the English housecarls; from the Bayeux Tapestry. AAAC

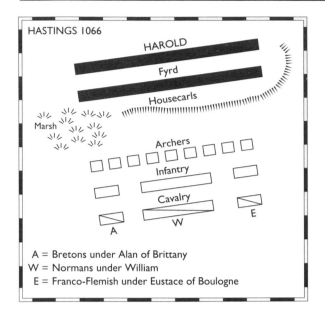

HASTINGS 1066

HAROLD

Fyrd

Housecarls

Marsh

Archers

Infantry

Cavalry

A

W

E

A = Bretons under Alan of Brittany
W = Normans under William
E = Franco-Flemish under Eustace of Boulogne

tumbling back down the slope in confusion. The archers had failed to make any impression on the grim line of warriors on the ridge and had, moreover, used up all their arrows. An hour had passed, and William had the extra frustration of seeing the English army reinforced by latecomers who had been marching all night to reach the battlefield.

William now ordered up his heavy infantry, Bretons on the left under Count Alan of Brittany, Normans in the centre, and Flemings on the right under Eustace of Boulogne. In the hand-to-hand fighting that followed both sides suffered heavy casualties, but the housecarls gained the upper hand and sent William's men-at-arms stumbling down the slope in shocked defeat. It was now time for the cavalry to move in to exploit the gaps forced by the infantry – but there were none. As the horses struggled up the steep slopes or through the marshes they lost their momentum, and many of them refused to face the terrible axes of the housecarls, weapons with blades a foot in width, capable of severing a horse's head with one blow. The attack collapsed and William's cavalry fell back in confusion. Now occurred one of the decisive moments of the battle. As the Breton knights retreated, crashing through their own infantry, the chaos they caused threw open the unguarded flank of the Norman centre. Here was a chance for the English to advance with a rush and drive the Normans off the field – but the king had given no order to advance. Whether Harold's brother Gyrth or some thane on the right took the initiative and ordered the fyrd to charge, or whether it was just a spontaneous rush of blood by the untrained shire

levies, we will never know. In the event, hundreds of fyrdmen swept aside the housecarls in front of them and charged down the hill in pursuit of the Bretons. At the same moment William fell or was knocked from his horse and the cry went up that the duke was dead. For a few seconds victory lay within Harold's grasp. A charge by the full English line might have so disordered the Normans that they could not recover. But Harold was not sufficiently confident that he had blunted the Norman threat to risk abandoning his strong defensive position. A minute passed. William had leapt to his feet, remounted and removed his helmet, bellowing to his men that he was unhurt. The crisis was over. The Breton cavalry now re-formed and massacred their English pursuers, who were trapped in the marshy ground at the bottom of the hill. It is doubtful if more than a handful survived to regain the English lines. It was a disaster for Harold and he knew it. The English line now contracted to take account of the missing fyrdmen.

The three arms of William's force – archers, heavy infantry and cavalry – had now been tried and all had failed in turn. He was left with no option but to engage in the kind of 'toe-to-toe' fighting at which the housecarls were the masters, and so the battle became one of attrition rather than man-oeuvre. The Norman cavalry, quite unsuited to the terrain, struggled through the marshy ground and up the steep slope, only to be turned back with heavy losses time and time again. Then, late in the afternoon, there was an incredible replay of the incident where the fyrdmen charged the Breton knights and were annihilated. So coincidental was this second 'mistake' by the English that many chroniclers have claimed that William's Fleming knights deliberately feigned flight in order to draw out the enemy. This is unlikely, but whatever the reason, the undisciplined English on the left charged down the slope only to suffer the same fate as their colleagues on the right earlier in the day. This second disaster, coming on top of the deaths of Harold's brothers Gyrth and Leofwine, was a hammer-blow to the English king, who now must have regretted his decision to give battle with such a depleted army. Yet, drawing in his dauntless housecarls he presented an unbroken wall of shields and axes to the Normans. William of Poitiers was impressed by the grim, immovable mass of the English:

. . . a strange manner of battle where the one side works by constant motion and ceaseless charges, while the other can but endure passively as it stands fixed to the sod. The Norman arrow and sword worked on: in the

English ranks the only movement was the dropping of the dead: the living stood motionless.

If Harold, on the ridge, was in despair, William was no happier at the bottom of the slope. Only when the English had broken formation had he been able to overcome them. The housecarls had resisted every attack by archer, knight or footsoldier. With only two hours of daylight left, he was afraid that the English would withdraw in the darkness and re-form elsewhere, and he knew that his own army could not face a second battle against a reinforced enemy. Victory would have to be won that day — at whatever cost.

Ordering his archers — now with a replenished supply of arrows — to fire in a high arc so that their missiles fell upon the heads of the English, forcing them to lift their shields, William sent in his infantry under this 'creeping barrage'. In the close-quarter fighting on the ridge casualties were again heavy. Inch by inch the Normans gained a foothold, breaking the English line in places and cutting off small groups of men, to be mopped up by the cavalry. In this last stage of the fighting occurred the famous incident of the 'arrow in the eye'. It is impossible to tell from the evidence whether it was Harold or merely a housecarl who was struck in the eye by the arrow. What is certain, however, is that Harold did not die that way. Before the battle a group of Norman knights had sworn to slay the oathbreaker, as they viewed Harold, and though many of them died trying to breach the English line, four eventually broke through the ring of housecarls and hacked Harold down, killing him beneath his banner of the Fighting Man, made for him by his mother Gytha.

With the death of Harold, English resistance gave way, and the remaining fyrdmen took to their heels and escaped into the forest. The housecarls retained formation and then began to fall back under the attacks of the Norman cavalry. Few leaders were left to organize further resistance — only Esegar the Staller and Leofric, abbot of Bourne, are mentioned. At this moment, in the growing dusk, the Normans suffered a disaster which, had it occurred earlier, would have cost them the battle. Pursuing the housecarls, a large number of riders crashed to their deaths in a ravine — the Malfosse — on the right of the ridge. But it hardly mattered now. While the Norman infantry amused themselves by stripping and hacking the corpses — only Harold's mistress Edith Swansneck could identify his body after the battle — William prepared the next stage of the invasion, the march on London. Harold's body was eventually laid to rest in Waltham Abbey, and William was crowned king in Westminster Abbey on Christmas Day 1066.

The Battle of Manzikert 1071

It was the Christians of Western Europe who fought to regain the Holy Land from the Muslims during the Crusades. Yet for centuries before that the protection of the Christian holy places had been the task of the Byzantine emperor in Constantinople. The decisive defeat of the Byzantines by the Seljuk Turks at Manzikert in 1071 changed all that. The Byzantine Empire lost its recruiting grounds in Anatolia and became too feeble to hold back the Turks. To save themselves the Byzantines were forced to call on the states of Western Europe for military help. And out of their appeals grew the Crusades – the great movement to free the holy city of Jerusalem.

Yet everything might have been different. The Seljuk leader, Alp Arslan, had no personal quarrel with the Byzantines. On the contrary, he stood in awe of their military power and the prestige of their emperors. But his failure to restrain Turkish war bands from raiding and pillaging Byzantine territory in search of booty convinced the Byzantines that the Seljuks had to be stopped. The ease with which these Muslim raiders captured city after city showed that the Empire was now only a shadow of its former self. Since the death of Basil II in 1025 stringent cutbacks in military expenditure and the collapse of the system of local defence meant that the Byzantines had to hire mercenaries to defend their lands. And with a series of emperors who were more administrators than warriors it became obvious that the Empire was becoming decadent. Strong government was imperative and when, in 1068, the feeble Constantine X Ducas died, his widow Eudocia chose as her husband and emperor a young general named Romanus Diogenes.

Romanus set about rebuilding the Byzantine army, aiming to recapture the strategic cities of Armenia lost to the Seljuks in the previous decade. But he faced strong opposition to his policies from the Ducas family, who saw him as a usurper and were determined to overthrow him. A more ruthless man than Romanus would have eliminated them. Instead he merely exiled his most bitter opponent, John Ducas, the dead emperor's brother, hesitating to secure his throne by shedding blood.

In early March 1071 Romanus left Constantinople to rendezvous with the huge army assembling near Sebastea, numbering more than 100,000 combatant troops. His mind was set on regaining the strategic cities of Armenia and he had bankrupted the treasury to raise a force large enough to achieve this aim. Arab chroniclers wrote in astonishment of the huge siege engines, which needed vast teams of oxen to haul them. To lessen the rigours of campaigning Romanus took with him hundreds of mules laden with silver tableware, chandeliers, tapestries and silver ornaments, as well as his personal library and the extensive personal wardrobe expected of an emperor even on campaign. Nothing was overlooked – a complete pharmacy, Turkish baths made out of leather and a private chapel, complete with portable altars and icons, all found a place in the imperial baggage train.

Through the streets of the capital, crowded with cheering onlookers on that brisk March day, Romanus rode surrounded by the imperial cavalry of the Tagmata, regiments of cataphracts in all their regalia, which comprised the armoured fist of the Byzantine army. Following these knights on their mailed horses were the European mercenaries –

clean-shaven Normans with conical helms and kite-shaped shields, and rough red-bearded Rus, clad in mail coats with fur cloaks and striped baggy trousers. And in pride of place rode the Varangian Guard, the emperor's personal bodyguard, made up of axe-wielding Vikings and English housecarls.

Yet evil omens accompanied the start of Romanus' campaign. When a grey dove alighted on the emperor's hand during the brief sea-crossing of the Bosphorus it was felt by many to bode ill, and as the great army moved slowly through Anatolia it was dogged by bad luck. Near Dorylaeum the emperor's accommodation caught fire, destroying some of his carriages and personal equipment, as well as killing his finest horses, which ran through the camp screaming and burning like torches. Near Coloneia the Byzantines came upon the scene of Manuel Comnenus' defeat the previous year, and the troops became sullen and gloomy as they rode past the grisly evidence of a dreadful massacre, with the sun-bleached bones of old comrades lining their path for miles.

At Sebastea Romanus assembled his full army, which, besides his guards regiments and Varangians, included large numbers of Asiatic mercenaries from all over the Near East. Full-bearded Patzinaks in fur caps brushed shoulders with pigtailed Khazars, their faces hideously scarred from birth, while blond-haired Alans in brightly coloured jackets and trousers mixed with Cumans in thick sheepskin jerkins and heavily armoured Georgian and Armenian knights. It was a colourful and warlike assembly, but it served only to emphasize how little unity there was in the Byzantine army by that date. There were

pitifully few of the once-elite Anatolian soldiers who had formed the backbone of imperial armies for centuries. In fact there were far too many ill-trained levies and ill-disciplined mercenaries, who would break at the first clash of arms. More than ever Romanus would need to depend on the strength of the Tagmata and the Varangian Guard, as well as the loyalty of his commanders.

Reaching Erzurum, Romanus divided his army. He sent the Normans under Roussel of Bailleul and the infantry under Joseph Tarchaniotes to lay waste the territory west of Lake Van, while with the remainder he successfully stormed the city of Manzikert. But Romanus had miscalculated how soon the Turks would be ready to face him; sending out thousands of his men to scour the region in search of food, he left himself seriously depleted in numbers.

The first that Alp Arslan had heard of Romanus' advance into Armenia was when he was near Aleppo in Syria with his mind firmly on his campaign against the Egyptian Fatimids. He reacted with lightning speed, moving north towards Lake Van with the 4000 men of his bodyguard, calling in troops as he went. By the time he reached Khoi, to the east of Lake Van, he had perhaps 40,000 horsemen, less than Romanus, but still a substantial army. He sent the emir Sundak with a strong force of horsemen to reconnoitre the Byzantine position. Unexpectedly Sundak's men encountered the Byzantine scouting group of Roussel and Tarchaniotes and routed them, sending them fleeing in panic towards the west. How strongly they had resisted the Seljuks is open to doubt, and the suggestion of

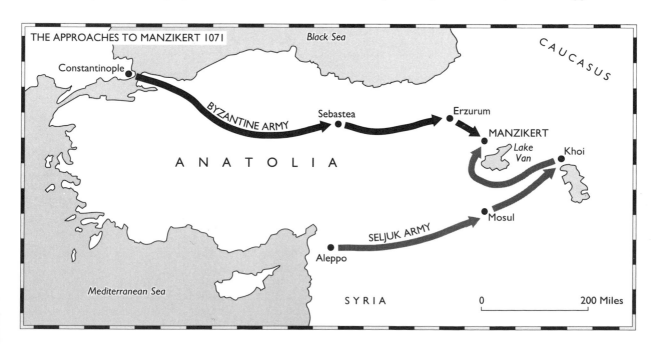

treachery by their commanders cannot be over-looked. Sundak now began skirmishing with Romanus' main force, and when Nicephorus Bryennius was sent to drive him off he found himself facing Seljuks in overwhelming numbers.

With Bryennius facing destruction and urgently demanding reinforcements, the thought must have briefly crossed Romanus' mind that perhaps he had misjudged his enemy. But he soon dismissed the idea. Alp Arslan could not have assembled his army so quickly or reached Manzikert in so short a time. Bryennius must be exaggerating the danger. Refusing to be ruffled by such alarmist reports and listening instead to the boasting of the Strategos Basiliakos that he could soon defeat these nomad vagabonds, Romanus foolishly gave the Armenian commander his chance, sending him out with a force of cavalry to rescue Bryennius. In the event the headstrong Basiliakos rode straight into an ambush and saw his entire command wiped out. At least Bryennius took the opportunity to disengage his forces and return to camp, bloodied but undefeated. News of the setback lowered morale in Romanus' camp. Many felt they had been defeated already, and confidence in the emperor fell. The Uz mercenaries, kin to the Seljuks and unwilling to be on what seemed likely to prove the losing side, deserted to the enemy en masse.

The next morning an embassy from the caliph of Baghdad came to the Byzantine camp to beg the emperor for a truce. Romanus foolishly assumed that this was a sign of weakness and refused to negotiate, insisting the Turks withdrew from the territory they held in Armenia. Having emptied his treasury to raise such a powerful army Romanus knew he would have to use it. If he returned home without a victory his throne and his life might well be forfeit.

With his peace offer rejected Alp Arslan was left with no option but to fight or withdraw in shame. In his war tent he assembled his emirs and asked them to swear allegiance to his son Malik-Shah, in case he himself fell in the fight. Then, handing over command of the army to the eunuch Tauraug, he took up the mace, the weapon of close combat, as a symbol that he would not leave the battlefield unless victorious.

The Byzantine army, meanwhile, was being drawn up in two lines, each several ranks deep. In the centre Romanus commanded his guards regiments, while on his left Nicephorus Bryennius led the troops of the European themes, and on the right were the mercenaries and the levies from Anatolia, under Alyattes. The crucial reserve line was commanded by Andronicus Ducas, son of the exiled John Ducas, a fine commander but a bitter enemy of Romanus.

The battle began with Romanus charging the Seljuks with the heavy cavalry of the Tagmata, trying to use his armoured knights to smash the Turkish centre. Amidst supplications to Allah the Almighty the Seljuks rode straight towards the Byzantines, firing their arrows, but at the last moment swinging away and riding out of range, using their favourite tactic of the feigned retreat. The air was filled with a cacophony of sound. In the front rank of each Seljuk regiment rode men clanging with all their might on timbrels, rattles, gongs and cymbals, while others blew loudly on trumpets. These were the men whose duty it was to terrify the enemy with their noise and to inflame the passions of their own warriors.

As the Turks raced back and forth across the open plain, drawing ever closer towards the distant foothills, Romanus became desperate to come to close quarters with them. He knew there was a likelihood of ambushes yet he could think of no alternative but to press on. The Turks kept up a barrage of arrows on the Byzantines from long range to which Romanus could only respond with his Patzinak and Cuman mercenaries, as fast and as mobile as the Seljuks, but incapable of delivering a telling blow. Hour followed hour as the Byzantines pressed on with their advance, periodically halting to fight off the swarms of Seljuk horse-archers, until

---

Byzantine cavalry depicted on an 11th-century ivory relief. AAAC

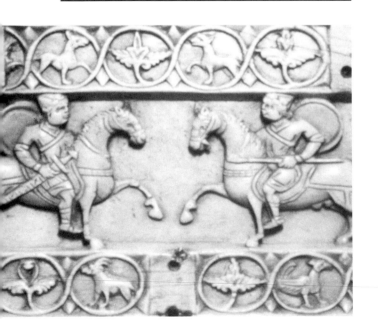

they reached the now-abandoned Seljuk camp. With dusk falling Romanus decided that he had come far enough for one day. He had left his camp undefended and was afraid that the enemy might capture his baggage train. He therefore called a general halt and ordered his commanders to reverse the imperial standards as the sign for an orderly withdrawal. But on a battle-front stretching perhaps five or six miles from right to left and in the heat of battle, parade-ground manoeuvres were almost impossible to interpret. On both flanks the Byzantines were heavily engaged with the enemy, and seeing the standards reversed men began to cry that the emperor had been beaten and was retreating. Panic spread all along the line and the Byzantine flanks started to waver.

Watching from the hills, at the edge of the plain, Alp Arslan could hardly believe his eyes. The huge Byzantine army was beginning to break up in confusion. He sent for his horse and rode out at the head of his reserve cavalry. In a great sweep of colour the Seljuks burst upon the Byzantines from the surrounding heights, the yellow standards of the royal Mameluke regiments easily identifiable, each bearing the insignia of its commander. Behind them came the horse-archers, in silk tunics over their cuirasses, darting in and out, filling the air with their arrows, which thudded into the round shields of the Varangian Guards or ricocheted away from the lamellar or plate armour of the cataphracts. But the horses of the Byzantines were the Seljuk's main target, and the screams of these animals, bucking and tipping their riders, mixed with the cries and curses of men and the infernal noise of naqqara, horns and cymbals.

The Seljuks circled around Romanus' division in the centre, cutting it off from the wings. The emperor was trapped and fighting for his life. In this moment of crisis Romanus called on Andronicus Ducas to lead the reserve to his aid – but Ducas took no notice and continued retreating, unmolested by the Turks. Seeing that the emperor was in difficulties he had set up the cry that Romanus was dead and ordered his men to retreat to the camp. He had chosen his moment supremely well: the Ducas clan was avenged – but at what cost to his people and nation. With both Byzantine wings in full retreat pursued by thousands of triumphant Muslim warriors, Alp Arslan concentrated his attacks on the cream of the imperial army, which was trapped and fighting desperately around the emperor. Pouring volleys of arrows into the fast-diminishing circle of defenders, the Seljuks soon identified Romanus himself, surrounded by a ring of Varangian Guards in their scarlet cloaks and

THE HORSE ARCHER AND THE ARMOURED KNIGHT

The battle of Manzikert was a forerunner of many similar battles that would be fought during the Crusades. It illustrates the difficulty faced by the heavily armoured Byzantine knights (cataphracts and klibanophoruses) in coming to grips with the more lightly armoured Seljuk horsemen. The Muslim horse archers were fast and mobile, but their arrows could not often penetrate armour except at short range — and here they risked being overwhelmed by the strength of the knights. Unless the line of armoured knights broke, as at Manzikert, it was almost impossible for the Seljuks to force a victory unless the Christian commander made a mistake, such as being drawn into an ambush or travelling too far into waterless desert.

swinging their deadly axes. Some of them were replaying the tragic scene of five years before when they had fought around Harold Godwinson's banner of the Fighting Man at Hastings. Romanus himself fought furiously until his horse was killed by an arrow and fell, pinning him to the ground. A Mameluke warrior dragged him clear, taking prisoner for the first time in the history of the Empire a living Byzantine emperor. As Romanus was led away from the carnage the last remnants of the Byzantine regular army were being routed by the Turks. Some mercenaries fought to the end, but others, like the Uzes, had deserted to the enemy or joined Ducas in his treacherous flight.

Alp Arslan treated the captive emperor with more kindness than his own people were to show him. When news of the disaster reached Constantinople the exiled John Ducas seized power, deposing Romanus in favour of the young Michael VII. Shortly afterwards Romanus was released and allowed to return home, but the traitor Andronicus Ducas led an army against him and, in spite of giving him a guarantee of safety, seized the ex-emperor and blinded him so horribly that he died from his wounds. It is said that Alp Arslan wept at the news.

But the damage was done. The Byzantine Empire had been fatally weakened, and Turkish freebooters raided openly, even up to the outskirts of Constantinople. Christian pilgrims were prevented from visiting the holy places and Jerusalem was now more firmly than ever in the hands of Islam. Only a great response by the Christians of the West – by people and princes – could reverse the consequences of the battle of Manzikert.

The Battle of Hattin 1187

Hattin

Crusaders

Commander:	King Guy of Lusignan
Vanguard:	Count Raymond of Tripoli
Centre:	King Guy
Rearguard:	Balian of Ibelin and Gérard of Ridefort
Numbers:	1500 knights, 3000 turcopoles, 10,000 archers and infantry

Saracens

Commander:	Sultan Saladin
Left wing:	Keukburi
Centre:	Saladin
Right wing:	Taqi al-Din
Numbers:	20,000

The fall of Jerusalem to the First Crusade in 1099 had been a great blow to the Muslim world. Jerusalem was the third most holy city of Islam and, during the next century, it became the central aim of *Jihad* – or holy war – to regain it. But after 1100, Christian settlers and pilgrims flooded into the newly won lands of Outremer – Syria and the Levant – and, supported by the major states of Western Europe, it seemed the Christian settlements would become permanent. The Muslims refused to accept this, yet until they found a leader who could unite them, they would never be strong enough to drive the infidels out.

By 1187 the Muslims had found such a leader in Sultan Saladin, ruler of Egypt and Syria, who called on all Muslims to join him in a *Jihad* to regain Jerusalem. His victory at the battle of Hattin virtually destroyed the Christian states of the Middle East and ensured that these areas would remain Islamic for the next 800 years.

To hold down a mainly Muslim population and to resist the threats from surrounding Muslim states, the Crusaders had built powerful castles throughout the kingdom of Jerusalem, allowing a few knights to dominate the countryside. In the event of a siege, the defenders of a castle were able to signal for help by lighting beacons. In this way, large Crusader armies could be assembled where they were most needed. The Saracens knew that they could not hope to beat the Crusaders if they stayed within these castles, or in fortified towns like Acre, Kerak and Tyre. Only by drawing them out into a pitched battle could they destroy them. Afterwards, they would be able to take the castles easily, once their garrisons were gone.

In 1187 Saladin invaded the kingdom of Jerusalem, hoping to exploit the splits in the Christian ranks. The Christian king, Guy of Lusignan, was a weak man who had taken the throne by a trick, and whose power was deeply resented by native nobles such as Raymond of Tripoli and Balian of Ibelin. Guy was influenced by men like the ruthless Reginald of Kerak, whom Saladin had sworn to kill with his own hand, and Gérard of Ridefort, Master of the Knights Templar, both powerful warriors but impetuous commanders. Saladin needed to draw Guy away from the defences of his castles and out into the open. How could he do it ?

Saladin decided to lay siege to the city of Tiberias, knowing that it would be virtually defenceless, as Guy had already stripped the castle garrisons throughout the country to assemble the royal army at Saffuriya. Tiberias was the property of Raymond of Tripoli, who was with the royal army, while his wife, the countess Eschiva, was in the city protected by a tiny garrison. If Eschiva called on the king for help, Guy would have no option but to go to her aid. When a messenger rode from Tiberias to Saffuriya on just such a mission, Saladin made certain that he was not molested. Meanwhile, the Saracens occupied the high ground on either side of the waterless plateau that separated Saffuriya from Tiberias. There they would wait until the Crusaders walked into their trap.

At Saffuriya Guy called a war council and asked his senior commanders for their advice. Raymond of Tripoli spoke first and, surprisingly, argued strongly against a rescue bid. Like everyone present he knew that Saladin was planning a trap and that if the royal army advanced into the waterless desert the whole army could be lost as the result of one battle. He also knew that Saladin was a man of honour, who would not harm a defenceless lady. But such talk infuriated Gérard of Ridefort, the

Master of the Templars, who condemned Raymond as a coward. To Gérard it was a disgrace for the army to sit doing nothing while the Saracens sacked a Christian city. But the king, and the rest of the lords, were swayed by Raymond's arguments, and the decision was taken to resist the temptation to rush to the relief of Tiberias.

As the Christian camp slept, Gérard went to Guy's tent just as the king was retiring for the night. Guy was uneasy in the presence of the Templar, always aware of the part that Gérard had played in helping him to the throne. Gérard told him that if he did not march to the relief of Tiberias the military orders – Templars and Hospitallers – would withdraw from the army. Under pressure like this Guy simply caved in and reversed his earlier decision not to march. When the rest of the camp heard that the king had changed his mind they were dumbfounded. Everyone knew that a march to Tiberias in the heat of midsummer was madness and certain to end in disaster. But the king's word was law.

The Christian army, probably the largest ever assembled in the 88-year history of the kingdom, comprised some 1500 knights, 3000 or so other horsemen – sergeants and turcopoles – and just over 10,000 footsoldiers, some in hauberks (long coats of chainmail) and heavily armed with sword and shield, others with crossbows, and still more with bows and slings. On 3 July 1187 the entire force set out from Saffuriya just before sunrise for the 15-mile journey to Tiberias. They were leaving the well-watered gardens of Saffuriya for the sunbaked plateau ahead where they knew the Saracens would be waiting for them. The vanguard was led by Raymond of Tripoli, with Balian of Ibelin and Gérard of Rideford at the rear and the king with his lords in the centre. At first, the Saracens confined themselves to hit-and-run attacks. The knights in the centre of the Crusader column were forced to move at the speed of the footsoldiers, who formed a protective sleeve all around them and shielded their horses from the Saracen arrows with their mail shirts or leather gambesons.

The sun was relentless and there were no trees to offer shade on the limestone road on which they travelled. The heavily armoured knights, with coloured surcoats keeping their hauberks from baking the flesh within, wiped dusty sweat from their eyes and peered suspiciously ahead, waiting for the attack they knew would come. All around them lumbered the footsoldiers, exchanging crude jests to relieve the tension. Some were well-equipped mercenaries from Genoa or the Low Countries, armed with crossbows, who earned their living by following the likeliest paymasters. Others were townsmen from the coastal cities who had answered the *arrière-ban* (a call to arms of all able-bodied citizens) and were fired up by the feeling that they were fighting not only for their faith but for their families back in Acre, Tyre and Beirut. Most of these wore tunics of quilted cloth or leather gambesons, which would resist the blow of a Saracen sword and deaden the impact of an arrow. The air was filled with many of the languages and dialects of Europe; the Christian army was truly an international force.

The column had no water carts – which would have slowed it down even further – and the men had to carry their own water bottles. Before the sun was at its height most had used up all their precious supply and could look for no more water until they reached the Sea of Galilee. Now that the column was well and truly committed to the march, and retreat would be as hard as going forward, Saladin launched the wings of his army, which charged down from the hills and ringed round the Crusader columns. The Christian crossbowmen kept the Saracens at a distance, but, in order to fight, the column had to slow almost to a standstill, and above their heads the sun was doing its work.

By 10 a.m. the Crusaders had been marching for nearly six hours and were becoming exhausted. Their last chance of water before Lake Tiberias was to the north at a spring near Mount Turan, but King Guy ordered his men to march on and the chance was missed. In the vanguard Raymond was convinced that the long, straggling column would never reach Tiberias before the men died of thirst and suggested to the king that they change direction and head into rising ground to the north where there were springs near the village of Hattin. It would mean abandoning Tiberias for the moment but it might save the column. The king agreed and the whole army now turned in a northeasterly direction near Meskenah. In the confusion of the turn some knights broke away from their infantry escort and

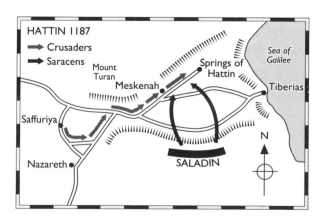

tried to quicken their pace towards the water. Sensing that his prey might elude him Saladin launched a large force of cavalry under his nephew Taqi al-Din to ride around the column and block its path to Hattin. Realizing that unless they could break through Taqi's men the whole column was doomed, Raymond prepared to charge the Saracens with his knights. However, before he could do so a desperate – and as it turned out fatal – message reached him from King Guy, ordering a halt and the setting up of camp. The exhausted rearguard – mainly Templars – could go no further that day. Without water Raymond knew that this was a sentence of death. 'Alas! alas! Lord God, the war is over. We are betrayed to death and the land is lost,' he told Guy – but the king was adamant and the camp was set up.

With his enemy trapped on the plateau, far from any water, Saladin's troops surrounded the Crusader camp, harassing the Christians all night with shouts of triumph and a cacophony of drums and trumpets. In the light of their fires the Crusaders could see the Saracens deliberately taunting them with offers of water, only to tip it in the sand as they held out their hands. To the horrors of their situation was added the presence of scorpions and poisonous spiders, which crept into their armour.

At first light the Crusaders began their march towards the springs at Hattin. Hundreds of horses had already died from thirst or from Saracen arrows, and so many knights were marching with the infantry. Morale within the Christian army was very low, and some knights deserted to the enemy. The fighting slowed the column's momentum until it was again halted. Suddenly the infantry gave way and with a great moan hundreds of them left the column and rushed up the rocky slopes towards where they thought the water could be found. Faced with the collapse of his whole column Guy had no option but to pitch his tent to act as a rallying point. Around him gathered most of the knights from the central column, but few infantry obeyed his urgent summonses to return to their duty. Even when the bishops called them back to defend the True Cross itself there was little response. To add to their suffering the Muslims had lit brush fires, which blew smoke constantly into their faces and worsened their maddened craving for water.

Sensing that the day was lost Raymond massed his own knights and those from Antioch and Sidon and charged the Saracens guarding the approach to the village of Hattin. Raymond's knights succeeded in cutting through and making their escape into the hills, but for King Guy and the mass of the army there was no escape. Without infantry to hold back the Muslims with their crossbows, Guy's knights were almost helpless. The Saracens now closed in on the grim circle of iron-clad warriors ringed round the True Cross. In the chaotic melee around the holy relic the Bishop of Acre was killed, and it was taken up by the Bishop of Lydda instead. Taqi al-Din now ordered his warriors to put aside their bows and, wielding sword, mace and lance, to charge the knights defending the bishop. By sheer weight of numbers they bore down the defenders and Taqi himself seized the relic and rode exultantly out of the fight. Al-Afdil, Saladin's 17-year-old son, saw this happen and thought victory was now certain. But his father corrected him and the Crusaders made another desperate charge, which was turned back only yards away from where they stood.

I cried out again: 'We have beaten them.' My father turned to me and said: 'Be silent. We shall not defeat them until that tent falls.' As he spoke, the tent fell.

With the loss of this holy relic, the symbol of God's support, Christian morale collapsed. So exhausted was Guy that he simply sat on the ground and awaited capture. With him were taken most of the lords of the kingdom, except for Raymond of Tripoli and Balian of Ibelin, who had escaped.

Saladin treated his noble prisoners well, except for Reginald of Kerak, whom he slew with his own hand; the common soldiers, on the other hand, were all sold into slavery, some for as little as the price of a pair of sandals. So complete was the Christian defeat that every city and castle within the kingdom – save Tyre – fell to Saladin in a single campaign. Guy had risked everything on a single battle, against the advice of more experienced soldiers. He had led his army into a trap, even though he had been warned against it.

The Christian defeat at Hattin was a catastrophe for the Crusading movement. The defeat was complete and irreversible. A Crusading army – the biggest that the kingdom of Jerusalem had ever fielded and fighting under the True Cross – had proved itself incapable of resisting the Muslims. To many true believers it was a sign that God had turned his face away from them. There were more Crusades – at least six of them – but they no longer possessed the religious zeal and values that had inspired the soldiers of the First Crusade whose reward – the Holy City itself – had now been lost by a faithless generation. Crusades were now excuses for territorial greed and aggrandizement. The Fourth Crusade in 1204 had moved so far away from the original aim to regain the Holy Land that it occupied itself with besieging and capturing the Christian city of Constantinople.

The Battle of Las Navas de Tolosa 1212

Las Navas de Tolosa

Spanish
Commander: King Alphonso VIII of Castile
Vanguard: Diego López de Haro, Lord of
              Viczaya
Centre: Pedro II of Aragon
Rearguard: Alphonso and Archbishop Rodrigo
              of Toledo
Numbers: 10,000 knights and heavy cavalry,
              60,000 infantry

Almohads
Commander: Miramamolin
Numbers: unknown

While Pope Urban was preaching the First Crusade at Clermont in 1095, urging the people of France to take up the Cross to regain Jerusalem and the Holy Land from the Saracens, a similar crusading spirit prevailed south of the Pyrenees, in the Christian kingdoms of León, Aragon and Castile. Spain had been first conquered by the Muslim Moors in 711, but by the 11th century the country was divided between the areas reconquered by the Christians in the north and the Moorish lands of the south (al-Andalus). The process known as the *Reconquista* — the crusading movement to liberate the south from Muslim control — was gathering strength, and Spain had in El Cid a crusading hero to match any from Outremer. In the following century, helped by Spain's crusading orders such as the white-robed Knights of Calatrava and the red-cloaked Knights of Santiago, the rulers of the Spanish kingdoms took the initiative against the crumbling Muslim power in al-Andalus.

Although in 1195 the great Almohad caliph, Yaqoob al Mansoor, inflicted a heavy defeat at Alarcos on the king of Castile, Alphonso VIII, Yaqoob's death in 1199 brought to the throne of the Almohad empire in Spain and Morocco his shy, nervous and unwarlike son, al-Nasir, known to the Christians as Miramamolin. This encouraged Alphonso to break the treaty he had signed with Miramamolin's father and begin raiding into Almohad territory, as far south as Granada. By 1211 Miramamolin had had enough and brought an army across from Africa, landing in Seville and threatening Alphonso with retribution.

The Archbishop of Toledo, Rodrigo Jiménez de Rada, with the backing of Pope Innocent III and the Spanish military orders, persuaded Alphonso to resume the *Reconquista* and take up the gauntlet thrown down by Miramamolin. Throughout Europe the call went out for crusaders to join Alphonso, and recruits soon flocked in from Italy, France, and even Germany. The kings of Aragon, Portugal, León and Navarre pledged to support Castile against the Muslims, and by Easter 1212 a great, cosmopolitan crusading army was assembling at Toledo. When the army marched south on 20 June, the vanguard — made up of crusaders from outside Spain — was led by Diego López de Haro, Lord of Viczaya. The central part of the army was commanded by Pedro II of Aragon, and the rearguard was led by Alphonso, with Archbishop Rodrigo and the knights of the military orders. It was an impressive force numbering perhaps 10,000 armoured horsemen and as many as 60,000 footsoldiers. Even so, they could expect to be outnumbered by Miramamolin's army of Berbers, African Negroes and Andalusians.

Unfortunately, the Christian army was very undisciplined and the French knights seemed more concerned with plundering Muslim castles and cities rather than facing the enemies of their religion in battle. On 24 June the French attacked Malagón and massacred the garrison. A week later the French broke ranks again and captured Calatrava, lost only recently to the Almohads by the Knights of Calatrava. Alphonso was pleased to regain the city, but he infuriated the French by forbidding them to loot the town and returning it instead to the Order of Calatrava. This was the final straw for the French knights, who were finding the weather too hot and the loot too small. Leaving behind their bishops, they deserted the crusade and returned to France.

Undeterred, Alphonso spurred on his army to Las Navas de Tolosa where, on 13 July, he encountered the Almohad army. For two days both armies sat watching each other, content to skirmish.

The Christian victory at Navas de Tolosa rang the death knell of the sophisticated and tolerant culture of Moorish Spain. CV

Finally on 16 July the Christian army formed up for battle in four divisions. At the rear, Alphonso VIII with the knights of the military orders formed a reserve, while in the front line the centre was held by the men of Castile and León under Diego López de Haro. On the left wing Pedro II commanded the troops of Aragon, and on the right Sancho VII led the men of Navarre.

The battle began with a series of frontal charges by the heavily armoured Leónese knights under Diego López, which were repulsed by the Muslims. The tactics of the Almohads were described by one of their warriors:

We formed a square on the flat land. On all four sides we placed a rank of men with long spears in their hands.

Behind them stood a second line with spears and javelins, while behind them were men with bags of stones [slingers]. Behind all stood archers.

However, when the Almohads counter-attacked – to the sound of huge kettle-drums, some several yards in diameter – with Andalusian heavy cavalry and Mauretanian light horsemen, they were held up by the infantry of the Spanish reserve, who peppered them with missiles from slings, bows and crossbows. There now occurred a vicious dispute between Miramamolin's Berber and Andalusian troops, and the latter suddenly deserted *en masse*, throwing the Caliph back on his African troops alone. Taking advantage of this Alphonso launched his reserve to join the two wings under Pedro II and Sancho VII and broke the Almohad line with his armoured knights, rolling up its left wing. King Sancho broke right through the Muslim defenders to Miramamolin's magnificent gold-embroidered tent, which was surrounded by a palisade held together by chains. The Caliph's Negro guards, armed with spears and enormous hide shields, fought ferociously around the royal tent, but the knights of Navarre hacked them down and seized the pavilion. It was a signal for Miramamolin to flee the field and make his way to Seville, with just 4000 of his soldiers remaining. The Almohad losses were large – possibly a third of their entire army – but in view of the desertion of the Andalusians it is possible to exaggerate their casualties. In spite of chroniclers, who speak of just 25 or 30 Spanish casualties, it is clear that in such a hard-fought battle Christian losses must have been heavy, particularly to the military orders, which had borne the brunt of the fighting. The booty was immense and the great tapestry that covered the entrance to Miramamolin's tent was sent to the monastery of Las Huelgas at Burgos, where it still hangs today as a symbol of this battle – Spain's greatest national victory.

Alphonso VIII's victory at Las Navas de Tolosa was 'the Waterloo of Arab rule in Spain'. The Muslim threat to Christian Spain was ended and the Almohad Empire's days were numbered. Miramamolin was dead within a year, and with his death the equilibrium in Spain between a Christian north and a Muslim south was permanently altered. Within 40 years the whole of al-Andalus had fallen to the Christians, leaving only the Muslim kingdom of Granada in the south beyond Christian control. Las Navas de Tolosa marked a turning point in the *Reconquista* and a tragic end to what General Glubb has called the 'refined and cultured civilization of Muslim Andalus . . . [which was] far in advance of both western Europe and northern Africa'.

The Battle of Ain Jalut
1260

Ain Jalut

Mongols
Commander: Kitbuqa
Numbers: 25,000 cavalry, including Crusaders, and Georgian and Armenian Christians

Mamelukes
Commanders: Kutuz and Baybars
Numbers: 100,000 Mamelukes, Egyptians and Syrian Muslims

The vast Mongol Empire created by Genghis Khan – an empire stretching across much of Asia – survived his death intact. Under his successors the empire extended even further, with waves of Mongol armies invading Korea, China, Russia and even Europe. In 1253, the fourth 'Great Khan' – Mongke – sent an army under his brother Hulägu to occupy Persia and to destroy the Assassins of Syria. At first this Mongol campaign was welcomed by the Abbasid caliph of Baghdad, because the Assassins were a heretical sect of Islam. But the Mongols were soon pressing at the gates of his own domain, and in 1257 they attacked Baghdad itself. Ironically, it was the schism within the Muslim world that helped Hulägu. The Shi'ite Muslims actually welcomed a Mongol victory over the hated Sunnite caliph. After a brief siege, in which the Mongols used catapults to fire the foundations of buildings surrounding the walls of Baghdad, the city was taken by assault. All Muslim soldiers were put to the sword, along with 3000 of the Caliph's courtiers. The Mongols sacked the city for seven days, sparing the Nestorian Christians in their churches but massacring Muslims, regardless of their sect. The riches of Baghdad – one of the most fabulously wealthy cities in history – were sent back in vast wagon trains to Mongke at Karakorum, the Mongol capital in Central Asia. With Baghdad in ruins, Hulägu ordered the caliph and his sons to be sewn up inside a carpet and then trampled to death under the hooves of Mongol horses. So many of the people of Baghdad were slaughtered – perhaps

100,000 or more – that the Mongols were forced to evacuate the area because of the threat of disease.

A contemporary Persian writer – understandably suffering from a certain degree of bias – described a typical Mongol warrior:

Their eyes were so narrow and so piercing that they might have bored a hole in a brazen vessel, and their stench was more horrible than their colour. Their heads were set on their bodies as if they had no necks and their cheeks resembled leather bottles full of wrinkles and knots. Their noses extended from cheekbone to cheekbone. Their nostrils resembled rotting graves, and from them the hair descended as far as the lips.

The Mongols placed little importance on personal cleanliness, living and often sleeping on their small horses, and dressing in the skins of whatever

A Mongol horse archer photographed in the 19th century, showing little change from his forefathers who fought at Ain Jalut. PN

animals they could find on the bleak and often frozen steppes from which they came. A nomadic people, their livelihood centred entirely around their horses. They fed on milk-curd and *kumis* (an intoxicating drink made from mare's milk) and often drank blood by opening a vein in a horse's neck.

The Mongol's favourite weapon was the composite bow, a weapon with a surprisingly powerful pull of 166 pounds (greater than the English longbow of the 14th century), and a range of 200–300 yards. The Mongols hardened their arrow-heads by plunging them red hot into salt water, and this enabled them to pierce armour. They often carried lassoes and a hook for unhorsing their enemies, while among other weapons they used lances and light sabres, and carried wicker shields. By the 13th century many Mongols wore armour of either leather or lamellar scales.

After the fall of Baghdad Hulägu's name became so terrifying that Muslim rulers throughout Syria and Iraq rushed to swear allegiance to him. The Prince of Mosul – having boasted that he would take Hulägu by the ears – saved his neck by claiming that he had only meant that he would wish to fix golden earrings to the Mongol's exalted ears. Another Muslim prince gave Hulägu a pair of socks with the prince's likeness printed on the soles so that Hulägu could walk daily on the man's face.

If the Muslim world was in uproar at the arrival of the Mongols, the Christians of Syria – notably those who lived in the Crusader enclaves – believed that Hulägu was the legendary Prester John, who had come to free them from the scourge of Islam. Hulägu's wife actually was a Nestorian Christian, as was Kitbuqa, his leading general. To the Latin Christians of Outremer any Christian was better than no Christian, and they prepared to ally themselves with the Mongols in their campaigns against the Muslims.

Hulägu now called on the Sultan of Syria – al-Nasir – to surrender Damascus to the Mongols. The sultan knew that he could not resist the power of Hulägu's army, now swollen by Christian Armenians and Muslim allies, and so in desperation he turned to the rulers of Egypt – the Mamelukes. The Mameluke leader, Kutuz, had no love for the Syrians, but he hoped to make the most of the emergency for his own ends. Hulägu, meanwhile, took Aleppo, and the Christians from Acre – including the Grand Master of the Teutonic Knights, Anno von Sangerhausen – rode out to join the Mongol army and serve with them on their 'crusade'. The Christian leader – Bohemond IV of Antioch – played his cards well and received Aleppo

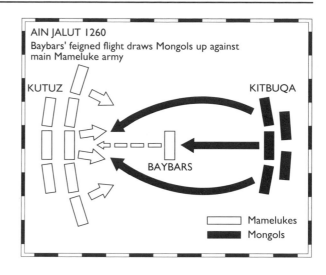

and Damascus from Hulägu. It seemed that the Mongols might achieve for the Crusaders everything that Richard the Lionheart and the Third Crusade had failed to do. Bohemond and Hulägu even began planning to move on to Jerusalem.

Then – out of the blue – occurred an event that changed the face of history. At his capital of Karakorum, south of Lake Baikal, the Great Khan Mongke died of dysentery. Although Kubilai had been proclaimed 'Great Khan' in succession, his right was disputed and another brother, Arik Boke, took up arms against him. It was vital for Hulägu to return to China to support Kubilai. The conquest of Syria would just have to wait. Leaving Kitbuqa in command of a much reduced army, Hulägu returned home with the majority of his Mongol warriors. The 'crusade' to take Jerusalem was cancelled and Kitbuqa now faced the difficult task of holding the gains Hulägu had made in Syria.

Before hearing of Mongke's death Hulägu had declared war on the Mamelukes of Egypt and demanded that they should surrender to him. At first Kutuz had despaired at having to face Hulägu's hordes, but when news reached him that the dreaded Mongol conqueror had evacuated most of his troops from Syria, his courage returned and he demonstrated his defiance by nailing the heads of the Mongol emissaries to the gates of Cairo. On 26 July 1260 the Mameluke army left Cairo led by the Bunduqdari Baybars and marched through Palestine towards Damascus. As it passed through areas devastated by Mongol raids, Muslim warriors of every sect flocked to join its ranks until the Mameluke army numbered close to 100,000 men.

Undeterred by mere numbers, Kitbuqa left Damascus and headed south with an army of about 25,000, made up of Mongols and Georgian and Armenian Christians. At Goliath's Springs, not far

An illustrated page from Rashid al-Din's history of the Mongols (16th century). PN

Baybars led the Mongols straight up against the entire Mameluke army, four times its size. Apparently unperturbed by his predicament, Kitbuqa ordered the Mongols to deploy in total silence, their movements controlled by the raising and lowering of black and white flags. Eventually, by a series of wheeling manoeuvres, Kitbuqa succeeded in defeating the Mameluke van and left flank. Kutuz now ordered a massed charge of the Mamelukes, which hit the Mongol centre with overwhelming force and broke it. Refusing to retreat Kitbuqa rode up and down trying to re-form his scattered army: 'It is here that I must die! Some soldier will reach the khan to tell him that Kitbuqa refused to make a shameful retreat and that he sacrificed his life to his duty. Nor must the loss of one Mongol army grieve the khan too deeply. Let him reflect that for a year the wives of his soldiers have not conceived, that the horses of his stud have sired no colts.' Kitbuqa was taken prisoner by the Mamelukes and brought before Kutuz, who laughed at him, 'After overthrowing so many dynasties, behold you now caught in the trap!' The Nestorian Christian replied, 'If I perish at your hand, I acknowledge that God and not you will be the author of the deed. Do not be intoxicated by a moment's success. When the news of my death reaches the ears of Hulägu-khan, his wrath will boil like a stormy sea. From Azerbaijan to the gates of Egypt the land will be crushed by Mongol horses.' Kutuz struck off his head, which was used by a number of Mameluke riders for a game of polo.

The Mongol army was virtually destroyed, and Kutuz entered Damascus in triumph. He was not to enjoy his victory, however, for he was murdered by servants of the ambitious Baybars, who became the founder of the Mameluke state. The Christians had gambled by siding with the Mongols, and with the defeat of these previously invincible warriors the Muslims were able to extinguish the last vestiges of a Christian presence in the Holy Land. The battle of Ain Jalut was decisive in that it condemned the Christian Crusaders to oblivion. The Mongol ruler of the Golden Horde in Russia – a Muslim, unlike the Nestorian Christian Hulägu – was soon on good terms with the Mamelukes in Syria and the chance of any future Mongol invasion of Syria and Egypt receded. The Mamelukes flourished in Egypt until dispossessed by the Ottoman Turks in 1517.

from Nazareth, the Mongols encountered Baybars' advance column of Mamelukes. The Mongols immediately charged into the Egyptian vanguard, scattering it and sending Baybars in confused flight with Kitbuqa not far behind. But Kitbuqa was falling for a typical Mongol ruse, a feigned flight.

The Battle of Crécy 1346

The causes of the Hundred Years War are both complex and tedious. Suffice it to say that on the death of the French king Charles IV in 1328, the royal line of Capet came to an end and the crown passed to Philip of Valois, whose claim was based on the Salic Law of the Franks that property inheritance could not pass through the female line. As it happened, Edward III of England claimed he had a better right to the throne than Philip of Valois through his mother Isabella, daughter of Philip IV. But this was not the only cause of friction between the French and the English. Philip of Valois had interfered with the wool trade between England and Flanders, as well as threatening English possessions such as Guienne in southern France.

When, on 11 November 1337, the English began the war – which was to last 116 years – by capturing the island of Cadsand off the coast of Flanders, Edward III cannot have dreamed of how close to conquering the whole state of France he and his successors would come before eventually being driven out in 1453. France was the largest and most prosperous state in Europe, with a population of some 20 million and a powerful feudal nobility bred

to war. In comparison, England had less than 4 million people, a small military nobility, and no European reputation in military terms. But such comparisons are misleading. England was a far more united state than France, and her highly professional soldiers, commanded by a series of brilliant officers, had experience from the Scottish wars. And in the longbow the English had a modern, democratic weapon – democratic in that at long range the meanest peasant archer could slay the greatest noble or the most skilful warrior in all France.

However, by the time of the battle of Crécy in 1346, the effectiveness of the English longbow should not have surprised the French knights. English victories at Dupplin Moor in 1332 and Halidon Hill in 1333 against the Scots had been won by a combination of men-at-arms and bowmen fighting in formation, while at Cadsand in 1337 the English archers had shown their superiority over Flemish crossbowmen. The French themselves had even suffered at the hands of English longbowmen in a number of encounters prior to Crécy, including the naval battle at Sluys in 1340, and the encounters at Morlaix (1342), Auberoche (1345) and St Pol de Léon (1346).

Edward III's expedition of 1346 landed near Cherbourg and marched inland, passing unhindered through the Norman countryside. The town of Caen was captured after a brief siege, and the

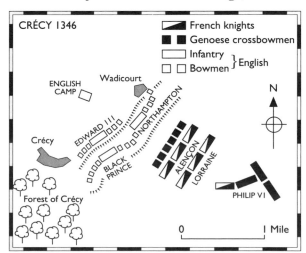

Constable of France was taken for ransom. The English then moved on towards Rouen, where they learned that King Philip VI was preparing his army and had taken the Oriflamme – the war flag of France – from the Abbey of St Denis in Paris, where it resided in peacetime. Edward meanwhile found the bridges across the Seine had been broken down, and headed north to rendezvous with his Flemish allies in Picardy. But Edward found his way blocked by the River Somme in full flood. He was now heavily pursued by overwhelming French numbers and was fortunate to find a crossing point near Blanchetaque. He quickly moved on towards the forest of Crécy, where he took up a defensive position to await a French attack.

Edward III's army of 12,000 men, two-thirds of whom were archers, had taken up a good position, on a gentle ridge with both flanks protected. On the right flank nearest to Crécy was Edward's son, the 16-year-old Black Prince, along with the earls of Warwick and Oxford, Count Godfrey of Harcourt, and four 'Garter knights' – Sir Thomas Holland, Sir John Chandos, Lord Stafford and Lord Burghersh. With the Black Prince were 1000 men-at-arms, 1000 Welsh footsoldiers and about 3000 archers. On the left, near the village of Wadicourt, were the earls of Northampton and Arundel, with the Bishop of Durham and 1000 dismounted knights, 3000 archers and some Welsh infantry. The king's reserve

'battle' was situated higher up the ridge, and was made up of 700 dismounted men-at-arms and about 2000 archers. The chronicler Froissart reports that the English archers adopted a 'harrow' formation for receiving the French charges, and it is clear that Edward III must have been aware of this formation, adopted by the Byzantine general Narses at the battle of Taginae in 552.

The French army under King Philip VI was both cosmopolitan and disorganized. As well as the nobility of France, the army included Charles, king of the Romans, the counts of Namur and Hainault, the duke of Lorraine and King Jaime II of Majorca, as well as hundreds of German and Bohemian knights under the blind King John of Bohemia. The French array consisted of probably 12,000 mounted men-at-arms, with a vast number of footsoldiers, who were, however, of little value and counted for nothing in French tactics. More significant was the contingent of 6000 Genoese crossbowmen who preceded the knights into battle, led by their own commanders, Odone Doria and Carlo Grimaldi. The French knights were contemptuous of such mercenaries and ignored their complaints that they were tired after 18 hours of marching and that the continuous rain had soaked their bowstrings.

It was late in the afternoon, and approaching the hour of vespers (6 p.m.) as the disordered French army came into sight of the English. Sir Charles

THE ENGLISH LONGBOW

The English longbow was adopted from the Welsh bow. It was between 5 and 6 feet long and generally made of yew, though sometimes of elm and ash. Contrary to modern usage the string was not drawn back to the ear; the bow was bent away from the body in a strong, continuous movement. Arrows were a 'cloth-yard' long and ranges of up to 300 yards could be achieved. Using the narrow chisel-pointed head the arrow was able to pierce chain mail with ease, and even plate armour at shorter ranges. Firing rates of 12 to 15 arrows per minute were often achieved, and this helps to explain the devastation caused by the arrow storm that hit the French knights in the first few minutes of the battle of Crécy.

Left: English bowmen at Crécy. Detail from the Chronicles of Froissart in the Bibliothèque Nationale, Paris. PN

Edward, the Black Prince; detail of the latten effigy of c. 1376 in Canterbury Cathedral. PN

Oman asserts that Philip, acting on the advice of Alard de Baseilles, wished to make camp in order to allow the rear of his army to catch up so that everyone might rest. However, the undisciplined French knights would not listen to him. According to Froissart's account,

... neither the king nor the marshals could stop them, but they marched on without any order until they came in sight of their enemies. As soon as the foremost rank saw them, they fell back at once in great disorder, which alarmed those in the rear, who thought they had been fighting ... All the roads between Abbeville and Crécy were covered with common people, who, when they were coming within three leagues of their enemies, drew their swords, bawling out, 'Kill, Kill' ... There is no man, unless he had been present, that can imagine, or describe truly, the confusion of that day.

Before leaving Abbeville the French host had been formed into nine or ten divisions, but so poor was the discipline that by the time they arrived at Crécy little sign of order remained. Despairing of being able to withdraw his army into camp, Philip decided to attack.

The Genoese crossbowmen advanced towards the English, followed by the first line of French men-at-arms under the counts of Alençon and Flanders. The first volley from the crossbows fell short and was answered by an overwhelming fire from the English archers and stone-firing English cannons. The Genoese panicked and tried to get out of range, but could not break through the masses of French cavalry, who refused to make way for them. In anger at being held up by such mercenaries King Philip called out 'Kill me those scoundrels, for they block our advance and serve no purpose!' There now followed an incredible scene as the king's brother, the count of Alençon, rode down the retreating Genoese. As Oman says,

This mad attempt to ride down their own infantry was fatal to the front line of the French chivalry. In spite of themselves they were brought to a stand at the foot of the slope, where the whole mass of horse and foot rocked helplessly to and fro under a constant hail of arrows from the English archery.

Few of Alençon's first line came to grips with the dismounted English knights, for most were brought down by arrows. Yet no attempt was made to clear the field before the second French line charged. This resulted in further confusion in which the blind king of Bohemia – fighting chained to a knight on either side – was killed.

Throughout the battle the French commanders showed no tactical understanding whatsoever. Each band of knights seemed to have the single idea of charging at the enemy head-on, with no thought of manoeuvre or flanking action. The only danger to the English occurred when some of Alençon's men-at-arms, avoiding the archers, managed to break into the division of the Black Prince, where they were beaten after a stiff fight. At one stage the young prince was thrown to the ground and was rescued by his standard bearer, Richard Fitzsimmons. Alarmed at the danger to the prince, Godfrey Harcourt appealed to the king for reinforcements, but Edward issued the famous instruction to 'let him win his spurs'. Even so, the king quietly sent the Bishop of Durham with 20 knights to bolster the prince's flank.

Edward III was himself engaged in single combat by Sir Eustace de Ribeaumont, and twice knocked to the ground. Overpowered and taken prisoner, Sir Eustace was later entertained at dinner by the king. Edward was so impressed by the Frenchman's valour that he gave him a string of pearls, saying, 'Sir Eustace, I give you this chaplet as the best warrior of the day, and I beg you to wear it in the love of me, and seeing you are my prisoner, I give you back your liberty.'

When the French had launched 15 consecutive charges, the last of which took place after dark, they eventually withdrew having suffered enormous losses, including the kings of Majorca and Bohemia slain, as well as 1542 lords and knights killed, and thousands of footsoldiers. Philip had been unhorsed twice himself in the fighting, but escaped with some ease as the English, maintaining tight discipline, did not pursue their beaten enemy.

The days of the feudal horscmen were numbered, for the longbow and later the handgun, combined with the pike, would give the advantage to the professional footsoldier fighting on the defensive. The French, however, clung to the traditional virtues of knighthood, and the lesson they drew from their defeat at Crécy was the wrong one, that it had been the dismounted English men-at-arms who had triumphed, not the lowly archers. The result was that at Poitiers in 1356 King John II dismounted his knights and advanced these heavily armed warriors towards the English lines on foot. Again the English archers carried out great slaughter, though this time the battle was more of a hand-to-hand melee than at Crécy.

If Calais was the only direct English gain from the battle of Crécy, it was a vital one, being seen as a kind of medieval Gibraltar, giving England a foothold on the continent from which to launch invasions, as well as becoming the main port for English wool exports. But more important than that, England had become a significant military power. Her combination of bow and pike was to win her innumerable victories over the French in the next 80 years, allowing her to absorb vast areas of French territory. For 100 years England became the dominant military power in Western Europe, and her soldiers were to win fame and renown as mercenaries in Spain, Italy and Germany as well as in France.

The Battle of Tannenburg 1410

The crusading movement of the Middle Ages was not confined to the struggle to regain Jerusalem and the holy places in Palestine. Equally vigorous attempts were made to drive the Muslims from Spain in what is known as the *Reconquista*, while along the shores of the Baltic the Teutonic Order – a religious order of knights like the Hospitallers and Templars in Outremer – conducted a ferocious campaign to convert the heathen Prussians and Lithuanians to Christianity. Atrocities were widespread: pagan Slavs were burned at the stake and, by way of retaliation, captured knights boiled in their armour. Eventually the Order established a powerful secular state, which by the 15th century was threatening the territorial integrity of Poland. The Teutonic Order was supported in its efforts by the rulers of England, France, Hungary and the Holy Roman Empire, who provided money, men and diplomacy where necessary. The threat of this German *Drang nach Osten* ('expansion to the east'), accompanied as it was by settlers, merchants and priests, was well understood by the Slavonic peoples of northeastern Europe, who united to repel the German invaders. In 1386 the states of Poland and Lithuania were bound together by the marriage of Queen Jadwiga of Poland to the Grand Duke Wladyslaw of Lithuania, and the Slavs – long since Christianized – were able to present a united front to the Germans.

The spark came when a Lithuanian-backed revolt broke out in the Teutonic Order's territory of Samogitia, in the last few months of 1409. King Wladyslaw of Poland and his ally, Grand Duke Witold of Lithuania, agreed to take the offensive against the Order, by invading Prussia and seeking to capture Marienburg (Malbork), the capital of the Teutonic Knights. This strategy, they felt certain, would bring on a decisive encounter that would settle the affairs of the area for generations to come. To prevent the Knights from concentrating all their strength, Wladyslaw made a series of feint attacks into Pomerania, West Prussia and towards Tilsit, forcing the Germans to divide their forces. In fact, whereas Ulrich von Jungingen, Hochmeister of the Teutonic Order, anticipated a Polish thrust towards Pomerania, Wladyslaw outmanoeuvred him by striking due north towards Marienburg on the River Nogat.

On 9 July 1410 Wladyslaw and Witold crossed into Prussia with an army numbering over 50,000 men, made up of 20,000 Polish cavalry, 11,000 Lithuanian light horsemen, 1500 Crim Tartars, as well as large numbers of Polish infantry, Bohemian mercenaries under Ziska, Russians, Wallachians and Serbs. They moved towards the River Drweça, where the Hochmeister had taken up a strong defensive position. Wladyslaw's spies calculated that the German army numbered some 40,000 men, with 20,000 horsemen and 20,000 infantry and archers. They also reported that the German defences were impregnable, and so Wladyslaw decided to head further north towards the city of Dabrowno, in the hope of drawing the Germans out. The Poles easily stormed the fortress of Dabrowno and massacred the defenders, before pulling away to await the German reaction. Detaching a force of 3000 men under Heinrich von Plauen to strengthen the garrison at Marienburg, the Hochmeister bridged the River Drweça in 12

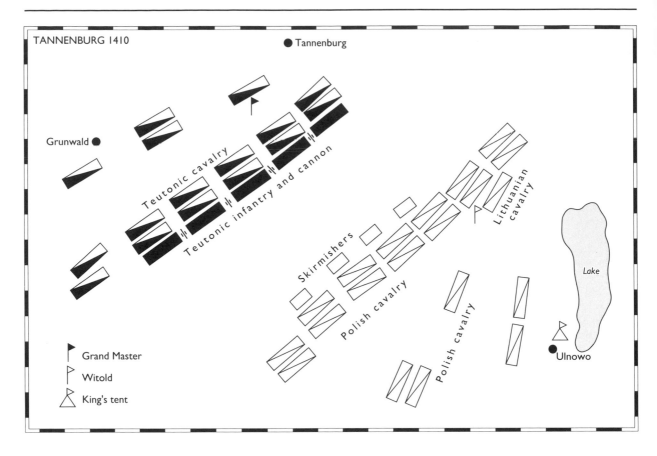

TANNENBURG 1410 ● Tannenburg

Grunwald ●

Teutonic cavalry

Teutonic infantry and cannon

Skirmishers

Polish cavalry

Polish cavalry

Lithuanian cavalry

Lake

Ulnowo ●

Grand Master

Witold

King's tent

places, and advanced with his army towards the villages of Grunwald and Tannenburg, determined to force Wladyslaw to fight.

On the night of 14/15 July 1410 the tempestuous weather must have convinced both Slavs and Germans alike that even the heavens were at war. Tents were blown over in the Polish camp and omens were eagerly interpreted – in one, a king was seen fighting a monk on the moon: to the delight of the Poles, the monk was defeated, just as the Hochmeister would fall before King Wladyslaw.

But for all the good omens, the Poles seemed completely oblivious to the whereabouts of the Teutonic army, which by first light on 15 July was marching towards them intent on forcing a battle without more ado. Excited messengers rode into the Polish camp with the alarming news that the Germans were no more than a mile away. But Wladyslaw 'would not be put off by such a sudden and unexpected arrival of the enemy and believing that matters divine should come before matters martial, entered the chapel and most devotedly heard two masses said by his chaplains'. Duke Witold, on the other hand, was alarmed by the imminent threat of an attack by the Germans and tried to hurry his pious ally to complete his devotions. The Polish army now raised its banners and began to assemble to the south and west of Lake Lubien.

The German army had occupied a strong position on high ground to the east of the Poles, the knights themselves grouped into 52 'banners' or units. The wind brought alive hundreds of pennants, some bearing Christian symbols, others a riot of heraldic dragons, bulls and lions, while above all flew the great banner of the Teutonic Order, a white flag nearly two yards square with a gold cross outlined in black, in the centre of which a golden shield bore a black eagle. In front of his knights the Hochmeister had ordered a line of obstacles to be laid to hinder his enemies, behind which his crossbowmen and mercenary English longbowmen were massed. Clearly von Jungingen had decided to adopt a defensive strategy. But in doing so he missed his best opportunity for success. Seeing the Poles and Lithuanians in disorder by the lake, his commanders pressed him to attack immediately, while Wladyslaw was at prayer. But the Hochmeister obstinately clung to his position and gradually the opportunity disappeared.

Once Wladyslaw had completed his prayers he put on his magnificent armour and joined Witold in surveying the German lines. The thought of the terrible battle ahead seemed to weigh heavily on all the commanders – it is even recorded that the Hochmeister broke down in tears, while the pious Wladyslaw could not bring himself to order the killing to start. But von Jungingen knew that his strategy depended for success on the Poles assaulting his lines, and so he used a skilful ruse to force Wladyslaw to take the initiative. From the German lines two knights were sent towards the Polish royal party, bearing swords without scabbards. These, they told Wladyslaw, were sent by the Hochmeister to help the king in the fight as he obviously had none of his own. Thus armed, would the Poles now stop hiding in the trees and come out and fight? The Polish knights were enraged by this insult, but Wladyslaw himself was unruffled, donning his helmet and accepting the challenge. Battle was now imminent. Wladyslaw's bodyguard of 60 chosen knights took up their position around him, though Witold, disdaining protection, rode up and down his lines urging his men to greater efforts.

Just after 9.00 a.m. a great fanfare of trumpets was heard from the Polish camp, and with thousands of soldiers singing hymns the Slavonic armies advanced towards the serried ranks of the Germans, with every Polish knight wearing a field sign of a knot of straw on the upper arm as identification. The white surplices and mantles of the Teutonic Knights with their black crosses tipped the distant ridge as if with snow, and above this their weapons glinted in the sunshine. In contrast with the Christian emblems on the flags of the Poles, many of the Samogitians in the Lithuanian ranks followed

standard bearers who swung severed heads on poles. As they neared the front ranks of the enemy, the wild Lithuanian horsemen, wielding lances and hurling javelins, charged full tilt at the left of the German line nearest to the village of Tannenburg. So furious was their charge that they overran the German footsoldiers, scattering their cannons, but were then struck by a counter-charge from the knights of the Grand Marshal of Prussia, Friederich Wallenrod, whose better mounts and heavier armour soon gave them the advantage. The Lithuanians were driven in disorder towards the lake, pursued by the German horsemen, and only the three Smolensk banners survived the rout, riding round to join their Polish allies in the centre. Here, and on the right of their line, the 20 banners of knights commanded by the Grand Commander, Conrad von Lichtenstein, were being forced back in heavy hand-to-hand fighting with the Polish knights,

---

The knights of the Teutonic Order regarded themselves as crusaders against the Slavic pagans of the east. But by 1410 the Poles and Lithuanians had long been Christianized, and the Order had effectively lost the reason for its existence – but not its resented secular power in the region. PN

many of whom wore the fantastic winged and crested helmets for which they were famous. With the battle at a decisive stage Witold, horrified by the collapse of his own army, rode to Wladyslaw begging him to move forward from his safe position near the village of Ulnowo, a mile from the front. With his standardbearer carrying the great banner of Cracow, a long flag in red silk bearing a silver lion, Wladyslaw and his bodyguard spurred their horses forward.

Across a wide front of two or three miles the battle swayed this way and that. Wallenrod's victorious knights on the left, who were returning from driving the Lithuanians off the field, saw that their centre and right were under pressure and charged to their aid, forcing back the Polish right, which was rallied with some difficulty by Witold, who seemed to be everywhere in the fight. Near the village of Grunwald, the Hochmeister von Jungingen could see that the result of the battle was in the balance, and personally led his reserve of 16 banners of heavy cavalry in a great charge that nearly broke the Polish centre. At this stage some German knights broke off from the fray to charge at the royal party surrounding King Wladyslaw on a nearby hillock. A single knight in white tabard charged the king, but the king's secretary, fighting only with a broken lance, upended the German, who was despatched by the king's guard.

It was as if this single incident encapsulated the whole battle. The splendid ranks of German knighthood were now struck from an unexpected quarter. A large force of Lithuanians and Tartars, who had earlier fled the battle, were somehow collected together by Duke Witold, who brought them back to the field to strike the Germans in the rear. This final blow was decisive and the flower of the Order succumbed in the melee that followed. Among the slain were the Hochmeister himself, as well as his deputy, the Grand Marshal, and hundreds of the senior brothers of the Teutonic Order.

With their leaders dead or taken, the rank and file of the German army fled, pursued by the Lithuanian light horsemen. The numbers engaged and killed at Tannenburg make it one of the largest and bloodiest of all medieval battles, and its 10-hour duration shows how intense the fighting had been. Estimates of 18,000 Germans killed and 14,000 taken prisoner seem astonishingly high, but, in view of the encirclement of their troops in the final stages of the battle, these estimates may not be far from the truth. Of the 700 'white-cloaks' – brothers of the Order

– no more than 15 were taken alive, while every one of the Order's 52 banners were taken by the Poles and hung in Cracow Cathedral.

King Wladyslaw was greatly moved when he received news of the death of Ulrich von Jungingen, and saw God's work in the overthrow of the vain Hochmeister. He ordered a herald to spread the news throughout the camp that mass would be held the next day to celebrate the victory and to honour the dead on both sides. Once the prisoners had been paraded they were generally paroled, except the wealthiest nobles and knights, who were held for ransom. Two days after the battle the Poles began their advance on Marienburg, some 75 miles away from the battlefield. In the eight days it took them to reach the capital of the Teutonic Knights, Heinrich von Plauen – undaunted by the news of the catastrophe that had struck the Order and its Hochmeister – had so strengthened the citadel that though Wladyslaw easily captured the surrounding town, he could make no inroads on the castle's 27-foot thick walls. Eventually the Poles were forced to retire after reinforcements from the Order's garrisons in Livonia arrived to raise the siege of Marienburg. But the damage was done. The once-great Teutonic Order had been humbled on the battlefield by an alliance of Slav states that no informed observers anywhere in Europe had thought would have been equal to the task.

The Teutonic Order had suffered other defeats in its history, but none as great as Tannenburg. Previously its reverses had been at the hands of pagan tribesman and its casualties were counted martyrs in the struggle to spread the Christian faith. But by 1410 the Lithuanians were themselves Christian, and the original religious aims of the Teutonic Knights – some of whom oppressed their own people like secular princes – no longer appeared valid. The defeat of the Order was interpreted by many as God's punishment for its pride and arrogance. The crusading spirit in Germany was dying, and volunteers from Western Europe were no longer willing to help the Order in its territorial aggression against fellow Christians. In 1466 the Order surrendered West Prussia to Poland by the Treaty of Thorn, and withdrew from Marienburg to a new capital at Königsberg. The Order went into a gradual decline, and in modern times it was reduced to a mere 20 noble members. Its final act was to support the attempt to assassinate Hitler in the July Bomb Plot of 1944, after which 12 of the brothers were executed.

The Siege of Orléans
1429

Orleans

English
Commander: Earl of Suffolk
Numbers: 5000 infantry and archers

French
Commanders: The Bastard of Orleans, Joan of Arc
Numbers: unknown

The wars between England and France that have earned the general title 'The Hundred Years War' had begun as a dynastic dispute, but by the 15th century they were clearly part of a national struggle. Hatred of the English was endemic in France, and Joan of Arc spoke for many Frenchmen in referring to the English as 'goddams'. In the eyes of the French the English were 'false, damnable and treacherous . . . they are an accursed race, opposed to all good and all reason, ravening wolves, proud, arrogant hypocrites, tricksters without any conscience, tyrants and persecutors of Christians, men who drink and gorge on human blood, with natures like birds of prey, people who only live by plunder'. And the English did not like the French either.

By the end of the 14th century many of the gains made by England in the early campaigns of Edward III and the Black Prince had been lost. But the death of the Lancastrian king Henry IV in 1413 brought to the throne of England a man whose single-minded ambition for foreign conquest persuaded him to exploit the internal divisions in France – between the Burgundian and Armagnac factions – in order to seize the throne of France for himself. Henry V first made an alliance with Duke John 'the Fearless' of Burgundy in May 1413 and, having neutralized this powerful noble, he felt strong enough to invade France two years later. At Agincourt, in October 1415, the English inflicted a terrible defeat on the French, and in the next two years Henry completed the conquest of Normandy. The ailing French king Charles VI – disowning his own son, the mentally immature Charles the Dauphin – married his daughter Catherine to the

English king and, on the birth of a son, accepted the future Henry VI as heir to both the French and English thrones. The English position was further strengthened by the murder of John the Fearless by supporters of the Dauphin. In 1519 a Carthusian monk at Dijon showed the duke's shattered skull to the then king, Francis I, and pointing to its death wound said, 'This is the hole through which the English entered France.' The duke's son, Philip 'the Good', now became a *de facto* ally of the English. But the sudden death of Henry V left his 9-month-old

Siege tactics in the 15th century; an illustration from a work by Viollet-le-Duc, the 19th-century architectural historian. HDC

Joan of Arc at the coronation of Charles VII, following her success at Orléans. This painting by Ingres (1854) epitomizes Joan as national heroine and saint – although she was not actually canonized until 1920. AKG/LOUVRE, PARIS

notably the supremacy of their bow and pike tactics, was too strong for any combination of French knights. At Cravant in 1423 Bedford routed the Dauphin's Armagnac supporters, while the following year at Verneuil he inflicted a great defeat – virtually the equal of Agincourt – on another of the wretched Dauphin's armies. As after Crécy and Poitiers, the English longbow imposed a reign of terror on the French nation. By 1426 Bedford was being drawn into a more widespread campaign aimed at nothing less than the total conquest of the Dauphin's holdings in central and southern France.

Both Berry and Anjou were now targets for English conquest, and in October 1428 Thomas de Montacute, earl of Salisbury, with an English force of 5000 men, began the siege of the populous city of Orléans, on the River Loire, striking at the very heartland of the Dauphin's strength. If Orléans were to fall to the English, France would be virtually extinguished as an independent kingdom. But two unexpected events were to change the situation completely. On 23 October the earl of Salisbury, whose very name held terrors for the French, was killed by a stone splinter while overseeing the siege. Even so, French fortunes had further to slip before they recovered. When an English supply column of 300 wagons was approaching the city it was attacked at Rouvray by a large French army. The English commander, Sir John Fastolf, formed up his wagons into a laager, like the Gothic laager at Adrianople but on a smaller scale, and the escorting English archers destroyed the French in what became known as 'the battle of the herrings'.

As the English tightened the siege around Orléans, establishing an arc of six stockaded forts to the north of the Loire, it seemed only a matter of time before the city was forced to surrender. So bleak did the situation seem by the early days of 1429 that the Dauphin's supporters advised him to leave France completely and find refuge in Scotland or Spain. Yet the city had become a symbol of French resistance to English domination, and at this low point the second of the unexpected events occurred: a 17-year-old peasant girl from Domrémy in Lorraine became convinced that it was her destiny to save France from the English.

Joan claimed that she had heard the voices of the Archangel Michael, St Margaret and St Catherine telling her to go to the Dauphin's court at Chinon and tell him that it was her task to raise the siege of Orléans and drive the English out of France. Afterwards she was to take the Dauphin to Rheims, where he would be crowned king of France. Having convinced Robert de Baudricourt of her sincerity she was taken by him the 300 miles to meet the

son Henry as king of England under the regency of his uncle the duke of Gloucester. And when Charles VI died in turn and was buried at Saint Denis in Paris, the crown of France was there for whoever was strong enough to take it.

The Dauphin proclaimed himself King Charles VII of France, but could not summon up the courage to risk a coronation at Rheims, which was too near English-controlled territory. His weakness seemed to symbolize the state of France at the time. The duke of Bedford, with his Burgundian allies, held Paris, while English soldiers like the atrocious Richard Venables and his gang of ruffians roamed freely in lawless bands through much of the country. The military strength of the English,

76

Dauphin at Chinon. It is doubtful if anyone living or writing in the 20th century can fully understand the appeal of this inspired girl. Modern views of her probable epilepsy or psychological disturbance are irrelevant. She was what France needed at the time, and her inspiration was enough to convince hard-bitten soldiers like Dunois, Alençon, de Xantrailles, La Hire, Gilles de Rais and de Richemont – hideously wounded at Agincourt and now with a face like a frog – to follow her as if she were a divine talisman.

Arriving at Orléans, Joan immediately upbraided the Bastard of Orléans for his inadequate defence of the city, and set about doing a better job herself. She appealed to the English commanders to raise the siege but received only abuse and threats that if she were caught she would be burned as a witch. Undeterred, she led assaults against the English positions, was wounded in the neck by an arrow, but refused to be confined to bed and was with the French soldiers as they overran the English cantonments and raised the siege.

The news of 'the Maid' and her miracles at Orléans astounded both English and French together. The duke of Bedford wrote of the 'enchauntements and sorcerie . . . of the Feende, called the Pucelle'. But the English had not abandoned hope of success at Orléans and reinforcements under Lord John Talbot and Sir John Fastolf were hurrying from Paris. On 19 July the French army, fresh from its triumph at Orléans, met the English at Patay. Afraid to meet them in an open battle the French commanders asked Joan's advice. She told them to attack straight away and that they would need their spurs – not to flee, but to pursue the English when they turned tail. Under Joan's inspiration the French defeated the English for the first time in living memory. Town after town now fell to the French army as it moved north, including the great cathedral cities of Troyes, Chartres and Rheims – where Charles VII was duly crowned on 16 July. Bedford feared that even Paris might fall. And when his army met the French at Montépilloy, Bedford visibly quailed at the sight of Joan's banner among the French flags. Captured by the Burgundians and presented to the English for trial and execution as a witch, Joan of Arc became a martyr for France, a martyr whose inspiration survived her death. Through her efforts France regained its self-respect and French soldiers learned to believe in themselves once more.

The raising of the siege of Orléans was the decisive moment in the Hundred Years War. The example of Joan of Arc freed the French people from their obsession with defeat at the hands of the English. Without Joan's inspiration it seems unlikely that Orléans could have resisted for much longer and, having fallen, it would have heralded the collapse of the French monarchy and the fragmentation of the country at the hands of not only the English but of great noblemen like the duke of Burgundy. In the words of John Payne:

The heroic peasant girl of Lorraine . . . created the French people. Until her time France had been inhabited by Bretons, Angevins, Bourbonnais, Burgundians, Poitevins, Armagnacs; at last the baptism of fire through which the land had passed and the breath of heroism that emanated from the Maid of Orleans had welded together the conflicting sections and had informed them with that breath of patriotism which is the beginning of national life. France had at length become a nation.

The Siege of Constantinople 1453

Constantinople 1453

Byzantines
Commander:	Emperor Constantine XI and Giovanni Giustiniani
Numbers:	8000, including 3000 Italians, and 26 ships

Turks
Commander:	Mehmed II and Admiral Baltoglu
Numbers:	150,000 men, including engineers and camp followers, and over 300 galleys

The accession of the last emperor to the Byzantine throne on 6 July 1449 was no matter for rejoicing. It merely opened the final sombre chapter in a thousand-year history, in which, despite occasional triumphs and conquests, the old Eastern Empire of Ancient Rome had been gradually whittled away. The new emperor, Constantine XI Dragases, was taking over responsibility less for an empire than for a city – Constantinople, the last bastion of Christianity against the ever-expanding empire of the Ottoman Turks. Many times the Turks had tried to remove this last enclave only for the city's massive land walls to prove too strong for them. But when Sultan Murad II died in 1451 he was succeeded by Mehmed II, the 'Conqueror', probably the greatest Ottoman ruler in a line which, down to Suleiman the Magnificent in the 16th century, was noted for its able rulers. Nicknamed 'Drinker of Blood', Mehmed was a ruthless and brutal despot, drowning his infant brother on taking the throne and marrying his mother to a slave. His macabre sense of humour made him admire his contemporary, the Transylvanian prince Vlad Dracul, for nailing the turbans of the Ottoman envoys to their heads. But most of all Mehmed loved war. He lived for it and strove to emulate the achievements of great conquerors like Alexander the Great and Julius Caesar. To him it was an insult that Constantinople should remain unconquered within his territory, and he made it his life's aim to take the city as his capital.

His resources for doing so were enormous. Not only did he have the largest and best-trained army of the 15th century – his janissaries (Christian slaves bred for war) were the finest troops in Europe – but he had the most important artillery train of any living monarch. He loved huge cannons, the more massive the better, and he richly rewarded the Hungarian renegade Orban for designing some of the biggest guns ever built: one vast bombard or basilisk used in the siege of Constantinople was capable of firing a stone ball weighing 1500 pounds.

Against Mehmed's army of 150,000 men – this time the chroniclers were not exaggerating – the Byzantine emperor could muster just 4973 men willing to fight, out of the city's population of 100,000. Fortunately the cowardice of his people

Mehmed II, the Ottoman sultan. This delicate portrait by Sinan Bey, painted c. 1475–80, belies Mehmed's ruthlessness and brutality. PN

did not depress Constantine, and support from the Italian maritime cities under leading condottieri (mercenaries) like Giovanni Giustiniani – appointed commander-in-chief by a thankful emperor – helped swell the number of the defenders to about 8000. In the harbour of the Golden Horn the imperial fleet, under Gabriel Trevisano, even with help from Venice, Pisa and Genoa, numbered just 26 ships, which were outnumbered more than 12 to 1 by the Turks.

In early April 1453 the Turks began a massive land assault, supported by their portentous if relatively harmless heavy guns. The noise was enormous but the damage to the walls slight, and when the masses of heavily mailed janissaries and poorly armed bashi-bazouks tried to scale the city walls they were met by devastating short-range fire from Giustiniani's handgunners and crossbowmen. The first ranks of the Turks were simply swept away – to Mehmed's fury. Officers with chain whips and heavy maces thrashed the Turkish soldiers back to the walls, but the momentum of the attack was broken. Further assaults floundered under the impact of Greek fire, which was poured on the attackers from the walls or fired from siphons and catapults.

Frustrated, Mehmed next resorted to the expedient of having part of his fleet carried overland, to bypass the defensive chain across the harbour of the Golden Horn. Once inside the harbour he knew that he could bring troops to assault the previously invulnerable northern walls, stretching Giustiniani's garrison to its limits. The amazing sight of the Turkish boats being moved overland almost broke the spirit of the defenders: in countless previous sieges of Constantinople the control of the Golden Horn had always saved the city, but now that advantage was lost.

Further land assaults in early May were supported by a huge Turkish siege tower called 'City-Taker', but nothing seemed to depress Giustiniani, who destroyed the monster by rolling barrels of gunpowder under its supports. Mehmed was heard to exclaim, 'What would I not give to win that man over to my side!' Meanwhile, all Mehmed's attempts to drive mineshafts under the city walls had been foiled by the German mining expert and artillerist Johann Grant, who had detected each mine in turn and destroyed them with gunpowder or stinkpots (containers full of suffocating fumes) or by flooding them.

The final assault on the city was curiously anti-climactic. While Mehmed's janissaries fought hand-to-hand on the city walls with Giustiniani's pikemen, a chance discovery of a small, undefended

TURKISH ARTILLERY

The Ottoman Turks made greater use of artillery and firearms than any other Muslim power. From the 1420s the Turks employed artillery to besiege cities and recruited gunners and engineers from among the Balkan peoples they conquered. The most famous of these Balkan gunners was the Transylvanian named Orban, whose guns enabled Mehmed II to finally capture Constantinople in 1453. During the 16th century, Jews fleeing from the Inquisition in Spain and Italy brought the latest techniques in gun-making to the Turks, and soon English and Dutch gunners were selling their services to the Ottoman sultans. The Turks specialized in guns of enormous size, casting the great gun-barrels at the site of the siege rather than transporting such weighty machines. By mid-century ranges of well over a mile were being achieved, with shot of half a ton. Ottoman master-gunners belonged to the Kapilku Corps and numbered 1000 by 1575.

Ottoman cast-iron cannons of the 15th century, outside the Military Museum, Istanbul. PN

postern gate by the Kerkoporta allowed first a few and soon hundreds of Turks to burst into the city. At the same moment Giustiniani was struck down by a shot and carried away from the walls. With his inspiration gone and the Turks already moving through part of the city, resistance crumbled. The emperor, flanked by Don Francis of Toledo and Theophilus Palaeologus, charged sword-in-hand into the press of janissaries and died there, calling out 'God forbid that I should live an emperor

without an empire! As my city falls, I will fall with it.' What followed was a general massacre in which some 4000 Christians were slaughtered before Mehmed managed to regain control. The sultan later amused himself by paying the ransoms of noble prisoners captured by his men and then personally beheading them.

The Byzantine Empire had ceased to exist. A thousand years after Rome's Western Empire had fallen, the Eastern Empire had succumbed to the inevitable. For three days the city of Constantinople was given over to plunder; countless priceless artefacts were destroyed, along with manuscripts and books containing the wisdom of the ancient world. As Christobolus of Imbros wrote,

Immense numbers of sacred and profane books were flung on the fire or torn up and trampled under foot. The majority, however, were sold at derisory prices, for a few pence. Saints' altars, torn from their foundations, were overturned. All the most holy hiding places were violated and broken in order to get out the holy treasures which they contained . . .

But it was not just the pillage of a captured city,

The Turks bypass the defensive chain across the Golden Horn by dragging their ships overland. AKG

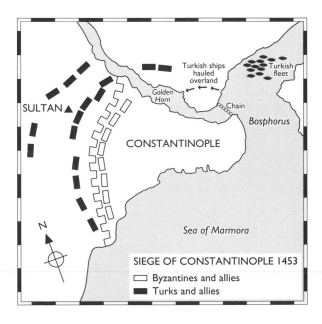

or even the rape of a civilization, it was the metamorphosis of an idea. Constantinople, the citadel of Christendom, had now become the bastion of the Turks. The Turks had not just come to destroy and ride home this time, sated but essentially unchanged. With Constantinople – later renamed Istanbul – as their new capital these Asiatic conquerors had become a European power, with extensive lands in the Balkans. They were a young, virile, expansionist power, and other European states could no longer ignore the Turk now that the Byzantines were not there to keep them at bay. This time the Turks had come to stay, and the problem of the Ottoman Empire in Europe was one that would engage the minds of European diplomats until the First World War and after.

For the Christian world the fall of the 'Queen of Cities' brought them face to face with some harsh realities. Economic dispute and religious schism – between Western Catholicism and Eastern Orthodoxy – had prevented the Christian states from offering a unified front to the Turks, and the result of such disunion had been clearly demonstrated. In the coming century the Turks would have to be held on the Danube instead of the Dardanelles. For the Greeks it was the end of a glorious civilization and the peoples of Greece were not to regain their freedom for four centuries. The classical traditions of which Constantinople had been guardian were now blown to the winds. Fortunately, the knowledge of the ancient world resided in the hearts and minds of many of the scholars who fled the city before the final apocalypse and found fruitful ground in Italy, France and other areas where the Renaissance had already taken root in the previous fifty years.

The Battle of Bosworth Field 1485

If ever a battle was decided by treachery it was the one fought near the small Leicestershire town of Market Bosworth on Sunday 21 August 1485. It was a ragged and desultory affair, pitching foreign mercenaries and traitors on the one hand against pressed men and fainthearts on the other. If there was courage it was the courage of desperation, and if there was any military skill it was just the professional one of slaughtering *en masse*. Yet few English battles have had greater consequences, and for only the second time in English history a reigning monarch was to meet his death at the head of his army.

Henry Tudor's accession to the throne of England in 1485 as Henry VII was the culmination of a series of fortunate chances. His own claim to the throne was not strong; it derived from his mother Margaret Beaufort, who was descended from Edward III via the marriage of Edward's son John of Gaunt to Catherine Swynford. And although from 1471, when King Henry VI and his son were murdered by the Yorkists after the battle of Tewkesbury, Henry Tudor was the head of the Lancastrian faction, his Yorkist rival, Edward IV, had two sons,

as well as brothers, all of whom had a prior claim to the throne. In the event, Henry spent a frustrating 14-year exile in Brittany with his uncle Jasper Tudor, while the Yorkists ruled in England. But he did not abandon hope and kept in touch with other exiled Lancastrian lords, waiting for his chance to return to England.

In April 1483 King Edward IV died, leaving the crown to his 12-year-old son Edward, and the government of the country to his brother Richard of Gloucester as protector. Richard had been loyal to his brother while he lived, but now he had no intention of allowing the new king's Woodville relations to oust him from power. In May, with the support of the duke of Buckingham, Richard placed the young king and Richard of York, his brother, in the Tower of London 'for their comfort'. Then, proclaiming his brother's marriage to Elizabeth Woodville invalid in view of Edward's earlier relationship with Eleanor Butler, Richard declared Edward's two young sons bastards. After they had been secretly murdered (on whose orders is still a matter of fierce debate) Richard had himself declared king on 6 July 1483. But taking the throne was easier than keeping it. Both at home and abroad Richard III faced many enemies. In France the Lancastrian lords had gathered around Henry Tudor as their champion, while in England the king had reason to fear that powerful families, such as the Stanleys in the northwest and the Percys in Northumberland, would prove false in a crisis. As news of Richard's unpopularity reached France, Henry Tudor's advisers convinced him that his chance had come.

Henry Tudor's fleet left Harfleur on 1 August, carrying with it a force of some 2000 French mercenaries under the command of Philibert de Chaundé. With Henry were a number of English lords who had shared his exile, including his uncle Jasper Tudor, John de la Vere, earl of Oxford, and the Bishop of Ely. Six days later, 'with a soft southern wind', a landing was made at Milford Haven in Pembrokeshire, part of Jasper Tudor's earldom, where Henry had spent his own boyhood. Local support was strong. His first major ally was Rhys ap Thomas, but many other Welsh gentry rallied to Henry's cause and his army had soon swelled to over 5000, still less than the king could muster but a sizeable force for the 15th century.

The reports that reached the king of his rival's progress must have been galling. As the rebels marched through Wales it was clear that neither Sir Walter Herbert in the south nor Sir William Stanley in the north had attempted to bar Henry Tudor's way. Richard could not be sure of his friends and made stringent efforts to tie them to him. When Lord Stanley asked permission to return to his estates in Lancashire on the grounds of ill health, Richard only agreed on condition that his son, Lord Strange, should remain as a hostage.

Meanwhile, Henry Tudor had reached Shrewsbury – where he was joined by Sir Gilbert Talbot with 500 men – and next turned south, passing through Staffordshire. Ominously for the king, both Lord Stanley and his brother William met with the rebels at Atherstone; Richard now knew that they could not be relied on for support in the coming struggle. Only the fact that the king held Lord Stanley's son might persuade them at least to remain neutral. From his headquarters at Nottingham castle Richard had been following the progress of the invaders, but once they moved into Leicestershire he decided that the time had come to strike in case they slipped by him and made a dash for London. On 19 August he set off – resplendent in his crown-encased helm and riding a white charger – at the head of the royal army for Leicester. He still had a substantial advantage of numbers, and his force of about 8000 men marched in three separate 'battles': the vanguard of 1200 archers and 200 knights was led by John Howard, duke of Norfolk; the main battle of 2000 pikemen and 1000 men armed with halberds and bills was in his own charge; while the rear battle, led by Henry Percy, earl of Northumberland, consisted of 2000 billmen, with 1500 horsemen, who also rode along the flanks of the march. It was a strong, professional force under proven commanders – both Richard and Norfolk had gained battle experience under Edward IV – but its loyalty was doubtful.

Richard's army encountered the invaders near the village of Sutton Cheney, and Norfolk's vanguard, following the silver lion banner of the Howards, took up position on a commanding ridge about 400 feet above sea level, named Ambion Hill. The Stanley brothers, with perhaps 5000 of their retainers, were also in the vicinity, Sir William to the north of the royal army and Lord Stanley to the south. They were either maintaining a neutral position until they saw which side was likely to emerge victorious, or else merely awaiting the right

moment to strike down the king. On the morning of 22 August the royal army took up its battle positions and the king sent his last message to Lord Stanley, telling him that unless he joined the royal army his son's life was forfeit. Some chroniclers report that he replied to the king that he had other sons and would not come. In the event Lord Strange was not killed – a surprising oversight for a king with such a ruthless reputation.

The earl of Oxford led the vanguard of the rebel army, which, before it could reach Norfolk's men on Ambion Hill, had to negotiate swampy ground at the foot of the ridge. The tricky terrain threw Oxford's men into disorder, and for a moment the advantage lay entirely with the king. A sudden charge down the hill onto Oxford's disordered ranks would have probably driven the rebels from the field in complete rout, but the opportunity was missed. Either Richard was overconfident and underrated his opponents – particularly Henry Tudor, whom he held in little esteem as either warrior or general – or else he did not trust his own troops. If the latter, he had good reason to be suspicious for, as the Croyland Chronicle relates, there were many of the royal army 'who rather coveted the king dead than alive, and therefore

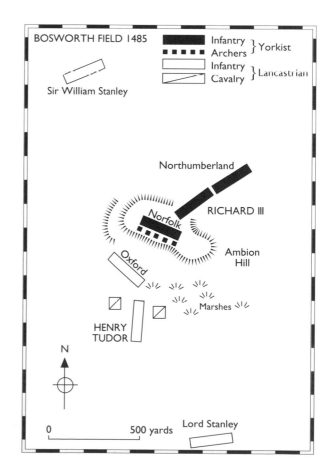

fought faintly'. In the event, Oxford soon restored order to his troops and, bringing up some artillery, he opened fire on the static ranks on the hill above him. It is doubtful if the cannon caused much damage, nor even the arrows fired by the bowmen, for the armour of the late 15th century was as effective as it ever was likely to be before the widespread use of firearms.

Oxford now concentrated his men around the de Vere standard – a star with streams – ordering no man to break ranks. As the rebels advanced up the

hill in a phalanx of pike and billmen the fighting began in earnest, a hand-to-hand struggle that lasted for the best part of two hours. It was a desperate struggle between men fighting less for a cause than to save their own lives. Tactics were simple: as the front lines fell more men were fed into the melee from the main bodies behind; in such fighting weight of numbers would eventually tell. But morale was as vital a factor as numbers, and when the duke of Norfolk was killed – one report says at the hands of Oxford himself – the royal army began to waver. A messenger was seen riding to Sir William Stanley with the news of Norfolk's death and the capture of his son, the earl of Surrey. It was enough for the Stanleys: the king was doomed.

At this crucial moment the king found that his worst fears were justified. His rearguard, commanded by Northumberland, refused to move up to his support. What happened next is not certain, although some chronicles suggest a royal 'death-ride'. Since the beginning of the fight Richard had

The Tudor chroniclers – and the play of Shakespeare – have provided very partial and inaccurate accounts of the character of Richard III and of his death at Bosworth Field. Although Richard did indeed charge at Henry Tudor in one final do-or-die bid to save the battle, he was pulled from his horse and impaled on a mass of Welsh pikes before he could confront his rival for the crown. HDC

been calling on men of keen sight to pick out the exact whereabouts of Henry Tudor in the rebel army. Convinced that only the demise of his rival on the field could change his fortunes, Richard mounted his white charger and, battleaxe in hand and with his personal bodyguard of 80 knights around him, he rode down the slopes of Ambion Hill, heading straight for Henry Tudor. Hacking his way through the ranks of Welsh footsoldiers, Richard struck down first Sir John Cheyney, a man greatly his superior in height and strength, and then Sir William Brandon, Henry's personal standardbearer. But at this moment, Sir William Stanley's men, who had been mere spectators in the struggle so far, attacked the right flank of the royal army. In the confused fighting around Henry Tudor's standard, Richard III was pulled from his horse and impaled on a mass of Welsh pikes before he could cross swords with his enemy.

All around the royal army was breaking up under the combined weight of Henry's French and Welsh troops to their front and the retainers of the Stanley brothers now worrying their flanks. Shakespeare's memorable picture of a hunted Richard Crookback calling out 'A horse, a horse, my kingdom for a horse' is fine theatre but pure fiction. The king was never far from enemies in this battle; he had little time for speeches. With Richard dead, Oxford was able 'to put to flight them that fought in the forward, whereof a great many were killed in the chase. But many more forbare to fight, who came to the field with King Richard for awe and for no goodwill and departed without any danger, as men who desired not the safety but destruction of that prince whom they hated'. The crowning of Henry Tudor on the battlefield by Lord Stanley was a fitting climax to a lurid tale of treachery and dishonour.

Casualties were light, for there was little point in fighting once the king was dead. The royal army lost perhaps 1000 men to the rebels' 200, though as was usual in battles of this period, casualties were proportionately higher among the nobles. In death Richard was exposed to a shame that mirrored the hatred felt for him by his many enemies: his naked body was slung across the back of a horse and exposed publicly in Leicester for two days before being buried at Greyfriars church.

Thus died the last Plantagenet king of England, but his death did not mark an end to the fighting nor a guarantee of security for the new Tudor dynasty. A further pitched battle at Stoke in 1487 was needed to quell the Yorkists, and Henry VII spent much of his reign holding on to what he had won at Bosworth. But he did hold on, and by marrying Edward IV's daughter, Elizabeth of York, he reconciled the warring factions of York and Lancaster and bequeathed a more united and financially sound state to his son Henry VIII. England's security in the 16th century – no foreign troops set foot on English soil during this period – enabled his descendants, notably his granddaughter Elizabeth I, to rule England during a period of unparalleled splendour. The Tudor dynasty established by Henry's victory at Bosworth ushered in a period of greatness for England – now no longer linked to continental Europe but opening the seaways to world empire.

The Siege of Tenochtitlán 1521

Tenochtitlán

Spanish

Commander: Hernán Cortés

Numbers: 86 cavalry, 118 crossbow and arquebusmen, 700 sword and pikemen, 18 cannon, 15 brigantines, plus Tlaxcalan and other allies totalling 75–80,000

Aztecs

Commander: Great Speaker Cuauhtémoc

Numbers: unknown

The discovery of the New World by Christopher Columbus in 1492 created a sensation in Europe. Stories of rich civilizations and untold wealth encouraged many young and otherwise rootless men from Italy, Spain and Portugal to cross the Atlantic to seek their fortune. Hernán Cortés and Francisco Pizarro were perhaps just the two luckiest of thousands of such aspiring conquistadors, ruthless soldiers and explorers who came to South and Central America looking for gold and conquest, and paving the way for priests and traders to follow them. Within fifty years of first establishing a foothold in the New World the Spanish were well on the way to extending their rule over a whole continent; in addition, the wealth they sent back to Europe from silver and gold mines in Mexico and Peru caused such a rise in prices that it nearly wrecked the relatively primitive financial system of the 16th century. It is estimated that Cortés extorted from the Aztecs \$6,300,000 in gold (on a 1950s estimate) and that within forty years of his victory at Tenochtitlán Spain had received from her new possessions 100 tons of gold, which was double the previous amount held in the whole of Europe. In the same period 6785 tons of silver crossed the Atlantic to Spain. From their new lands the Spaniards also gained wealth in the form of jewels, feathers, artefacts, precious woods, spices, foods (including chocolate) and skins. All this was enough to fund the wars of Charles V and Philip II and underpin the Counter-Reformation, making the 16th century the century of Spain.

Of all the peoples the Spaniards met in the New World it was the ferocious Aztecs of Mexico who presented the greatest obstacle to Spanish power. In fact, it was only through a stroke of luck that Cortés was able to enter Aztec territory at all. Although in some respects a stone-age people – not even possessing the wheel – the Aztecs had evolved an astounding civilization. They had built in the middle of Lake Texcoco (the site of present-day Mexico City) not only one of the largest cities in the world at that time but also one of the most beautiful. Tenochtitlán had a population of at least 250,000, and was just one of a number of such cities in the extensive Aztec Empire. The Aztec ruler – the Revered Speaker – was a man of immense power, able to equip an army of 250,000 warriors with little difficulty. But for the Spanish soldiers and the priests who travelled with them, the great cloud that hung over Aztec society was its religion, which was based on human sacrifice. Its pantheon of gods, notably the Aztecs' particular god, Huitzilopochtli, demanded a continuous supply of human hearts, which were cut out of the victims on the Aztecs' great stone pyramids. Thus the Aztecs were con-

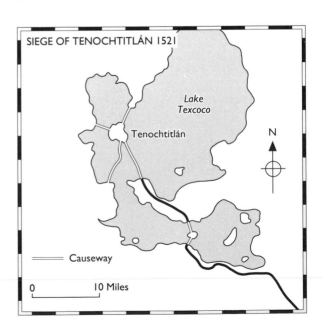

SIEGE OF TENOCHTITLÁN 1521

Lake Texcoco

Tenochtitlán

N

Causeway

0   10 Miles

MUTECZUMA

Rex ultimus Mexicanorum

Motecuhzoma II – more popularly known as Montezuma –
the king of the Aztecs (*left*); and his conqueror, Hernán
Cortés (*right*). AKG/PN

stantly at war with their neighbours, taking prisoners to replenish the supply of hearts. Curiously enough, it was the Aztec habit of capturing enemies in battle for sacrifice rather than killing them immediately that saved many Spanish lives.

The Aztecs believed in a prophecy that one of their gods – originally the Toltec god Quetzalcóatl, who opposed human sacrifice – had been driven out by the other gods and had sailed away to the east. It was predicted that one day he would return, in what the Aztecs called a 1-Reed year on their calendar. This occurred every 52 years, and the Aztecs always became fearful when the date approached in case a vengeful Quetzalcóatl – Feathered Serpent – should choose that year to return to punish the Aztecs. As it happened, Quetzalcóatl was always pictured with a white face, wearing dark clothes and having a feather in his hat. The next 1-Reed year was 1519, and in that year, and on the very day predicted – 22 April – the Spaniard Hernán Cortés, dressed unwittingly in the style of Quetzalcóatl, landed on the coast of Mexico at Vera Cruz. With him he had a Tabascan Indian girl named Malinche – or Dona Marina – who spoke

Nahuatl, the Aztec language, and acted as adviser and translator to the expedition. Cortés also brought with him 550 Spanish soldiers with pikes, crossbows and arquebuses, as well as 16 cavalry, and a pack of fierce staghounds. When the Aztecs saw this assembly of men on the beach they were astounded and immediately assumed that Cortés was Feathered Serpent returned. The Spanish horses amazed the Aztecs, who believed – for there were no horses at that time in the whole of the Americas – that the man was joined to the horse and the whole was a different species of animal. The Aztecs had dogs – but they were tiny ones for eating – and found the great Spanish hounds fearsome. But it was the Spanish weapons that were truly terrifying. Against the Aztec wooden swords tipped with obsidian the Spaniards deployed swords, pikes and armour all made of steel, while their firearms and cannons seemed a guarantee of Cortés' divinity.

When representatives of the Aztec leader Motecuhzoma II met Cortés they gave him gifts, including a huge disc of the sun, the size of a cartwheel and made from solid gold. This was all the Spaniards really needed to know – here was wealth undreamed of back home. The Aztecs had hoped that the god would take the gifts and depart, but the sight of all the gold had exactly the opposite effect. In fact it was the gold that doomed the Aztec people. Cortés wrote to King Charles in Spain: 'I intend to advance and see him [Motecuhzoma] wherever he might be found and bring him either dead or in chains if he will not submit to your Majesty's crown.'

Cortés then began his march to the Aztec capital, sinking his entire fleet to show his men that there was no way home without complete victory. When news of the god's arrival spread, tribes who hated the Aztecs came and offered to serve the Spaniards. As the invaders entered the powerful state of Tlaxcala they were attacked by the Tlaxcalan army, and for the first time the Indians were able to see European tactics and weapons in action. Outnumbered 50 to 1, Cortés won an overwhelming victory, his cannon terrifying the natives and his cavalry spearing the unresisting foe. The beaten Tlaxcalans promised to serve him against the hated Aztecs. When Cortés reached Cholula, servants of Motecuhzoma tried to poison him. In retribution he massacred the population of the city. Eventually reaching Tenochtitlán, Cortés first pretended friendship with Motecuhzoma, but then held him as hostage against the good behaviour of his people – for Cortés was fully aware of his precarious position, surrounded as he was by a quarter of a million hostile Aztecs. Eventually Motecuhzoma was killed by his own people, who chose as their new leader a strong warrior named Cuauhtémoc. Cortés and his men were besieged in Tenochtitlán, and on 30 June 1520 – ever after known by the Spaniards as *La Noche Triste* ('the night of sorrows') – they tried to break out of the city and cross the lake to the mainland by marching down one of the causeways. As they did so they were attacked by thousands of Aztecs. Half of the Spanish force was captured and sacrificed, and their skulls and those of their horses were added to the great skull rack in the main square of Tenochtitlán. Cortés barely escaped with his life. Pursued by the Aztec hordes the Spaniards turned on them at Otumba, and in an amazing battle completely routed them.

Cortés now prepared to return to conquer Tenochtitlán and establish Spanish power once and for all in Mexico. While he was preparing a fleet of small brigantines to control the lake during his assault, he was reinforced by fresh troops from Spain. In April 1521 he had 86 horsemen, 118 crossbowmen and arquebusiers, 700 sword and pikemen, as well as 18 cannons. In addition he had as many as 75,000 Tlaxcalan allies. It was still a stiff task, for the Aztecs numbered at least 250,000 men, and this time he could not rely on their native superstition to win the fight for him.

Arrayed against him was the cream of Mexican military power: Eagle knights, Jaguar knights wearing the skins of jaguars with the head of the animal acting as a helmet, and Arrow knights. Serving under the knights were thousands of men bred to war, men prepared to fight the Spaniards house by house up the causeways and throughout the huge city. The main Aztec weapon was the razor-sharp obsidian-edged *maquahuitl* sword, the wooden *macana* club, the *tepuztopilli* lance and the *cuauhololli* axe. Some Aztecs used bows, but they were relatively feeble and could not penetrate the Spanish armour.

To triumphant shouts of 'Castile' and 'Santiago', and to a cacophony of native instruments Cortés launched his brigantines on the lake and began his assault on Tenochtitlán. He had divided his forces into three sections: his deputy, Pedro de Alvarado, took 30 horse, 18 crossbowmen, 150 infantry and 25,000 Tlaxcalans and advanced down the causeway that ran from Tacuba in the northwest; Cristóbal de Olid, with 33 horse, 18 crossbowmen, 150 infantry and 25,000 Tlaxcalans advanced on the causeway from Coyoacan in the southwest; and Gonzalo de Sandoval, with 24 cavalry, 4 arquebusiers, 13 crossbowmen, 150 infantry and 30,000 Indian allies, advanced on the causeway from Itzapalapa in the southeast. Cortés himself commanded the brigantines in which the rest of the Spanish forces – crossbowmen and arquebusiers – were placed. It was a carefully planned exercise, showing a thorough appreciation of Aztec strengths and weaknesses. Cortés even left one causeway free, so that the Aztecs would have an escape route and would not fight to the death. In the event, few took this route; most preferred to die with their city.

At the start of the siege Alvarado and Olid destroyed the freshwater supply to the city. The Aztecs retaliated by pelting the Spaniards with the arms, legs and heads of the prisoners they had sacrificed, screaming 'Bad men, your blood shall appease our gods and will be drunk by our snakes.' The Aztecs had realized the horror that their sacrificial practices had for the Spaniards and played on this psychological weapon throughout the siege.

When Cortés' brigantines appeared on the lake the Aztecs attacked them from over 500 canoes, but the firepower of the Spaniards was just too violent for the fragile Indian craft. Yet with great ingenuity Aztec divers plunged stakes into the floor of the shallow lake to keep the brigantines away from the causeways, where Cortés hoped to support his soldiers in their advance. Other Aztecs frequently tried to swim up on the Spaniards by surprise, but few succeeded. By 9 June Alvarado, in particular, was making good progress up his causeway. Every 400 yards or so the Spaniards had to fill in the gaps where the Aztecs had broken down the bridges. This was hard work and at night the Aztecs frequently destroyed the work that had taken the Spaniards and their allies all day. The fighting on the causeways was ferocious, and the Aztecs could only be forced back foot by foot. Cortés ruthlessly destroyed every Aztec house he passed and used the rubble to fill up the gaps. As the work went on the brigantines scoured the lake destroying every Aztec canoe they met and hanging the warriors from their masts. It was a bitter and intense struggle, unlike any war that the Mexican Indians had known before. Accustomed to 'Flower Wars', in which prisoners were taken alive for sacrifice, they could not understand the war of extermination the Spaniards were waging. But the Aztecs were not slow to learn, and their hatred of Cortés and his men was amply demonstrated by the delight they took in sacrificing the Spaniards they captured to the ominous beat of a huge drum. The Spaniards would shiver involuntarily as they heard that drum, knowing that some of their comrades were at that moment having their living hearts torn out by blood-blackened priests. Bernal Diaz leaves us this description:

We saw them put plumes on the heads of many of them, and then they made them dance with a sort of fan in front of Huitzilopochtli. Then, after they had danced, the priests laid them on their backs on some narrow stones of sacrifice and, cutting open their chests, drew out their palpitating hearts which they offered to the idols before them. Then they kicked the bodies down the steps, and the Indian butchers who were waiting below cut off their arms and legs and flayed their faces, which they afterwards prepared like glove leather, with their beards on, and kept for their drunken festivals. Then they ate their flesh with a sauce of peppers and tomatoes.

On one occasion the Aztecs came close to taking Cortés. He had advanced too far beyond the last opening and was ambushed by an Aztec force, which drove him back to the brink of a 60-foot gap. Many of his own men were killed or taken, but Cortés' life was saved when Christobál de Oled cut off the arm of the Aztec chief who was dragging Cortés towards a canoe. The Aztecs threw Spanish heads at the Spanish leader, cursing him and saying

FLOWER WARS

The Aztec armies of the Triple Alliance (Tenochtitlán, Texcoco and Tacuba) often fought battles for the purpose of capturing prisoners to sacrifice to their war god Huitzilopochtli. In the reign of Great Speaker Motecuhzoma I (1440–68) a form of limited warfare known as the Xochiyaoyotl – or Flower War – began to be practised. These ceremonial combats – akin to European tournaments – allowed warriors to gain prestige and to demonstrate their prowess by capturing rather than killing enemy soldiers. Prisoners taken in the fighting acknowledged their captor as their 'honoured father', and it was the latter's responsibility to take them back to Tenochtitlán. After the sacrifice the warrior who had achieved the capture was allowed to eat select portions of his enemy, thereby gaining from his strength and courage. In one such Flower War in 1515 between the Aztecs and the Tlaxcalans, Motecuhzoma II committed over 100,000 soldiers from the Triple Alliance and still suffered defeat.

that they had slain Dona Marina. But Cortés remained resolute and immovable. Step by step he was destroying the city and forcing the diminishing number of defenders into a small part of the centre of Tenochtitlán. Many Aztec warriors had so little food that they were no more than living skeletons, but the light of battle still burned in their eyes and they fought until they were killed. Thousands throughout Tenochtitlán were dying of starvation, and disease – particularly the smallpox introduced by the Spaniards – was rampant. Without adequate drainage the city was a cross between a cesspit and a charnel house, with bodies rotting unburied in the streets.

Smoke began rising from various parts of the city as the three Spanish columns burned their way into the centre of the city, converging on the great market place. When the vast pyramid of Huitzilopochtli fell to the Spaniards they found at its peak a mass of congealed blood and flayed human remains, as well as the heads of sacrificed Spaniards, many of which were still recognizable. Day after day the Tlaxcalans led away prisoners in their thousands. Cortés writes that one day the number was 12,000, the next day 40,000. So terrible was the scene that even Cortés' hard heart relented and he tried to persuade the warrior-king Cuauhtémoc to surrender. But the king threatened death to anyone who spoke of peace, and it was not until nine-tenths of the city was in Spanish hands that Cuauhtémoc was captured trying to escape by canoe. Cortés had him tortured to reveal the

The Spanish conquest of the Americas was accompanied by innumerable atrocities. Here the Spaniards set their war dogs on some Aztecs. PN

whereabouts of the huge amounts of gold the Spanish had assembled before they had been forced to flee on *La Noche Triste*. On 13 August 1521 Cortés led one final assault on the last few defenders and the city was taken. The Aztecs had been destroyed.

Cortés had conquered the greatest Indian power in the western hemisphere and his example inspired a whole series of conquistadors to spread Spanish power both south and north. Three years later the Mayas of Yucatán fell to Alvarado, and between 1531 and 1533 Pizarro conquered the Inca empire of Peru. It was the death knell of the great Indian civilizations of the Americas. In the wake of the conquistadors came the devastating scourges of disease, slavery, forcible religious conversion and cultural collapse. The Europeans had come to stay.

The Siege of Vienna 1529

Vienna

Austrians
Commanders: Count Nicholas von Salm and Wilhelm von Rogendorf
Numbers: 16,000 foot and 600 horse, including 700 Spanish arquebusiers under Luis de Avalos

Turks
Commander: Suleiman the Magnificent
Numbers: 120,000

The threat to Europe posed by 'the Turk' was an ever-present one from the 15th to the 18th centuries. It fell to the House of Habsburg to act as a bastion against Ottoman expansion, and on several occasions there was a very real possibility that the Turks would succeed in breaking through into Central Europe. But no occasion was more perilous than when Suleiman the Magnificent, fresh from his great victory over the Hungarians at Mohács in 1526, reached Vienna in 1529. With Francis I of France in secret alliance with him, most of the Balkans in Turkish hands and with the renegade Hungarian ruler John Zapolya lending him aid, only the ancient and not very formidable walls of Vienna seemed to stand between Suleiman and his dream of conquering Germany.

Suleiman had left Istanbul in May 1529 with an enormous army, estimated at up to 120,000 fighting men and with 20,000 camels for transport. Like the movement of lava down a hillside he moved relentlessly through Hungary and into Austria, with city after city capitulating or succumbing to his massive cannons. Thousands of Hungarian and Austrian peasants – mostly women and young boys – were taken as slaves and marched overland back to his capital on the Bosphorus; some areas were depopulated for a generation to come. Only the fortress of Pressburg resisted Suleiman, but he knew that if Vienna fell then the defenders of Pressburg would be forced to surrender, so he wasted little time on besieging this strongpoint.

Meanwhile, the power of the Habsburgs was divided. The emperor Charles V was entangled in a war with France, and this occupied the bulk of his German and Spanish troops. His brother Ferdinand, archduke of Austria, appealed to him for help when news of the Turkish invasion reached him, but Charles could spare very little: just 700 elite Spanish arquebusiers under Luis de Avalos. These gaudily dressed professionals each carried a bandolier round his neck containing the 'Eleven Apostles' – cartridges and powder for eleven shots – and it was often said that each handgunner carried eleven lives on his shoulders. The imperial diet (assembly) voted troops to help the Viennese, with Frederick, the elector of the Palatinate, as their commander. However, Frederick had only got as far as Krems when he heard that the Turks had ringed Vienna, and he was unable to get through to the city. The Viennese were thrown back on their own not

An Ottoman cavalryman with crescent-and-star pennant; from a 16th-century German woodcut. PN

insubstantial resources, in the form of a large garrison of 16,000 foot and 600 horse. To relieve the soldiers from duties like fire-watching, labouring and transport, a civic guard was raised, but it was rarely called upon to fight in the days ahead. It was less in the quantity than the quality of the garrison that Vienna was fortunate. Whereas the Turks had easily overpowered the numerous but undisciplined horsemen of Hungary and Serbia, they had not yet faced in battle the highly professional Spanish arquebusiers, the German Landsknechts with their 18-foot pikes and halberds, or the Doppelsöldners (literally 'double mercenaries') with their massive double-handed swords – and they were in for a shock.

In 1529 Vienna did not seem to present a great problem to the Turkish artillery and engineers. With medieval walls just six feet thick it should have succumbed easily. After all, seventy years before, Turkish cannons had broken down the massive fortifications of Constantinople. In the intervening years the Turks had perfected the art of siege warfare and had captured many stronger cities than Vienna. What could stop them now?

The northern walls of Vienna were protected by the River Danube, and the eastern side by a small river known as the Wiener Bach, which prevented an approach from that flank. This reduced the Turkish attack options to two: the south and west walls. Curiously the Turks decided to concentrate on just the southern wall, merely covering the western wall with artillery batteries and a few

entrenched troops. This decision greatly simplified the task of the defenders, who assembled their best troops around the Carinthian Gate in the south.

The defence of Vienna was in the hands of two seasoned campaigners, the 70-year-old Count Nicholas von Salm, and the Marshal of Austria, Wilhelm von Rogendorf. Before the Turks had completely encircled the city the Austrians destroyed all the houses outside the walls to reduce the cover available to the attackers. Inside the city, thatched roofs were stripped from houses to reduce the risk of fire, and a huge earthwork thrown up behind the south and west walls to provide a second line of defence in case the walls were breached. The defenders massed their guns and best arquebusiers around the Carinthian Gate, expecting the Turkish assaults to single it out for attack.

On 23 September the Turkish army arrived outside the city, and in the next three days completed their encirclement, setting up batteries of 300 cannon. Soon Vienna was completely cut off from the rest of Europe, with a Turkish flotilla stationed on the Danube. An intricate array of zigzag trenches was dug, and Turkish sharpshooters were pushed forward within range of the walls. But the defenders had no intention of remaining passive; only six days after Suleiman's arrival, 2500 footsoldiers emerged from a gate in the eastern wall and took the Turks by surprise, wrecking their trenches and killing their engineers. The Turkish commander-in-chief, the Grand Vizier Ibrahim Pasha, barely escaped with his life.

On 1 October the Turkish bombardment began. But although it knocked down bastions and ripped up walls it was surprisingly ineffective. Instead of defending stone walls the German and Spanish soldiers took up their positions behind piles of rubble, which were even more difficult to assault. Day and night the cannonade continued, while thousands of Turkish janissaries, armed with arquebuses and bows, peppered the walls – again with little effect. But the real battle was being fought underground. The Turks were famed for their mining operations, and the Habsburg commanders were determined to counter-mine wherever possible. Having detected a Turkish mine the Austrians dug counter-shafts and waited in them until the Turks drew near; then the intervening wall was broken down and the Turkish miners were killed at sword or pikepoint. Sometimes barrels of gunpowder were rolled in and exploded. It took a special kind of courage to fight and die twenty feet below the surface.

On 6 October Count von Salm sent 8000 men – nearly half the garrison – on a mission to wreck

SIEGE OF VIENNA 1529

Branch of Danube

Turkish piquets and some batteries

VIENNA

Main Turkish front of attack

Turkish piquets

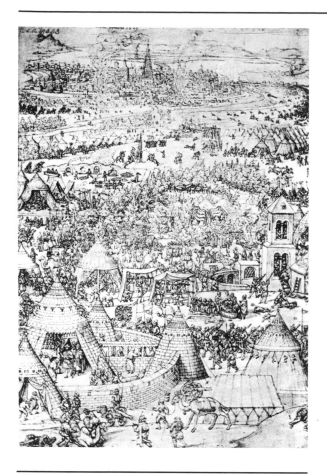

A view of the massive Turkish encampment, with Vienna in the distance. PN

The Turks were growing despondent. The weather was becoming colder and there was snow in the air as the Turks decided on one last effort. On 12 October two more mines were exploded around the Carinthian Gate, but the defenders filled the gaps with barrels of wet earth. Suleiman tried to encourage his men with great rewards, offering to ennoble the first man to enter the city – but to no avail. There was no fire in the attackers, and the Viennese could see that most of the Turkish troops were being thrashed and flogged by their officers to make them go forward. After a few hours of mostly desultory efforts the Turks finally gave way and fell back in disorder. That night the inhabitants of Vienna could see the sky lit up by the burning tents and pavilions of the retreating Ottoman army. To add to the eerie sight of flickering lights in the darkness, there were the screams of the prisoners massacred by the Turks before they went. The next morning an Austrian cavalry detachment came across the bodies of thousands of Christian peasants. Infuriated, the Austrian horsemen pursued the Turks, turning Suleiman's retreat into a rout. Half-starved Turkish soldiers succumbed to the cold conditions, for by 17 October snow was falling. Abandoned carts, dead horses and camels, and the numerous corpses of soldiers marked the route of the retreating army. Even the Turkish naval flotilla, sailing down the Danube, suffered heavy damage under the guns of the fortress of Pressburg.

The moral effect on the Turks was immense. They had not just been beaten, they had been humiliated by an enemy scarcely a quarter their number. If it was only the first of a great number of battles between the Habsburgs and the Turks, it was the one occasion when a Habsburg defeat would have been irreversible. The loss of Vienna in 1529 would have enabled Suleiman to winter in Central Europe, before beginning a new campaign in Germany in the spring of 1530. With Germany rent by the religious divisions of the Reformation, it is doubtful how united German resistance to the Turks would have been. The defenders of Vienna, notably old Nicholas von Salm, had saved Europe and inflicted on the Turks a decisive defeat.

the Turkish trenches opposite the Carinthian Gate. At first the raid was very successful and the Turks routed, but as the defenders hurried back into the city it was found that the gate was too narrow to accommodate such a flow of men and many were killed by the Turks under the walls. Four days later a huge Turkish mine blew a hole in the defences near the church of St Clara, but an attempt by Albanian troops to enter the breach was hurled back with heavy losses, and the gap filled with beams of wood prepared for just such an emergency.

The Battle of Lepanto 1571

Lepanto

Christians

Commander:	Don John of Austria
Vanguard:	Juan de Cardona with 6 galleasses and 7 galleys
Left wing:	Agostini Barbarigo with 53 galleys
Centre:	Don John, Sebastien Veniero and Marco Antonio Colonna with 62 galleys
Right wing:	Giovanni Andrea Doria with 50 galleys
Reserve:	Marquis of Santa Cruz with 30 galleys. There were also 70 fast-sailing frigates, too weak to join the battle line.
Marine numbers	28,000

Turks

Commander:	Ali Pasha commanding the fleet and Pertev Pasha commanding the soldiers and marines
Right wing:	Mohammed Sirocco with 54 galleys and 2 smaller galliots
Centre:	Ali Pasha with 87 galleys and 8 galliots
Left wing:	Ulugh Ali with 61 galleys and 32 galliots
Reserve:	8 galleys and 22 smaller ships.
Marine numbers:	25,000

After the fall of Constantinople to Sultan Mehmed II in 1453 the Turks set out to extend their dominion in the Mediterranean. This involved them building a fleet to match their power on land. During the following century the Ottomans became the dominant naval force in the eastern Mediterranean and the seas off the North African coast. Fleets of fast Turkish galleys, rowed by thousands of Christian slaves, preyed on the ships of Spain and Venice, forcing Christian vessels to carry black sails for use at night in an effort to escape the marauders. Only a united Christian response would have been strong enough to combat the Turks, but in a Europe torn by dynastic and religious quarrels such unity

was unattainable. While the pope might preach the idea of a crusade as in earlier times, the French kings often allied themselves to the Turks in their struggle against the Habsburgs of Spain and Austria. Even Italian maritime states like Genoa and Venice would not make common cause against the Turks, each glorying in the discomfiture of its rival, forgetting its own setbacks at the hands of the common enemy.

The death of the great sultan Suleiman the Magnificent in 1566 was a turning point, not just in the history of the Ottoman Empire, but in Europe as a whole. Until that time the Osmanli dynasty had produced an unfailing line of able rulers, and this process seemed set fair to continue until Suleiman ordered the murder of his brilliant son Mustafa to make way for another son by a jealous but beautiful junior wife, Roxelana. On the death of Suleiman he was succeeded by the boy, an imbecilic weakling known as Selim the Drunkard, and the great line of Osman ended. Power now devolved on the sultan's generals and admirals, whose task it was to pursue traditional Ottoman policy. The next target they selected was the Venetian island of Cyprus. The Doge of Venice appealed to Pope Pius V to call on Christian countries to aid his people in their peril and, after much petty bickering, a Holy League was set up by the pope, Venice and Philip II of Spain, as well as many minor Italian states and the crusading Knights of St John, to raise a fleet of 300 ships and 50,000 fighting men.

While the diplomacy went on, the heroic Venetian commander of Cyprus, Antonio Bragadino, held the Turks at bay, inflicting heavy casualties on them in men and ships. Only after he had run out of food and powder was he forced to accept Turkish terms. He and his men were allowed to march out of the citadel of Famagusta with the honours of war, but the Turks immediately broke their word. Once the Venetians were disarmed, the common soldiers were sold as slaves, the officers beheaded, and Bragadino barbarously mutilated – his ears and nose were cut off, then he was rowed around the Turkish fleet and flayed alive, his skin being stuffed with straw and sent to Selim the Drunkard in Constantinople. Yet the fate of Bragadino and his courageous example were to inspire Christians throughout the Mediterranean to resist the Turks as nothing else could have done.

The Christian success at Lepanto owed much to the unity of command that was achieved when the pope selected the little-known Don John of Austria to lead the fleet. Don John was the bastard son of the late emperor Charles V and his mistress Barbara Blomberg, and had lived in obscurity until brought to court and acknowledged as his half-brother by Philip II of Spain. Although inexperienced in 1571 Don John was a natural leader, an unsullied champion of Christendom, who had studied with the great Spanish general, Alessandro Farnese, and was now to have the experience of such veteran admirals as the papal commander Marco Antonio Colonna and the Venetian Sebastiano Veniero.

The Christian fleet assembled at Messina in Sicily, nearly 300 vessels crowding into the harbour. As well as the galleys, which made up most of the fighting strength of the fleet, there were 70 fast-sailing frigates and six curious hybrids – Spanish galleasses – which were to play a significant part in the battle ahead. Whereas galleys in the 16th century carried guns at bow and stern, their chief tactic was to ram, grapple and board. The galleasses, on the other hand, carried guns amidships and were able to keep up a heavy fire on the approaching Turkish galleys to which the enemy could not reply. Placed in front of the galley-line, they could inflict heavy casualties at comparatively long range. Although slow sailers, each galleass bristled with guns of all calibres.

The Christian fleet was to consist of five divisions. The main line of battle comprised a left wing of 53 galleys commanded by Agostino Barbarigo, a centre of 62 led by Don John himself, assisted by Colonna and Veniero, and a right wing of 50 under the Genoese admiral Giovanni Andrea Doria. In front of the battle line the galleasses were commanded by Juan de Cardona, and behind the battle line a reserve of 30 ships was led by the Marquis of Santa Cruz, Spain's greatest sailor.

Don John flew his flag in the largest of the Spanish galleys, the *Reale*, a magnificent vessel with her stern sculpted by the famous Vasquez of Seville. The *Reale* had a crew of over 700, of whom 300 were oarsmen and the rest Spanish pikemen and arquebusiers. On the left of the *Reale*, the papal admiral, Colonna, flew the pope's flag of crossed keys, and on the right of Don John, the great lion banner of St Mark flew proudly over the flagship of Sebastiano Veniero, admiral of Venice. Also in the centre was the flagship of the Knights of Malta under their Grand Master, Giustiniani. In all, 272

Christian ships were assembled, holding 28,000 elite fighting men, many Italian and Spanish veterans, but also some 2000 Germans, and on the decks of one of Colonna's galleys stood a young officer who would never forget this last manifestation of European chivalry in arms against the infidel Turk. Miguel de Cervantes was to fight, shed blood and conquer alongside Don John of Austria at Lepanto. It was as if Shakespeare had served with Drake at Gravelines, and lived to record his experiences.

The great fleet left Messina on 15 September and headed towards the Gulf of Corinth, where the Turkish fleet had last been sighted. In fact, the Turks had been spying on the Christian fleet without being noticed. The Muslim corsair Kara Khodja, flying black sails, and with every part of his vessel painted black, had slipped into Messina harbour and counted the strength of the Christians. The Turks were reassured by his report and were confident that with the fleets evenly matched the

Don John of Austria, bastard son of the emperor Charles V, and victor of Lepanto. AKG

greater experience of their commanders would bring them victory. Of the 274 vessels in their fleet, all but 20 of the light craft could fight in the battle line, unlike the 70 Christian frigates. Like their opponents, the Turkish fleet was divided into three parts: the right wing – 54 Egyptian and Levantine galleys – were commanded by Mohammed Sirocco; the centre – 87 galleys from the Greek islands and North Africa – was under the Ottoman commander-in-chief Ali Pasha; the left – 61 galleys from Syria, Constantinople and North Africa – was led by the much-hated corsair, Ulugh Ali, a renegade Italian from Calabria. Aboard the ships there were 25,000 Turkish soldiers, many of them militia, more often armed with bows than firearms, and a few elite janissaries.

On 7 October, near the entrance to the Gulf of Corinth, Don John's lookouts reported 'enemy in sight', and the young commander ordered the banner consecrated by Pope Pius V – depicting a crucifix and the figures of the apostles Peter and Paul – to be broken out at the mainmast of the *Reale*. Throughout the Christian fleet chaplains – grey-gowned Franciscans and the black-robed Dominicans – heard the confessions of thousands of sailors and marines, while Don John – clothed in a magnificent

suit of armour – was rowed from ship to ship holding up a crucifix and exhorting his men to fight well in the holy cause. Christian oarsmen aboard the vessels – some criminals, others men who rowed for pay – were freed and armed, to swell the numbers of combatants on the Christian side. The Turks could take no such risk, as all their rowers were pressed men and slaves who would have turned on them if they could.

So swiftly did the Turks close on the Christian fleet that they found it unprepared. Many of the ships of Doria's right wing and Santa Cruz's reserve found that the fighting had started even before they had rounded Cape Scropha. About midday the galleasses opened the battle by firing broadsides at the approaching Turkish squadrons, scoring an immediate and important hit on the enemy flagship. But the Turks refused to face these floating batteries and sailed past them to come to grips with the sort of enemy they understood. On the Christian left the Venetian ships were rammed and grappled by Mohammed Sirocco's Egyptian galleys. The valiant Barbarigo, fighting with his visor raised, was killed by an arrow in the face, and soon hordes of Turkish soldiers were aboard his flagship. The fighting was hand-to-hand and there was no room for quarter. With Barbarigo's flagship in Muslim hands the Venetians counter-attacked and occupied the flagship of the Egyptians, killing Sirocco and sweeping his decks with arquebus fire. At point of pike the Venetian flagship was regained by Barbarigo's nephew Contarini, though he too fell at the moment of victory. When the Venetian flag was raised aboard Mohammed Sirocco's great galley many of his captains lost heart and ran their ships ashore, escaping into the interior, pursued in some cases by their own freed galley-slaves.

The battle was really decided in the centre, where the fighting was most intense. The Ottoman commander, Ali Pasha, flying a white pennon from Mecca, bearing in gold lettering verses from the Koran, steered straight for Don John's flagship, raking his rowers' benches with grape-shot and killing many of the helpless men below decks. When the two huge galleys collided the *Reale* was rocked by the impact and many of her crew thrown down or tipped overboard. Soon the entire centre of the Christian line was engaged and ships grappled like drowning men clinging to each other while trying to force the other under. In the confusion commands went unheeded amidst the screams and rending sounds of masts splintering and banks of oars snapping like matchwood. Drums and trumpets added to a cacophony that was painful to the ears. Aboard the *Reale* 400 Spanish arquebusiers

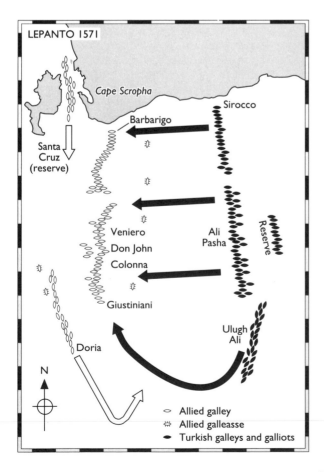

LEPANTO 1571

Cape Scropha

Sirocco

Barbarigo

Santa Cruz (reserve)

Veniero

Don John

Colonna

Ali Pasha

Reserve

Giustiniani

Ulugh Ali

Doria

N

○ Allied galley
⚏ Allied galleasse
● Turkish galleys and galliots

fired volleys into the heaving mass of Turks aboard Ali's ship, while freed oarsmen with sword and pike repelled boarders who swarmed up the rigging and swung from ship to ship. Ali's janissaries engaged Don John's Spaniards with bow and musket from unmissable range, and some of the finely dressed Turks had their clothing ignited by the fire of the Spanish handpieces. Yet inch by inch the *Reale* was losing its fight against the veteran marines in the service of the Turkish admiral.

The decisive moment of the battle was the intervention by the Prince of Colonna in the struggle between the flagships. The papal admiral, having boarded and captured a galley commanded by the Bey of Negropont, saw that the *Reale* was in difficulties nearby. Ordering his rowers to give him full speed, Colonna drove his prow deep into the stern of Ali Pasha's galley, sending boarding parties onto the Turkish flagship and relieving pressure on Don John. Assaulted from a new direction, Ali had to recall some of his boarders to defend his own ship.

There are many eye-witness accounts of the battle and some extraordinary cameos survive, like that of the 70-year-old Venetian admiral, Sebastian Veniero, standing by the pooprail of his ship and

Lepanto was the last major naval battle fought between galleys. This contemporary Venetian painting evokes the intensity of the hand-to-hand fighting. AKG

firing a blunderbuss full of bullets and nails into the crowded Turkish ships alongside. With arrows and shots flying around him, he calmly gave the weapon to a young boy nearby to reload for him. At another point, Don John's pet marmoset picked up a smoking hand grenade thrown by the Turks aboard the *Reale* and then either dropped it safely in the sea, or, according to other sources, threw it back at the Turks. A third account speaks of Turkish janissaries, out of powder and arrows, pelting the Christian soldiers with oranges – and laughing.

There was little to laugh about as the bitter fight between Don John, Colonna and Ali Pasha reached its conclusion. Disciplined Spanish pikemen under Vasquez Coronada and Gil d'Andrada first cleared their own decks and then swarmed onto the Turkish galley to rout their janissary opponents at push of pike. Not one Turkish soldier survived the struggle, Ali Pasha himself being felled by an arquebus ball.

The Turkish admiral's head was cut off and presented triumphantly to a bloodstained Don John, but the Christian general was horrified at the sight and ordered it dropped overboard. Ali's holy standard of Mecca was hauled down and replaced by the flag of the Holy League, a sight that spread panic throughout the Turkish fleet. With the fight in the centre drawing to a close there was just time for the young Cervantes to suffer a wound that cost him his left hand, while Admiral Veniero put aside his blunderbuss long enough to ram and sink two Turkish galleys, before the enemy turned to flee.

The most controversial part of the battle involved the struggle between Andrea Doria and Ulugh Ali. The corsair's attempt to outflank the Genoese admiral caused Doria to head too far south (some of his critics accusing him of cowardice), allowing Ulugh to turn back suddenly and crash straight into the unprotected right flank of the Christian centre. Seven Turkish galleys overwhelmed the flagship of the Knights of Malta, while Venetian and papal vessels nearby were hard-pressed by Ulugh's men. The heroic Grand Master Giustiniani, with five arrows firmly stuck in his body, and lying under the piles of corpses, was one of only three men to survive on his ship, as Ulugh Ali hauled down the flag from his mainmast to present as a trophy to Selim in Constantinople. But the corsair did not have it all his own way. Viewing the danger in the centre Santa Cruz brought up the Spanish reserves, while Don John personally led 12 galleys to the rescue. Finally the arrival of the laggardly Doria put Ulugh Ali to flight, but the corsair made his escape with 14 ships and the flag of the Knights of Malta.

The losses in a galley battle were always enormous, for there was no chance of escaping from the melee that followed a boarding, and few prisoners were taken. The Christians lost 7500 men killed, including many of noble rank – 60 of the Knights of St John died around Giustiniani aboard his flagship. But the Turkish losses were devastating: 15 galleys sunk and 190 captured, with Ali Pasha and over 30,000 men killed or drowned. And the 12,000 Christian galley-slaves freed after the battle would have echoed G.K. Chesterton's words that 'Don John of Austria has set his people free.'

The battle of Lepanto was decisive more for the effect it had on the Christian West than on the Turks. The Ottomans were able to rebuild their fleet and once again menace the Mediterranean lands, but they no longer posed the invincible threat that they once had. They had passed their highpoint and under the leadership of increasingly corrupt and depraved sultans the Turkish Empire began a relentless decline. Don John's victory showed that the Turks could no longer hold a united Christendom in thrall.

The Spanish Armada 1588

Spanish Armada

Spanish

Commander: Duke of Medina-Sidonia

Divisions	Ships	Tons	Guns	Soldiers	Sailors	Total Men
Armada of Portugal	12	7737	347	3330	1293	4623
(Duke of Medina-Sidonia)						
Armada of Biscay	14	6567	238	1937	863	2800
(Juan Martinez de Recalde)						
Armada of Castille	16	8714	384	2458	1719	4171
(Diego Flores de Valdés)						
Armada of Andalusia	11	8762	240	2327	780	3105
(Don Pedro de Valdés)						
Armada of Guipuzcoa	14	6991	247	1992	616	2608
(Miguel de Oquendo)						
Armada of the Levant	10	7705	280	2780	767	3523
(Martin de Bertendona)						
Urcas (storeships)	23	10,271	384	3121	608	3729
(Juan Gomez de Medina)						
Patasses and zabras (fast craft)	22	1121	91	479	574	1093
(Don Antonio Hurtado de Mendoza)						
Galleasses	4	unknown	200	773	468	1341
(Don Hugo de Moncada)						
Galleys	4	unknown	20	Nil	362	362
(Diego de Medrano)						
Rowers (galleys and galleasses)						2088
Total	**130**	**57,868**	**2431**	**19,295**	**8050**	**29,453**

English

Commanders: Lord Howard of Effingham, Sir Francis Drake

At Gravelines:

Left wing: Lord Henry Seymour (*Rainbow*) and Sir William Winter (*Vanguard*)

Centre: Lord Howard (*Ark Royal*) and Sir John Hawkins (*Victory*)

Right wing: Sir Francis Drake (*Revenge*) Sir Martin Frobisher (*Triumph*)

Numbers of ships varied throughout campaign, a total of 197 being used, including 34 galleons, 34 merchantmen, 30 London barques, 30 Royal barques, 20 coasters, 23 voluntary ships.

The Spanish Armada that sailed against England in 1588 was the final recognition by King Philip II that his relations with his sister-in-law Elizabeth Tudor could never be normalized. Elizabeth I had begun her reign as an ally of Spain and for many years, in spite of conflicting interests in the area of trade with South America and the Caribbean, England and Spain had subdued their hostility. However, by the 1570s it was becoming clear to Philip that England would not return to Catholicism under Elizabeth, and as a result he began to support the claims to the English throne of the Catholic Mary Stuart – Mary, Queen of Scots – whom Elizabeth had imprisoned in England. But it was events in the Netherlands that brought the break with England into the open. The revolt of the Protestant Dutch against their Spanish masters was encouraged and supported by the English and when, in 1585, Elizabeth sent an army into the Netherlands to fight against the Spanish, war between England and Spain became

The Spanish Armada in crescent formation being attacked by the English fleet. The captains of the Spanish ships were under threat of death from their commander if they broke rank. AAAC

open. Philip realized that unless he could neutralize England, and prevent her from supporting the Dutch rebels, it might be impossible to defeat them. The Armada was aimed not at invading and conquering England, which would have been impossible, but to help Philip's general, Alessandro Farnese, duke of Parma, to ship an army of Spanish veterans across the Channel and force Elizabeth out of the war by capturing parts of southern England, even perhaps London. Such at least was the plan, but many Spaniards feared English seapower and thought the Armada's chances of success very slim. One of them was Spain's best sailor, Juan Martinez de Recalde:

It's very simple. It is well known that we fight in God's cause. So when we meet the English, God will surely arrange matters so that we can grapple and board them, either by sending some strange freak of weather or, more likely, just depriving the English of their wits.

Unless God helps us with a miracle the English, who have faster and handier ships than ours, and many more long-range guns, and who know their advantage just as well as we do, will never close with us at all, but stand off and knock us to pieces.

Victorian accounts of the Armada often misrepresent the struggle as a kind of Spanish Goliath against an English David. This could not be further from the truth. The English fleet that followed Howard and Drake was as large and heavily armed as its Spanish counterpart. Nor were all the English ships small and manoeuvrable as some accounts imply. In 1588 the English used 197 ships in the campaign, including the huge 1100-ton *Triumph*, flagship of Sir Martin Frobisher. Lord Howard's *Ark Royal*, the fleet flagship, was an 800-tonner, with 44 guns, including 4 massive 60-pounders, as well as a complement of 396. Few of the Spanish ships could match this armament. Indeed, taken as a whole, the English fleet had 2 ships of over 1000 tons, 1 of 900 tons, 2 of 800, and 8 more over 500 tons. In fact, the main difference between the fleets was in the emphasis the Spaniards placed on military personnel; the English ships carried mainly sailors, with far fewer marines and soldiers than the Spaniards. The Armada consisted of 130 ships in all, including 20 galleons, 4 galleasses, 4 galleys, 44 armed merchantmen and 58 smaller vessels. It carried a total complement of 8050 seamen and

18,973 soldiers, plus 3000 or so specialists and servants.

On 30 May 1588 the Armada set sail from Lisbon, only to be dispersed by storms. When the scattered ships made harbour at Corunna in northern Spain, the fleet admiral, the Duke of Medina-Sidonia, wrote to the king proposing that the whole enterprise be abandoned:

We have now arrived in this port so scattered and shaken that we are much inferior in strength to the enemy, in the opinion of all who are competent to judge.

How do you think we can attack so great a country as England with such a force as ours is now?

The king took this calmly, encouraged his commander-in-chief to continue, and left the rest to God. The ships were refitted, and by the beginning of July the fleet set out to sea again.

Meanwhile, preparations in England were taking their erratic course. The lord-lieutenants of the counties were raising local militias, and garrisons were being established in the south-coast ports, while in the coastal shires beacons were set up on cliffs and hills to spread the word of the Spanish approach. The queen's naval advisers, notably Lord Howard of Effingham, Sir Francis Drake, John Hawkins and Thomas Fenner, had convinced Elizabeth that the Spaniards must be beaten at sea, for if they were to effect a landing her brave but incompetent army, led by the ailing earl of Leicester, would be no match for the Spanish veterans.

As the Armada approached the Lizard in Cornwall on 29 July a council of war was held aboard Medina-Sidonia's flagship, the *San Martin*. Here the formation of the fleet was determined: the Spanish ships were to form a crescent, which all captains were to maintain at the risk of their lives. The Spaniards knew that from now on they would be subject to harassing attacks and that this formation would be the most difficult for the English to break. That same day Lord Howard in the *Ark Royal* was in action against De Leyva's tall galleon, the *Rata Coronada*. At once the differences in firepower were apparent. While the Spaniards sprayed the *Ark*'s sails, the English ship – firing three shots to every one from the Spaniard – pounded the enemy hull, weakening her and killing her crew. During the battle Hawkins in the *Victory* and Martin Frobisher in the huge *Triumph* inflicted punishment on Juan Martinez de Recalde's *Santiago*, as well as the *Capitana* and *Rosario*. One of Oquendo's best ships, the 1000-ton *San Salvador*, was badly knocked about and burst into flames when a flash exploded the powder in her magazine. After three hours' fighting

the English drew away leaving the Spaniards bloodied but undefeated.

That evening Drake in the *Revenge* revealed something of his buccaneering nature when, posted to lead the English fleet through the night by showing a lantern at his stern, he extinguished the light and abandoned the rest of the fleet in order to pursue the damaged Spanish galleon *Rosario*, Pedro Valdes' flagship. Drake forced Valdes to surrender and towed the prize into Weymouth, ensuring his own claim to the prize money. Meanwhile Howard, Hawkins and the others were floundering around in the darkness, looking for Drake. So infuriated was Frobisher that he later challenged Drake to a duel over the incident. It is because of incidents such as this that one can quite understand Elizabeth's preference for Lord Howard over Drake as commander of her fleet. In the Spanish fleet such dereliction of duty would have cost Drake his head.

As the Armada sailed along the coast, Lord Howard received constant supplies of food and ammunition from the English seaports, as well as extra ships. Off the Isle of Wight there was another sharp skirmish. Hawkins in the *Victory* almost

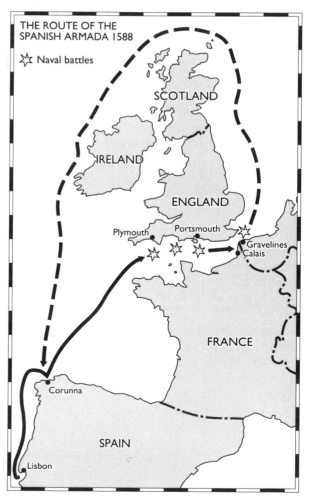

THE ROUTE OF THE SPANISH ARMADA 1588

☆ Naval battles

SCOTLAND

IRELAND

ENGLAND

Plymouth   Portsmouth

Gravelines
Calais

Corunna

FRANCE

SPAIN

Lisbon

MAJOR ENGLISH SHIPS AT THE BATTLE OF GRAVELINES 1588

Ship	Commander	Tons	Mariners	Gunners	Soldiers
Ark Royal	Lord Howard	800	270	34	126
Revenge	Sir Francis Drake	500	150	24	76
Victory	Sir John Hawkins	800	270	34	126
Triumph	Martin Frobisher	1100	300	40	160
Elizabeth Bonaventure	Earl of Cumberland	600	150	24	76
Rainbow	Lord Henry Seymour	500	150	24	76
Golden Lion	Lord Thomas Howard	500	150	24	76
White Bear	Lord Sheffield	1000	300	40	150
Vanguard	Sir William Winter	500	150	24	76
Elizabeth Jonas	Sir Robert Southwell	900	300	40	150
Antelope	Sir Henry Palmer	400	120	20	30
Dreadnought	Sir George Beeston	400	130	20	40
Mary Rose	Edward Fenton	600	150	24	76
Nonpareil	Thomas Fenner	500	150	24	76
Hope	Robert Crosse	600	160	25	85
Swiftsure	Edward Fenner	400	120	20	40

succeeded in taking the *Santa Ana* and the *San Luis*, but was driven off by De Leyva in the *Rata Coronada*, assisted by the galleasses. Soon the *Golden Lion* and the *Ark Royal* were involved in the fight, the latter receiving some damage.

Medina-Sidonia was running short of ammunition as the result of the running fights, and now had the frustration of seeing a further 36 English ships under Lord Henry Seymour and Sir William Winter join Howard's fleet off Portsmouth. He wrote to Parma:

My stores are beginning to run short with these constant skirmishes, and if . . . the enemy continues his tactics, as he certainly will, it will be advisable to load a couple of ships with powder and ball of the sizes noted . . . and despatch them to me without delay.

English seapower was clearly every bit as dangerous as he had feared, and at times like this he must have dreamed of his peaceful orange groves in Andalusia, which he had been loath to leave when offered the command of the Armada. Nevertheless, the fleet was still intact and was nearing Calais, where he hoped he would be able to contact Parma about the next stage of the mission. Had he known the problems facing Parma his morale would have fallen even lower. The Spanish commander in the Netherlands had assembled the flat-bottomed boats to carry the troops to England, but there was no way that they would be able to leave shore. He was being hemmed in by 50 Dutch ships, and to have sailed to meet Medina-Sidonia would have been suicide. Unless the Armada could defeat Lord Howard and scatter his ships the military operation was doomed.

While the Armada anchored in Calais Roads, the morale of the English was not much higher than that of the Spanish. In spite of advantages in command, firepower and ship-handling, the English had been quite unable to break up the Spanish formation. And it was proving very difficult to sink ships with gunfire alone. Boarding, which would have been normal practice, was quite out of the question against the heavily defended Spanish vessels, whose marines and soldiers were more than a match for the English sailors. Whether it was Drake who now suggested fireships we cannot be sure. But since the previous year, when the Dutch had used a floating mine against Parma's troops with devastating effect, the Spaniards were paranoid about the damage of such 'mines' to their ships. When the English floated eight fireships at night into Calais harbour, all hell broke loose. Although the fireships were themselves a failure, the Spaniards took them for more floating mines, cut their own anchor ropes, and rushed hither and thither, colliding with each other. The *San Lorenzo* ran aground and was later boarded by Richard Tomson of Ramsgate with a party of soldiers. As dawn came the sight that met Medina-Sidonia's eyes must have come close to breaking his heart. After all his care to keep the fleet together over so many days his captains had simply panicked and were now spread far and wide.

Howard took his chance and led the English into action off Gravelines. In a full-scale attack, Drake and Frobisher headed the right wing of the English fleet, Howard and Hawkins the centre, and Lord Seymour and Sir William Winter the left. This time the English decided to abandon their long-range bombardment, which was doing little harm, and close to such short range that they could not miss. As the fleets moved together the casualties started mounting on both sides, with the great galleons battering each other's hulls. Pedro Coco Calderón describes Drake's battle with Medina-Sidonia's flagship, *San Martin*, which lasted all day:

The enemy then opened a heavy artillery fire on our flagship, which was continued for nine hours. So tremendous was the fire that 200 balls struck the sails and hull of the flagship on the starboard side, killing and wounding many men, disabling and dismounting three guns, and destroying much rigging. The holes made in the hull between wind and water caused so great leakage that two divers had as much as they could do to stop them up with tow and lead plates, working all day.

During the fight the *San Juan de Sicilia* turned over and sank, carrying most of her crew to the bottom, and the *San Felipe* and the *San Mateo* were disabled and ran aground on the shore. Yet in spite of nine hours of firing they were the only terminal victims of the English guns. Howard withdrew and called a council of war.

Meanwhile, the Spanish ships were far more damaged than the English realized. Few still had their anchors, while many others lacked sails and rigging, or were listing from damage below the water line. As the crippled fleet turned into the North Sea the weather began to change and the seas grew rough. Medina-Sidonia in his leaking galleon *San Martin* was coming to the conclusion that the mission could not succeed. It would be impossible in their present condition to fight their way back into the Channel and link up with Parma. The only alternative was to escape around the north coast of Scotland. Several captains, including Recalde and De Leyva, argued that such an action was disgraceful and tried to persuade the admiral to continue with the mission. But the Armada was now completely out of cannon shot, and without that it could not even defend itself against the English ships. In addition, food was short, water foul, and disease breaking out on some ships. In the end, Medina-Sidonia's was the only sensible course, without which it is doubtful if any of the Spanish ships would have reached home.

Lord Howard and the English commanders were still frustrated at their inability to destroy more of the enemy. As Howard wrote to the queen's chief adviser, Lord Burghley, 'Their force is wonderful great and strong, and yet we pluck their feathers by little and little.' The English continued their pursuit of the Armada as far as the Firth of Forth, when the decision was taken to let the Spaniards risk the difficult coasts of Scotland and Ireland. Burghley was disappointed: 'I am sorry the Lord Admiral was forced to leave the prosecution of the enemy through the wants he sustained. Our half-doings doth breed dishonour and leaveth the disease uncured.' Unknown to Burghley – or to Drake and Howard – the winds and the seas were going to complete the task that they had started. Many Spanish ships floundered in the next few weeks and those sailors who did come ashore received little pity. At Galway the governor of Connaught massacred 400 shipwrecked Spaniards, while Lady Denny of Tralee Castle executed 23 wretched survivors who had surrendered to her, enjoining her mercy.

Of the 130 ships that had left Lisbon, some 63 Spanish ships, including many of the best galleons,

Sir Francis Drake: swashbuckling but irresponsible? PN

The *Ark Royal*. Launched in 1587, she served as Howard of Effingham's flagship during the Armada. Contrary to popular opinion, the major English ships were of a similar size to those of the Spaniards. PN

were lost on the expedition. The English did not lose a single ship during the entire campaign. Yet, although the defeat had been a staggering one, King Philip accepted it as God's will, saying 'I could easily if I chose place another fleet upon the sea.' In fact he did, for there were several more Spanish armadas against England in the 1590s. But they stood no more chance of success than Medina-Sidonia's. The kind of amphibious attack that the Spaniards planned was beyond the power of a 16th-century ruler, just as it defied both Napoleon and Hitler in more modern times.

The defeat of the Armada was the greatest disaster of King Philip's reign, and a body blow to the Counter-Reformation in northern Europe. Had Elizabeth of England succumbed to the Spanish threat in 1588, the future for both the Protestant Dutch and the Huguenot cause in France would have been grim. Further, the prestige of the English as the champion of Protestantism was increased, and the English seafarers carried the war from European waters out into the Atlantic and the Caribbean, laying the foundations of Britain's North American empire.

The Battle of Breitenfeld 1631

Short of stature, he was meagre and terrible in aspect; his cheeks were sunken, his nose long and pointed, his eyes fierce and dark. When not sheathed in gilded armour, he usually wore a slashed doublet of green silk, a preposterously broad brimmed and conical hat, adorned by a red ostrich feather; a long beard, a long dagger and mighty Toledo sword . . .

Tilly was a widely respected general who had yet to taste defeat. But he had never before faced an enemy like the king of Sweden.

Gustavus Adolphus, the Swedish king who pioneered a revolution in military organization and tactics; portrait by the great Dutch painter Albert Cuyp. PN

The Thirty Years War, which raged throughout Germany between 1618 and 1648, was the last of the great religious wars in Europe. But more than religion was at stake in the fighting: the whole political future of Germany was in the balance. In 1629 the armies of the Austrian Habsburgs under Tilly and Wallenstein had carried the flags of the Counter-Reformation as far north as the Baltic coast, and there seemed every chance that the whole of Germany would become a province of Catholic Austria. Without Swedish help the Protestant cause in Germany – and probably the Low Countries too – seemed doomed. The intervention of Gustavus Adolphus of Sweden – the 'Lion of the North' – at this juncture and his subsequent victory at Breitenfeld in 1631 saved Protestant Europe from, in the words of one Protestant historian, 'an impending reign of Jesuits'.

On 16 September 1631 the Swedes located the Catholic army, under their veteran commander Johann, Graf von Tilly, between the villages of Breitenfeld and Stenberg, just north of Leipzig. A Scotsman with the Swedes has left us a description of the elderly Habsburg commander, now over 70 years of age:

Gustavus Adolphus camped a mile from Tilly's position and spent that night discussing the proposed battle with his Swedish and Scottish generals. At first light the Swedish soldiers assembled and, peering through the haze of the early autumn morning, they could just see the Imperial camp fires as a string of red dots along the ridge. As the light improved one Swedish officer observed through his spy-glass that his own men looked 'ragged, tattered and dirty . . . besides the glittering, gilded and plume-decked Imperialists. Our Swedish and Finnish nags looked but puny, next their great German chargers. Our peasant lads made no brave show upon the field when set against the hawk-nosed and mustachio'd veterans of Tilly.'

Tilly had carefully chosen his position to give him the advantage of 'ground, wind and sun'. He set his army across a ridge controlling the roads into Leipzig, and overlooking marshy ground through which the Swedes would have to advance to drive him from his position. His army numbered approximately 40,000, in the centre of which, under his own command, was his infantry – drawn up in 17 huge

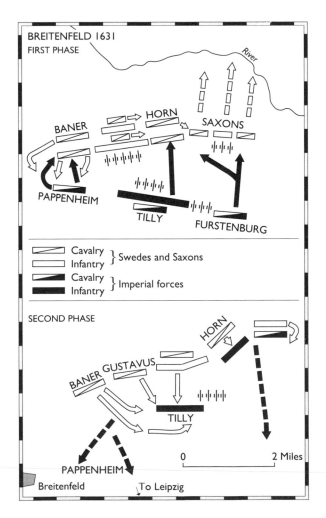

battalions, each of 1500 to 2000 men. On the left wing were 5000 heavy German cavalry – *Schwartz-Reiters* – commanded by the brilliant but impetuous Graf Gottfried Heinrich zu Pappenheim; on the right was a similar group of mixed cuirassiers led by Graf von Fürstenberg. Tilly's artillery was massed in the centre of the ridge, and his entire front extended in total to some 6000 yards.

Gustavus faced the problem of integrating his allies, the 18,000-strong Saxon army, into the Swedish tactical system. In the end, wisely, he decided not to place too much reliance on them and allowed them a free hand on the extreme left of his line, covering the Düben road. The rest of his army – numbering 26,800 men – were positioned with great care. At first sight the Swedish formation resembled that of Tilly, with an infantry centre and cavalry on the wings. But appearances were deceptive. The Swedish centre was not a solid block but a series of mobile units under the king's personal control. In the first line were four infantry regiments of interspersed musketeers and pikemen, behind whom was a reserve cavalry regiment and a Scots infantry regiment. Behind them was a second line of three more infantry regiments, with a further general reserve of two cavalry regiments in the rear.

On the Swedish right wing Field Marshal Baner commanded a front line of five cavalry regiments, interspersed with units of 200 musketeers, and with a reserve cavalry regiment behind. There was also a second line of four more cavalry regiments. Gustavus had made his own left wing under Field Marshal Horn weaker than his right, as the Saxons were covering the area opposite Fürstenberg. Yet he had not neglected it and, as events were to show, this part of the Swedish army was to play a vital role after the collapse of the Saxons.

Both sides had completed their preparations by about noon, but neither was prepared to make the first move, and for two hours or so they were content to bombard each other with their cannon. In this phase the Swedes were far more successful than the Imperialists, and Pappenheim's left wing took a galling fire. In the words of Colonel Robert Monro, who was with the Scottish regiment,

With trumpets sounding, drums beating, and colours advancing and flying . . . the enemy was thundering amongst us, with the noise and roaring whistle of cannon-bullets; where you may imagine the hurt was great; the sound of such music being scarce worth hearing . . . then our cannon begun to roar, great and small, paying the enemy with the like coin, which thundering continued alike on both sides for two hours and a half, during which times our battalions of horse and foot stood firm like a wall . . .

In folchem Habit Gehen die 800 In Stettin angekommen Irrlander oder Irren.

Irish soldiers in the service of Gustavus Adolphus. Mercenaries were a crucial component in many European armies at this period. PN

Firing three times as quickly, the Swedish artillery was far more effective than that of the Imperialists. Unable to restrain his men any longer, Pappenheim ordered his whole wing of over 5000 cavalry to advance at a trot. From his vantage point in the centre Tilly was furious, calling out that Pappenheim had robbed him of his honour. The German heavy cavalry trotted to within 30 yards of the Swedes before beginning their *caracole*, by which the front rank fired their pistols then made way for the second rank and so on; it was like an elephantine ballet. Unimpressed by this archaic manoeuvre the Swedish musketeers poured a heavy fire into the almost static German cavalry, emptying saddles by the hundred. Seven times Pappenheim's cavalry charged until, sensing his opponent was weakening, Field Marshal Baner ordered his reserve cavalry to charge at full tilt into the Germans, hacking and slashing at them with their swords and sending them reeling back in disorder. Soon Pappenheim's entire wing was being driven in headlong flight down the road to Leipzig.

Two miles away, at the other end of the field, matters had taken an entirely different turn. Seeing Pappenheim's charge on the left, and assuming Tilly had ordered an advance, Fürstenberg attacked the Saxons with his cuirassiers only for the entire Saxon

army — 18,000 strong — to turn tail and run at the first clash of arms. In minutes the left flank of the Swedish army was laid bare. Tilly, sensing his opportunity, now detached the right wing of his infantry and ordered it to advance and fall on the exposed Swedish flank, while Fürstenberg fell on the Swedish rear. However, Gustavus Adolphus had been expecting little more from his Saxon allies and had prepared for just such an emergency. Moving with much greater speed than the ponderous Imperialists could manage the Swedish reserve under Horn wheeled to the left and welcomed Tilly's infantry with shattering volleys from their musketeers and light regimental cannons.

Gustavus himself, convinced that the front was stabilized, now rode across to Baner's cavalry on the right and ordered the West Gothland Horse to attack the Imperialist infantry fighting Horn, while he personally led four regiments against Tilly's artillery on the ridge. Charging up the slope through

GUSTAVUS ADOLPHUS – THE LION OF THE NORTH

Gustavus Adolphus was a military genius whose character and career have earned him comparisons with Alexander the Great. He set out to build a new kind of army, encouraging soldiers to see themselves as professionals and individuals. Though discipline was still strict, it was based on good sense and justice, and men's lives were not squandered at the whim of incompetent captains. His soldiers were given uniforms – the first in modern military history – and were well paid; in addition, there were good medical services, and every regiment had its own chaplain. With Sweden's small population limiting his pool of manpower, Gustavus hired mercenaries – many of them Scots – whom he treated as if they were honorary Swedes, and from whom he expected the same performance as from his native troops.

Gustavus revolutionized European warfare, breaking the supremacy of the massed pike formations – Swiss phalanxes and Spanish *tercios* – that had dominated battlefields since the 15th century. Rejecting these formations as too ponderous and rigid, Gustavus emphasized flexibility and mobility, establishing the 1000-man battalion as his basic unit and mixing musketeers and pikemen within it. Unlike the Spaniards and Germans, who fought in ranks of 10, Gustavus reduced the depth of his units eventually to just three ranks. Instead of the heavy matchlock, fired from a rest, his musketeers were armed with lighter wheel-lock firearms, as well as paper cartridges in which powder and ball were combined, saving time and increasing the rate of fire. His pikemen, equipped with shorter pikes than the traditional 16–18-foot Spanish ones, and stripped of unwieldy armour, fought better at close quarters with their sabres. Unlike the German heavy cavalry – the *Reiters* – who advanced at no more than a trot and fired their pistols in the *caracole* manoeuvre, the Swedish cavalrymen charged at full tilt and fought with the sword, relying on maximum shock rather than firepower. Again, rather than charging in deep columns, Gustavus taught his cuirassiers to charge in line, with a depth of just three troopers. As with other arms of the service, his artillery was far more modern than that of any other European army, and with the help of the young Lennart Torstensson, Gustavus established a permanent artillery service of six regiments. He also introduced the 'leather-gun' – a regimental four-pounder – which was light and manoeuvrable, and two of these accompanied every regiment into battle.

Overall Gustavus added flexibility to his army and effectively coordinated the various arms of infantry, cavalry and artillery. His methods were widely imitated, but Gustavus had at his service a series of great Swedish captains, of whom he was inifinitely the greatest.

a hail of fire, the Swedes overran the guns, killing their crews, and turning them round to fire into Tilly's infantry. The Imperialist *tercios* were now caught in a savage cross-fire: while Torstensson fired the Swedish guns to their front, their own guns raked them from their left. As Tilly's army began to disintegrate the entire Swedish centre now advanced, driving his veterans off the field like vast flocks of sheep.

After the fighting had died down Monro recounts that his 'bonfire was made of the enemy's ammunition waggons and pikes left, for want of good fellows to use them; and all this night our brave comrades, the Saxons, were making use of their heels in flying, thinking all was lost . . .'

It was an astonishing and complete victory, the Swedes losing under 2000 men to the Imperialists' 7000 killed and 6000 wounded or captured. Tilly's entire artillery train was taken, as well as his baggage camp and 90 regimental flags; but far more than that, the 'invincible' Tilly – wounded three times in the fighting – had lost his reputation. His old-fashioned methods, of mass and weight and slow, statuesque manoeuvres, had been shattered by the new mobile and flexible methods of a more modern commander. The battle of Breitenfeld heralded the end of an era in military history and Gustavus Adolphus' victory decided, once and for all, that 'Germany was not to become a Catholic power under the House of Austria'.

The Battle of Rocroi 1643

Rocroi

French

Commander:	Prince of Condé
Left wing:	La Ferté-Senneterre and L'Hôpital
Centre:	d'Espenan
Right wing:	Gassion
Reserve:	Sirot
Numbers:	23,000 cavalry and infantry

Spanish

Commander:	Don Francisco Melo
Left wing:	Albuquerque
Centre:	Fontaine
Right wing:	Isembourg
Numbers:	27,000 cavalry and infantry

The 16th century had been the great age of Spain, her well-trained armies achieving numerous successes on battlefields in both the New World and the Old. But the prolonged religious wars in Europe had placed a great strain on Spain's economy and her manpower, so that by the last years of the Thirty Years War her military strength was on the wane. The victory of the young duke of Condé at Rocroi in 1643 changed the fortunes of France and annihilated Spanish military power – a defeat that toppled Spain from her position as one of the great powers and paved the way for French supremacy in Western Europe under Louis XIV.

Condé's appointment – at the age of 22 – to the command of the French army of Picardy in 1642 came not a moment too soon. French morale, after a string of defeats at the hands of the Spaniards, was at rock bottom, and their army was an undisciplined rabble in which 'everyone came and went as he would, one to look after his affairs, another to seek some favour at court'. The French generals were incompetent courtiers in the main, and desertion was widespread in the ranks. As the Duc d'Aumale wrote, 'the army lacked enthusiasm and confidence; it had that appearance of gloomy resignation that comes of being accustomed to defeat'.

From the outset Condé changed all this. Intelligent, headstrong, and with the arrogance of youth,

he took the army by the scruff of the neck and shook it into shape. He was a man unprepared to compromise – he would win or he would perish. This was essential, for the Spanish army of 1643, under the command of the governor of the Netherlands, Don Francisco Melo, was a powerful machine. Built around a hard kernel of experienced Walloon and German pikemen and Spanish and Italian musketeers, it was fortunate in having excellent professionals in command, some of whom had risen through the ranks, like Fontaine, son of an inn-keeper, and Beck, who started life as a shepherd.

On hearing that the Spaniards were besieging the fortress of Rocroi on the frontier between France and the Spanish Netherlands, Condé set out to meet them, determined to force a decisive battle, even though royal instructions had only told him 'to discover the enemy's plans and prevent their execution, but at no time to take any action unless it seems certain to redound to the glory of his Majesty's arms'. King Louis XIII was dying, and Condé refused to be tied by the cautious words of a man who would soon be dead. Condé looked ahead to a new and more glorious era for France.

The fortress of Rocroi was built in a clearing in the vast forest of the Ardennes, and was surrounded by marshy, flat terrain. When the Spaniards heard of the French approach, Melo, confident that his veterans – some 27,000 strong, and the finest in Europe – could gain a victory, planned to form up on a slight ridge two miles from the town. But Condé came on like a whirlwind and seized the strategic ridge for himself. Falling back, the Spaniards now assembled across the French line of approach to Rocroi.

Condé arranged his army of 23,000 men in what appeared to be a traditional formation, with two lines of infantry in the centre under the command of d'Espenan, and cavalry on the wings. But he placed a third line of infantry and cavalry in reserve under his most reliable general, Sirot. The right-wing cavalry was commanded by the fiery Gassion and the left by the incompetent La Ferté-Senneterre. The aged and senile l'Hôpital, sent along to oversee the young Condé's behaviour, joined the French left

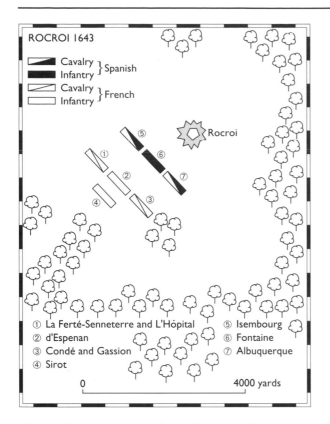

ROCROI 1643

Cavalry } Spanish
Infantry

Cavalry } French
Infantry

Rocroi

① La Ferté-Senneterre and L'Hôpital   ⑤ Isembourg
② d'Espenan   ⑥ Fontaine
③ Condé and Gassion   ⑦ Albuquerque
④ Sirot

0   4000 yards

wing and, in doing so, almost brought disaster on the whole army. Befuddled by the speed and energy of his protégé, he preferred to avoid a battle and thought that if he could relieve Rocroi there would be no need to fight at all. As the French front extended beyond the Spanish one by some hundreds of yards on both left and right, l'Hôpital found that he had a clear path ahead of him to Rocroi, and he persuaded La Ferté-Senneterre, who should have known better, to make a dash with his cavalry towards the town. Condé watched in horror as thousands of his horsemen charged off without orders on what appeared to be a 'death-ride'. Unsupported by the centre or right they faced annihilation if the Spanish commander threw his whole strength at them. The French were lucky, however, as no doubt suspecting some more threatening motive from this absurd manoeuvre, Melo contented himself with 'bloodying the French nose' and sending La Ferté-Senneterre's troopers back in headlong retreat to the French lines. Condé had had a clear demonstration of what might be in store for the French if he failed to impose his authority on his generals.

There was to be no further fighting that day and the two armies spent an uncomfortable night in position on the battlefield. Condé had one piece of good fortune when a Spanish deserter brought him news that an ambush had been planned for the next day, with Spanish musketeers occupying a copse of

dense trees and undergrowth on the French right. Just before dawn on the day of battle a company from the Picardy regiment fell on the Spaniards in the copse and cut them to pieces.

At first light Condé made an important adjustment to the cavalry on the French right, dividing them into two separate squadrons, one under Gassion to move around the left flank of the Spanish army, forcing the commander there, Albuquerque, to turn to face him, while Condé would lead his elite squadrons of Gendarmes de la Garde to hit the Spanish cavalry on the flank. The plan worked brilliantly, and in this one manoeuvre Condé earned his place in the pantheon of great commanders. Hit from both sides the Spanish left wing was shattered and fled from the field. Showing perfect control of himself and his elated troopers, Condé was now able 'to check his men without impairing their courage, to control them in the very heat of action, to give them their heads while yet retaining his hold on them'.

Although triumphant on their right wing, matters did not go so well for the French elsewhere. Not content with his nonsense of the previous day, La Ferté-Senneterre started his charge too early and reached the Spanish positions with his horses winded and in total disorder. His Gendarmes were easily routed by Isembourg's troopers and swept off the field. The triumphant Spaniards next circled round and fell on the unprotected French infantry, capturing all the French guns. L'Hôpital, as if to exculpate his dismal role in the previous day's disaster, bravely recaptured the guns, only to lose them again as his few remaining squadrons of light horse were swept away. The Spaniards now turned the French guns as well as their own on the massed infantry in the French centre, and cut terrible swathes through the helpless pikemen there. The French centre began to disintegrate under the fire of 30 cannon. It seemed that the day was lost and many Frenchmen threw down their weapons and took to their heels. Only Condé's thoughtful creation of a third line of infantry under Sirot saved the day, as this resourceful officer moved forward to plug the gaps in the French centre.

Now, at the very moment of greatest French danger, like Alexander the Great falling on Darius at Gaugamela, Condé appeared at the head of his right wing cavalry, circling round the back of the enemy infantry and falling on them like a thunderbolt. Easily identifiable by the white plume he wore in his hat, and, according to one French soldier 'carrying victory in his eyes', he was an inspiration to every Frenchman that day. Seeing the waving white plume in the distance, a great cheer rose from

the French ranks, and Sirot led his infantrymen forward, crushing the Spaniards between himself and Condé's cavalry in their rear. Taken by surprise, and assaulted from both sides, the Spanish army gave ground.

Then something strange happened. As if at a signal the fighting men disengaged and took breath, and silence descended on the battlefield. D'Aumale writes, 'To the din and tumult of battle there succeeded some minutes of silence and calm, almost as terrifying. Men and horses were exhausted, and all needed a few minutes of repose. All seemed to be taking breath for a last struggle.'

The elite Spanish infantry were now encircled by the French, but their commander, the Count of Fontaine, wounded and directing his forces from a litter, fought back with his few remaining cannon, mowing down hundreds of the advancing French

Condé at Rocroi. Appointed at the age of 22 to the command of the army of Picardy in 1642, the next year the supremely able and confident young duke was to put an end to Spanish power in northern Europe for ever.
GIRAUDIN/BAL

pikemen, until he was hit again and killed by a musket ball. Condé was not deterred and tightened the noose round the doomed Spanish centre, which had formed up into squares of pikemen to keep the French cavalry at bay. The French musketeers were brought up to close range and poured a deadly fire into the Spanish *tercios*, which had no way of responding. At last the French could see some Spanish officers waving their hats frantically, indicating they wished to surrender. Condé and his aides rode towards the now-silent Spanish squares, only to be met by a sudden hail of fire by some hidden musketeers. Outraged by such dishonourable behaviour, the French now fell on the remaining Spaniards, offering no quarter. So great was the slaughter of the infantry that when asked how many men were left in his command, one Spanish officer replied, 'Count the dead and the prisoners – they are all.'

French losses had been heavy, with over 2000 men killed and many more wounded, but the Spanish army had suffered a complete disaster, losing 8000 men dead, 7000 taken prisoner, and thousands more wounded. Such losses of experienced and battle-hardened veterans could not be made good. Spanish military power ended on the marshy plain of Rocroi, while for France it was the start of a glorious rise to power, which, in less than fifty years, would see her ruler – Louis XIV – as the dominant prince in Europe.

The Battle of Marston Moor 1644

Marston Moor

Royalists

Commanders:	Prince Rupert of the Rhine and the Earl of Newcastle
Left wing:	Lord Goring and Sir Charles Lucas with the Northern Horse
Centre:	Lord Eythin with 10,000 infantry including Newcastle's Whitecoats
Right wing:	Lord Byron with 2,600 cavalry
Reserve:	Rupert with 700 cavalry
Numbers:	17,000 cavalry and infantry

Parliamentarians

Commanders:	Earl of Leven, Earl of Manchester, Lord Fairfax
Left wing:	Sir Thomas Fairfax with 3000 cavalry from the Northern Army
Centre:	Crawford and Baillie with 18,000 foot, many of them Scottish
Right wing:	Oliver Cromwell with 5000 cavalry from the Eastern Association
Numbers:	27,000 cavalry and infantry

The decisive battle of the English Civil War was fought at Marston Moor, just outside York, on 2 July 1644. Defeat cost Charles I his northern capital and most of his northern army. From that point onwards the Royalists were forced onto the defensive against the overwhelming superiority of the anti-Royalist alliance of Scots and Parliamentarians. Until 1644 the king could still envisage a victory in the war, but after Marston Moor it was only a matter of time before he lost his throne – and eventually his life. Absolutism had failed in England, but it was to constitutional monarchy and not republicanism that the English people would eventually look.

In June 1644 three parliamentary armies were besieging the city of York, held by Charles's northern commander, the earl of Newcastle. The king sent his brilliant nephew, Prince Rupert of the Rhine, to relieve the city. Rupert believed that the king had instructed him by letter to seek out and destroy the enemy armies. However, this was a misunderstanding. Charles felt that if York could be saved without a battle, then Rupert should avoid the risk of fighting at a numerical disadvantage. But the headstrong prince was spoiling for a fight against an enemy he held in contempt.

On the morning of 1 July Rupert completely outmanoeuvred the enemy and reached York, linking up with Newcastle's army in the city. King Charles would have been the first to tell Rupert that enough was enough; there was no need to risk a battle that had already been won by manoeuvre. But Rupert was feeling over-confident, and rather than resting his troops and attempting to weld a unified command with Newcastle, he decided to bring on an immediate battle.

The Royalist commanders in York were alarmed

Prince Rupert of the Rhine. Inspired but impetuous, he was probably the most able man on the field on 2 July 1644 – apart from the commander of the Parliamentary left wing, a certain Oliver Cromwell. PN

by Rupert's plan and tried to dissuade him from seeking battle. Lord Eythin told him that the gates of the city had been blocked by earth and masonry during the siege, and this would take a long time to clear. And would it not be better to wait for the 5000 reinforcements Newcastle was expecting from the north under Colonel Clavering? Rupert refused to listen, insisting that he had a 'command from the King to fight the Scottish army whereso'er he met them'.

Meanwhile, the allied Parliamentary and Scots leaders had heard of the king's victory at Cropredy Bridge in Oxfordshire, news that had not yet reached the prince, and believed that Rupert would now strike south to join his uncle's army. In the early hours of 2 July they began to withdraw towards Tadcaster in order to bar Rupert's path. However, Rupert had no intention of going south until he had destroyed his enemies, and sent out his own advance guard onto Marston Moor. The Parliamentarians, only now realizing their mistake, were in danger of being attacked while on the march. They hastily sent messengers to recall their infantry, which was stretched out in straggling columns on the road south, expecting at any moment to be attacked by a torrent of Rupert's cavalry. What they did not know was that Rupert was being deliberately obstructed by Lord Eythin, who did not want the prince to risk a battle.

Rupert had his own troops in position by early morning on 2 July, but he had agreed to wait for the rest of the army to march out from York. Gazing in frustration across the broad moor, Rupert's officers could see that the enemy was in complete confusion, assembling amidst standing corn and hedges and with little room to manoeuvre on ground turned marshy by the summer rain. When Newcastle and his Lifeguards at last arrived on the moor it was approaching midday. Rupert found it difficult to conceal his own frustration: 'My Lord, I wish you had come sooner with your forces.' Newcastle told him that the York garrison were still plundering the enemy trenches but that Eythin would soon get them in order. This news delayed Rupert's plan even further. He allowed himself to be dissuaded by Newcastle from attacking immediately on the promise that Eythin would soon be there with more than 4000 foot. Rupert's decision not to attack was a decision he would regret to the end of his days.

Across the moor the Parliamentarians were in a shambles as troops took up position more or less as they arrived, with the Scottish infantry, which had headed the march to Tadcaster, being the last to return. But by about 2 or 3 p.m. they had completed their preparations, and by the time Eythin arrived at about 4 o'clock, with 3000 foot and not the 4000 Newcastle had promised, it was to find the enemy confidently singing psalms. Rupert had missed his chance of winning a decisive victory through the deliberate obstruction of Lord Eythin, and now faced an enemy army that outnumbered him by 27,000 to 17,000.

On the right of the Parliamentary army were the 3000 cavalry of Lord Fairfax's Northern Army, commanded by his elegant son, Sir Thomas Fairfax. These horsemen – either cuirassiers with breast and back plates, helmets, pistols and carbines, or dragoons, who were more lightly armoured and were accustomed to fighting on foot – were arrayed in regiments of about 500, and into smaller troops of about 70. Apart from their regimental colours and the white scarves adopted by the Parliamentarians before the battle, the cavalry on each side was equipped in an almost identical fashion.

In the centre of the Parliamentary army was the mass of footsoldiers, some 16–18,000 strong, containing a majority of Scots. Most of the footsoldiers were pikemen, but there was also a proportion of musketeers. The pikemen were gathered together in regiments of 1000 men and, armed with 16–18-foot pikes, they formed a formidable obstacle to the enemy cavalry. The musketeers, armed with matchlocks, fired from rests they carried with them. When fighting at close quarters they often used their muskets as clubs, or used their swords.

On the left of the Parliamentary army was the elite cavalry of the Eastern Association commanded by Oliver Cromwell, numbering over 5000 men. The enormous strength on this flank persuaded Rupert that he would need to strengthen his own right wing, where Lord Byron had a mere 2600 horsemen.

As overall commander of the king's army, Rupert did not lead the cavalry as was his custom, and took a risk in choosing the brave but impetuous Byron to command the right wing. Byron's unreliability was well known: his headstrong charge at Edgehill in 1642, in support of Rupert, had done much to deprive the king of a complete victory on that day. Yet so important was Byron's responsibility that the prince gave him explicit instructions on how to receive the charge of Cromwell's cavalry. It was common tactics at that time to intermingle musketeers with cavalry on the pattern of King Gustavus Adolphus of Sweden, and Byron's front line was made up of 1100 horse, with 500 musketeers in platoons of 50 placed between the regiments of cavalry. As a flank guard for Byron, Colonel Tuke's regiment of 200 horse was placed on his right.

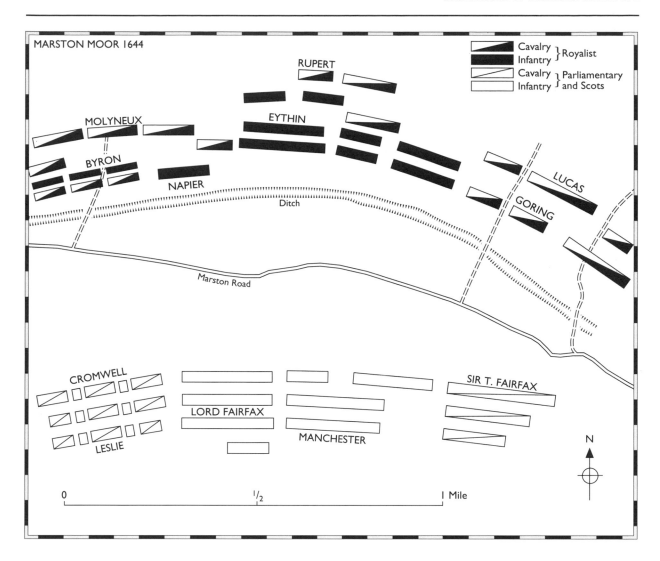

Behind the front line was a second line of 1300 horse, under Lord Molyneux, containing Prince Rupert's own regiment. However, Rupert went further than this and improvised a 'forlorn hope' of musketeers under Colonel Thomas Napier, some 1500 strong, along the ditch that crossed the battlefield parallel with the Marston road. Under no circumstances, Byron was told, should he charge out against Cromwell. He was to wait until the Roundheads had been disordered by the terrain and the fire of the musketeers before joining battle.

Rupert had placed both his and Newcastle's infantry – to the number of about 10,000 men – in the centre, under the command of Lord Eythin. The quality of these troops varied greatly, from the recently recruited Lancashire men, who threw down their arms in many cases at the first clash, to the veteran 'whitecoats' – Newcastle's 'lambs' – who were the best infantry on the field, and fought to the last.

On the left Rupert gave the command to the general of the Northern Horse, George Goring, a drunkard away from the battlefield but a brave and shrewd general, and to his stalwart lieutenant-general, Sir Charles Lucas. Here the Royalists enjoyed a considerable advantage in terrain, which they were to put to good use. Rupert kept personal control of a reserve of 700 horse.

As the day drew towards a close, battle seemed unlikely and the Prince declared that he would not attack until the next morning. When Newcastle asked if he was certain that the enemy would not attack him, Rupert arrogantly dismissed the possibility that a dullard like Leven – the Parliamentary commander-in-chief – could take him by surprise. Indeed, so confident was he that there would be no fighting that day that he told Newcastle to 'repose himself', which the earl did by smoking a pipe in his coach on the edge of the field. Rupert meanwhile ordered food to be brought from York for the whole army, while he and his cavalry dismounted and began their meal.

Alexander Leslie, 1st Earl of Leven, was a self-made man. Although illiterate and of humble stock he had far more professional experience than Rupert. Perhaps he had none of the prince's flair, but he had learned his craft in the Swedish service under the best European captains, and he knew when his enemy had dropped his guard. Just as a storm of rain began, discomforting Rupert's musketeers, Leven ordered his cannons to fire, and signalled the entire Parliamentary army to advance. In moments, 'the main bodies joining, made such a noise with shot and clamour of shouts that we lost our ears and the smoke of powder was so thick that we saw no light but what proceeded from the mouth of guns'.

On the left Cromwell had been bombarding Byron's position for some while, and the Royalist cavalry, which had been in position most of the day and was eager to charge, must have pressed Byron to take some retaliatory action. Byron needed little persuasion to disobey his orders and, at the sight of Cromwell's cavalry charging down towards him, he set out to meet them, scattering his own musketeers whom Rupert had placed with such care.

This was a disastrous mistake. Everything so carefully prepared by Rupert to disorder Cromwell's charge was now turned by Byron against his own men. It was they who were disordered in crossing the ditch and slowed by the marshy ground. Moreover, Napier's musketeers in the ditch had to move aside to let Byron's squadrons pass. As a result of Byron's foolhardy action all the musketeers on the Royalist right were wasted, and when Cromwell's troopers smashed into Byron's line in the marshy area and broke it, sending its scattered remnants fleeing from the field, there was no concentrated fire power to turn them back. With Byron beaten, the second line led by Viscount Molyneux now made a determined resistance, standing like an 'iron wall' against the Roundheads. Cromwell was himself wounded at this stage and temporarily forced to leave the field for treatment. Molyneux and his brother, both 'blood-thirsty Papists', fought with particular bitterness against David Leslie's Presbyterian Scots until overwhelmed by sheer weight of numbers.

When the fighting started, Rupert was 'set upon the earth at meat a pretty distance from his troops, and many of his horsemen were dismounted'. In a matter of minutes, he gathered his Lifeguards and rode towards the right wing in time to see Byron's troops beaten and his own regiment fleeing. Yelling above the tumult, 'Swounds, do you run, follow me,' he managed to re-form them and lead them back into the fray, but they were beaten men. Even the personal example of Rupert could do little to stem the rout of his right wing.

On the other side of the field, Sir Thomas Fairfax's cavalry faced serious man-made obstacles. In order to reach the moorland Fairfax was forced to channel his cavalry, which contained many raw recruits, through a narrow lane, which the Royalists had lined with musketeers. As he tried to do this Goring led a counter-charge that drove the Parliamentary cavalry off the field. Fairfax found himself alone, slashed through the cheek and without a command, so complete was his discomfiture. But instead of fleeing with his men he remained to play a prominent part in the later stages of the fighting. Removing the 'signal out of my hat' – a white scarf for identification – 'I passed through for one of their own commanders' and rode unnoticed across the battlefield before joining up with Cromwell on the other side of the moor.

Goring's Northern Horse had meanwhile reached the ridge from which Fairfax had set off. Here he 'possessed many of their ordnance and, if his men had been kept close together as did Cromwell's, and not dispersed themselves in pursuit, in all probability it had come to a drawn battle at worst . . . but Goring's men were much scattered . . . before they could know of the defeat of the Prince's right wing'. Many of Goring's men were plundering enemy baggage tents and it is doubtful if he had even 1000 men under control as night drew on. Sir Charles Lucas, leading the second line of Goring's wing, found the flank of the Parliamentary infantry completely open and savaged the unguarded Scottish pikemen, spreading such panic through the right of the allied army that all three of its commanders fled from the field: Leven to Leeds, Lord Fairfax to his house at Nun Appleton, where he went to bed, and the Earl of Manchester, who was eventually prevailed upon to return. Rumours of defeat spread down the road with them, and in the Royalist town of Newark the church bells signalled a great victory for the king. But as a Scottish army chaplain commented, 'God would not have a general in the army; He himself was general.'

And if God needed a tool that day, he chose Oliver Cromwell. As Cromwell wrote, 'God made them as stubble to our swords.' Having scattered the Royalist right wing, he led his cavalry round the back of the Royalist infantry so that he now took up the position originally occupied by Goring's Northern Horse. Darkness was closing in and, on a battlefield thick with the smoke of thousands of muskets, it must have been almost impossible to see what was going on. But Cromwell had chosen the right moment to strike the decisive blow. With nearly 4000 cavalry still in hand, he was looking up the slope at Goring's victorious – but disordered – Northern Horse, probably no more than a quarter of his own strength.

This time Goring would have to fight on the disadvantageous ground that had proved too much for Fairfax earlier in the fight, and with greatly inferior numbers. Drunk, if this time only on the adrenalin that must have flooded his veins at the sight of Cromwell's massive force, Goring flung his troopers down the slope towards the enemy, only to be shattered by the impact. As the Northern Horse fled from the field, Cromwell reined in as many squadrons as he could. The battle might be won; but there was killing to do.

In the centre of the moor the heavily outnumbered Yorkshire infantry had refused quarter and, with no cavalry left to support them, prepared to fight to the death. As one observer wrote, 'Our foot play'd the man, but the horses jades.' To save the useless slaughter of brave men, Sir Thomas Fairfax rode into the fray, beating up the weapons of his own men and shouting 'Spare your countrymen',

but Newcastle's own whitecoat regiment fought on until overrun by Parliamentary cavalry. Their coats of undyed woollen cloth led their enemies to gloat that they had 'brought their winding-sheets about them into the field'. Just three of their number survived the battle. The last stand of Colonel Lambton's regiment was described by an eyewitness:

. . . by mere valour, for one whole hour, [they] kept the troops of horse from entering among them at near push of pike. When the horse did enter, they would have no quarter, but fought it out till there were not thirty of them living; those whose hap it was to be beaten down upon the ground as the troopers came near them, though they could not rise for their wounds, yet were so desperate as to get either pike or sword, or piece of them, and to gore the troopers' horses as they came over them.

With the Parliamentary leaders having fled it was

Cromwell, with a wounded knee, leading the elite cavalry of the Eastern Association; after the picture by Abraham Cooper. PN

MUSKETS

The early musket was a heavy and unwieldy weapon, taking two minutes to reload and weighing so much (at 28 pounds) that it had to be fired from a forked rest. In order to use it a soldier needed to carry powder charges for each shot, a priming flask, a slow-burning cord with which to fire the priming powder, and a mould to make his own bullets. Nevertheless, it was a powerful weapon, which could kill at 400 yards – although its accuracy was poor. It was also dangerous to use. If too much powder was used in the charge it was possible for the barrel to blow up in one's face, while wet weather virtually put the musketeers out of action. For old soldiers the musket was simply a joke, and even into the 17th century some Englishmen still preferred the longbow. A modern historian has suggested that if either side in the English Civil War had rejected the musket in favour of the longbow they would have won every battle with ease.

A musketeer of the early 17th century. PN

---

left to Oliver Cromwell to complete the victory. York, so recently relieved, now fell to Parliamentary forces along with most of the north of England. The earl of Newcastle, the king's main supporter in the north, fled to the continent, along with Lord Eythin and many prominent Royalists. Prince Rupert began the depressing task of rallying the remnants of the king's army. When he next met his monarch it was not as the liberator of York but as the commander who had lost the cream of the Royalist army in an unnecessary battle and, in doing so, made the Civil War unwinnable for the king.

The Battle of Blenheim 1704

During the second half of the long reign of Louis XIV, France came close to securing hegemony in Europe. The fact that this was eventually denied her was due to the resistance of France's most indomitable foe, William III of Great Britain, and to the genius of John Churchill, the first duke of Marlborough. Yet it was a close thing. The War of the Spanish Succession, which broke out in 1702, coincided with the death of William and the accession of his daughter, Anne. Louis XIV refused to recognize her, accepting instead the Jacobite candidate, James Stuart – the Old Pretender – as the rightful king of Britain. Moreover, France had provocatively banned English imports into France. England's allies – the United Provinces in the Netherlands and the Austrian Habsburgs – were broken reeds, and with France's ally the Elector of Bavaria coveting the Imperial throne at the expense of the Habsburgs, the future for the English cause in Europe seemed bleak indeed. Yet in one of the greatest campaigns in military history, Marlborough was to march an army 350 miles from the English Channel to southwest Germany and inflict a defeat at Blenheim on the Franco-Bavarian forces threatening Vienna, shifting the entire balance of power in Europe in favour of Britain and away from France for the next hundred years. In the words of Marlborough's most distinguished descendant, Sir Winston Churchill, the battle of Blenheim 'changed the political axis of the world'.

In early May 1704 Marlborough marched south along the eastern bank of the Rhine, confusing his French opponents, who entirely failed to divine his purpose. Reaching the Danube with his army in prime condition, he found the French and Bavarians in possession of all the river bridges and was forced to capture a crossing point at Donauworth at the cost of 5000 men. At dawn on 11 August 1704, Marlborough and his Austrian ally, Prince Eugène of Savoy, met in the tiny Danubian village of Tapfheim, not five miles from the strongly fortified Franco-Bavarian camp. Eager to review the enemy position through a telescope, the two men climbed to the top of the village churchtower. They had a panoramic view of the fast-flowing River Danube and the nearby village of Blenheim on the left of the French position, and the low hills and wooded slopes around Lützingen on their right. But between the river and the woods was a broad plain, perhaps four miles wide, made up of cornfields which, at that time of the year, were showing merely stubble after the harvest. In front of the French camp and flowing across the plain towards the Danube was a stream, the Nebel, which made some of the low-lying parts of the plain swampy. Both commanders were highly satisfied with this position as a suitable battlefield, and Marlborough issued instructions for an attack the following day.

The duke had been plagued by a nervous headache in the days leading up to the battle, but when he rose on the morning of 13 August he felt completely recovered. After prayers he ordered the drums to sound to rouse the soldiers from their slumbers and to prepare them for the struggle ahead. In nine columns the Allied troops assembled on the battlefield, numbering about 52,000 men, of whom some 9000 were British. Closest to Blenheim and the Danube were the British troops under Lord Cutts, known to all as 'the Salamander'. Marlborough commanded the centre, and on the right was Prince Eugène with his white-coated Austrian troops, Danes, Hanoverians, and well-drilled Brandenburgers in blue.

The French were taken by surprise. They had expected Marlborough to withdraw from what they saw as an untenable position, and the thought of him attacking their strong defences never seemed to have entered their heads. In the French camp everything was chaos. Soldiers, woken from their sleep, rushed hither and thither seeking their officers, while cavalry squadrons bowled them over and collided with baggage wagons rushing to the rear. Soon order grew out of chaos and the French drummers began to beat out defiance to their opposite numbers, now less than a mile distant. Cannons fired exploratory rounds, and in Blenheim the French defenders knocked holes in the walls of houses to act as loopholes for their muskets. Facing Cutts in the village was the Marquis de Clérambault, while on the far left towards Lützingen was Marshal Marsin with the Elector of Bavaria facing Prince Eugène. Marshal Tallard had taken command of the centre facing Marlborough himself, who, magnificently attired in a scarlet coat and wearing his Order of the Garter, was conspicuous on his white horse. Content with his preparations, the duke dismounted and, in spite of attracting a few shots from the French guns, enjoyed lunch with his senior commanders.

Marlborough's keen eye had seen that the entire French position was hinged at two points – the strongly held villages of Blenheim and Oberglau. Here the French had massed their infantry, and if his proposed counter-attack in the centre was to be successful, he would need to keep the garrisons of the two villages fully occupied. He therefore committed his two wings to assaulting the villages and keeping the French busy there. Meanwhile, the Allied soldiers of the centre and left had to stand in silence while the French artillery cut swathes through them. Marlborough had heard nothing from Eugène's right wing to say that it was in position to begin the attack. At last a galloper arrived to say that Eugène was ready and, mounting his horse, Marlborough announced, 'Gentlemen, to your posts!'

The battle was about to begin. Lord Cutts' redcoats marched towards Blenheim, while in the centre the duke's brother, Charles, was leading the Allied infantry across the swampy ground and into the stream, which, to their surprise, was far more shallow than expected. Incredibly, Tallard – shortsighted but too vain to admit it – could see little of Churchill's attack and gave no orders to check it until the Allied foot were on dry land again. If Charles Churchill was remarkably fortunate, Cutts' English redcoats had run into a storm of French fire outside Blenheim. Clambering over barricades hast-

ily erected by the French defenders, the redcoats fought with sword, bayonet and often musket butt to force their way into the village. But the French fire was overwhelming and over a third of the attackers fell. Next, Lord Orkney directed five more battalions – including the Royal Scots – to force their way into Blenheim.

Tallard was convinced that his right flank, pivoted on Blenheim, could hold for the moment, while on the extreme left Marsin and the Elector were involved in a bloody clinch with Eugène's Austrians and Brandenburgers. Tallard decided to ride to the left to see if Marsin was confident of holding the prince, before returning to deal with Marlborough in the centre. But in his absence, the Marquis of Clérambault made a disastrous decision whose effects would help to determine the outcome of the whole battle. Alarmed at the ferocious English assault on Blenheim he ordered first 7 battalions from the centre to join the defenders of the village and then, as if that were not enough, a further 11 reserve battalions. Soon over 12,000 French troops were massed in Blenheim, so tightly packed that they could scarcely move; more importantly they were out of the fight at a time when they were needed in the centre. Robert Parker, one of the British soldiers in Blenheim, wrote:

We mowed them down with our platoons . . . and it was not possible for them to rush out at us . . . without running upon the very points of our bayonets. This great body of troops was therefore of no use to Tallard, being obliged to keep on the defensive in expectation that he might come to relieve them.

When the true enormity of his blunder struck him

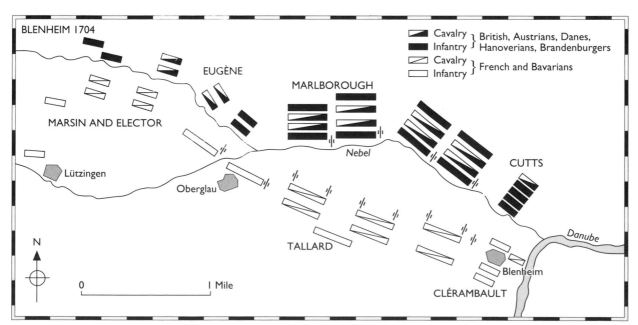

the Marquis rode in anguish into the Danube and drowned himself.

Just as the Allied troops had, not surprisingly, failed to break into Blenheim, so Eugène's men had been bloodily repulsed from Oberglau. The two villages that Marlborough had thought so important to his success were still firmly in French hands. The battle was not going in the way that Marlborough had expected. But generals need to be able to exploit the unexpected. As Tallard watched from his central position, the French heavy cavalry – squadrons of Gendarmes and the men of the King's Household – resplendent in their scarlet coats, were riding down the slopes to destroy a line of English dragoons waiting to receive their charge outside Blenheim. It was a mismatch – the English were certain to be overwhelmed by sheer weight of numbers. But nobody had read the script to Colonel Palmes, commanding the five squadrons of dragoons. As the Gendarmes approached, Palmes ordered the dragoons to charge them head-on, and in seconds he had routed the finest cavalry in Europe, sending them reeling back in panic. All

along the French line a groan of amazement was heard. The Elector of Bavaria, on the left, could not believe his eyes: 'What! The Gendarmerie fleeing!' It was the turning point of the battle. French confidence sank and Tallard traced his ultimate defeat from that moment.

Outside Oberglau a murderous fight was taking place between the 'Wild Geese', an Irish brigade that fought under the French flag, and 10 Allied battalions under the Prince of Holstein-Beck. The Irish gained the upper hand and the prince was killed, but Marlborough refused to give way and kept feeding in men from his centre. There was a crucial moment when Marsin launched 60 squadrons of French horse at Marlborough's flank, but

The battle of Blenheim in full swing. In the right foreground Prince Eugène directs the attack towards Oberglau, while on the left in the distance can be seen Blenheim in flames, and Marlborough attacking with his cavalry. ME

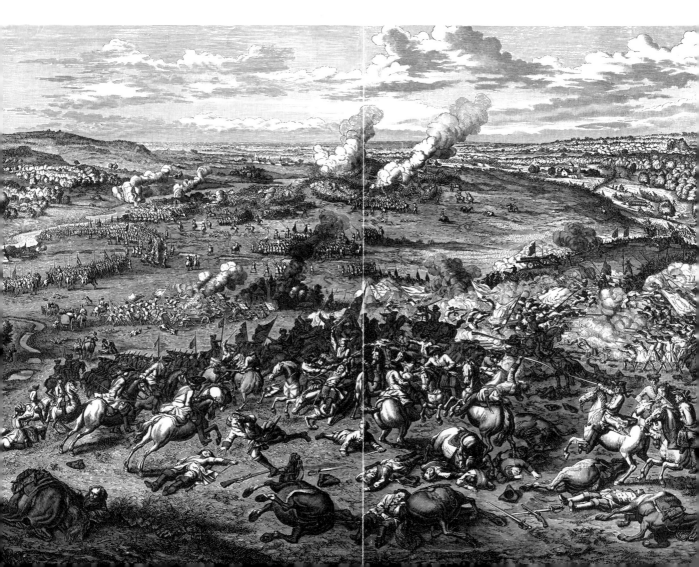

Eugène timed a counter-charge by his Austrian cuirassiers to perfection and the French were scattered. The fighting around Oberglau was confused but terrible in its intensity. One French soldier described it in later years:

From a church-tower you would have seen the enemy repulsed on one flank and we on the other, the battle rippling to and fro like the waves of the sea, with the entire line engaged in hand-to-hand combat from one end to the other – a rare enough occurrence . . . This spectacle, lit by bright sunshine, must have been magnificent for any spectator to view it with *sang froid*.

Marlborough was now ready for the great attack that he had been planning from the previous day. The villages of Oberglau and Blenheim were neutralized, and Eugène was holding the Franco-Bavarian left wing in check. The duke now planned to crush the French centre. To do so he had assembled roughly twice the manpower that the French had available, partly through the unwitting assistance of the Marquis de Clérambault, who had isolated so many men uselessly inside the village of Blenheim.

At 5.30 p.m. the trumpets sounded the charge and Marlborough, still conspicuously on his white horse and with his Order of the Garter flashing in the sunlight, led the Allied centre – a mile in width and with 8000 cavalry and 15,000 infantry – in a massive assault on Tallard's centre. 'The two long lines, perfectly timed from end to end, swung into a trot, that quickened ever as they closed upon the French.' The French tried vainly to hold back the torrent, but they were swept away. Tallard was taken prisoner and the cream of Louis XIV's army routed. Nine French battalions of raw recruits were caught in the open and massacred almost to a man. Robert Parker saw them the next day, 'dead, in rank and file'. One French officer wrote, 'We were borne back on top of one another. So tight was the press that my horse was carried along some three hundred paces without putting hoof to ground right to the edge of a deep ravine.'

The battle was as good as over, though Lord Cutts had an embarrassing time trying to persuade the French masses in Blenheim to surrender to his much smaller command. But with bluff and a little Scots cunning the thing was done and the French gave up the struggle. But the victory had been bought at a high cost. The Allies had lost 4500 men dead and 7500 wounded. The French losses were enormous: 38,609 killed, wounded or captured.

Few battles have ever had more significant effects than Blenheim. In many cases the consequences of a defeat for one side may be terrible but for the other far less significant. But at Blenheim defeat meant disaster for whichever side lost. Had Marlborough been defeated then the Austrian Habsburgs would have been ruined and the Elector of Bavaria would have replaced Leopold I as Holy Roman Emperor. The whole development of Germany might have followed a different pattern, with a French client-state, Bavaria, upstaging both Habsburgs and Hohenzollerns in the future of the country. In Britain the throne of the young Queen Anne would have been weakened and the claims of the Old Pretender immeasurably increased. But Marlborough's victory instead ruined the Elector of Bavaria, whose lands were annexed to Austria. The fame and reputation of the French army and its commanders had received a blow from which they could scarcely recover. At the end of the War of the Spanish Succession Britain's gains from the Treaty of Utrecht made her supreme not only at sea but also set her on the path to world empire.

The Battle of Poltava 1709

During the 15th and 16th centuries Russia had been essentially a backward Asiatic state, little known in the West. But under the rule of the Romanovs, and particularly in the reign of Peter the Great – tsar from 1682 – things began to change. Peter combined a gigantic body – not far short of seven feet tall – with a huge curiosity. His childlike innocence when confronted by the wonders of Western European science and technology contrasted with his demonic fury when faced with opposition to his reforms. He could be a brutal tyrant on occasions, personally flogging and executing his own people, while at other times he could be charming and avid to learn about English shipbuilding and Dutch commerce. He was a man driven by a furious energy, his aim to Westernize Russia whatever it cost in human suffering. He built the great city of St Petersburg as his 'window on the West', and in the Great Northern War fought Sweden for domination of the Baltic Sea.

Sweden, the greatest power in the north for almost a century – and a nation with a great military tradition – found after 1697 a man strong enough to resist the emerging Russian colossus: Charles XII – the 'Swedish Meteor'. A general of amazing ability and energy, Charles humiliated the Russians in a series of battles and, in 1707, planned an invasion of Peter's territory to put an end once and for all

to the tsar's ambitions. Peter, always in awe of the young Swedish king, hoped to invoke 'General Winter' to defeat the Swedes, using 'time, space, cold and hunger' as his allies. Yet so high did Charles' military reputation stand in 1707 that few doubted that he would soon be dictating terms to a defeated Peter in the Kremlin.

Charles began his invasion in January 1708, crossing the Vistula from his base in Poland with a powerful Swedish army of 24,000 cavalry and 20,000 infantry. He had two choices before him: either to clear the Russians from the shores of the Baltic, or to head south into southern Russia to pursue and destroy Peter's main army. Ever the man of action, Charles decided on the latter course, a decision that was to cost him the war. In July 1708 he came to an agreement with Mazeppa, Hetman of the Ukraine, by which Sweden would guarantee Ukrainian independence in return for the support of 30,000 Cossacks. But this was a chimera: Mazeppa eventually brought just 1500 men with him, and the march south took the Swedes further and further away from their supply base in Poland. The demon driving Charles to follow the Russians wherever they went even made him refuse to wait for a major supply column of 11,000 men under General Lewenhaupt, which had set out from Riga on the Baltic shore. While his generals advised him to fall back on his supplies, Charles recklessly marched on towards his appointment with destiny, ordering Lewenhaupt to follow him into the Ukraine – a virtual death warrant for Lewenhaupt as it turned out, for a large Russian army stood between him and the king. On 9 October the Swedish supply column was cut up by the Russians at Liesna, losing its artillery, ammunition wagons and most of its food supplies. Lewenhaupt managed to struggle through to meet Charles 12 days later, with just 6000 men and no supplies. After this disaster the other Swedish generals were convinced that a retreat into Poland was the only safe course remaining, but again Charles overruled them, insisting on spending the winter of 1708 – probably the coldest ever experienced in Europe – in Russia. The weather was so severe that the Baltic froze over, as did the canals in Venice, while in the Ukraine birds

Peter the Great at Poltava; painting by Martin Le Jeune (1731). PN

fell from a lead-grey sky, frozen solid. Three thousand Swedes died of cold, while thousands of others were crippled by frostbite.

Yet nothing broke Charles' dauntless spirit. In February 1709 he defeated 7000 Russians with just 400 men near Kharkov, and in another skirmish, 5000 men with just 300; it was the magic of his name that inspired his soldiers to win these improbable victories. He wrote back to Poland that his army was in splendid condition, but he was lying; his prime minister, Count Piper, described his troops as being in 'an indescribably pitiful state'. Of his original 40,000 he now had fewer than 20,000 men, including cripples; his artillery was down to 34 guns and his gunpowder virtually ruined. Yet Charles had convinced himself that once he could come to grips with Peter everything would change – if only he could persuade the Russians to stand and fight.

In June 1709, the Swedes began to besiege Poltava, hoping to draw Peter's main army into a battle to relieve the city. During a skirmish on the River Vorskla Charles was shot in the foot. The wound proved to be a serious one and fever developed, with the king passing into a coma. Field Marshal Rehnsköld took command but – able as he was – he did not inspire terror in Russian hearts as his master had. Nor was Rehnsköld's command of his own army unchallenged, and there were frequent quarrels with his second-in-command, General Lewenhaupt, and the prime minister, Count Piper.

From his sickbed Charles discussed with Rehnsköld a plan to attack Peter's army of 40,000, which was in an entrenched camp near Poltava. Admittedly the Swedes were heavily outnumbered by the Russian army, probably by more than 2 to 1, yet he believed their high morale and record of success against Russian troops was enough to offset the disparity in numbers. However, Peter was no longer the man who had allowed 8000 Swedes to defeat his 40,000 men at Narva in 1700. He had learned his military lessons – his Swedish conquerors had been good teachers. To protect the

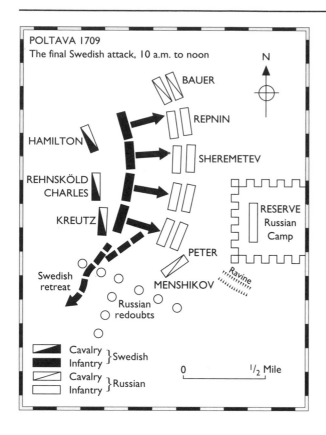

POLTAVA 1709
The final Swedish attack, 10 a.m. to noon

N

BAUER

REPNIN

HAMILTON

SHEREMETEV

REHNSKÖLD
CHARLES

RESERVE
Russian
Camp

KREUTZ

PETER

Swedish
retreat

Ravine

MENSHIKOV

Russian
redoubts

Cavalry } Swedish
Infantry

Cavalry } Russian
Infantry

0   ½ Mile

approaches to his camp he had prepared a powerful line of six redoubts facing the Swedish camp. These would have to be overcome before an enemy could reach the main Russian encampment. Rehnsköld knew this but hoped to bypass these strongpoints in a secret night assault.

Darkness came very late in the Russian summer and it was not until 11 p.m. on the night of 27 June that the Swedes began to move to the assembly points prior to their attack, each soldier wearing a piece of straw in his cap for identification in the confusion of battle. While the Swedish regiments mingled confusedly in the moonless dark, the unmistakable sounds of hammering could be heard from the forward Russian redoubts. Surprise was vital to the Swedes but had they been discovered? Rehnsköld, with all the strain of this climactic encounter weighing on his mind, rode forward alone to investigate. He found that the Russians had constructed a new line of four redoubts at right angles to the existing six, to form a 'T' shape. The Swedish advance would have to move on either side of the four advanced redoubts and in doing so be struck by a flank fire from them. To make matters worse, the Russian sappers had spotted the Swedes assembling in the darkness and had opened fire on them. The element of surprise had been lost.

It was not until first light that the 7000 blue-coated Swedish infantry fixed bayonets and began

their march towards the Russian redoubts. In the centre the Delacarlian regiment overran the first redoubt at bayonet point, while Stackelberg and the West Bothnians cleared the second redoubt. However, the third and fourth redoubts were very stubbornly defended, and soon Roos's six battalions of Swedish infantry were involved in bitter fighting, while the rest of the army kept marching, leaving them far behind.

While the fighting raged round the redoubts, the Russian general Menshikov launched a massive cavalry attack, which Rehnsköld countered with his own squadrons. Soon 20,000 horsemen were thrusting and hacking at each other in a confused melee. Confidently Menshikov held his own against Kreutz's troopers and sent back 14 captured Swedish standards to his tsar. But Peter's confidence failed him, and he ordered his cavalry commander to withdraw, which Menshikov did most unwillingly.

Having repelled the Russian cavalry, Rehnsköld was able to order the Swedish infantry on the left to occupy the open fields beyond the redoubts, facing Peter's camp. Charles, carried on a stretcher, was pleased by the ease with which the plan had worked so far, but where were the remaining 12 battalions of infantry? Far away on the extreme right, 6 infantry battalions – a mere 2400 men commanded by Lewenhaupt himself – were fighting a war of their own, assaulting the Russian camp, which was defended by 40,000 men. Bypassing a ravine and under heavy fire, Lewenhaupt overran two Russian redoubts, without cavalry or artillery support, and was on the point of storming over the southern rampart of the Russian camp with sword and bayonet when a messenger from Rehnsköld arrived to recall him. Furious with Rehnsköld for robbing him of the chance of a complete victory, he obediently re-formed his columns and marched across to the open fields to take up position with the main army.

By 6 a.m. Rehnsköld and Charles had the cavalry and two-thirds of the infantry in position, opposite the Russian entrenchments, but nobody knew the whereabouts of Roos and the other six battalions. The answer was that with extreme tenacity Roos was still attacking the redoubts. Aware that he was now alone and with no idea where the rest of the army had gone, Roos concentrated on what he believed was his duty and continued striving to win positions that were of no tactical importance whatsoever. In this fierce fighting the Delacarlian regiment, pride of the Swedish army, was destroyed, and Roos suffered nearly 40 per cent casualties before he was surrounded and forced to surrender.

At this stage Rehnsköld had two options open to

him. He could continue with his original plan and attack the Russian camp, although now with a much depleted infantry force; with surprise gone and in the face of 70 guns and 30,000 infantry this would be hazardous to say the least. The second option – a bitter one – was to march back the way he had come, try to rescue Roos, and then concentrate his forces for a later attempt on Peter's camp. It appears that Charles favoured the first option, but Rehnsköld decided on a retreat. As the Swedes began to leave their positions Peter seized his chance and ordered his green-coated infantry out of the camp and into battle formation, led by Sheremetev and Prince Repnin. They were flanked by cavalry formations, on the right by Bauer's 18 regiments of dragoons, and on the left by Menshikov's 6 regiments, among whom Peter had placed himself, in the uniform of an officer of the Novgorod regiment. In the face of this threat Rehnsköld could not continue the retreat without risking disaster. He had to wheel his whole force back into line. The Swedish cavalry squadrons on the left, under Hamilton, found it difficult to form up on the marshy ground, and it was therefore

left to Lewenhaupt's fast-diminishing infantry – little more than 5000 strong now – to open the battle by attacking 30,000 Russian infantry, supported by 70 cannon, massed in front of their camp.

With drums beating and in perfect order, the blue-coated Swedes marched into the face of the Russian cannons, which Peter's Scottish general, Bruce, had placed in front of the Russian lines to bear directly on the thin blue line. Lewenhaupt's only chance was to strike a hard blow to one part of the Russian line and then attempt to roll it up, supported by the cavalry. Without firing a shot the Swedes marched on, never wavering in their forward motion, even though cannon-shot cut swathes through their line and volleys of musket fire poured out from the Russian infantry. Then, incredibly, the Swedes burst through the first Russian line at bayonet point, sending the green-coats reeling back in panic. They captured a cannon, swung it round,

Russian 'strelitzi' at the time of Peter the Great. PN

Captured Swedish standards at Poltava: the end of Sweden
as a great European power. ME

and began to fire into the Russian flanks. Having achieved what seemed impossible, Lewenhaupt looked round for the Swedish cavalry to sweep forward and enlarge his breakthrough, rolling up the wavering Russian line. But no cavalry came.

The moment of panic in the Russian lines passed and as Lewenhaupt looked to the left wing of his infantry he saw that they had been shattered by a torrent of cannon shot, losing 50 per cent of their number before even reaching the enemy. Moreover, the further his right wing cut into the Russian masses, the more they were engulfed on all sides. The Swedish army was breaking in half, and as the Russian infantry moved forward the remnants of the blue-coats went down fighting or took to their heels. Lewenhaupt himself rode up and down trying desperately to rally his men, but the battle was now lost beyond recall. Heroic bands of cavalry at last attacked, but in 'penny packets', like the 50 Household troopers of the Nyland Horse under Count

Anders Torstensson, grandson of Gustavus Adolphus' great friend, who charged heroically into the Russian infantry and were shot down to a man.

Fortune certainly favoured Russia on that day: while Charles XII could only lie in frustration gazing up at the sky and contributing nothing to the battle as 21 out of his 24 bearers were shot, Tsar Peter – an unmissable target as he towered above all around him – survived three bullet hits, one ball knocking off his hat, another lodging in his saddle, while a third ricocheted from a silver icon that he wore on a chain round his neck.

Rehnsköld, seeing disaster all around, shouted to Piper, 'All is lost', and galloped into the thick of the fighting, where he was taken prisoner. The king was lifted onto a horse and helped from the field, his wound bleeding copiously, to take refuge in Turkey. It was left to Lewenhaupt to rally the remains of the Swedish army. But for most of the Swedes there was nowhere to go, and on 1 July 1709 Lewenhaupt surrendered what was left of the army – over 14,000 officers and men – to Menshikov, without striking another blow. It was a sad end for an army that had dominated European battlefields for the previous 80 years.

The battle of Poltava was a defeat from which the Swedes never recovered. Over 10,000 men were left on the battlefield, killed or wounded, and Field Marshal Rehnsköld and Count Piper, Sweden's prime minister, were taken prisoner, along with five generals. It was as if a great weight had been lifted from Peter's shoulders: no longer need he fear total defeat at the hands of Charles XII, with the consequent disintegration of the country he had worked so hard to modernize. After innumerable adventures in Turkey, Charles got back home to Sweden, but he was never again the force he had been, and died at the siege of Frederiksten in 1718 – a brilliant but unstable soldier.

There had been a fundamental shift in the balance of power in northern Europe: Sweden's decline became terminal; Russia's rise irresistible. In his tent after the battle Peter proposed a toast to his teachers. Field Marshal Rehnsköld asked him who they were, and Peter gallantly replied, 'You are, gentlemen.'

SALAMIS *(top)* A romantic depiction of the great naval battle by Wilhelm von Kaulbach (1862). AKG/NEUE PINAKOTHEK, MUNICH

SALAMIS *(above)* A Greek coin celebrating the victory. AAAC

SYRACUSE *(right)* A Greek helmet from the 5th century BC. AAAC

ACTIUM (*above*) The victor, Octavian, who went on to become the first emperor Augustus. PN

GAUGAMELA (*left*) Alexander and Darius, as recreated by a 15th-century Italian painter. CV

ZAMA (*below*) Scipio Africanus captures Carthage; Urbino plate, 1540. AAAC

TEUTOBURGER WALD *(above)* A relief from the 2nd century AD showing a Roman legionary and a barbarian. AKG/MUSÉE DU LOUVRE, PARIS

HASTINGS *(left)* A scene from the Bayeux Tapestry showing Norman cavalry riding north to fight the English. AAAC

AIN JALUT *(opposite)* Mongol horsemen in battle; from a 16th-century Persian history of Genghis Khan. PN

Banderium — Cuitatis finsbergensis quod ducebat Ucemarsialcus
seu Uicecomendator finsbergensis ubie   Sub quo erat
scu aliqui fres de ordine milicaret et aliqui proprii asinu. Sed podium
Insigne aut vexilli daqui constab fuit Leo vet albus per Johanne
bohemie rege tuc in pruffia miles agentez in bobaros
                                    longitudo

Nota hoc bandorum ptinet in longitudine tres
vluas In latitudine vero duas vluas ai medio
qrtali. Cauda aut protuhit in longitudine
vuis ai qrtali in latitudine vuis et vlue mius
qrtali quito infoil tauto stris t fine sitissime

Banderium Comendarie de Antiquo castro quod ducebat
Wilhelmus Anpfen Comendator de Antiquo castro ze
Sub quo erat talia ze ordine fres et proprii milits sed
ones fere internarp

latitudo

TANNENBERG *(opposite top)* Flags of the Teutonic Order flown at the battle. AKG

ORLÉANS *(opposite bottom)* Joan of Arc arrives at Chinon a year before her greatest victory. AAAC

TENOCHTITLÁN *(right)* The stone-age technology of the Aztecs was no match for the firearms, steel swords and horses of the Spanish. PN

VIENNA *(below)* Turkish janissaries on their way to the siege. AAAC

LEPANTO A contemporary painting of the decisive clash between Turkish and Christian fleets. PN

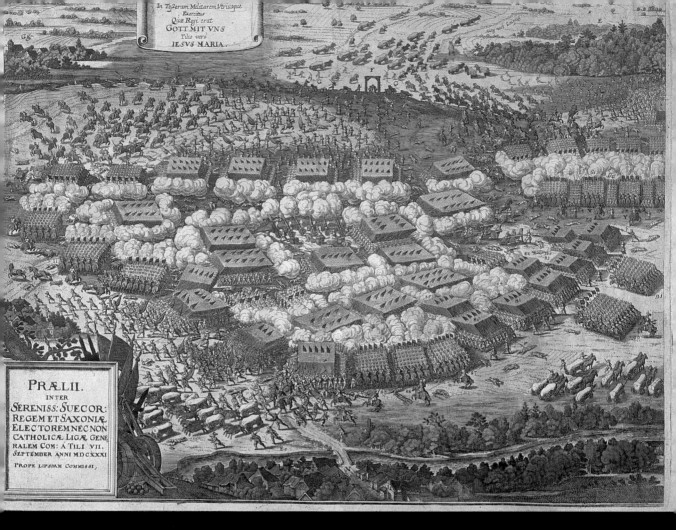

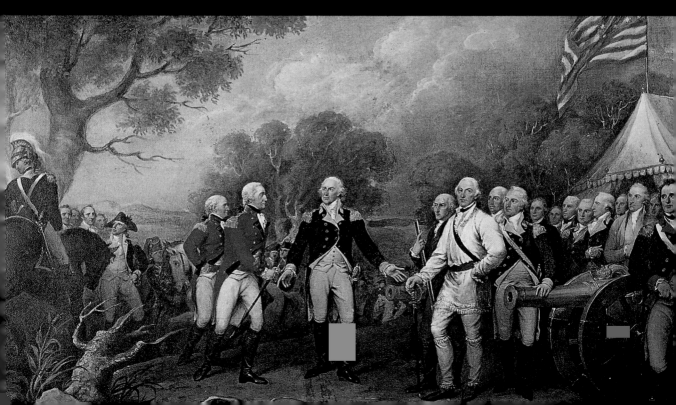

WATERLOO The general advance of the British lines. RC

GETTYSBURG *(above)* Section of the cyclorama painting by Paul Philippoteaux (1884), on display at the Gettysburg National Military Park. PN

SEDAN *(below)* Hand-to-hand fighting between French and Prussian troops. AKG

帝國艦隊旅順攻擊手

TSUSHIMA *(above)* The Japanese fleet in action off Port Arthur. AKG

BATTLE OF BRITAIN *(below)* British soldiers watch a German plane shot down; painting by R. Bunch (c. 1940). BAL/IMPERIAL WAR MUSEUM

STALINGRAD (*above*) German troops in the shattered city. AKG

GULF WAR (*below*) The Iraqis set light to over 500 oil wells before abandoning Kuwait. GAMMA

The Battle of Plassey 1757

> **Plassey**
>
> **British**
> Commander: General Clive
> Numbers: 900 British, 200 Portuguese and 2100 Sepoys
>
> **Bengalis**
> Commander: Surajah Dowlah
> Left wing: Mir Murdin
> Right wing: Mir Jaffir
> Numbers: 35,000 infantry, 18,000 cavalry and 50 guns

One effect of Robert Clive's victory at Plassey in 1757 was that, in Macaulay's words, 'the treasury of Bengal was thrown open to him'. And to what use was this vast accumulation of wealth put? The answer: to fuel the industrial and agricultural changes already taking place in Britain in the mid-18th century. By 1760 the British had made many technological advances, but where was the finance necessary to exploit them? The answer: in the hands of the East India Company and its numerous British investors. Inventors like Cartwright, Hargreaves, Watt and others at last found financial backing for their ideas, and Britain prospered as no other country. As one writer observed, 'It is not too much to say that the destiny of Europe hinged upon the conquest of Bengal.' And this transformation – almost magical in both its cause and effect – was the product of a tiny skirmish at an Indian village where the victors bought their success with the lives of just 23 of their own men and no more than 500 of the enemy.

The decisive struggle between France and Britain in India took place in Bengal. In 1756 the able nawab of Bengal, Alivardi Khan, died and was succeeded by his nephew, Surajah Dowlah. Surajah was disturbed to hear that the British merchants in Calcutta had begun to fortify the city, ostensibly against the threat of a French attack. But Surajah feared that it could be the first step in a British takeover of his land, and warned the merchants that 'if they do not fill up their ditch and raze their fortifications I will expel them totally out of my country'. The British foolishly ignored this warning, and Surajah felt compelled to take action. On 9 May his troops attacked Calcutta. At first they were driven back by the British defenders, who were vastly outnumbered. Unaware – or dismissive – of European standards in warfare, Surajah then advanced on the British under a flag of truce and overran them, capturing and then imprisoning 145 men in a room designed for just three. In a single torrid night, 121 of the British prisoners died in the appalling crush of the 'Black Hole of Calcutta'. Having committed a crime for which the British would never forgive him, Surajah re-garrisoned Calcutta with 3000 of his own troops and returned to his capital at Murshidabad, unaware that his actions would trigger a series of events that would topple him from his throne and place his lands under British rule for two centuries.

Returning from a spell of sick leave in England, Lieutenant-Colonel Robert Clive of the army of the East India Company found he had a crisis on his hands. News of the disaster at Calcutta reached Madras in August 1756, and a decision was reached to retake the city and punish Surajah Dowlah for his crimes. Clive was given command of an expeditionary force of 900 British soldiers and 1500 sepoys, to be ferried to Bengal by a squadron under the command of Admiral Watson. On 31 December the British fleet reached the mouth of the Ganges and sailed up the River Hooghli. Under cover of the ships' guns the 39th Foot, led by Captain Eyre Coote, stormed into Calcutta and took the city at the cost of just a handful of wounded.

Clive then received news that Britain and France were at war in Europe. This – the start of the Seven Years War – changed the strategic situation. The French had 300 troops with artillery at Chandernagore and in the event of a British attack on the nawab it was predictable that the French would come to Surajah's aid. In any case, on hearing of Clive's arrival, Surajah had raised an army of 40,000 men and was advancing on Calcutta. On 3 February, just outside the city, Clive launched a surprise attack on the Bengalis at dawn. At first all was confusion and the British suffered 150 casualties – most of the

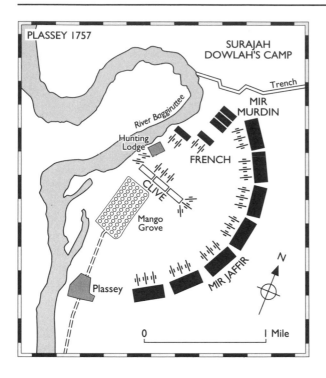

PLASSEY 1757

SURAJAH DOWLAH'S CAMP

Trench

River Bagginuttee

MIR MURDIN

Hunting Lodge

FRENCH

CLIVE

Mango Grove

Plassey

MIR JAFFIR

N

0   1 Mile

War with France freed him to attack the French base at Chandernagore, which he succeeded in taking by assault on 14 March. News of this enraged Surajah Dowlah, who, fearing the British were becoming too strong in Bengal, opened negotiations with the Marquis de Bussy, the French commander in the Carnatic. Both Clive and Admiral Watson were now convinced that Surajah could not be trusted and looked for a way to remove him from power. Events played into their hands. Unlike his uncle of fond memory, Surajah was regarded by his people as a cruel, debauched tyrant, who had inflamed the hatred of a group of his nobles, led by his commander-in-chief, Mir Jafar. The conspirators saw in Clive the means by which the nawab might be deposed. They approached Clive and Admiral Watson in Calcutta to ask if the British would support their plot to overthrow Surajah. Clive – with a ruthlessness that marked him as closer to the empire-builders of the 16th and 17th centuries than those of his own time – replied that he would. In return for control of all French trading posts and settlements in Bengal, possession of

wounds inflicted by 'friendly fire' – but at last the Indians were defeated and Surajah agreed to make peace with the British. On 9 February Surajah agreed to reinstate the merchants of the Company in Calcutta.

But Clive already had other things on his mind.

The Black Hole of Calcutta, an atrocity that provided the British with an opportunity to extend their power in India. PN

Calcutta and its environs, and compensation for the 'Black Hole' atrocity, Clive promised to place Mir Jafar on the throne of Bengal.

Clive advanced on Surajah's capital at Murshidabad, his force swelled to 900 British, 200 half-caste Portuguese, 2100 sepoys and 10 artillery pieces. But how much trust could he place on the word of Mir Jafar? Clearly if things went badly Mir Jafar for all his oaths and protestations would stay loyal to the nawab. In fact, within days, a message arrived for Clive from Mir Jafar still professing loyalty to the British but indicating that he hoped to stay neutral in the coming fight. Undeterred, Clive moved his small army across the River Baggiruttee and reached the small village of Plassey on 23 June. The British soldiers took refuge in a grove of mango trees and tried to get some sleep, but found their slumbers disturbed by the appalling cacophony made by the drums and cymbals of the nawab's approaching army.

The next day, Surajah deployed his whole army in a huge arc around the small British force, apparently trapping it in the mango grove. A total of 35,000 Bengali infantry and 18,000 cavalry, with 50 guns pulled by oxen and pushed into position by elephants, faced Clive's minuscule force of just 3200. In addition, a small group of French soldiers had joined the nawab with four extra field guns. To Surajah it must have seemed like a good day for a massacre. To Clive, who was viewing the scene from the roof of a hunting lodge alongside the river, it must have seemed like a good day for a miracle.

Clive decided that boldness was the best policy. He marched his entire force out and lined them up facing the enemy division commanded by the nawab's only really loyal officer, Mir Muddin. He concluded that if he could win here, other commanders – notably Mir Jafar – would almost certainly give up the fight. The firing began when the French opened up with their light guns and the British replied, silencing them in a short time. But soon the full arc of Surajah's army was firing at the British and, after just 30 minutes' combat and a mere 30 men injured, Clive retired his men behind the walls of the mango orchard, telling them to keep their heads down. Meanwhile, the British gunners were firing through holes cut in the wall of the orchard and were scything down the nawab's men in hundreds. Still the Bengalis refused to advance, and Clive decided to wait under cover until nightfall and then attack the enemy camp. It was at that moment that the miracle that Clive had been waiting for occurred. Seemingly out of a clear sky a rainstorm swept the entire area. The British, sheltering under tarpaulins in the orchard, kept their

Surajah Dowlah, nawab of Bengal (*top*); as much a victim of treachery as of the determination of the heavily outnumbered Robert Clive (*above*)? PN

weapons and powder dry, but out in the open the nawab's army was drenched and the fire of their cannons fizzled out. Mir Muddin chose this moment to charge towards the orchard, but was hit by a torrent of grapeshot and killed, and his men panicked and fled.

Surajah now called on Mir Jafar for advice. Mir Jafar could hardly credit his luck. Advising the nawab to leave the field and return to his capital he promised to 'mop up' the British troops for him. As Surajah left the field, Mir Jafar sent a message to Clive suggesting that he should attack now and the day would be his. Whether he needed this advice is a moot point, for Clive took the initiative and brought his troops back into the open. The Bengali army was now leaderless – with the nawab fled, Mir Murdin dead and Mir Jafar a traitor – and Clive was able to rake their ranks with grapeshot and massed musketry. By 5.00 p.m. the British had taken Surajah's camp and the battle was over. Clive had looked for a miracle, and it had happened: 3000 men had put to flight 50,000.

The next morning the slippery Mir Jafar came into camp to congratulate Clive on his victory. Clive welcomed him as the new ruler of Bengal, and the former nawab was pursued by Mir Jafar's son and executed in cold blood. Clive reached Murshidabad on 29 June, officially installing the new nawab. He was soon seen – as Clive had always intended it – as a puppet of the East India Company, with a British resident at court guiding his hand.

Never have such enormous consequences flowed from so tiny a cause. The battle of Plassey was no more than a skirmish, and the British victory was earned less by the fighting qualities of the British troops than by the indomitable willpower of Robert Clive, who had the courage to outface a force nearly twenty times his own in size. Nor must the treachery of Mir Jaffa be forgotten. Without his 'help' it is possible that the British could have lost the battle, and with it their hold on Bengal. And from this skirmish both political and economic advantages flowed: the Company became landlords of the 'twenty- four Parganas' – 900 square miles of land around Calcutta – which yielded fabulous wealth in rents. With Warren Hastings as resident at the court of Murshidabad the British were supreme in Bengal; and with such power the nature of the East India Company undertook a significant change. From a company of merchants emerged a powerful political force that was to govern large parts of India for the next hundred years.

The Fall of Quebec 1759

The final struggle between France and Britain for control of Canada may have been started by a shot fired by 21-year-old George Washington on 28 May 1754, at Great Meadows, the junction of the Ohio and Allegheny rivers. True or not, the career of the young Virginian was to be closely linked with Britain's colonial struggle against France and, though he could not have foreseen it, he – rather than William Pitt or James Wolfe – was to be the greatest beneficiary of Britain's success at Quebec in 1759.

By 1759 Britain's prime minister, William Pitt ('the elder'), was convinced that the French empire in North America was breaking up. Vastly outnumbered by the British colonies to the south – French Canada had a population of just 82,000 against the 13 British colonies with 1,300,000 – and surrounded by enemies on all sides, the French colonies were abandoned to their fate by the mother country, which was facing severe problems of its own in Europe. But the French commanders in

Canada, Louis Antoine de Bougainville and Louis de St Véran, Marquis de Montcalm, were not the kind of men to give up easily. At Ticonderoga the previous year, Montcalm – greatly outnumbered – had crushed a clumsy assault by the British general Abercrombie, and unless the British could find better commanders, Montcalm was confident of holding his bases along the St Lawrence River against whatever the British could send.

William Pitt devised an ambitious three-fold assault on Canada in 1759. While General Amherst was to capture Ticonderoga and Crown Point on Lake Champlain, General Prideaux was to take Fort Niagara, sail down Lake Ontario, and capture Montreal. But the main strike was to be against Quebec on the St Lawrence River, and was to be carried out by the brilliant but unorthodox, 32-year-old General James Wolfe, son of one of Marlborough's veterans. Wolfe was a frail-looking man who suffered from tuberculosis and kidney problems, but his eyes burned with a furious intensity. Wolfe it was who gave rise to George II's most celebrated saying: when told by jealous rivals that Wolfe was mad, the king replied, 'Mad is he? Well, I wish he would bite some of my other generals.' The death of Wolfe at Quebec undoubtedly robbed his country of a brilliant commander

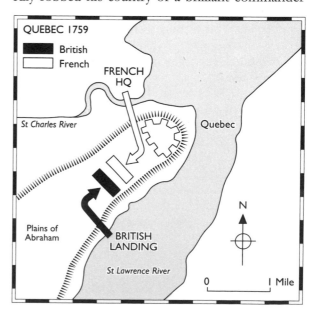

who might have made all the difference in the later War of American Independence.

Wolfe left England aboard the *Neptune* on 14 February 1759 with a fleet of 70 ships under Admiral Saunders, and by May the force that was to assault Quebec was assembling at Louisbourg, in the Gulf of St Lawrence. There were to be 8500 regular British troops under young brigadiers chosen by Wolfe himself: one observer called it 'a boy's campaign', but it was not going to be child's play. Quebec was a powerfully fortified town on a rocky headland, hundreds of feet above the St Lawrence, and defended by a garrison of 14,000 men with 106 guns. Montcalm was confident that any British attack would have to be made on the eastern side of the town, and he dug his trenches and gun emplacements there, between the Beauport and St Charles rivers, manning them with the majority of his men. But the French had grounds for additional confidence. It was believed by the best French naval opinion that the St Lawrence could not be navigated beyond Quebec without great risk. However, Wolfe was blessed with seamen of unusual quality, and one young officer, James Cook – later of even greater fame than his general – took soundings and mapped the river so accurately that his work was not superseded for a hundred years.

Having successfully landed his troops at Ile

d'Orléans, Wolfe initially agreed with the views of his opposite number, that the best way to attack Quebec was from the east. But he soon recognized that this was exactly where the French wanted him to attack and that Montcalm had a powerful force dug in there. After weeks of scanning Quebec through a telescope Wolfe was rescued from his dilemma by the Royal Navy. On 18 July some ships, including the *Sutherland*, penetrated the river beyond Quebec. Montcalm was horrified, realizing now the possibility that a landing could be made to the south of the town. To cover this he sent troops under Bougainville to patrol this area. It was a battle of wits between two able generals, both praying that the enemy would succumb to hunger before his own troops did. From his study of the area Wolfe concluded that there was only one possible place where he could force the French to give battle in the open, away from their massive defences to the east, and that was the Plains of Abraham, to the south of the city, named after a French sailor who had once owned the land. The problem was that the only way to reach the plains was by scaling a cliff that towered 200 feet above the river.

On further investigation, Wolfe learned that there was a path to the top of the cliff, so with a force of 4500 men, he set off in a series of longboats to follow behind the *Sutherland,* which was showing just two lamps at her stern. The first boat carried Wolfe with 24 light infantry, who would make the first ascent. Behind came 1300 men from Monckton's and Murray's brigades. In the second wave came 1910 men of Townshend's brigade, with 1200 men kept in reserve. During the slow and dark journey down the river Wolfe was heard to recite Gray's *Elegy,* surprising everyone with the admission that he would rather have written that poem than take Quebec.

French sentries patrolling the beach noticed the dark shapes on the river. *'Qui vive?'* called one. A Highland officer, Captain Donald McDonald, replied in perfect French, *'La France.' 'Quel régiment?'* enquired the guard. *'De Reine,'* said McDonald, naming one of Bougainville's regiments. Satisfied, the sentry returned to his patrol. At 4.00 a.m. the British boats reached the beach below the cliff. The beach was deserted. Clearing away the tree trunks and bracken with which the French had concealed the path, the British troops, with their Indian scouts, began clambering up towards the top of the cliff. The whole operation had been a triumph for the navy, which had negotiated a difficult river in almost total darkness and delivered its human cargo safely to its destination.

Within two hours the full complement of 4828 men was on the heights. But Wolfe knew there was no time to waste. He must bring Montcalm to battle before the Frenchman could assemble his full strength. Wolfe's final orders to his assault troops have the ring of Nelson about them:

A vigorous blow struck at this juncture may determine the fate of Canada . . . The officers and men will remember what their country expects from them, and what a determined body of soldiers inured to war are capable of doing.

The French officer who should have been guarding the Anse de Foulon, where the British came ashore, had been so confident that it was impossible for a landing to be made there that he had carelessly dismissed 40 of his men to help with the harvesting at a nearby village. While he slept the impossible had happened.

For perhaps the only time in his life Montcalm panicked. The last thing he had expected was to see British troops fully drawn up for battle on the Plains of Abraham. With just 5000 of the town's garrison

he hastened out to give battle, not giving Bougainville time to join him with a further 3000 front-line troops. Both sides opened fire at long range and Wolfe was hit in the wrist, but not incapacitated. As the lines of British and French troops advanced towards each other, it was noticeable that the British were proving steadier. At just 50 yards the British stopped and, when ordered, fired according to Sir John Fortescue 'the most perfect [volley] ever fired on any battlefield, which burst forth as if from a single monstrous weapon, from end to end of the British line'. The result was shattering – and the French had no chance to recover as the redcoats and Highlanders hurled themselves upon their enemies. As Wolfe led the 28th Foot into the fray he was first shot in the groin and then soon afterwards through the lungs. Desperate that his men should not see him fall he asked an officer to support him. Carried to the rear, he lived just long enough to hear a soldier shout, 'See how they run.' 'Who run?' enquired Wolfe. 'The enemy, sir,' replied the soldier. 'Now God be praised, I will die in peace,' murmured Wolfe, as he slipped into a coma from which he did not awake.

Less than a mile away a similar tragedy was being enacted. Montcalm, mounted and attempting to rally his troops, was shot through the body and only held in his saddle by an aide. Riding back into Quebec so that no one should see that he was hit, the brave French general did not even have the consolation of victory that had eased Wolfe's passing. He lingered painfully, only dying the following morning. He was buried in a British shell hole in the Ursuline Convent in Quebec.

But the battle was not yet over. With the main actors removed from the scene it was up to the supporting cast to consolidate the British gains. The French, had they but known it, still had a substantial numerical advantage. But Brigadier Townshend never let them settle long enough to regroup. If Wolfe was the victor on the Plains of Abraham, it was Townshend who captured Quebec. The battle ended with the British having lost just 630 casualties and the French 830. After all the blood that had been spilled in the previous hundred years of Anglo-French warfare in North America it was incredible that the future of Canada should have been decided so cheaply. On the afternoon of 17 September the French flag was lowered in the citadel of Quebec to be replaced by the Union Flag.

The Treaty of Paris in 1763 only put the stamp of legality on the work of Wolfe and his redcoats at Quebec. France ceded to Britain the whole of Canada. In the words of Chateaubriand, 'France has disappeared from North America like those Indian

GENERAL JAMES WOLFE

The dying Wolfe on the Plains of Abraham. ME

It has been suggested that the death of General James Wolfe at Quebec in 1759 robbed Britain of the brilliant general that she so clearly needed during the American War of Independence. But history is full of such 'ifs' and it should be remembered that Wolfe was suffering from tuberculosis, which may well have shortened his life.

Wolfe joined the army in 1741 and had a metoric rise, fighting at Dettingen in 1743 and at Culloden in 1746. By 1750 he was a full colonel and the training methods he introduced made his regiment one of the best in the British Army. In 1757 he took part in the Louisbourg expedition in Canada and – serving under Amherst as a brigadier – he won many of the laurels of the victory. Returning to London he was promoted to major-general and given command of the expedition to seize Quebec. He met his death on the Plains of Abraham and his loss at the young age of 32 gave the public the hero they were seeking. Wolfe's last year of life has taken on such a romantic – almost legendary – character that it is difficult sometimes for historians to assess his military record fairly. It is sufficient to note that his gamble in climbing the Plains of Abraham in search of a decisive engagement with the enemy would undoubtedly have won him the approval of Napoleon Bonaparte. No higher praise is possible.

tribes with which she sympathized.' The future lay with Britain, which was now 'the greatest maritime and colonial power in the world.' Yet with Wolfe and Montcalm in their graves, it was time to remember the young Virginian, George Washington, who had fought with the British and now shared their victory. The American colonists had welcomed the help of the mother country in their struggle against the French, but now that threat had been removed it was time for the redcoats to go home. In 1761 an astute British observer had noted, 'I don't know whether the neighbourhood of the French to our North American colonies was not the greatest security for their dependence on the mother country, which I feel will be slighted by them when their apprehension of the French is removed.' The French were equally convinced. In 1763 de Vergennes wrote, 'Delivered from a neighbour whom they always feared, your other colonies will soon discover that they stand no longer in need of your protection. You will call on them to contribute towards supporting the burthen which they have helped to bring on you; they will answer you by shaking off all dependence.' The battle on the Plains of Abraham had given Britain Canada and control of the Newfoundland fisheries, but it had also brought the independence of the American colonies very much nearer. And defeat had helped to plunge France into the downward spiral that led to revolution in 1789.

The Battles of Saratoga 1777

The battles of Saratoga were lost in the clubs and drawing rooms of London months before 'Gentleman Johnny' Burgoyne set out for the Americas in April 1777. The British strategic plan for that year was a particularly bad one, aiming at unrealizable targets by dividing British forces in America and allowing commanders to follow separate and conflicting policies. It was the product of minds of little talent, notably those of Secretary for the Colonies, Lord George Germain, and the vain playwright-general Sir John Burgoyne, whom Horace Walpole dubbed 'Julius Caesar Burgonius'. To compound these faults the plan would make it impossible for the commanders in America – Burgoyne himself and Sir William Howe – to communicate with each other or even with Germain back in London without an unacceptable delay. It was a formula for disaster.

There were really two plans to put an end to the American Revolution in 1777. The British commander-in-chief in America, Sir William Howe, had decided that his best chance of defeating the rebels would be to move on Philadelphia, the rebel capital,

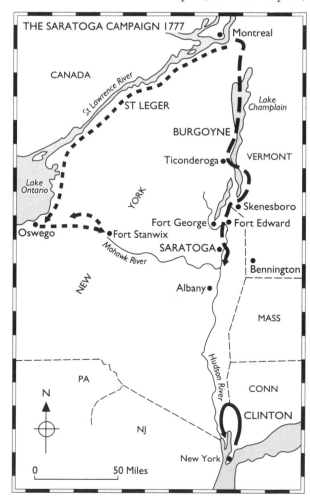

THE SARATOGA CAMPAIGN 1777

and draw George Washington's army into a decisive battle in defence of the city. However, Howe had carelessly given support to a rival plan by Burgoyne to advance from Canada down the Hudson River to Albany to meet Howe's own forces advancing from New York. Either plan was feasible but – given that Albany is 100 miles north of New York and Philadelphia 100 miles to the southwest – not both. How Germain could have allowed his commanders to believe that both could go ahead simultaneously defies explanation. Howe, in fact, did not believe that the advance from Canada was the main strategical thrust of 1777, nor did he intend to delay for a moment his own assault on Philadelphia. If Burgoyne wanted to advance from Canada then he would be on his own.

Burgoyne began his own operation on 31 June

with a force of 7213 regulars, comprising three brigades of British and three of Hessians and Brunswickers. In addition, he took 250 Canadians and American loyalists, as well as about 500 Indians. It was a colourful display, with the redcoats of the British line regiments and the blue of the Germans standing out sharply against the background of the Canadian forests. The fact that the British artillerymen and the German Jägers wore green was coincidental and no concession to camouflage. Burgoyne's column was encumbered by a massive artillery train of 138 guns and a host of camp followers, many of them women. Keeping a diary of the expedition – and accompanied by her three young daughters – was the redoubtable Baroness von Riedesel, wife of the Brunswick general.

The first part of the journey was by boat on the glistening waters of Lake Champlain, with the Indians in their brightly painted birch canoes leading the way for the armada and Burgoyne and his fellow generals, Phillips and Riedesel, following in their pinnaces. As a display of British naval might it was impressive, but the expedition was ill-prepared for the march overland: once the lake was

'General Burgoyne addressing the Indians'. The British recruitment of Indian allies turned many American loyalists to the revolutionary cause. ME

past the lack of carts and wagons made for painful progress. As an ominous presage the column was frequently interrupted by heavy storms, which were followed by a plague of black flies. To Burgoyne's soldiers in their woollen uniforms, with tight gaiters on their legs and stiff leather collars keeping their heads up, it must have seemed that even nature was helping the rebels. For the Brunswick Dragoons it was even worse. Bereft of their horses these huge men in thick jackets, stiff leather breeches and ornate elbow-length gauntlets were marching in 12-pound jackboots and trailing their long swords, weighing 10 pounds each, behind them. The long plumes in their cocked hats inspired the envy of the Indians, but also caught in the foliage and attracted enemy sharpshooters, perched high in the trees.

As a diversion, Burgoyne had sent Colonel Barry St Leger – founder of the first English horseracing classic in 1776 – with 875 regulars via the St Lawrence River to Fort Oswego, on Lake Ontario, where he met 1000 Indians under the brilliant, English-educated Mohawk chief, Joseph Brant. It was proposed that St Leger would first take Fort Stanwix before marching down the Mohawk Valley to join Burgoyne before Albany. Burgoyne had hoped the appearance of British troops would encourage loyalists to come out in his support; in fact, he was quite wrong and the sight of so many Indians had the reverse effect, with settlers thronging to join the rebel militias.

Burgoyne's main column reached Fort Ticonderoga on 1 July. The fort was held for the rebels by Major-General St Clair with just 2500 troops, but the size of the British force persuaded St Clair to abandon his post and retreat to Fort Edward. In England news of the fall of Fort Ticonderoga caused King George III great excitement; he rushed into the Queen's apartments exclaiming, 'I have beat them, I have beat all the Americans.' Lord George Germain announced the fall of Ticonderoga to Parliament as if it was the final nail in the coffin of the American revolt. Nothing could have been further from the truth. Although Burgoyne was just 70 miles from Albany and could have continued by water to Fort George, just a short march from the Hudson River, he allowed himself instead to be persuaded to march his troops overland from Skenesboro, apparently on the advice of loyalist major Philip Skene. Skene's advice was not entirely disinterested: the building of a road through the wild terrain by the British troops would link his colony with the Hudson and improve his trade once the war was over. But it was hell for the redcoats and German mercenaries. The American general Schuyler used scorched-earth tactics to

delay the British advance, cutting down thousands of trees and even damming and redirecting streams across their path. One British soldier reported that the Americans had destroyed no less than 40 bridges, including 'one which crossed a morass two miles in extent'. Swarms of mosquitoes rose from the swamps to attack the suffering British soldiers, adding to the misery of the hundreds already suffering from dysentery. In fact, Burgoyne wasted three weeks in completing a march that should have taken a matter of days. At Fort Edward he halted his exhausted men for almost a month, uncertain how to proceed in the absence of news from Howe in New York. His supply line stretched over 150 miles back to Montreal and food was becoming short. To go back or to go on was now Burgoyne's choice: one alternative offering safety but humiliation, the other the chance of glory but also of disaster. Short of horses and wagons, Burgoyne desperately sent back appeals to Montreal for help. Meanwhile, the region was inflamed by the murder and scalping of beautiful 18-year-old Jane McCrea by two of Burgoyne's Indians, whom the British general refused to punish in case it led to mass desertions by their fellows.

Burgoyne desperately needed mounts for his dragoons, for without horses they were just a liability. Hearing that there was a plentiful supply of horses near Bennington in Vermont, Burgoyne sent Colonel Baum with a force of 500 men, including 150 of the Brunswickers, to collect the horses and whatever stores they could find. The raid was supposed to be conducted with stealth, yet the Germans marched off behind their regimental bands playing patriotic tunes. After being harassed by snipers on the march, Baum sent back to Burgoyne for reinforcements and a further 650 men under Colonel von Breymann were sent. Warned that there was a force of 1500 New Hampshire militia in the area, commanded by General John Stark, Burgoyne dismissed the threat as insignificant. In fact, after a dispute with Congress, Stark was acting on his own authority, not on the orders of his commander, General Schuyler.

On 16 August Stark infiltrated Baum's column by disguising some of his men as loyalists with white paper badges in their hats. Roaring 'There, my boys, are your enemies. You must beat them, or Molly Stark is a widow tonight,' his troops drove off the loyalists and Indians, killed Baum, and wiped out most of his force. Breymann arrived with his reinforcements only to be set upon by Stark's militia, who inflicted a further 230 casualties on the Germans before sending them scattering.

Meanwhile, many miles away to the west, St

Leger's column had moved down the Mohawk Valley and besieged Fort Stanwix, which was held by 750 Americans under Peter Gansevoort and Marinus Willet. An American relief force of 800 New York Militia, led by General Nicholas Herkimer, was ambushed by Mohawk Indians under Joseph Brant at Oriskany and badly cut up. Herkimer was wounded early in the fighting but was propped up against a tree and, continuing to smoke his pipe contentedly, gave orders to the last. During the skirmish an extraordinary cloudburst so dampened everyone's powder that for an hour no shots were fired. Eventually Brant called off his Indians, leaving the remnants of Herkimer's force to withdraw. When news of this setback reached General Schuyler at Stillwater he sent Benedict Arnold with a further 900 men to relieve the fort.

Meanwhile, a sortie from Fort Stanwix had taken the Indian and loyalist camp by surprise, sending Indian squaws scampering in terror and the loyalist commander, Sir John Johnston, fleeing barefoot and dressed only in his shirt. The Americans wrecked the Indian tepees and captured all Johnston's private papers as well as his wardrobe. Supplies of every kind were taken as well as five standards, which were displayed from the parapets of the fort.

To relieve Fort Stanwix Benedict Arnold used a clever trick, sending into the Indian camp a half-witted Dutchman named Hon-Yost Schuyler to spread rumours that a huge American force was advancing towards them. The Indians regarded half-wits as being in touch with the spirit Manitou, so when Hon-Yost pointed at the leaves of the trees to indicate the American numbers, they abandoned the siege and deserted, leaving St Leger with such a depleted force that he had no option but to pull back to Canada. On their way the Indians broke into the rum store and became so drunk that St Leger had to conduct a fighting retreat against his erstwhile allies. To add insult to injury two Indians, intent on mischief, came upon St Leger and Johnston engaged in a bitter argument. Knowing that the ground ahead was swampy they rushed up behind the officers shouting that Benedict Arnold was upon them, whereupon the two officers rushed headlong into a bog.

Burgoyne's situation was now hopeless, with his western force in retreat and his German troops decimated, but with the desperation of an inveterate gambler he decided to push on towards Albany, where he hoped to be able to winter his army. He already knew that he could expect little help from Howe's deputy, General Clinton, at New York. Although Clinton had not said as much to Burgoyne, he had no orders from Howe, now advancing on Philadelphia, to help the Canadian army, and he was not prepared to act on his own authority.

Burgoyne decided to march his depleted force of 7000 men down the west side of the Hudson River, crossing over a bridge of boats and bringing it into direct confrontation with the Americans. Congress had blamed Schuyler for the loss of Ticonderoga and had replaced him with Gates, an ex-British regular officer, known to Burgoyne as 'the old midwife'. Midwife or not, Gates had taken up a strong defensive position on Bemis Heights, near the village of Saratoga, and Washington had reinforced him with Colonel Daniel Morgan's corps of buckskin-clad sharpshooters from Virginia and west Pennsylvania. Morgan was a gnarled veteran of Braddock's fateful expedition to the Monongahela in 1755 and still bore the scars of the 500 lashes he had once received for striking a British officer. His light infantry, often fighting stripped to the waist Indian-style, were reputed to be able to sever a squirrel's tail at a hundred paces with their long-barrelled flintlock rifles.

The British assaulted the American position on 19 September in what became known as the battle of Freeman's Farm, with the Brunswick general Riedesel commanding the British left, Burgoyne and Hamilton the centre, and the Scottish general Fraser the right. Fraser's advance guard was decimated by Morgan's impetuous sharpshooters, but the Americans were too eager and were hit and scattered by a volley from Hamilton's brigade, leaving their commander in tears and trying to regroup his men with his famous turkey call. Heavy fighting around Freeman's Farm involved a see-saw struggle, with the Americans seizing the British guns but being driven back at the point of the bayonet, while American snipers in the trees shot down the majority of the British officers, easily identified by their gorgets and epaulets. But the Americans missed the chance of striking a decisive blow when Gates refused Benedict Arnold the men he needed to break Burgoyne's centre. The British commander called on Riedesel to bring up men and guns, and by the late afternoon the Brunswick artillery was firing grapeshot into the quivering American ranks. At last Gates was forced to pull back his men, leaving the British victorious but bloodied, having lost over 600 men to the Americans' 300.

Burgoyne had gained little by this Pyrrhic victory and retired to lick his wounds. In London Germain was quite aware that Burgoyne was on his own: 'I am sorry,' he said, 'the Canada army will be disappointed in the junction they expect with Sir William Howe, but the more honour for Burgoyne

if he does the business without any assistance from New York.' With starvation a real possibility, and with packs of wolves roving at night to dig up the recently buried corpses, Burgoyne now overrode the advice of his generals – who favoured retreat – and decided on another attack on the American position at Bemis Heights on 7 October. This time the attack would be spearheaded by just 1600 men – a desperate move, even for this reckless commander.

Meanwhile, a bitter row had broken out in the American camp between the two senior American officers, causing Gates to dismiss his most able commander, 'that son-of-a-bitch' Arnold. However, Arnold was not to be removed so easily and a round-robin among the other American generals urged him to stay in camp. No sooner had the fighting begun than Arnold rode out of the camp to the cheers of his men, pursued by one of Gates's aides with orders for him to return. Conscious of the effectiveness of the famous Scottish officer, Simon Fraser – who had been with Wolfe at Quebec – Arnold ordered a backwoods sharpshooter, Tim Murphy, to pick him off. Fraser was undismayed by Murphy's first two near-misses and, mounted on a white horse, continued leading his

men. However, Murphy's third shot hit its mark. With Fraser mortally wounded British resistance faded. Arnold seemed to be everywhere, 'more like a madman than a cool and discreet officer', racing from one end of the battlefield to the other, leading assaults, overriding other generals' orders and capturing Breymann's redoubt, before being shot in the thigh and carried from the field. If any one man's example won the fight that day it was Benedict Arnold's.

Burgoyne withdrew, having suffered 600 losses to 150 by the Americans. The weather was appalling – it rained incessantly and his men were exhausted by battle and by lack of food. Baroness Riedesel recorded details of the last few days of the campaign, with General Fraser dying in great pain on her dining table: 'I spent the night . . . looking after my children whom I had put to bed. As for myself, I could not go to sleep, as I had General Fraser . . . in my room, and was constantly afraid children would be carried to safety by a mounted officer. In the cellar below the dining room, wounded soldiers kept little Frederica von Riedesel in shrieks of laughter by imitating farmyard animals.

But there was to be no happy ending for Burgoyne and his army, and on 17 October he surrendered his remaining 5000 troops and their stores to Gates, who offered generous terms, allowing the British to march out with the honours of war and enjoy free passage to Great Britain on condition they did not serve again in the war. He even invited the British officers to dine with him. The table may have been plain (two planks laid across some barrels) but the fare seemed splendid: ham, goose, beef, mutton and New England rum. The meal ended with toasts – Burgoyne drank to General Washington and Gates to the King. Yet although Burgoyne was permitted to return to Britain on parole, Congress repudiated Gates's terms of surrender and the British troops were taken to prison camps in the south. Back home, Burgoyne was for a while a laughing stock, with London coffee houses resounding to a satirical rhyme:

> Burgoyne, alas, unknowing future fates,
> Could force his way through woods but not
> through Gates.

Burgoyne's defeat at the battles of Saratoga was 'a thunderclap, which resounded round the world'. The American victory encouraged Congress to adopt the Articles of Confederation, strengthening the national feeling of the 13 separate colonies. In the long run this was to prove a decisive event in American history. In the short run, Saratoga prompted Louis XVI to recognize the new republic and brought France into the war against Britain, quickly followed by Spain and the Netherlands. Foreign aid flooded into the American colonies and at sea Britain now faced the united fleets of several countries – which were eventually to force the final British surrender at Yorktown in 1781. But even more than this, the battles of Saratoga were proof that a new state had been born. As Gates wrote to his wife after his victory at Saratoga, 'If old England is not by this lesson taught humility, then she is an obstinate old slut, bent upon her ruin.' In fact, it took six more years for Britain to accept the lesson of Saratoga and recognize American independence. 'Rebellion,' as a contemporary observer noted, 'which a twelvemonth ago was really a contemptible pigmy, is now become a giant.'

Horatio Gates, chivalrous in victory. PN

that my children would wake up and cry and thus disturb the poor dying man, who so often sent to beg my pardon for making me so much trouble.' Burgoyne now retired with the utmost secrecy to a fortified camp at Saratoga: 'Little Frederica was afraid and would often begin to cry,' wrote the Baroness, 'I was, therefore, obliged to hold a pocket handkerchief over her mouth, lest our whereabouts should be discovered.' For a while Burgoyne tried to drive away thoughts of his predicament by carousing with plundered liquor at the captured mansion of General Schuyler at Fishkill. The Baroness indignantly describes the house ringing with, 'singing, laughter and the jingling of glasses'. While Burgoyne drowned his sorrows with his companions and his mistress, the Baroness was arranging that in the event of a breakout each of her

The Battle of Trafalgar 1805

Trafalgar

BRITISH

Commander: Vice-Admiral Horatio Nelson with 27 ships of the line carrying 2148 guns

Ships	Guns
Windward line	
Victory (Vice-Admiral Nelson)	100
Téméraire	98
Neptune	98
Conqueror	74
Leviathan	74
Ajax	64
Orion	74
Agamemnon	64
Minotaur	74
Spartiate	74
Britannia	100
Africa	64
Leeward Line	
Royal Sovereign (Vice-Admiral Collingwood)	100
Belleisle	74
Mars	74
Tonnant	80
Bellerophon	74
Colossus	74
Achille	74
Polyphemus	64
Revenge	74
Swiftsure	74
Defence	74
Thunderer	74
Defiance	74
Prince	98
Dreadnought	98

FRANCO-SPANISH

Commander: Vice-Admiral Villeneuve with 33 ships of the line carrying 2626 guns

Ships	Guns
(French)	
Bucentaure (Vice-Admiral Villeneuve)	80
Formidable	80
Neptune	80
Indomptable	80
Algéciras	74
Pluton	74
Mont-Blanc	74
Intrépide	74
Swiftsure	74
Aigle	74
Scipion	74
Duguay-Trouin	74
Berwick	74
Argonaute	74
Achille	74
Redoubtable	74
Fougueux	74
Héros	74
(Spanish)	
Santíssima Trinidad	130
Principe de Asturias	112
Santa Ana	112
Rayo	100
Neptuno	80
Argonauta	80
Bahama	74
Montanez	74
San Augustin	74
San Ildefonso	74
San Juan de Nepomuceno	74
Monarca	74
San Francisco de Asis	74
San Justo	74
San Leandro	64

In the study of history it is vital to be aware of the part played by geography in the lives of great nations. Few states have enjoyed the strategic advantage possessed by Britain through its 22-mile-wide moat known as the English Channel. While Britain maintained a navy strong enough to patrol the Channel she could feel confident that no foreign power – however strong on land – could effect a successful invasion. In her long history Britain faced three substantial threats from Continental Europe

– in 1588 from Spain, in 1805 from France, and in 1940 from Nazi Germany. On the second occasion a French victory over Britain would have removed the final and most formidable hurdle to Napoleonic hegemony in Europe. Coupled with Napoleon's victory at Austerlitz only a few weeks later, it would have marked the highpoint of French power and put an early end to Britain's economic and imperial domination of the 19th century. That the threat was defeated is due to Lord Nelson's decisive victory at Trafalgar, which established British naval supremacy for a century.

Since the failure of the Peace of Amiens in 1803 Napoleon's mind had been taken up with the idea of an invasion of Britain. Unlike earlier attempts by Philip II of Spain and later ones by Hitler, Napoleon's plans for an invasion were eminently realistic and held out the best chances of success. Between Dunkirk and Le Havre he had assembled an armada of barges and had encamped an army at Boulogne waiting for his fleet to win him just 24 hours of control in the Channel, which was all that he needed to effect a crossing. He knew that his veteran soldiers would be far too good for the English militia if he ever could get them ashore. But the English kept a stranglehold on the French naval bases at Toulon, Brest and Rochefort, as well as Cadiz and Cartagena, where French ships were anchored alongside their Spanish allies. If only the French fleet could break out and give the English the slip, it might be possible for them to reach Boulogne and assist Napoleon's troop-transports to make their short but crucial journey. The strain was telling on all the admirals by 1805: Admiral Collingwood in the *Royal Sovereign,* for example, had not once been ashore in 22 months, while Nelson in the *Victory* kept a round-the-clock watch on the French commander, Admiral Villeneuve, and his fleet at Toulon.

However, on 30 March 1805, Nelson's frigates reported that Villeneuve's fleet had broken out of Toulon, and Nelson concluded that they would head for the eastern Mediterranean. But he was wrong: the French passed through the Straits of Gibraltar, heading for the West Indies. Nelson set off in pursuit but was still well behind when Villeneuve stopped briefly at Martinique and then turned for home. Had he given Nelson the slip this time? If so, he was hoping to head into the Channel to link up with Napoleon at Boulogne. But Nelson had sent home by a fast sailing brig the news that Villeneuve had evaded him, and the Admiralty in England ordered the British Brest and Rochefort squadrons to unite and protect the Channel from Villeneuve, should he come that way. The result was

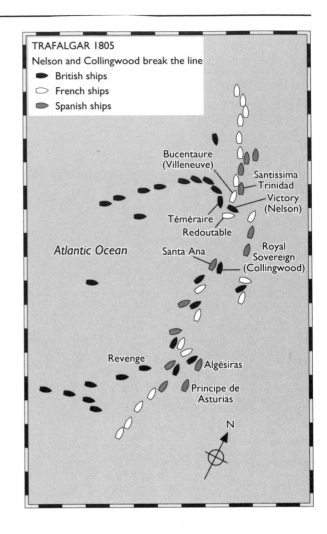

TRAFALGAR 1805
Nelson and Collingwood break the line
- British ships
- French ships
- Spanish ships

Bucentaure (Villeneuve)
Santissima Trinidad
Victory (Nelson)
Téméraire
Redoutable
Atlantic Ocean
Santa Ana
Royal Sovereign (Collingwood)
Revenge
Algésiras
Principe de Asturias
N

that on 22 July Sir Robert Calder fought a night battle with Villeneuve off Cape Finisterre. The battle was indecisive but it was enough to make Villeneuve abandon his plan to break into the Channel. Instead he headed for Cadiz. Napoleon had hopefully sent him a note at Brest:

Admiral, I trust you have arrived at Brest. Start at once. Do not lose a moment. Come into the Channel with our united squadrons, and England is ours. We are all ready. Everything is embarked. Come here for twenty-four hours and all is ended, and six centuries of shame and insult will be avenged.

When he heard instead that Villeneuve was in Spain, Napoleon was beside himself with fury. The invasion of England was abandoned and he began to plan the campaign against England's allies, Austria and Russia, which was to lead to his victory at Austerlitz, perhaps his greatest triumph. Before he left, however, he sent Admiral Rosilly to replace Villeneuve, and on hearing this news the French commander realized that unless he did something he would end his career in disgrace. It was with this in mind that he accepted battle with Nelson at Trafalgar, even though he knew that his chances of victory were slight.

On 19 October 1805, with Nelson leading the windward line of 12 British men-of-war and Collingwood in the *Royal Sovereign* leading the leeward line of 15, the British approached the Franco-Spanish fleet of 33 ships-of-the line off Cape Trafalgar, south of Cadiz. Although Villeneuve had the advantage in numbers of ships and guns, the British were superior in leadership, seamanship and morale.

As the day dawned the lookouts on the British men-of-war could see the whole horizon covered with enemy ships. Although the two fleets were just nine miles apart the wind was so slight that it took nearly six hours for them to come into gunnery range. Approaching in two columns, led by their admirals, the British fleet was planning to cut through the Franco-Spanish line in two places and engage the enemy at close range so that escape would be impossible. Advancing as they were, virtually at right angles to the enemy, meant that the French and Spanish ships would have the chance to fire several broadsides without the British being able to reply. The French found these tactics incredible and against all normal practice. But Nelson wanted to make certain that this battle was fought to a finish, and so he was prepared to accept early damage and casualties in order to get so close

that his broadsides would destroy the enemy.

Aboard the *Victory* Nelson had a premonition of death, and asked Captain Blackwood of the frigate *Euryalus* to witness his will, saying that this would be his last battle. In spite of the advice of his officers he insisted on wearing his finest uniform with all his decorations, making him a certain target for snipers in the rigging of the French ships.

Aboard the *Neptune* a midshipman described the sight as the two fleets came together:

It was a beautiful sight when their line was completed, their broadsides turned towards us, showing their iron teeth, and now and then trying the range of a shot to ascertain the distance that they might, the moment we came within point blank (about 600 yards), open their fire on our van ships – no doubt with the hope of dismasting some of our leading vessels before they could close and break their line. Some of the enemy's ships were painted like ourselves with double yellow streaks, some with a broad single red or yellow streak, others all black, and the noble *Santíssima Trinidad* with four distinct lines of red, made her seem to be a superb man-of-war.

Soon there was no time for such reflection. From

The lower gundeck of Nelson's *Victory*. Housing thirty 32-pounder guns, this deck was the broadest on the ship, and it was here that most of the crew ate and slept. PN

the *Victory* the signal was being made 'England expects every man will do his duty.' This caused a lot of muttering from the British sailors, who asked when they had ever failed to do their duty. Now the French and Spanish line began to thunder out their shots, at first mainly at the *Victory* and the *Royal Sovereign*, but soon ships further back in each line were being hit. Nelson pressed relentlessly on and the British fired no shot in reply. Soon eight ships were firing at the *Victory*, but still Nelson held his fire, until he came through the enemy line and fired a shattering broadside into Villeneuve's flagship *Bucentaure*. Collingwood meanwhile had opened fire on the *Fougueux* and the *Santa Ana* simultaneously. Soon other English ships were in the action, *Conqueror* and *Téméraire* supporting Nelson, and

Belleisle and *Mars* astern of Collingwood. While Nelson's and Villeneuve's flagships fought alongside each other, the heroic French captain Lucas in the *Redoubtable* came up and tried to board the *Victory*, but was repulsed after a fierce struggle between the marines. The leading ships of the Franco-Spanish column under Admiral Dumanoir continued on their heading and escaped almost unhurt from the terrible melee that was now taking place. The *Victory* had dreadfully mauled the *Redoubtable* and of a crew of 643 there were more than 500 casualties, with 300 men dead. But the *Victory* had lost a mast, her wheel had been shot away, and her upper deck was awash with blood and the remains of men shattered by chain and grapeshot, as well as the heads of those decapitated by solid shot. At 1.20 p.m. Nelson himself was hit by a sniper in the rigging of the *Redoubtable* and carried below. He knew the wound was mortal but lived long enough to hear that he had won a complete victory. Soon the *Redoubtable* struck her colours, followed by the *Fougueux*. With Nelson dying aboard the flagship, Collingwood took command of the battle, and in the next hour nine enemy ships were taken or destroyed. The French flagship was just a burning hulk, crewed by corpses, when the *Conqueror* sent a boarding party to accept the surrender of Admiral Villeneuve himself. The magnificent Spanish man-of-war *Santíssima Trinidad* was hunted by the English ships in packs. Battered by as many as eight at the same time she was eventually taken by the *Prince*, 'her beams covered with blood, brains and pieces of flesh, and the after parts of her decks with wounded; some without legs and some without an arm', according to Midshipman Badcock, who helped to board her.

The battle of Trafalgar was over. What had started as a hard-fought battle between fleets of equal size ended as a massacre. The French and Spanish ships had been knocked to pieces by superior British gunnery, and their casualties were proportionately heavy for a naval battle: 4408 killed and 2250 wounded. British losses of 449 killed and 1214 wounded were mainly suffered in the early part of the battle. Many French and Spanish sailors drowned in the confused melee which made rescue difficult, but it is pleasing to note the gallantry of the British seaman who rescued one lady from the water – a survivor from the *Achille* – who was, curiously, dressed as a harlequin. A lieutenant of marines aboard the *Britannia* found her a nice warm dressing gown.

With the battle over, the weather now completed Nelson's work, wreaking havoc on the wrecked French and Spanish ships that were being taken by the British as prizes. Few of them reached harbour and so thousands of British seaman were robbed of their rewards. Nevertheless, the battle marked a turning point in the history of Europe. Napoleon's naval power was broken for all time and his hopes of defeating Britain – his most resolute enemy – were ended. Confined to a European battleground, his victories, though impressive, could not alter the balance of power between Britain and France. Britain was henceforth able to use her seapower to control trade with Europe, as well as to maintain her armies in Spain or wherever else they were needed. In the long run Trafalgar was as fatal to Napoleon as Waterloo.

The Battle of Austerlitz 1805

Austerlitz

Austro-Russians

Commanders:	Emperor Francis II of Austria and Tsar Alexander I of Russia
Chief of Staff:	General Weyrother
Right wing:	General Bagration, with Prince Lichtenstein
Centre:	General Kutuzov
Left wing:	General Buxhowden
Numbers:	85,400 infantry, cavalry and 278 guns

French

Commander:	Emperor Napoleon I
Left wing:	Marshals Bernadotte, Lannes and Murat
Centre:	Marshal Soult
Right wing:	Marshal Davout
Numbers:	66,800 infantry, cavalry and 139 guns

On 14 March 1804 the First Consul of France, Napoleon Bonaparte, sent troops into the neutral state of Baden and kidnapped the emigré nobleman, the Duke of Enghien, returning him to France and executing him there for treason. This ruthless demonstration of his power was, in the words of one contemporary, 'more than a crime; it was a mistake'. The murder of the Bourbon prince served to alienate Napoleon's young admirer, Tsar Alexander I of Russia, and to shatter the Peace of Amiens that had kept Europe free from armed conflict for the previous two years.

The resulting struggle between Britain and France, after the collapse of the Peace of Amiens in 1804, can be defined by the two decisive battles fought in 1805. After the battle of Trafalgar, Britain no longer had to fear a French invasion, but after the battle of Austerlitz Britain could no longer hope to secure a victory over Napoleon by financing his military enemies, Austria, Prussia and Russia. Austerlitz made Napoleon not only supreme in France but in Europe, and it would take a decade of economic pressure and desperate fighting to unseat him.

Yet the Third Coalition devised by the British prime minister William Pitt ('the younger') in April 1805 had held out the hope of overthrowing the 'Corsican bandit', who had crowned himself emperor as recently as December 1804. Immense forces were gathering in Central Europe under Francis II of Austria and Alexander I of Russia, and the British were not without hope of persuading Prussia to join them. Determined to prevent this at all costs, Napoleon reacted with astonishing speed. Abandoning his planned invasion of Britain he opened negotiations with Prussia, offering her Hanover to keep her out of Britain's net. Furthermore, he warned the Austrians that if their military preparations did not immediately cease he would enter Bavaria with overwhelming force. On 3 September Francis II rejected his ultimatum with scorn and 85,000 Austrian troops crossed the River Inn into Bavaria under Quartermaster General Mack and the Archduke Ferdinand.

But Allied preparations for the campaign of 1805 had become unnecessarily complex. The Austrians had divided their forces between four theatres, and a total of three Russian armies were lumbering through Bohemia and Moravia to rendezvous with the Austrians on the Inn. So sloppy was the planning that the Austrian staff had failed to allow for the fact that the Russians used the old Julian calendar and were thus 10 days behind the Austrians, who used the Gregorian one. The result of this blunder was that while the Russian commander Kutuzov was only just entering Moravia, Mack was expecting his arrival any day at Ulm, 300 miles to the west.

Napoleon took the Allied threat very seriously. The main Austrian force in Bavaria could pose a threat to Alsace, while the Archduke Charles, with a further 95,000 men in northern Italy, could invade southern France. And when the ponderous Russian armies eventually arrived, Austro-Russian strength might be overwhelming. Napoleon's response was positive as always: he would strike first at Mack on the Danube before going on to destroy the tsar's armies in Austria. With 210,000 men, operating in a vast new formation – La Grande Armée – he would defeat his enemy in detail.

By brilliant manoeuvring Napoleon forced Mack to surrender at Ulm with 27,000 men, at virtually no cost to himself. He then pressed on into Austria,

entering Vienna – abandoned by the Habsburgs and regarded as an 'open city' – and was able to replenish his supplies there, as well as capturing 500 cannon and 100,000 muskets. When news reached him that the Russian generals Buxhowden and Kutuzov had joined forces at Olmütz, there was a chance that the Russian and Austrian allies might outnumber him heavily, particularly if the Prussians decided to intervene. Fortunately for the French, the young Tsar Alexander was headstrong, and pressed for an immediate attack. This was playing into Napoleon's hands. He had already located the area where he wished to fight, east of the Moravian city of Brünn, near the village of Austerlitz.

Napoleon had already made a detailed inspection of the Austerlitz battlefield before committing himself to fighting there. He planned to allow the Austro-Russians to occupy the Pratzen Heights at the outset but to lure them away from the centre by offering an apparently weak right wing – though Davout's Corps would be near enough to reinforce this flank when the time came. Meanwhile the bulk of the French army under Soult would be kept partially hidden by the Zurlan Heights, and once the enemy had been lured away from the centre this force would crack them in half by advancing onto the Pratzen Heights. The French left wing would fight a holding operation, supported by Murat's cavalry. It was an interesting script, but would the enemy play their parts?

By early morning on 1 December the Austro-Russian forces were occupying the ground to the east of the Goldbach stream, with Russian troops on the Goldbach Heights and a large body on the Pratzen Heights. By nightfall the Allies numbered 85,400 men, with 278 guns, against Napoleon's 66,800 and 139 guns. But the emperor was expecting Davout's Corps to reinforce him at any time. Napoleon's two imperial enemies – the aged and indecisive Francis of Austria and the young and able Tsar Alexander – had established their headquarters at Krzenowitz. Of the Allied commanders some, like Mikhail Kutuzov, favoured caution, but others more aggressively followed the tsar's headstrong approach. Alexander had supreme faith in the Austrian chief-of-staff, Weyrother, an advocate of the offensive, and most of the planning was done by that officer. On the other hand, most of the Russian generals had a low opinion of the Austrians and refused to give Weyrother a fair hearing when he went over the battle plans on 1 December. The scene, described here by a Russian general present, was so absurd that it deserves to be recorded for posterity as the way for allies not to behave on the eve of battle.

When we had all assembled, General Weyrother arrived, unfolded upon a large table an immense and most accurate map of the environs of Brünn and Austerlitz

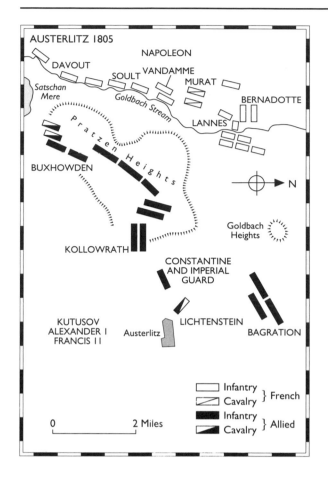

confident too. In his order of the day he told them:

Soldiers, I shall in person direct all your battalions; I shall keep out of range if, with your accustomed bravery, you carry disorder and confusion into the ranks of the enemy; but if the victory is for a moment uncertain, you shall see your Emperor expose himself in the front rank . . .

Note that no man shall leave the ranks under the pretext of carrying off the wounded. Let every man be filled with the thought that it is vitally necessary to conquer these paid lackeys of England who so hate our nation . . .

Having issued his orders, Napoleon retired to dine with his officers – on his favourite fried potatoes with onions – and was soon reassured by the arrival of a travel-stained Davout with his full corps.

The morning of 2 December dawned cold and misty, making visibility poor, particularly along the Goldbach stream. On the French right heavy Russian attacks soon overran the villages of Telnitz and Zokolnitz, but Napoleon was not alarmed. Things were going to plan. As the mist rose above the Pratzen Heights he saw to his great satisfaction the sight of torrents of Russian and Austrian troops – already more than 40,000 of them – pouring diagonally towards the French right, thinning their centre. Napoleon was supremely confident now. 'How long will it take you to move your divisions to the top of the Pratzen Heights?' he asked Soult.

and read the dispositions to us in a loud tone and with a self-satisfied air which indicated a thorough persuasion of his own merit and of our incapacity. He was really like a college teacher reading a lesson to young scholars. Kutuzov, seated and half asleep when we arrived, at length fell into a sound nap before our departure.

Weyrother's strategy, in fact, could have been written for him by Napoleon. As expected the weak French right wing had attracted his attention. Weyrother was proposing that as many as 54,000 of his troops would eventually concentrate on this weak flank, leaving the centre of the army on the Pratzen Heights so thin that he would be virtually inviting the French to attack him there, so enabling them to break the Allied army in half. When, at the briefing held by Weyrother, one Russian general had pointed out this possible flaw in his plans, the Austrian had dismissed it with scorn. Napoleon was already half-beaten, Weyrother insisted, or else why did he abandon the Pratzen Heights in the first place? Napoleon's deception had worked, and the battle ahead now took on an air of inevitability, interspersed with the minor mischances that occur in any prolonged struggle between armies.

Napoleon was confident, and that made his men

THE OLD GUARD

The Imperial Guard occupied a special place in Napoleon's Grande Armée. From its origins as a household guard to the monarch it grew to a maximum of 100,000 men by 1814. In 1799 Napoleon – as First Consul – set up the Garde des Consuls as a model for the rest of the army. Admission was severely restricted, candidates needing to be over 25 years of age, between 1.74 and 1.88 metres (5 ft 8 ins to 6 ft 2 ins) in height, and having had to demonstrate their courage in battle. The Guard was to be the cream of the army, and of the Guard the 'Old Guard' was to be the elite. The 'Old Guard' was made up of the 1st Grenadiers and 1st Chasseurs à Pied. After its triumphant performance at the battle of Marengo in 1800, where it had stood as firm as granite while all around other French regiments panicked, its reputation was made. At Austerlitz in 1805 the 'Old Guard' had cried at being denied a prominent part in the battle, and ever after they were known as *les grognards* (the grumblers). Members of the 'Old Guard' were identified by their tall bearskin bonnets.

'Less than twenty minutes, sir,' said Soult, 'for my troops are hidden at the foot of the valley, hidden by fog and campfire smoke.' Napoleon decided to wait until even more of the Allies had moved off the heights, and issued a triple spirit ration to the French soldiers, who were stamping their feet on the frosty ground and eager to be given the order to advance. At 9.00 a.m. Napoleon gave the go-ahead, and to a steady drumbeat the French began to attack the Pratzen Heights. At that very moment a blood-red sun emerged above the mist – the sun of Austerlitz was shining on the French. The Allies were shocked by the sight of dense columns of French troops emerging from the mists with bayonets bristling. Hasty orders were sent out from Allied headquarters to halt the march to the right, but it was already much too late – just two battalions managed to turn back in time, and they were swept away by the flood of French infantry.

On the French left a hard slogging match between French forces under Bernadotte and Lannes, with Murat supporting them with his cavalry, and the Russians led by Bagration, was only gradually turning in the French favour. At one stage Kellermann's light cavalry dismounted and drove off ten times their number of Prince Lichtenstein's Austrian cavalry. Eventually Murat's heavy cavalry – armoured cuirassiers on their massive horses – broke Russian resistance on this flank, and by noon

Bagration's entire force of 17,600 men was cut off from the rest of the Allied army.

The hardest fight of all was on the French right, where Davout was heavily outnumbered by the Austrians and Russians. For a while it was touch and go for the French, but as soon as Soult's attack on the Pratzen Heights became clear to the Allied commanders their confidence slumped, and they began withdrawing troops from this flank to support their centre. By midday a French victory was certain, but how complete a victory would it be? Napoleon withdrew Bernadotte's corps from the French left and placed it in reserve, with the Imperial Guard, along the Goldbach stream. Moving his own headquarters onto the Pratzen Heights he now directed Soult to veer towards the right to virtually encircle the Allied masses on the left. To counter this the Russian Imperial Guard led by the Grand Duke Constantine stormed into the attack, but their bayonet charge – delivered at the end of a 300-yard run – lacked impetus, and these magnificent soldiers took heavy casualties from Vandamme's

General Rapp's Mameluke cavalry charging the Russian Imperial Guard, which was annihilated by the onslaught. PN

A meeting of emperors: Francis II of Austria and Napoleon after Austerlitz. PN

the pursuit. The massive Russian concentration on the left — at one stage amounting to nearly 54,000 men under Buxhowden — found escape difficult as it was being driven towards the frozen Satschan Mere. As thousands of Russians tried to cross the ice, Napoleon ordered 25 cannon to open fire, splitting it asunder. Hundreds, perhaps thousands, drowned or died of exposure in the freezing waters. To the north, Bagration was making a more disciplined withdrawal, though any thought of continuing the struggle was far from his mind. Within two days both he and his men would be over 40 miles from the battlefield.

The French had won a stupendous victory. A battle that had seemed hopeful at 9.00 a.m., and promising by midday, was by 4.30 p.m. concluded in the most satisfying manner possible. Napoleon had out-thought his opponents and made them dance to the tune he played. His manipulation of his forces had been immaculate, and it was a truly Napoleonic victory — one from which the legend of his personal invincibility would grow. Against French losses of 1305 killed, 6940 wounded and a mere 573 captured, the Allies had suffered approaching 15,000 men killed (11,000 Russians and 4000 Austrians), as well as some 12,000 prisoners captured, along with 180 guns and 50 colours. The army of the two emperors had been annihilated, and one of Napoleon's most important enemies — Austria — had been knocked out of the war at a single stroke. Pitt's Third Coalition was on the verge of collapse.

The political significance of the battle of Austerlitz was clearly understood by William Pitt. When he heard of Napoleon's victory he ordered his servants to 'roll up the map of Europe. We shall not need it these seven years.' In Austria Francis II signed the Treaty of Pressburg, ceding large territories to Napoleon's recently created Kingdom of Italy, as well as to France's ally, Bavaria. Alexander I sent a eulogy to Napoleon:

Tell your master that I am going away. Tell him that he has performed miracles . . . that the battle has increased my admiration for him; that he is a man predestined by Heaven; that it will require a hundred years for my arms to equal his.

In France the many children orphaned in the fighting were officially adopted by the emperor himself and were allowed to add the name 'Napoleon' to their own. It was the beginning of the Napoleon legend that was to inspire French generals throughout the 19th century and beyond with the belief that the 'sun of Austerlitz' would always shine on French arms.

marksmen. But there was no stopping the Russian guardsmen and they overran two of Vandamme's battalions, sending many proud French soldiers running to the rear. As they passed Napoleon some of them even dared to shout, '*Vive l'Empereur!*' What Napoleon thought is not recorded; what he did is. He called up the cavalry of the Imperial Guard under Bessières, and after a titanic struggle the Russian guardsmen were overwhelmed by General Rapp's Mameluke cavalry: 500 of them died, along with 200 of the tsar's own personal escort, all of noble birth. Napoleon reflected, 'Many fine ladies of St Petersburg will lament this day.'

The fighting had been intense on both the right and left wings, and even on the Pratzen Heights in the later stages of the battle. General Thiebault reported, 'Up to the last hour of the battle, we took no prisoners, it would not do to run any risk; one could stick at nothing, and thus not a single living enemy remained to our rear.' The cry had been heard throughout the French army at Austerlitz, 'Let no one escape.'

With the enemy in full retreat the French began

The Battle of Waterloo 1815

Waterloo

Allies

Commanders:	Duke of Wellington, Field Marshal Blücher
Left wing:	Prince Bernard of Saxe-Weimar
Centre:	Prince of Orange's I Corps, Sir Thomas Picton's reserve division and Lord Uxbridge's cavalry brigades
Right wing:	General Hill's II Corps
Numbers:	49,608, 12,408 cavalry, 5645 gunners, 156 guns. (Prussian strength: 30,000 and rising to 50,000 or more, with 44 guns, as evening drew on)

French

Commanders:	Emperor Napoleon I and Marshal Ney
Left wing:	General Reille's II Corps with General Kellermann's cavalry
Centre and right:	General d'Erlon's I Corps, General Lobau's VI Corps, the Imperial Guard
Numbers:	48,950 infantry, 15,765 cavalry, 7232 gunners. 246 guns

In military parlance 'Waterloo' has become a synonym for a decisive battle. When a general 'meets his Waterloo' everyone immediately understands that he has not just been defeated but that he has been destroyed. And so decisive was the defeat of Napoleon Bonaparte near the small Belgian town of Waterloo on Sunday 18 June 1815 that it ended not only the career of history's greatest military genius but also a 20-year period in which, through him, France had dominated European affairs as no single power had done since the days of the Roman Empire.

On 4 March 1815 news reached the congress of great powers meeting at Vienna that Napoleon had escaped from his exile on Elba, where he had been placed after his defeat and abdication in 1814. He returned to France and received popular acclamation and the support of Marshal Ney, who had been sent by the restored Bourbons to arrest him. King Louis XVIII fled from Paris and the campaign of the 'hundred days' had begun. By the end of May Napoleon had raised France's military strength to 284,000 men, and had an effective army of 124,500

on the Belgian border. The Allies responded quickly, raising armies of Austrians and Russians that looked impressive on paper but might not materialize for some time. The task of containing Napoleon fell to Field Marshal Blücher's 115,000 Prussians and Wellington's 93,000-strong Anglo-Dutch forces. Napoleon crossed into Belgium and struck first in the direction of Brussels on 15 June, but the following day his left wing under Ney was held up by Wellington at Quatre Bras. Meanwhile, on the same day, Napoleon defeated the Prussians under Blücher at Ligny, sending Marshal Grouchy's corps to pursue them and prevent them joining with Wellington, who had taken up a new position at Waterloo.

The battlefield at Waterloo had been carefully chosen by Wellington as suitable for the sort of defensive battle at which he was a master. It was very small, stretching for no more than three miles from Hougoumont in the west to the town of Papelotte in the east. The Allied and French armies occupied two opposing ridges, separated by a mere 1300 yards, and into this cauldron of little more than three square miles 140,000 men and 400 guns would soon be pitched. It was a killing ground *par excellence*

'On the Morning of Waterloo'. The sounding of the last reveille of Napoleon's cuirassiers; from the painting by Lady Butler. PN

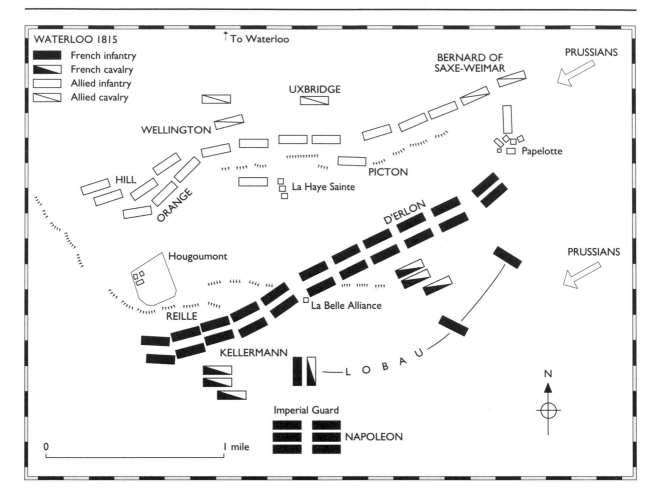

and offered Napoleon few opportunities for the kind of manoeuvring at which he excelled. He would be faced with few options but to assault Wellington's strong position head-on.

As the French deployed on 18 June, General d'Erlon's powerful corps of four divisions – 20,000 men – took up a position on the right, while to his left was General Reille's corps of three divisions, and behind him the mass of French cavalry under Kellermann. Further back was Lobau's VI Corps of 10,000 men, as well as more cavalry and the Imperial Guard. In total the French fielded 48,950 infantry, 15,765 cavalry, and 7232 gunners with 246 guns.

Wellington's dispositions were based on the assumption that Blücher would come to his aid sometime during the battle and would reinforce his left wing. As a result he had concentrated his own strength on the right wing and in the centre. As was his usual habit he had drawn up his troops on the reverse slopes of the ridge to reduce casualties from the French artillery. The right of the Allied line between Merbraine and the Nivelle road was held by 'Daddy' Hill's II Corps, while to his left was the Prince of Orange's I Corps and Sir Thomas Picton's reserve division. The extreme left of the Allied line was held by Prince Bernard of Saxe-Weimar with the cavalry brigades of Vandaleur and Vivian. In support of the centre was Lord Uxbridge's cavalry. Wellington had also occupied several advanced positions to act as breakers to the waves of French attacks, the most important of which was the château of Hougoumont, held by Nassauers, Hanoverians and units of the Coldstream Guards. Another was the farmhouse of La Haie Sainte, held by men of the King's German Legion. In total Wellington's force comprised 49,500 infantry, 12,500 cavalry, and 5500 gunners with 156 artillery pieces, being made up of about 21,000 British, 5000 King's German Legion, 11,000 Hanoverians and Nassauers, 24,000 Dutch and Belgians, and 6500 Brunswickers.

Such were the troops who were actually on the battlefield. But just as important were the ones who were not present, like Marshal Grouchy's corps of 30,000 men, which was supposed to be pursuing the Prussians from Ligny and yet failed either to keep Blücher from reaching Waterloo or to reach the battlefield itself. Much of the fault rested with Napoleon himself, whose messages to Grouchy were unclear and failed to entertain the possibility that the Prussians might evade the marshal and return to help Wellington. When Soult had suggested recalling Grouchy without delay before the battle of Waterloo began, Napoleon had pooh-poohed the idea. And when it was suggested that Blücher was planning to come to Wellington's aid, which explained the weak Allied left wing, Napoleon exploded with anger. He was working to his preconceptions, and this time he was wrong.

Napoleon was far from well and was suffering from the piles that plagued him in his later years. He was short-tempered and snappy and, worst of all, contemptuous of his enemy. Wellington was a bad general, or so Napoleon claimed, and his army would be driven off its ridge by massive frontal assaults. When Soult reminded him of Wellington's record in Spain it only seemed to make the emperor more determined to break him by main force.

The rain of the previous few days had made the terrain heavy and difficult for both infantry and cavalry assaults, and so Napoleon decided to delay his attack until as late as possible to allow the ground to dry. But every minute wasted added to the danger that the Prussians would come to Wellington's aid. An attack by mid-morning might have stretched the Iron Duke too far and made his defeat by mid-afternoon inevitable. Unknown to Napoleon, Blücher – a battle-scarred veteran who veered between fits of drunkenness and senile melancholia – had detached Bülow's IV Corps with instructions to make all possible haste to reach Waterloo, and the Prussian II Corps was following. In a message to Wellington, received early on the morning of the battle, Blücher had written 'Say in my name to the Duke of Wellington that, ill as I am, I will march at the head of my army to attack without delay the right flank of the enemy, if Napoleon should attempt anything against the Duke.' With Gneisenau watching Grouchy, 'Old Forwards' Blücher rode through the muddy, sunken roads of Belgium to join Bülow, shouting to his men as he passed, 'Lads, you will not let me break my word!' and, 'If things go well we shall soon all be bathing in Paris.' Grouchy, meanwhile, was having a late breakfast at Walhein, convinced that all the Prussians were massing at Wavre. When gunfire was heard to the west at 11.30 a.m. some of his generals advised him to 'march to the sound of the guns', but Grouchy refused and continued his breakfast. What he had heard was the start of the battle of Waterloo – and the death knell for Napoleonic France.

Prince Jerome Bonaparte's division began the battle with a diversionary attack on the château of Hougoumont, hoping to persuade Wellington to thin his centre to support the position. But Jerome's stupidity was to have entirely the reverse effect. Sensitive to his own modest military record when compared with his brother, he wanted very much to capture Hougoumont at whatever the cost and mulishly besieged the château and its outbuildings as if the fate of the whole empire depended on his success. The Allied defenders fought from within the buildings, firing through prepared loopholes, taking a steady toll of the French attackers. Soon Jerome had to call up help from General Foy's division, and the vicious struggle in and around the château escalated until it soon involved most of General Reille's II Corps, weakening the whole French left centre. To support Hougoumont had cost Wellington just 13 companies of the Coldstream Guards, while it had robbed Napoleon of a quarter of his infantry. On a day of swaying fortunes the Allies held Hougoumont by prodigies of valour throughout the battle.

Meanwhile, Napoleon had drawn up 84 guns to support d'Erlon's attempt to drive a hole straight through Wellington's centre. But he soon found that the wet ground simply absorbed the heavy shot, muffling explosions and preventing the solid shot ricocheting. In addition, Wellington's tactic of positioning his men on the reverse slope meant that they suffered few casualties from the French barrage. At 1.00 p.m. d'Erlon's massive corps was ready to go, but Napoleon now received reports that troops were unexpectedly appearing from the northeast – not Grouchy's men but the advance guard of Bülow's corps of 30,000 men. Napoleon at last wrote a peremptory order to Grouchy to march to Waterloo – but it was too late now and only reached the marshal at 5.00 p.m. For Napoleon there was no time to waste; Wellington must be driven off his ridge without delay.

Sending part of Lobau's infantry and cavalry units under Domont and Subservie to hold the right flank against Bülow, at 1.30 p.m. Napoleon ordered d'Erlon's Corps to advance across the valley towards the Allies on the ridge. But at the start a terrible mistake was made. Instead of advancing in battalion columns – presenting a narrow front – d'Erlon's men advanced in massive division columns, 200 men wide and with a depth of 24–27 men, offering the British gunners unmissable targets. The French casualties were truly shocking as they crossed the 1300 yards separating them from the Allies on the ridge. To make matters worse d'Erlon's men were advancing without adequate artillery or cavalry cover. On the ridge the British guns had been set up behind a strong hedge and fired with impunity through holes hacked in the thicket. As d'Erlon's depleted columns reached the top of the slope they were met by Picton's 3000 British redcoats, who fired a volley with their old 'Brown Bess' muskets and charged into them at the point of the bayonet. It was the first crisis of the battle and, though Picton was killed – shot through his top hat – his men swept the French back. D'Erlon's corps was simultaneously hit by two of Lord Uxbridge's heavy cavalry brigades: Somerset's Household Brigade of Life Guards, Dragoon Guards and Horse Guards, and Ponsonby's Union Brigade of Royal Scots Greys, Blues and Royals and Iniskillings. Three thousand of d'Erlon's men were taken prisoner at this time and the rest were driven back across the valley. Napoleon's sledgehammer attack had failed completely. However, the over-excited cavalry of Ponsonby's Union Brigade, having defeated d'Erlon, then charged the French guns only to be counter-attacked by Napoleon's lancers and cuirassiers: over 1000 of Uxbridge's

---

The charge of the Scots Greys – part of the massive counter-attack by Lord Uxbridge's heavy brigades in the early afternoon. PN

2500 British cavalry were lost in this moment of madness, including Ponsonby, killed by a French lancer.

By 3.00 p.m. Napoleon knew that he could expect no help from Grouchy. To continue the battle meant increasing numbers of Prussians would join the Allied left wing until the French were overwhelmed by weight of numbers. Yet he refused to withdraw, telling Marshal Ney that the position at La Haie Sainte would have to be taken at whatever the cost. Ney led an assault on the ridge during which he noticed Allied troops retreating – they were probably ambulance workers or men collecting ammunition – but Ney got it into his head that Wellington's army was on the point of breaking up. There now occurred one of the most extraordinary and yet majestic incidents in Napoleonic warfare, commemorated in dozens of paintings since 1815. Without infantry or artillery support, Ney called up 5000 French cavalry to assault the ridge in what he believed would be a decisive attack. The British responded by forming squares to receive the cavalry – in fact 20 large rectangles would be a better description – and the tide of French horsemen simply washed over these 'rocks' without doing much harm. The Allied gunners stayed outside the squares until the last possible moment in order to fire their pieces with shattering effect into the masses of men and horses riding towards them. The impressions of Ensign Gronow are worth recording:

Not a man present who survived could have forgotten in after life the awful grandeur of that charge. You perceived at a distance what appeared to be an overwhelming, long moving line, which, ever advancing, glittered like a stormy wave of the sea when it catches the sunlight. On came the mounted host until they got near enough, while the very earth seemed to vibrate beneath their thundering tramp. One might have supposed that nothing could have resisted the shock of this terrible moving mass. They were the famous *cuirassiers*, almost all old soldiers who had distinguished themselves on most of the battlefields of Europe. In an almost incredibly short period they were within twenty yards of us, shouting '*Vive l'Empereur!*' The word of command, 'Prepare to receive cavalry', had been given, every man in the front rank knelt, and a wall bristling with steel, held together by steady hands, presented itself to the infuriated *cuirassiers*.

The French cavalry rode over the British guns, but apparently did not think to disable them. Once the French retreated the gunners emerged from the squares and began firing again. It had been a magnificently picturesque but ultimately pointless exercise. Napoleon, viewing the destruction of his cavalry from a distance, was infuriated at Ney's stupidity. Meanwhile, by 4.00 p.m. the Prussians were emerging from the woods on the French right and engaging Napoleon's covering troops. Time was running out. A second – and even larger – cavalry assault, 10,000 strong, on the British squares was at that moment being defeated around La Haie Sainte. But at this – France's most desperate moment – Ney recovered his nerve and organized a coordinated attack on the strategic farmhouse, with artillery cover for an infantry and cavalry assault, and succeeded in driving the King's German Legion from the buildings they had held since early morning. Bringing up a battery of guns Ney now began to smash the British squares with artillery fire. This was the greatest crisis of the day. The exhausted Allied troops on the ridge really were on the point of breaking this time, and Ney sent urgent gallopers calling Napoleon to send up more troops. But Napoleon was beside himself with rage at the way Ney had squandered his cavalry, and refused to release the Imperial Guard, replying to Ney's urgent call with the scornful words, 'Troops! Where does he expect me to get them from? Make them?'

If Napoleon was missing his chance of victory by not supporting Ney, Wellington was nevertheless aware that the marshal's men had to be silenced at all costs. Taking personal command of a brigade of Brunswickers he rode across to plug the hole that Ney had smashed in his line. He need not have worried, for more and more Prussians were reaching the field now, including Pirch's II Corps and Zieten's I Corps, which rode round to support the Allied left on the ridge. It was too late for Napoleon to do anything more than extricate his army before it was destroyed. But he refused to concede the battle. Believing that his Imperial Guard could still break Wellington's hold on the ridge, he ordered his officers to tell their men that the troops arriving on their right were Grouchy's and not Prussians – a lie that was soon discovered and caused morale to collapse. Nevertheless, the Imperial Guard advanced with measured tread to the sound of the drums; according to Benjamin Haydon they were 'tall bony men with black moustachios, gigantic caps, depravity, indifference and bloodthirstiness burnt in their faces; more dreadful-looking men I had never seen'. As they marched up the slopes Wellington ordered his men to lie down so that the shot from the French artillery flew harmlessly over their heads. When the magnificent veterans of earlier Napoleonic battles reached the top of the ridge 'with high, hairy caps and long red feathers nodding to the beat of the drum', they were hit at

THE BRITISH SQUARE

The 'square' as an infantry defence against cavalry attack is not essentially British; its origins are deep in ancient history. Its aim was to repel enemy horsemen – something the 19th-century rifleman was unable to do unless formed up into a unit that protected both his flank and his rear. The hedge of bayonets that faced the cavalry was merely an extension of the ancient phalanx and the 16th-century *tercio*. Squares were hollow to allow officers, musicians, wounded men and even – at Waterloo – the gunners to shelter within. The sides of each square were usually four deep to allow volley firing, with the front rank on one knee holding their muskets upwards to present their bayonet point to the horses' chests. Although proof against cavalry attack the square was impotent against horse artillery. Marshal Ney's failure to coordinate his great cavalry attacks on the British squares at Waterloo with infantry or artillery support was a fatal error. The tactic of the infantry square became standard tactical procedure in Britain's 19th-century colonial wars, notably in the campaigns in the Sudan in 1885 and 1898.

short range by a fusillade of musket fire and grapeshot. At Wellington's order the British Guards leapt to their feet and at just 20 yards' range fired a volley into the French ranks, then charged them with the bayonet. Whether Wellington really said 'Up Guards and at 'em' is less important than the fact that Maitland's Guards brigade did exactly that. To the French soldier the Imperial Guard represented all that was best in his army and his nation. Yet, incredibly, the guardsmen were being driven back all along the line. The cry went up, '*La Garde recule!*' and the news spread like wildfire. Sensing the moment had come to attack, Wellington, mounted on his grey, Copenhagen, raised his hat and ordered a general advance. From the ridge to which they had been pinned all day, the whole Allied line moved forward. It was too much for the Imperial Guards and many raised the cry of beaten French troops throughout history: '*Sauve qui peut!*'

Napoleon's army was disintegrating and the emperor was persuaded to leave the stricken field to try to rally the survivors at Genappe. Many famous regiments had lost all cohesion and become mobs of terrified and beaten men. Still on the battlefield, General Cambronne showed great courage when called upon to surrender the Guard. He is quoted as replying, 'The Guard dies but never surrenders,' but some claim he merely shouted

'*Merde!*' Meanwhile, as it grew dark, Blücher and Wellington met at La Belle Alliance, the old Prussian grasping Wellington's hand with the words, '*Mein lieber Kamerad! Quelle affaire.*' Under Gneisenau's directions the Prussians took up the pursuit of the remnants of Napoleon's Armée du Nord.

The casualties in this memorable but savage encounter had been heavy on both sides. Out of a total force of 72,000 the French had lost 41,000 men killed, wounded or taken prisoner – 57 per cent, the highest percentage losses ever suffered in a Napoleonic battle – as well as 220 guns. Wellington's army had lost 15,100 and the Prussians 7000 – more than in many a defeat. In every sense Waterloo had been a fight to the finish. No one had much stomach for any further campaigning after this bloodbath. Wellington had been shocked by his experience: 'In all my life I have not experienced such anxiety, for I must confess I have never been so close before to defeat.'

Whether Napoleon could have won at Waterloo is a question frequently asked and, if he had, what would have been the consequences? Wellington, for one, was in no doubt that the French could have won at Waterloo, and by defeating him – the best general by far that the Allies had – Napoleon's prestige would have regained much of what had been lost by his defeats in 1813 and 1814. Nor can it be assumed that the large Russian and Austrian armies under Kutuzov and Schwarzenburg would have done any better than Wellington against a revitalized Napoleon. And if the Austrians and Russians, as had happened before, had been prepared to come to terms with France, then perhaps the British-led Seventh Coalition would have collapsed as had so many others in the previous 20 years. In the event, Napoleon did not win. But it had been 'a close-run thing'.

The battle of Waterloo ended an era – a period of transition between the 18th and 19th centuries, an age that bore the name and imprint of a man who had spread the legacy of the French Revolution throughout Europe. In the end the nationalism that he had helped to foster in Europe united to overthrow him. Yet ultimately it was the naval and economic power of Britain – first demonstrated at Trafalgar and then carried on by Wellington in Spain and finally on the ridge at Waterloo – that put an end to the era of Napoleon. And if it was not a wholly British army that triumphed at Waterloo – and the role of the Prussians must never be underestimated – it was British money that paid for the victory. The great age of Britain as a world power opened in 1815 as the door closed on France's imperial greatness. Wellington bequeathed Europe a century of relative peace after Waterloo, and his own country a century of unparalleled wealth and power.

The Battle of Gettysburg 1863

Gettysburg
Confederates
Commander:	General Robert E. Lee
Left wing:	Lt. General Ewell's II Corps
Centre:	Lt. General A.P. Hill's III Corps
Right wing:	Lt. General Longstreet's I Corps
Numbers:	76,224, including Major-General Jeb Stuart's cavalry division of 12,000, and 272 guns

Unionists
Commander:	Major-General Philip Meade
	I Corps under Major-General Reynolds
	II Corps under Major-General Hancock
	III Corps under Major-General Sickles
	V Corps under Major-General Sykes
	VI Corps under Major-General Sedgwick
	XI Corps under Major-General Howard
	XII Corps under Major-General Slocum
Numbers:	90,000, including Pleasanton's cavalry division

By May 1863 the Confederacy was facing a military crisis in its struggle to win independence from the Union. Although in Virginia General Robert E. Lee had won a series of brilliant victories over the Union armies there, in other sectors matters were less hopeful. Vicksburg, the great Southern fortress on the Mississippi, was blockaded and on the point of falling to General Ulysses S. Grant, while the Atlantic coastline of the Confederacy was actively patrolled by the Union navy, so that supplies and munitions from Europe were becoming rare. And there was the fear that at any time Union troops could make an amphibious landing somewhere on the coast of the Southern states, cutting the Confederacy in half. Confederate President Jefferson Davis was anxious to lift the prevailing mood of gloom and asked Lee, his commander-in-chief, to plan an offensive.

Ironically, the situation was no different in Washington. A series of disastrous defeats suffered by the Union Army of the Potomac had caused President Lincoln to shuffle his pack of generals like a Mississippi gambler. Unfortunately he always came up with a joker. Defeats at Second Manassas, Fredericksburg and Chancellorsville had created in the minds of Union generals such a fear of 'Bob' Lee that they were half beaten before they began each battle. Lincoln knew he needed a victory to restore confidence in the Union cause.

In May 1863 Lee was in favour of taking the initiative against the Union by invading the North and prosecuting the war there. Virginia had suffered devastation in the previous two years, and Lee considered it would be preferable to live off the rich lands of Maryland and Pennsylvania. The morale of his Army of Northern Virginia had never been higher, and further victories, with their consequent threat to the security of Washington, might force Lincoln's administration to negotiate a peace settlement. A display of Confederate strength in the heartland of the North might also encourage foreign powers like France and Britain to recognize the South and offer financial, even military assistance. In spite of the reservations of General James Longstreet, who thought the invasion plan too risky, Jefferson Davis gave Lee the go-ahead, and the Confederates began to prepare for the campaign.

The Confederate Army of Northern Virginia comprised three infantry corps: I Corps under Longstreet, II Corps under Ewell, and III Corps led by A.P. Hill. The cavalry division of 12,000 was commanded by the brilliant and dashing 'Jeb' Stuart, 'the best cavalry leader ever foaled in North America'. In all Lee had 76,224 men and 272 guns. Against him 'Fighting Joe' Hooker fielded 90,000 Union troops in seven infantry corps – each smaller than their Confederate equivalents: I Corps under Reynolds, II Corps (Hancock), III Corps (Sickles), V Corps (Meade), VI Corps (Sedgwick), XI Corps (Howard) and XII Corps (Slocum); Pleasanton was in command of the cavalry.

President Lincoln was not happy with his army commander, Joe Hooker. At Chancellorsville Hooker had been humiliated by Lee, and only the absence of an obvious successor prevented his replacement earlier. But Hooker seemed intent on professional suicide and, after a dispute with Halleck, he offered the president his resignation. To his surprise it was accepted. George Meade, woken from his bed by a presidential aide, asked, 'Am I under arrest?' 'No',

A Union battery at the battle of Gettysburg; photograph by Mathew Brady. PN

replied the aide, 'Hooker has resigned. You are appointed Commander-in-Chief of the Army of the Potomac.' Meade was its fifth commander in just 10 months. No sooner had Meade got used to his 'new hat' than he received alarming news: Jeb Stuart's cavalry division was raiding the outskirts of Washington and had captured a supply train of 125 wagons no more than 10 miles from the unfinished Capitol building. Meade had already been outmanoeuvred and was no longer standing between the enemy and the national capital. What Meade did not know was that Stuart was fighting a war all of his own, and was no longer in direct contact with Lee. Carefree Jeb Stuart, a showy dresser who often rode into battle accompanied by a man playing the banjo, sometimes had more courage than sense. And this

was one of those occasions. Content to cut telegraph lines, rip up railway tracks and generally enjoy himself, Stuart was not keeping Lee apprised of enemy movements. To an extent Lee, short of his cavalry 'eyes', was blindly groping his way north and had no idea of the whereabouts on the Union army. He decided to concentrate his forces around the towns of Cashtown and Gettysburg in Pennsylvania. Meade, on the other hand, was better informed, receiving constant reports from local people on the movements of the Confederates. Even so, the battle of Gettysburg began as an 'encounter battle', with neither commander wholly in charge of his troops at the outset.

The first encounter between blue and grey occurred because Confederate general A.P. Hill received news that a large consignment of Union army shoes were in a warehouse in the town of Gettysburg. Marching divisions like Hill's and Stonewall Jackson's got through their shoes at an incredible rate, and many Southern soldiers were forced to walk barefoot when their shoes had worn out. So the chance of seizing such vital supplies was enough to persuade Hill to order his troops into the town on 1 July 1863. As they marched down the road into Gettysburg, Hill's men encountered fire from two Union cavalry brigades, led by John Buford. Buford had dismounted his men and lined the hedgerows with marksmen. Knowing that he would soon be outnumbered, he sent a messenger to Reynolds, commanding I Corps, requesting he move his men up in support. Hill, meanwhile, had sent gallopers back to Lee to report that he had encountered the Union army at Gettysburg.

Buford's cavalrymen were at their last gasp when Reynolds came up at the double with his famous 'Iron Brigade', made up of Midwestern troops kitted out in black hats, and reputedly the toughest fighters in the Union army. Although Reynolds was killed by a sniper and the Midwesterners took over 60 per cent casualties, they held Hill's men in check. To the north of them Confederate general Ewell with his II Corps was being held up by Howard's 'Dutch' XI Corps, and in all some 24,000 Confederates were in action against 19,000 Federals. Lee arrived on the field before Meade and, though it was not a battle of his choosing, he ordered Hill and Ewell to pour in everything they had to try to win a quick victory. Under continuous assaults from Ewell, Howard's corps collapsed and fled back towards Cemetery Hill, leaving the remnants of Reynolds corps open to a flank attack. But Ewell — suffering severely from dyspepsia — seemed overwhelmed by his opportunity and did not take his chance to crack the Union I Corps. When Lee ordered him to pursue Howard and take Cemetery Hill, he fatally added the words 'if practicable'. Ewell took him at his word and decided it was not practicable; the Union position was too strong and the chance was lost. More and more Union troops were pouring into Gettysburg and deploying around Culp's Hill and Cemetery Hill in the north and right along Cemetery Ridge in the west for two miles before reaching the hill named Little Round Top in the south. Meade arrived after nightfall, and the day ended with the Confederates feeling that they had missed a great opportunity.

On 2 July Lee was convinced that he would achieve the great victory that had eluded him the previous day through Ewell's indecision. His confidence was high — too high, as he would later admit. He told one of his friends that he would 'throw an overwhelming force on their advance, crush it, follow up the success, drive one corps back on another, and by successive repulses and surprises . . . create a panic and virtually destroy the army

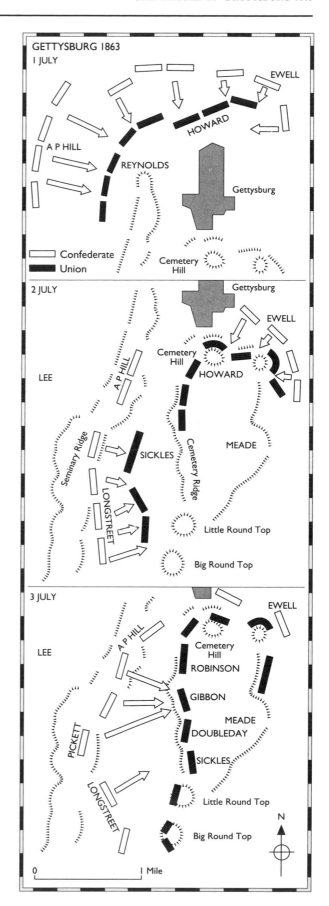

GETTYSBURG 1863
1 JULY

EWELL

HOWARD

A P HILL

REYNOLDS

Gettysburg

☐ Confederate
■ Union

Cemetery Hill

2 JULY

Gettysburg

EWELL

A P HILL

Cemetery Hill

HOWARD

LEE

Seminary Ridge

SICKLES

MEADE

Cemetery Ridge

LONGSTREET

Little Round Top

Big Round Top

3 JULY

EWELL

A P HILL

Cemetery Hill

ROBINSON

LEE

GIBBON

MEADE

DOUBLEDAY

PICKETT

SICKLES

Little Round Top

LONGSTREET

N

Big Round Top

0   1 Mile

... The war will be over and we shall achieve the recognition of our independence.' He was in danger of hubris.

General James Longstreet was at odds with himself on 2 July, and at odds with Robert E. Lee. He did not share Lee's confidence. Gazing through his telescope at the Union positions on Cemetery Ridge he thought them far too strong to attack. There was a danger that the battle could become a Fredericksburg in reverse, with his men dying on Cemetery Ridge just as Burnside's bluecoats had died on Marye's Heights the previous year. Surely it would be better to turn the Union's southern flank? But Lee was adamant: his men were eager and confident in their ability to beat the Unionists, as they had done so often in the past. Lee gestured at Cemetery Hill, saying 'The enemy is there, and I am going to attack him there.' Longstreet replied, 'If he is there, it is because he is anxious that we should

attack him; a good reason, in my judgement, for not doing so.'

But if Lee was having trouble with Longstreet, Meade was having his own problems. Although Union III Corps had been posted to Cemetery Ridge, their commander, Dan Sickles, had taken it upon himself to advance two divisions half a mile closer to the enemy to occupy what he considered a better position. Meade was furious, but it was too late to do anything about it. Sickles had left his men disconnected from the rest of the Union army, with both flanks open. Confederate gallopers brought Longstreet the startling news that both hills to the south – Little Round Top and Big Round Top – were unoccupied. His divisional commanders urged him to disobey Lee's orders and turn the Union's left flank. But Longstreet refused. He had already tried to change Lee's mind once on that score and would not try again. As a result, in a fit of pique, Longstreet ordered his corps to attack Sickles head-on. Some of the bloodiest fighting of the whole war took place before the Confederates punched a hole in III Corps. But Meade had reserves ready and fed them in when and where the gaps appeared.

The drama of the second day concerned Little Round Top. An Alabama brigade finally tried to occupy the hill and use it to enfilade Cemetery Ridge with their guns. But they were stopped by the fortunate intervention of Meade's chief engineer, General Gouverneur Warren, who happened by chance to be in the right place at the right time, collected troops from V Corps, including the 20th Maine Regiment, and rushed them up the slopes of the hill just in time to meet the Alabamians coming up the other side. The regiment's colonel, Joshua Chamberlain – a university professor in civilian life – summed up the situation quickly. His men – short of ammunition – were all that stood between the Confederates and the chance of rolling up the flank of the entire Union army. Ordering them to fix bayonets he led them in a charge that at least one soldier, Theodore Gerrish, was never to forget:

With a cheer and a flash of his sword, that sent inspiration along the line, full ten paces to the front he sprang ... 'Come on! Come on, boys!' he shouts. The colour sergeant and the brave colour guard follow, and with one wild yell of anguish wrung from its tortured heart, the regiment charged.

The rebels were confounded by the movement. We struck them with a fearful shock. They recoil, stagger, break and run, and like avenging demons our men pursue. The rebels rush towards a stone wall ... A band of our men leap over the wall and capture at least a hundred prisoners.

A dead Confederate sharpshooter at Round Top. The American Civil War was one of the first wars in which the horrors of battle were captured by the camera; photograph by Alexander Gardner. PN

While Longstreet's men were bearing the brunt

ROBERT E. LEE

No general in the history of warfare has been more loved by friend and foe alike than Robert E. Lee. His death in 1870 was an event for national mourning, even so recently after a bitter and divisive civil war. Lee was born into the Virginia aristocracy, son of the famous Revolutionary War general 'Light Horse Harry' Lee. After graduating from West Point he saw service in the Mexican War, along with most of his colleagues and opponents in the Civil War to come. When Civil War came in 1861 he was offered – and declined – command of the Union Army; instead he showed his loyalty to Virginia by resigning his commission and joining the army of the Confederacy. In 1862 he was given command of the Army of Northern Virginia and soon established a sound working relationship with brilliant subordinates like 'Stonewall' Jackson and 'Jeb' Stuart. Always fighting at a numerical and logistical disadvantage, Lee won a series of great victories – Second Manassas, Fredericksburg, Chancellorsville – before suffering defeat at Gettysburg in 1863. A modest man, Lee took the blame for this Southern disaster and offered to resign. Confederate president Jefferson Davis was wise enough to know he could not spare 'Marse Robert', and Lee continued to command Southern armies in the defence of Richmond, fighting Ulysses Grant to a standstill in dreadful attritional battles in 1864 and 1865, battles that must have broken the heart of such a generous soul. Lee surrendered to Grant at Appomattox on Sunday 9 April 1865, to save his nation further bloodshed.

Robert E. Lee, photographed in 1862. AKG

---

of the fighting along Cemetery Ridge, Ewell was facing an altogether easier situation around Cemetery Hill and Culp's Hill. Meade, as Lee had expected, was transferring troops from the north to support the hard-pressed Sickles. But again Ewell showed a lack of initiative and the chance to assault these two positions was missed. At the end of the second day honours were even, but Lee was convinced that on the third day he would sweep the Unionists off Cemetery Ridge.

Lee was tired and ill with diarrhoea. He had allowed Cemetery Ridge to become an obsession with him, and instead of planning to outflank Meade he was content to batter away at the Union defences in search of a decisive victory. For the third day of the battle he planned a huge artillery bombardment of the ridge to be followed by a frontal attack by three divisions. Longstreet was horror-struck. He could not understand Lee's

obsession and continued to argue for an attack on Meade's weak left flank. Lee refused to listen, instructing him to attack with 15,000 men against the Union centre on the ridge. 'General Lee,' Longstreet told him, 'there never was a body of fifteen thousand men who could make that attack successfully.' Lee simply replied that his men could do it. Longstreet reported later, 'That day at Gettysburg was one of the saddest of my life.'

The third day of the battle is remembered for one of the epics of American military history – a transatlantic 'Charge of the Light Brigade' on a grand scale. After a massive artillery duel involving some 300 guns, the Confederate assault force assembled, led by General George Pickett, a handsome but unimaginative soldier who passed out bottom of the class at West Point. At 3.00 p.m. Pickett led his three brigades forward into the 'valley of death' – in fact, across open fields and orchards. They had three-quarters of a mile to cover before they could come to grips with the Unionists and all that time they would be exposed to grapeshot and canister shells fired by 200 Union guns and the bullets of tens of thousands of riflemen. It was a tall order, but Pickett was apparently unperturbed. The next 30 minutes were hell. The veteran Confederate troops, in perfect order and with flags flying, marched towards the Union lines into a storm of shells. In the hot summer sun their bayonets glistened menacingly, and when the terrifying 'rebel yell' was heard the attackers broke into a run. They cut through the first Union line, with General Armistead memorably pointing the way with his hat perched on the end of his sword, but Armistead fell alongside a Union gun and his men wavered as the Union reserves charged them. It was the high point of Pickett's charge, but already the men in grey were streaming back down the slope. Over half of the Confederate force became casualties, including 70 per cent of Pickett's own division. Lee was there to welcome back the stumbling survivors, muttering in a hopeless voice, 'It's all my fault . . . I'm sorry.'

The battle was lost. Lee had squandered the hard-fought gains of the first two days and was now in danger of succumbing to a Unionist counter-attack. He desperately worked to restore his defensive lines, always with half an eye on Cemetery Ridge, expecting every moment to hear a loud cheer that would signal that Meade was going over to the attack. But Lee need not have worried; Meade had no intention of risking the defensive victory that he had won. He was not a gambler by nature and, just six days in the job, it was too much to expect him to pursue the man who had hypnotized the whole Union army at Chancellorsville. Lincoln was furious that Meade allowed Lee to escape, and it eventually cost Meade his job. In fact, Lincoln had at last found a general he could work with – Ulysses S. Grant. Union victory in the war was still some way off, but after Gettysburg there was no longer any doubt that victory would be achieved.

Although Lee was able to withdraw from Gettysburg he knew that he had lost not just a battle but the war. There would be no more Southern offensives; it would be backs-to-the-wall from now on. The men he had thought invincible were now lying dead and injured along Cemetery Ridge. He had suffered 28,000 casualties to Meade's 23,000 – 39 per cent of his entire force. His best troops, veterans of all his victories, had been squandered and could not be replaced. Lee offered his resignation to Jefferson Davis, who refused it. The master had 'nodded' but there was no one who could serve the South better.

The battle of Gettysburg was a turning point in the Civil War and in American history. Washington was no longer in danger, and the chances of foreign powers recognizing the Confederacy had gone. Southerners understood the implications well. One wrote:

Events have succeeded one another with disastrous rapidity. One brief month ago we were apparently at the point of success. Lee was in Pennsylvania, threatening Harrisburg, and even Philadelphia. . . . Yesterday we rode on a pinnacle of success – today absolute ruin seems to be our portion. The Confederacy totters to its destruction.

In the North the newspapers crowed: 'Victory! Waterloo Eclipsed' cried one; 'The charm of Robert Lee's invincibility is broken' observed another. After Gettysburg the defeat of the South and of slavery was certain. Lincoln had fought the war to preserve the Union, and Lee's defeat meant that the United States would remain one nation. On 19 November 1863 Lincoln spoke these words at the dedication of the Northern Cemetery at Gettysburg:

Four score and seven years ago, our fathers brought forth upon this continent, a new nation, conceived in Liberty, and dedicated to the proposition that all men are created equal.

Now we are engaged in a great civil war, testing whether that nation, or any nation so conceived, and so dedicated, can long endure. We are met on a great battlefield of that war. We have come to dedicate a portion of it, as a final resting place for those who here gave their lives that that nation might live . . .

Meade's victory at Gettysburg ensured that Lincoln's nation did live.

The Battle of Königgrätz 1866

Königgrätz

Austrians

Commander:	Field Marshal Ludwig Ritter von Benedek
I Corps:	General Eduard Count von Clam-Gallas
II Corps:	Lt. Field Marshal Karl Count von Thun-Hohenstadt
III Corps:	Ernest, Archduke of Austria
IV Corps:	Lt. Field Marshal Tassilo Count Festetics de Tolona
VI Corps:	Lt. Field Marshal Wilhelm Freiherr von Ramming
VIII Corps:	Major-General von Weber
X Corps:	Lt. Field Marshal Ludwig von Gablenz
Numbers:	250,000 men, including 25,000 Saxons

Prussians

Commanders:	King Wilhelm I, General von Moltke
1st Army:	Prince Friederich Carl with 115,000 men (II, III, IV Corps)
Army of the Elbe:	General von Bittenfeld with 48,000 men (3 divisions)
2nd Army:	Crown Prince Friederich Wilhelm with 93,000 men (I, V, VI Corps)
Numbers:	256,000 men

The destruction of the main Austrian army by the Prussians at the battle of Königgrätz in 1866 acted like a bombshell on European statesmen. For centuries Austria had spoken as the voice of the German-speaking peoples in international affairs, and the equilibrium of Central Europe had seemed to depend on a healthy Habsburg state. Now everything had been thrown into the melting pot. British newspapers produced shock leaders: 'Events of so startling a character have taken place in the theatre of the war and present such an aspect of importance towards the future that the mind is dizzied by its attempt to estimate their real importance.' The *Spectator* claimed that 'Thirty dynasties have been swept away, the fate of twenty millions of civilized men has been affected for ever . . .' The French, for once more measured than their British counterparts, noted 'One of those formidable battles which declare the irrevocable verdict of

force upon the destiny of nations has been fought in Bohemia. The battle of Sadowa [Königgrätz] has revealed the armed might of Prussia and has struck a perhaps irreparable blow at the political power of Austria.' The French were right. The battle of Königgrätz had changed the face of European politics in so fundamental a way that it made an eventual world war inevitable. The German historian Wilhelm Schüssler went further: 'A figure like Hitler is hardly to be explained without Königgrätz, for the result of that battle for Austria was an increasing decline of its German element, the rise of the Slavs, and the inflamed nationalism of the border struggles.'

War between Austria and Prussia for control of Germany came in 1866 as the culmination of a struggle that had started far back in the 17th century, with the development of Brandenburg-Prussia under Frederick William, the 'Great Elector'. During the 18th century Frederick the Great of Prussia had fought two lengthy wars against the Habsburgs to win from them and keep the rich province of Silesia, and though the Austrians and Prussians had found common ground against Napoleon, by 1830 their paths were diverging again. Prussia saw her future within a Germany united around her; Austria, with her millions of Hungarians, Italians and Slavs, preferred a federated German state. It was the diplomacy of Otto von Bismarck that was to untie the 'Gordian knot . . . of friendly dualism' and put the issue of Prussian or Austrian domination of Germany to the test of war.

In 1866 Austria's military reputation was much higher than that of Prussia. The steadiness of her white-coated infantry and the dash of her Magyar cavalry had been demonstrated in wars against Piedmont in 1848, France in 1859 and Denmark in 1864. In each of these wars her troops had fought with élan and some success. Her artillery was of an excellent standard and in 1866 she could field 736 rifled cannon and 58 smooth-bore guns, against Prussia's 492 rifled cannon and 306 smooth-bores. Her artillerists had recent experience of war – in 1859 and 1864 – and had carried out trials in Bohemia, on the ground where the decisive battle would be fought. The Prussians were also heavily outnumbered, but Bismarck's skilful diplomacy had brought Piedmont into the war against Austria with the promise of Venetia, and the Austrians had to deploy 3 of their 10 corps against the Italians. But the main difference between the armies lay in the infantry weapon and doctrine. The Austrian 'white-coats' were equipped with the Lorenz muzzle-loader, accurate up to 400 yards and during the war against France in 1859 considered better than the French rifle. But as a muzzle-loader its rate of fire was only a fifth that of the Prussian needle-gun. Ironically, the Austrians had rejected the needle-gun as they said it wasted bullets with its high rate of fire. But the Prussians disagreed, drilling their men to conserve ammunition and only use rapid fire at close quarters. When the Austrians saw the Prussian weapon used in the Austro-Prussian war against Denmark in 1864, they evolved an answer to the heavy rate of fire produced by the needle-gun. It was called the *Stosstaktik* and involved the Austrians

coming quickly to close quarters and using the bayonet. This could be effective in some situations, but was enormously costly in terms of casualties. The greatest difference between the two sides was in the quality of military command. Austrian leadership was often very poor: unlike their Prussian counterparts, the Austrian generals were aristocratic and amateurish, and many were incompetent and defeatist. At the head of the army the brilliant Magyar, Field Marshal Ludwig Ritter von Benedek, the 'Bayard of the Austrian Army', became profoundly depressed at his army's prospects. Against him, the Prussian commander, General Helmuth Karl Bernard von Moltke, though old in years, was young in spirit and mind, aggressive and prepared to gamble.

When war broke out on 15 June 1866 Prussia knew that the sympathies of many of the German states would be with Austria, and a number of them allied with her in the coming struggle. But Moltke disregarded the threat from this quarter and concentrated on the main struggle against the Austrians in Bohemia. Using the efficient Prussian railway system – the first time in military history that trains had been so used – he assembled three armies: the 2nd Army of 93,000 men under Crown Prince

Bismarck at Königgrätz – one of the last politicians to be present on a battlefield. IPA

Wilhelm in Silesia; the 1st Army of 115,000 men under Prince Friedrich Carl on the Saxon frontier; and the Elbe Army of 48,000 men under General von Bittenfeld further west in Prussian Saxony. The whole Prussian force amounted to 256,000 men, covering a front of 260 miles. To any student of Napoleonic warfare it was a colossal mistake. To divide and disperse armies in this way invited destruction by a concentrated enemy striking at each part in turn. But Moltke was gambling on the fact that the Austrian commander, Benedek, would wait to be attacked. Moltke was right – but, as Bismarck realized, it was a big risk.

The Austrians had assembled their full strength of seven corps at Olmütz in Moravia, and at first Benedek was indeed content to wait for the Prussians to make all the moves. First Bittenfeld crossed into Saxony, and the Elector of Saxony, an ally of Austria, withdrew his army of 25,000 men into Bohemia. Moltke now decided that his armies were too dispersed and ordered them to converge on the town of Gitschin in Bohemia. But as the Austrians were now marching in that same direction, Moltke was planning to unite his forces in the face of the enemy – a very brave and potentially fatal strategy. The two western Prussian armies – the Elbe and the 1st – now united under Prince Friedrich Carl and moved towards Gitschin, defeating an enemy force there quite easily. But the 2nd Army was having a much tougher time. At Trautenau on 27 June the Prussian I Corps suffered a severe setback against Field Marshal Ludwig von Gablenz's X Corps, though the casualties – 4700 Austrian against 1300 Prussian – were an ominous pointer to what would happen when the needle-gun was used against the main Austrian army. On the same day, the Prussian V Corps under General Steinmetz successfully beat off attacks from Ramming's VI Corps – again the needle-gun proving its efficiency in Prussian hands.

Benedek must have known from these two encounters that he had stumbled on the whole Prussian 2nd Army, which he outnumbered by more than 2 to 1. The chance of total victory was in his hands. If he could fall on the crown prince and destroy his force before the Prussian 1st Army could join the battle he would be able to secure a decisive victory. But Benedek's thoughts were dark ones. He had not sought the command and felt inadequate to the task of manoeuvring troops on this scale. His successes in Italy in 1859 had been as a defensive general and he was afraid to commit himself to a wholesale advance in the face of an enemy who was better armed and trained than himself. His own Italian troops were now beginning

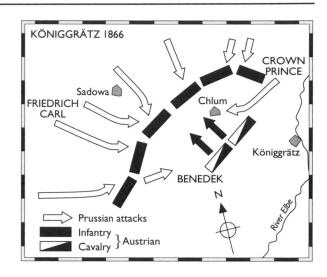

KÖNIGGRÄTZ 1866

CROWN PRINCE
Sadowa
FRIEDRICH CARL
Chlum
Königgrätz
BENEDEK
N
River Elbe

Prussian attacks
Infantry } Austrian
Cavalry

to crack, and his senior staff officers were panicking and advising him to retreat to protect Vienna. Instead of attacking the 2nd Army he ordered a retreat southwards and took up a new position facing the Prussian 1st Army, with the fortress of Königgrätz at his back.

Prince Friedrich Carl, commanding the 1st Army and the Army of the Elbe, attacked the new Austrian position on 3 July, with only a vague request to the crown prince to cover his flank. What Benedek had been afraid to do, the impetuous young prince was doing for him. When Moltke heard of what had happened he experienced his worst feelings of the entire campaign. Could Benedek even now achieve what he had missed so far and defeat the Prussians in detail? Moltke immediately sent peremptory orders to the crown prince to advance with all speed 'to the sound of the guns'. It would take him several hours to arrive; could the 1st Army hold out long enough to allow the 2nd Army to administer the *coup de grâce*?

Intense fighting had started at 8.00 a.m. along the Bistritz River. Historian Gordon Craig describes the splendour and variety of the Austrian troops:

The infantry with its white coats and blue trousers, green-clad Jaeger wearing cross-belted greatcoats and broad-brimmed hats decked with capercailzie feathers, hussars with yellow-trimmed *tshakos*, and uhlans with red-bordered *schapkas* and gaily-flagged lances, brown-coated artillerymen and high-booted cuirassiers with crested helmets – all shouting together as the staff with its gold-laced cocked hats and light green plumes rode by.

But towards this gaudy array was marching, deliberately and methodically, a sea of men in grey-green uniforms. It was the advance of the 19th century over the patchwork quilt of the Middle Ages. Firing

THE NEEDLE-GUN

It is often claimed that Prussia's victory at Königgrätz was due to the fact that the Prussian infantry fought with the breech-loading 'needle-gun', while the Austrians still used the muzzle-loader – a weapon with a rate of fire only a fifth as fast. There is some truth in this, although Austria's superiority in artillery came close to offsetting the Prussian advantage in infantry arms.

Lest it be supposed that the breech-loader was a new idea it should be stressed that the notion had been in existence for 200 years, and only the failure to construct a barrel strong enough to withstand the explosion of the charge prevented it from being adopted before. In 1835 a gunmaker named von Dreyse devised a breech-loader with a needle-pointed striker that fired the cartridge, hence earning its name of 'needle-gun'. The Prussians adopted the gun from 1841 but the Austrians rejected it, preferring their own Lorenz muzzle-loading rifle, which had a far greater range. The needle-gun could fire five shots each minute with a 65% rate of accuracy at 300 paces. In 1866 all front-line Prussian units were equipped with the Dreyse breech-loader and most Austrian officers were aware of the dangers that they faced in relying on their single-shot Lorenz rifles. In fact, Austrian fears of the needle-gun persuaded Benedek to emphasize the need for his infantry to come to close quarters with the enemy and rely on the bayonet. This cost many Austrian soldiers their lives in the 1866 war.

accurately and rapidly the Prussians shot down the 'white-coats' in their thousands and turned back their increasingly desperate bayonet charges. From a hill near the village of Dub the Prussian king Wilhelm I and Bismarck, the latter dressed in the uniform of a major in the Landwehr cavalry, watched the fighting with some trepidation. Moltke, stuffed up with a cold and with a handkerchief pressed to his nose, stood alongside them, waiting for news of the 2nd Army. When the king asked Moltke what arrangements had been made for a possible withdrawal, the old man replied, 'Here there will be no retreat. Here we are fighting for the very existence of Prussia.' It was Bismarck – with a telescope – who first noticed that the Austrian artillery had shifted their attention to what he had at first taken for a line of trees to the north. But the trees were moving. He handed his telescope to Moltke triumphantly. Moltke looked long and hard and then turned to the king: 'The campaign is decided and in accordance with Your Majesty's

desires!' It was the 2nd Army coming into action on the Austrian right flank.

Benedek had lost personal control of the battle, and some Austrian generals were making decisions of their own. Field Marshal Ramming launched an independent counter-attack and drove the Prussians out of Rosberitz and Chulm. The fighting in the village was described by an Austrian officer:

The air was literally filled with shells, shrapnel and canister; branches of trees, stones and splinters flew around our ears and wounded many, and for extra measure, Prussian shells landed not infrequently also. The shells crashed through the buildings; walls collapsed and buried the sound and the wounded; big clouds of dust rose in the air, made up of pulverized plaster and bricks mingled with the smoke of the powder. It was as if the world was coming to an end. But nothing could make the brave fusiliers quail; they fell in rows, but they were worthy of the old breed . . . they didn't waver a foot's breadth.

But with the Prussian 2nd Army pouring onto the battlefield Ramming could not hold on and the Prussians retook the villages. Although the battle was lost, the Austrians fought on with a fanatical courage that deserved a better cause and better leaders. By 3 p.m. Benedek had ordered a full retreat. Ironically, the Austrian commander came to life when it was too late and organized a brilliant withdrawal over the Elbe towards Olmütz under cover of his excellent artillery – which had outshot the Prussians throughout – and his cavalry. During the Austrian withdrawal a vast cavalry battle took place in which over 10,000 horsemen from both sides drove and hacked at each other in a swirling mass of dust. Once over the Elbe, the Austrians waited for the next round of fighting. Their losses at Königgrätz were enormous: 43,000 casualties, including 5658 killed. The Prussians had lost just over 9000 men, with under 2000 killed, mostly in the 1st Army, which had borne the brunt of the early fighting.

Better news for Austria came from the Italian front, where at Custozza the Archduke Albert had soundly thrashed the Piedmontese, and in a naval battle Admiral Tegetthoff had beaten the modern Italian fleet off the island of Lissa in the Adriatic. If the three Austrian corps from the Italian theatre had now marched north to join Benedek's army at Olmütz – and Albert had replaced the broken Benedek – the Prussians might have faced a second round far more dangerous than the first. But the emperor Franz Joseph had had enough and asked for terms.

Whereas Wilhelm I and some of his generals wanted to press on to take Vienna and humiliate

Austria, Bismarck was adamant that victory at Königgrätz was enough for what Prussia needed – leadership of Germany. Afterwards, he foresaw that a united Germany would need Austria as a friend against the probable enmity of France and Russia. The generals gave in and Bismarck had his way. But having 'killed' Austria, Prussia was tying herself to a corpse. Without a role in Germany, Austria looked increasingly to the Balkans, where she came into conflict with the national aspirations of Serbia and the long-term policies of Russia. With Germany standing at her back, ready to support her, Austria felt encouraged to pursue aggressive policies in the

The 1st Prussian Guards Regiment helping to retake the village of Chlum from the Austrians. AKG

Balkans that were bound to earn her the hostility of Russia. And a Prussia – dominant in northern Germany – was bound to come into conflict with France along the Rhineland. All it needed was for these trends to become set in stone by alliances and ententes, and the way to a major European war would be clearly marked. That war was to come in 1914.

The Battle of Sedan
1870

Sedan

French
Commanders: Emperor Napoleon III, Marshal
                  MacMahon, General Wimpfen
Numbers: 130,000 men (I, V, VII, XII Corps) 419
                  guns

Prussians
Commander: General von Moltke
Army of the Meuse: Crown Prince of Saxony
III Army: Crown Prince Friederich
                         Wilhelm, General Blumenthal

The exclusion of Austria from German affairs after 1866 had made Prussia the dominant German state. But Germany was still a confederation in which Prussia was just one – even though the most important – member. Prussian chancellor Otto von Bismarck was not content with this and needed a way of making the other German states unite with Prussia to form a single entity, with the Prussian king, Wilhelm I, as emperor of a united Germany. In the war of 1866 the south German states had sided with Austria against Prussia, and Bismarck decided that a war with France would be the best way of tying the German states together. He was fortunate in that the French emperor, Napoleon III, was facing severe domestic problems and was hoping to achieve a major foreign-policy success to boost his popularity at home. The issue of the Spanish succession would hardly have provided a *casus belli* for states that were not committed already to the path of war. Bismarck had prudently consulted the Prussian commander-in-chief Moltke and the minister of war Roon and gained their assurance that Prussia could defeat France, before he made his famous emendation to the Ems telegram. When France declared war on Prussia on 19 July 1870, it was almost by mutual consent.

France was going into war in 1870 for the most frivolous of reasons: the ill-health and declining vigour of a very vain man. Napoleon III still lived under the shadow of his uncle, the great Napoleon Bonaparte. France still expected him to undertake glittering foreign adventures, even though his personal experiences at the battles of Magenta and Solferino in Italy in 1859 had sickened him and disabused him of the notion of military glory. Nevertheless, war was popular with the French masses: 'The idea of war with Prussia is warmly received by the bulk of the population . . . No one for a moment doubts the results of the war. Everywhere in town and village, the same confidence is shown.' Crowds marched through Paris singing the *Marseillaise* and shouting '*A bas la Prusse!*' and '*A Berlin!*' The French had the confidence of ignorance, but they had entered the war without allies and without a proper appreciation of the strength of their enemy.

On 28 July the emperor and the prince imperial set off by train for Metz, where Napoleon took supreme control of the eight corps comprising the French army, which was occupying a 150-mile front from Thionville to Belfort. The emperor had inspired his men with tales of earlier French successes: 'Whatever road we take beyond our frontiers, we shall find glorious traces of our fathers. We will prove ourselves worthy of them.' But instead of an army ready to spring over the frontier and grasp the Germans by the throat, Napoleon found chaos and incompetence. French numbers – which should have exceeded 385,000 – were less than half of the 430,000 at Germany's disposal, and there were shortages of every kind in munitions and supplies. Many reservists who were rushed into the front line to fill the gaps found there were no uniforms for them, while others had no weapons. Officers could not find their units; generals had maps of Germany but none of France. Everywhere was a shortage of ambulances, canteens and baggage wagons.

The Germans had expected to face an attack from the French and were surprised when it failed to materialize. They would hardly have believed the chaos over the border, for their mobilization had proceeded smoothly. On 1 August a British visitor to Oberammergau reported, 'I was going to see the Miracle Play; but Jesus has been taken off to serve in the artillery, with Judas Iscariot as his superior officer.'

French commanders like Bazaine, MacMahon and Canrobert were heroes of an earlier age of French military adventures – in Algeria, the Crimea, Italy and Mexico – but they were now facing professionals, who had seen service against Austria just four years before. These German generals had no illusions about '*La Gloire*'; they knew that modern war was a serious matter. On the borders at Wissembourg and Wörth the French suffered early defeats that set the tone for the war as a whole. Hopes of an offensive collapsed, and Marshal Achille Bazaine, with three army corps, fell back on the fortress of Metz, while Marshal MacMahon retreated to Châlons, where the emperor joined him. By 21 August France faced a crisis. Bazaine was now besieged at Metz and Napoleon had to

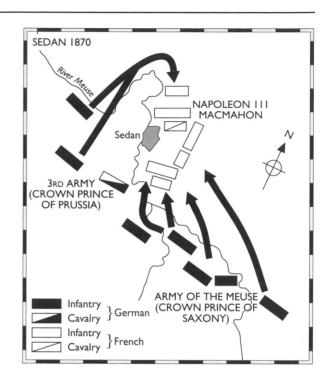

The Hessian 83rd Infantry Regiment in action against the Chasseurs d'Afrique. AKG

'Disabled!' A wounded French dragoon retreating during the Franco-Prussian War. PN

make an awkward decision: either to march to rescue Bazaine, which was what the French people demanded, or to fall back between the Germans and Paris, and so protect the capital. At a conference of war the emperor decided to fall back on Paris, only to have his order reversed by a furious telegram from the empress Eugénie, who told him that if he came back to Paris he would have to abdicate. While the French dithered, the Prussian commander-in-chief Moltke acted decisively to tighten the ring around Bazaine, who was defeated at two hard-fought battles at Vionville and at Gravelotte-St Privat, the latter the biggest battle of the war. Bazaine had had his chances in both battles, but by limp and inept leadership he had allowed an enemy almost as confused as himself to win decisive victories. Bazaine was now completely cut off from the emperor at Châlons.

MacMahon was still under orders from Paris to march to the relief of Bazaine, but Prussian armies were now driving him away from Metz towards the fortress town of Sedan, and on 31 August the marshal and the emperor found themselves penned up with 130,000 men in the town. The German commanders had no trouble tracking the French armies, as their movements were given daily in the

French newspapers. On 1 September the Prussians succeeded in encircling Sedan, and set up massive artillery batteries. A train bringing a week's food supplies to the stricken army arrived in Sedan, but, coming under gunfire, immediately returned to Mézières without unloading. Short of food and ammunition the French were doomed. As one soldier put it, *'Nous sommes dans un pot de chambre et nous y serons emmerdés.'* ('We're in a chamber pot and we're going to be shat on.') MacMahon was severely wounded in the fighting and surrendered command to General Wimpfen. The latter tried a break-out, but this failed. The French position was hopeless. A German officer relates:

The effect of our fire at such short range was truly terrible ... The spectacle of the carnage was horrible; the fearful cries of the victims of our shells reached as far as where we stood ... our superiority over the enemy was so overwhelming that we suffered no loss at all. The batteries fired as if at practice.

Napoleon ordered a white flag to be raised, but Wimpfen angrily tore it down. Eventually, however, even he knew there was no alternative but to surrender. Napoleon wrote to the Kaiser:

Sir, my brother,
    Not having died amidst my troops, there is nothing left for me but to hand over my sword into the hands of Your Majesty.
    I am Your Majesty's brother,
                                        Napoléon.

The entire French army of 124,000 men surrendered, along with 419 guns and *mitrailleuses* (an early form of machine gun). MacMahon's army of Châlons simply ceased to exist at a cost to the Germans of just 9000 men. Until 1940 this surrender at Sedan was the most disastrous in French history. Politically it marked the end of the Second Empire and was followed swiftly by the abdication of Napoleon III.

The war went on for a while, but France fought without hope. And Paris fought against the rest of the nation in the dreadful civil war of the Commune. But Napoleon III's surrender at Sedan had realistically ended the war. Defeat had humiliated France as never before, and when Bismarck insisted that Wilhelm I should be crowned Kaiser of the new German Empire in the Hall of Mirrors at Versailles he was ensuring that France would never forget that humiliation, nor the loss of Alsace and Lorraine that followed the Treaty of Frankfurt in 1871. But if a generation of Frenchmen looked longingly at the 'blue line of the Vosges', France knew that she could not regain her lost provinces without the help of an ally. Germany had grown too strong for any one European state to control, and so France looked to Russia as a future ally. Britain, too, had been surprised and alarmed by the ease with which the Germans had overcome France, hitherto Europe's pre-eminent military power. Britain's isolationist policy in Europe had depended on the continuing balance between European powers. Now that Germany had upset the balance it became essential for Britain to reverse the traditional hostility to France and see her as a potential ally against a Germany that, through her industrial, colonial and naval policies, was a threat to the *Pax Britannica* established by Britain in 1815. Thus Napoleon's defeat at Sedan paved the way for the division of Europe into armed camps of Triple Entente and Triple Alliance, needing just a spark to trigger off a general European war.

'Prussia's Royal Captive': Napoleon III and Bismarck on the morning after the French surrender at Sedan; from the painting by Camphausen. PN

The Battle of Tsushima 1905

Tsushima

Russians
Commander: Vice-Admiral Rozhestvensky
Battleships:

Name	Tonnage	Main Armament	Speed
Kniaz Suvorov	13,516	4 x 12 inch, 12 x 6 inch	17.6 knots
Imperator Alexander III	13,516	4 x 12 inch, 12 x 6 inch	17.6 knots
Borodino	13,516	4 x 12 inch, 12 x 6 inch	17.6 knots
Orel	13,516	4 x 12 inch, 12 x 6 inch	17.6 knots
Osslyaba	12,674	4 x 10 inch, 11 x 6 inch	18.3 knots
Sissoi Veliki	10,400	4 x 12 inch, 6 x 6 inch	15.7 knots
Navarin	10,200	4 x 12 inch, 8 x 6 inch	15.7 knots
Imperator Nikolai I	9672	2 x 12 inch, 4 x 9 inch	14.0 knots
Admiral Nakimov	8624	8 x 8 inch, 10 x 6 inch	16.6 knots

Japanese
Commander: Admiral Togo
Battleships and heavy cruisers:

Name	Tonnage	Main Armament	Speed
Mikasa	15,140	4 x 12 inch, 14 x 6 inch	18.0 knots
Asahi	15,200	4 x 12 inch, 14 x 6 inch	18.0 knots
Shikishima	14,850	4 x 12 inch, 14 x 6 inch	18.0 knots
Fuji	12,450	4 x 12 inch, 10 x 6 inch	18.0 knots
Idzumo	9750	4 x 8 inch, 14 x 6 inch	21.0 knots
Iwate	9750	4 x 8 inch, 14 x 6 inch	21.0 knots
Tokiwa	9750	4 x 8 inch, 14 x 6 inch	21.5 knots
Asama	9700	4 x 8 inch, 14 x 6 inch	21.5 knots

The emergence of Japan as a world power in the 20th century owed much to her development of a powerful navy. From the 1870s the Japanese had looked to Great Britain for naval instruction and advice on warship design, and, in 1871, 12 Japanese naval cadets attended the Royal Naval College at Greenwich. One of these was Heihachiro Togo, son of a samurai, and destined to be Japan's greatest sailor. In time he became the father of the modern Japanese navy, like Tirpitz in Germany, helping to build up a great fleet for his country.

The Russo-Japanese War broke out in 1904, essentially over Russia's presence at Port Arthur (on the Liaodong peninsula in what is now northern China) and her territorial claims in Manchuria – which conflicted with those of the Japanese. Without any formal declaration of war Japan attacked the Russian Far East fleet at Port Arthur on the night of 8 February 1904, torpedoing two battleships and a cruiser. From that moment the Japanese, although inferior in numbers, dominated the seaways, enabling them to transport their army to Korea and southern Manchuria, and to blockade the Russian fleet in Port Arthur. On 10 August the Russians tried to break out of the port, but were heavily defeated at the battle of the Yellow Sea. The remnants of the Russian fleet returned to Port Arthur, playing no further part in the war.

However, the Russians did not cut their losses and sue for peace, as most observers thought likely after this setback. Instead they reached the astounding conclusion that their salvation lay in their Baltic Fleet, which, by the shortest sea route, was 18,000 miles away. Admiral Rozhestvensky, commander of this northern fleet, was now presented with the unenviable task of sailing most of the way round the world to meet an enemy who had already defeated a naval squadron stronger than his own. But the immediate problem was that between the Gulf of Finland and Port Arthur there was no Russian base, and in time of war the ports of neutral nations and even those of Russia's ally, France, would be closed to him. Rozhestvensky had to rely for coal on prearranged meetings at sea with the commercial merchant vessels of the German Hamburg-Amerika line, and the coaling of warships in the open sea was an onerous and dangerous task. In addition to the low morale of his fleet there was a feeling that there was danger everywhere and that every hand was turned against them. One officer wrote, 'We shall have about as much chance as a gamecock would have in a battle with a vulture.'

In the North Sea a 'full-scale attack by Japanese ships' turned out to be a British trawler fleet from Hull. Incredibly the Russian battleships opened fire on the trawlers, damaging several and sinking one, as well as suffering hits that they inflicted on each other – the *Aurora* had four hits below the waterline and the ship's priest had his hand shot away. Rozhestvensky narrowly avoided causing a war between Britain and Russia, and was widely condemned and ridiculed in the newspapers of the world.

Meanwhile, at the Admiralty in St Petersburg, Rozhestvensky's enemy, Klado, had decided that reinforcements should be sent to join him. Anything would do, however unfit and derelict it might be. After all, it would increase the number of targets the Japanese would have to fire at. Rozhestvensky had originally condemned these 'old tubs' as worthless and nothing more than a millstone, which would hold back the rest of the fleet. They were jokingly called the 'sink-by-themselves' squadron by the Russian sailors. When the admiral heard that these ancient ships were to be sent to join him he decided to do everything in his power to avoid rendezvousing with them.

In spite of his efforts to mould his fleet into a fighting unit Rozhestvensky was constantly borne down by the inefficiency of his subordinate commanders. The fleet's repair ship, the *Kamchatka*, was a particular problem, having apparently fired 300 shells in a battle with three enemy ships: a Swedish merchantman, a German trawler and a French schooner, and later having signalled to the flagship, 'Do you see torpedo boats?' A general alarm was sounded throughout the fleet until the repair ship admitted it had used the wrong code and had simply meant, 'We are all right now.'

The worst problem for Rozhestvensky was that he knew – and the best of his officers knew – that they were all thoroughly incompetent and that they would have been better advised to turn back and risk being called cowards. They were not cowards, but they found it difficult to avoid appearing buffoons. To those who took their work seriously this was a heavy blow to morale. They would fight bravely when the time came but it would be futile because they were not trained to fight a modern naval battle. News that reinforcements were being sent under Admiral Nebogatoff was the final straw. Their present ships were not good enough. What was the use of sending unseaworthy hulks 18,000 miles to be sunk off Japan? To Rozhestvensky this was enough to bring on acute attacks of neuralgia, which confined him to his cabin.

At gunnery practice Rozhestvensky, who had been renowned for his gunnery as a young officer, watched while his destroyers scored not one single hit on a stationary target. When the battleships joined in, his flagship managed just one hit, which was on the ship towing the target. A formation of

Vice-Admiral Heichachiro Togo, commander of the Japanese fleet. PN

A Russian battleship sinking following an attack by a Japanese torpedo boat (foreground). PN

destroyers, ordered to form line abreast, scattered in every direction because they had not been issued with the new code books. Richard Hough describes the failure of the torpedoes:

Of the seven that left their tubes, one jammed, two swung ninety degrees to port, one ninety degrees to starboard, two kept a steady course but went wide of the mark, and the last went round and round in circles 'popping up and down like a porpoise' and causing panic throughout the fleet.

For Rozhestvensky the final insult occurred when he received an order from St Petersburg telling him to destroy the Japanese Fleet, sail on to Vladivostok, and there hand over command to Admiral Biriloff, who was travelling to the Russian Pacific port by the Trans-Siberian Railway. Biriloff was known as 'the fighting Admiral' even though he had never been in action. It was too much for Rozhestvensky to bear and despair turned to a mindless acceptance of fate. He knew that both he and his fleet were doomed. He would fight when the time came but it would be a reflex reaction, for everything he did seemed destined to fail. He was even being pursued by Nebogatoff's squadron of old ships, which he referred to as an 'archaeological collection of naval architecture'.

In Japan Admiral Togo was following the progress of the Russian squadron in the world's newspapers. He knew he would be outnumbered when the time came to fight. His fleet of 4 battleships, 8 armoured cruisers, 16 light cruisers, 21 destroyers and 57 torpedo boats could be outgunned by Rozhestvensky's 8 Russian battleships alone. But Togo was confident that he had the advantage in quality of crew and ships, and when at 5.05 a.m. on 27 May his scouts sighted the Russian fleet approaching the Straits of Tsushima, south of Fusan in Korea, he radioed back to Tokyo a confident message, 'I have just received the news that the enemy's fleet has been sighted. Our fleet will forthwith proceed to sea to attack the enemy and destroy him.'

The battle of Tsushima took place on the tsar's birthday, and the Russian officers aboard Rozhestvensky's flagship the *Suvorov* had just finished toasting their monarch when reports were received at 1.48 p.m. that Togo's warships were approaching fast. Rozhestvensky ordered the signal 'Steer north twenty-three degrees east' to be made from the flagship. Unfortunately the signal remained flying throughout the battle, causing much confusion.

Togo, aboard his flagship *Mikasa*, led his squadron of battleships and armoured cruisers down from the north on an interception course with the Russians. Before the engagement began the mainbrace was spliced aboard the Japanese ships – in typical British fashion – while the decks were soaked and sanded, and the men changed into clean uniforms to reduce the risk of infected wounds. At 2.45 p.m. Togo achieved the aim of all admirals: he crossed the Russian 'T', enabling him to fire broadsides against Rozhestvensky, while the Russians could only reply with their forward turrets. Showing great nerve and courage, Togo closed to a range of 6000 yards – point-blank range for his main armament – before opening fire. He had made his intentions quite clear: he had come to kill or be killed. And like a latter-day Nelson he signalled a message to his fleet, 'The rise or fall of the Empire depends upon today's battle. Let every man do his utmost.'

The Japanese concentrated their fire on the leading battleships of the two Russian divisions, Rozhestvensky's flagship *Suvorov* and the *Osslyablia*, and it was not long before they were scoring hits. The *Osslyablia* was reduced to a wreck within minutes by a storm of shells, and pulled out of line burning from stem to stern. Togo now shifted his fire to the ship second in the line, *Alexandre III*. Meanwhile the Russian flagship was in dire straits, 'burning like a peasant's hut', with both funnels and her mast gone and her steering gear so damaged that all she could do was turn full circles. She was listing badly when the seriously wounded Rozhestvensky was persuaded to transfer his flag to a waiting destroyer. A Russian officer, Commander Vladimir Semenoff, aboard the flagship described what it was like to be under Japanese fire:

It seemed impossible even to count the number of projectiles striking us. Shells seemed to be pouring upon us incessantly one after another. The steel plates and superstructure on the upper deck were torn to pieces, and the splinters caused many casualties. Iron ladders were crumpled up into rings, and guns were literally hurled from their mountings. In addition to this there was the unusually high temperature and liquid flame of the explosion, which seemed to spread over everything. I actually watched a steel plate catch fire from a burst.

In a desperate few minutes for the Russians, both the *Suvorov* and the *Alexandre III* went to the bottom, taking all of their crews with them except for a mere handful of survivors picked up from the sea by the destroyers. Even worse was to follow. The Japanese battleship *Juji* scored a direct hit on the magazines of the *Borodino*, which exploded in a terrible sheet of flame, pumping smoke thousands of feet into the air. As the smoke cleared it could be seen that the great vessel had turned turtle, trapping all her crew inside, before sliding finally beneath the waves.

Aboard the Japanese battleship *Asahi* the British naval observer, Captain Pakenham, was calmly seated on the maindeck taking notes on the battle when he was hit by a flying fragment – 'it was the right half of a man's lower jaw, with teeth missing.' A Russian shell had struck a guncrew nearby. The Japanese noted that Pakenham promptly went below – seeking shelter they assumed – only to

return a few minutes later in a new, immaculately white uniform, resume his seat, and continue taking notes.

The battle had turned into a massacre. The best Russian ships had already been destroyed, and the Japanese now turned their guns on Admiral Nebogatoff's feeble old battleship *Nicholas I*. Knowing himself outgunned and clearly believing that discretion was the better part of valour, the Russian admiral signalled to his squadron of 'sink-by-themselves' to head out of the battle and try to reach Vladivostok in the approaching darkness. Togo's battleships had also drawn away to leave the sea free for the Japanese destroyers to use torpedoes. The next Russian ship to sink, the *Navarin*, was overwhelmed by four Japanese destroyers firing from close range. The toll steadily rose as night drew on: the battleships *Sissoi*, *Nakhimoff*, and *Monomakh* all went down in the growing darkness.

The next morning at 10.30 a.m. Togo's battleships surrounded Nebogatoff's squadron south of the island of Takeshima, but before they were able to destroy them, the old Russian admiral hoisted a signal indicating that he wished to surrender. Realizing that the battle had become futile, Nebogatoff was unwilling to sacrifice the young lives of his sailors to save his own honour. He had decided to take the shame of surrender upon himself – even in the knowledge that he would be shot when he returned to Russia – saying to his men, 'you are young, and it is you who will one day retrieve the honour and glory of the Russian Navy. The lives of the two thousand four hundred men in these ships are more important than mine.' In the event the old man was not shot, but neither did his

TSUSHIMA 1905
Route of the Baltic Fleet October 1904 to May 1905

The remains of the Russian fleet in front of Port Arthur after the battle. CV

men regain the glory of the navy. Some of them later joined sailors in the Black Sea base at Odessa in seizing the battleship *Potemkin*, killing the officers and raising the Red Flag as a prologue to revolution in July 1905.

Of Rozhestvensky's 8 battleships, 6 had been sunk and the other 2 captured; of the 37 Russian ships that had gone into battle that day, 22 had been sunk, 6 had been captured, 6 had been interned at Manila and only 3 managed to reach the Russian port of Vladivostok. Russian casualties were 4380 killed, 5917 captured and 1862 interned. The Japanese lost just 3 torpedo boats, along with 117 men killed and 583 wounded. It was the Cannae of naval battles; never had a fleet been so completely overwhelmed.

Admiral Togo visited the wounded Rozhestvensky, imprisoned in a hospital in Japan, offering him the sage opinion that 'Defeat is a common fate of a soldier. There is nothing to be ashamed of in it. The great point is whether we have performed our duty.' The Russian government was unconvinced on this last point: on their return to Russia many of the senior officers, including Rozhestvensky and Nebogatoff, were tried by court martial.

The battle of Tsushima was a shattering blow to Russia and proved to her that the war was lost. But in Japan the battle won more than a war – it created a legend that was to haunt Japan's leaders for forty years. A British admiral once said, 'It takes three years to build a ship, but 300 years to build a tradition.' Japan thought that the victory had completed this task in a matter of a few years, while in Togo she thought she had a Nelson. It had all been too easy. Looking at Togo's victory over one of the world's great powers convinced some Japanese military men that with more ships, and bigger and better ones, similar victories could be won throughout the Pacific. Perhaps no power could resist the Japanese navy, not even Britain and the United States?

The importance of the battle of Tsushima must not only be seen in terms of the victory of an emergent Asiatic power over a declining European one, nor as another step on the weary road to Russian revolution in 1917. It was decisive because the result was so misleading. Certainly the Japanese navy had performed well, but its opponents had been weak, and it was not invincible. In the legend that grew up after Tsushima can be seen a pre-echo of future encounters like Pearl Harbor, Singapore, Midway and Leyte Gulf. Togo's victory set Japan on a path that would eventually lead her to the dreadful holocaust of Hiroshima and Nagasaki.

The Battle of the Marne 1914

Marne

Allies

Commander:	General Joffre
Left:	French 6th Army under General Manoury
Centre:	BEF under Field Marshal Sir John French and French 5th Army under General Franchet d'Esperey
Right:	French 9th Army under General Foch
Numbers:	1,082,000 men (56 infantry, 9 cavalry divisions)

Germans

Commander:	General Moltke
Left:	German 3rd Army under General von Hausen
Centre:	German 2nd Army under General von Bülow
Right:	German 1st Army under General von Kluck
Numbers:	900,000 menm (44 infantry, 7 cavalry divisions)

The battle of the Marne has been called 'the battle that never was', a curious description of one of history's most decisive encounters. But as Basil Liddell Hart has pointed out, the Marne was a 'psychological rather than a physical victory'. While it might do scant justice to the memory of the men who fought and died in September 1914, the fighting on the Marne was far less important than the state of mind of the commanders on both sides. In this case two personalities emerge from the fog of war: the French general Gallieni, a brilliant opportunist who saw his chance and took it, and the German commander-in-chief Helmuth von Moltke, nephew of the victor of Königgrätz and Sedan, whose nerve broke at the crucial time.

In 1914 the Germans had placed all their hopes on the famous Schlieffen Plan, a massive hook by five German armies which were to pass through Belgium, Artois, Picardy and then to the west of Paris before crushing the French against two remaining German armies in Lorraine. However, by violating Belgian neutrality the Germans unexpect-

edly brought Britain into the war alongside France, and by an irony of fate it was to be the tiny British Expeditionary Force that was to administer the *coup de grâce* to German hopes on the Marne in September 1914.

The Schlieffen Plan was a brilliant concept, aimed at winning the war in the west in six weeks, before moving German forces east to deal with the Russians, who, it was thought, would be slow to mobilize. Thus the Germans would avoid the old Prussian strategic nightmare – a war on two fronts. But the plan contained flaws that should have been ironed out before being used in 1914. Simple mathematics should have shown the German planners that General von Kluck's 1st Army, on the extreme right of the German 'hook', would have to travel much further – and much faster – than the crown prince's 5th Army on the inside of the wheel. Any delays encountered by von Kluck from unexpected Belgian – or British – resistance could be disastrous. In the event, it was resistance by the BEF at Mons and Le Câteau that disrupted the German timetable. Meanwhile, a thousand miles away in East Prussia an invasion by two Russian armies prompted Moltke to send two army corps from his right wing in Belgium to reinforce his beleaguered 8th Army. This was a catastrophic error. Moltke had made the cardinal mistake against which the dying Schlieffen had warned: he had not

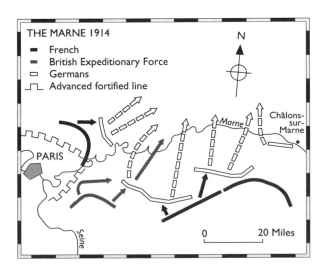

THE MARNE 1914
- ■ French
- ■ British Expeditionary Force
- □ Germans
- ⊓ Advanced fortified line

French infantry attacking in the early days of World War I. After the First Battle of the Marne, mobile warfare was to cease on the Western Front. PN

kept his right wing strong. Ironically, the troops he sent east did not reach Prussia in time to fight against the Russians at Tannenburg, and were in trains crossing Germany when the battle of the Marne was lost.

But all this was in the future as von Kluck's 1st Army drove the BEF and French 5th Army south. It looked as if the French had been beaten at all points of the line and that Germany was heading for her expected quick victory. But at army headquarters, Moltke was not confident. He received report after report of German successes – but where were the prisoners? Clearly this was not a re-run of 1870. The French were not going to sit down in Sedan and wait to be rounded up: they still had a lot of fight left in them. Meanwhile, Moltke's tortured imagination began to think the worst when two curious incidents occurred. In the first, Winston Churchill, First Lord of the Admiralty, ever eager to be involved, sent a brigade of 3000 marines to land at Ostend. Although they only stayed four days their arrival was so well publicized that the Germans believed that they were just the forerunners of massive British reinforcements – 40,000 strong – arriving on the Belgian coast to outflank them. Even more fantastic were the 80,000 Russians 'with snow on their boots', who were being brought through Scotland to bolster the Allies on the Western Front. The story that reached the Germans, and helped to convince Moltke that he must retreat, may have originated with a railway porter who overheard some Gaelic-speaking Highlanders

and spread the word that he had seen coaches full of Russians. Liddell Hart, with tongue in cheek, suggested the true hero of the Marne was that railway porter, even suggesting a statue in Whitehall be erected to 'The Unknown Porter'.

The military governor of Paris, General Joseph-Simon Gallieni, was one of France's most brilliant officers, who had been surprisingly passed over when Joffre was appointed commander-in-chief of the French army in 1911. In late August he temporarily took command of a new French army – the 6th – which was being formed near Amiens. At the same moment, von Kluck was reaching the conclusion that he lacked the strength necessary to swing west of Paris and take the city, and therefore instead passed the French capital to the east. On 3 September a British reconnaissance plane reported that von Kluck was now heading southeast, and this showed Gallieni that the flank of the German 1st Army was now open to a massive counter-attack from Paris. But Gallieni needed the cooperation of the British, who were still retreating. The British commander, Sir John French, was depressed to hear that the French government was abandoning the capital and moving to Bordeaux, and was at first unwilling to listen to Gallieni's plan. Gallieni, 'bespectacled and untidy, with shaggy moustache, black buttoned boots and yellow leggings', made quite the wrong impression on the British staff officers, who admitted that 'no British officer would be seen talking to such a —— comedian.' Gallieni now had to sell the plan to Joffre, whose peasant mind was slow to grasp the opportunity that was being offered. At last Joffre agreed, and after a difficult and emotional meeting with Sir John French the British were persuaded to cooperate in the counter-attack. Joffre had had to wheedle and cajole his difficult ally: 'I cannot believe that the British Army will refuse to do its share in this supreme crisis . . . history will severely judge your absence.' Then Joffre crashed his fist on the table, 'Monsieur le Maréchal, the honour of England is at stake!' Tears came to French's eyes at this astute Gallic stab and he mumbled, 'Damn it, I can't explain. Tell him we will do all we possibly can.' Joffre had got his way, and was able to announce to his staff, 'Gentlemen, we will fight on the Marne.'

On 5 September the French 6th Army under General Manoury struck von Kluck's flank. The famous story of how French taxicabs were used to rush troops from Paris to the front, though true, has been exaggerated. In fact just 600 cabs managed to shift 6000 French troops in two runs out to the battlefield. However, faced with this new threat the Germans were forced to turn west to meet it, and as they did so, von Kluck opened a gap of about 30 miles between himself and General von Bülow's 2nd Army to his left. Timidly – like a bather entering cold water – 20,000 men of the BEF advanced, supported by parts of Franchet-d'Espèrey's 5th Army. When news reached Moltke of this British offensive, 'he sat with a pallid face gazing at the map, dead to all feeling, a broken man'. On 8 September Moltke absolved himself of responsibility by sending a young staff officer, Oberstleutnant Hentsch, to check if it was true that the British were across the Marne. If he found that this was so Hentsch was to order a general retreat to the River Aisne. Hentsch confirmed the reports and by 9 September he had ordered von Kluck and von Bülow to pull back. In the words of war minister von Falkenhayen, 'Only one thing is certain: our General Staff has completely lost its head. Schlieffen's notes do not help any further, and so Moltke's wits come to an end.' The following day Moltke reported to the Kaiser, 'Majesty, we have lost the war.' He was right – but it took four years and millions of lives to convince the Germans that their hopes had vanished on the Marne.

But just as decisive was the attitude of the British to the breakthrough. Instead of ripping into the gap and turning the German setback into a disaster, Sir John French moved so slowly that it would appear that he did not want to force a decision. General Charteris wrote, 'Actually our own troops, though the men were very keen, moved absurdly slowly. The cavalry were the worst of all, for they were right behind the infantry.' And so although the Germans lost the battle of the Marne, the Allies failed to win it conclusively. Both sides were now condemned to four years of trench warfare, which consumed the lives of a whole generation.

A German victory at the Marne – or perhaps no battle of the Marne at all – would have enabled the Germans to achieve a virtual encirclement of the French armies. Before Britain could assemble the vast forces she would bring to France in 1915 and 1916 the war would have been over in the west, enabling Germany to concentrate all her strength on defeating Russia. A Russian collapse would have followed in 1915 rather than 1917, and there would have been no United States involvement in the war at all. Britain would have had to learn to coexist with a German super-state. German war aims had been promulgated by the German politician Matthias Erzberger, even before the battle of the Marne was fought. They included: Europe to become a confederation of states under German control; Poland, Belgium and the Baltic states would be annexed; the northern French coastline, from Dunkirk to Boulogne and Calais, would become German, as well as the ironfields of Briey, Longway and Belfort; and all French and Belgian colonies in Africa would be taken over. It seemed that German land-hunger knew no bounds. Above all, according to Erzberger, British 'hegemony' in world affairs would be ended.

THE BRITISH EXPEDITIONARY FORCE

The British Army was, in 1914, unusual in being a force of professional soldiers, unlike the vast conscript armies of France and Germany. All of its men were volunteers who had undergone a thorough training and were specialists in their field. Many had seen service in Egypt, South Africa and India, and their morale was high. They took the Kaiser's insulting description of them as 'a contemptible little army' as a compliment, and ever afterwards were proud to be known as the 'Old Contemptibles'.

In 1914 the British Army consisted of just six infantry divisions and one cavalry division, and only four of these divisions were sent to France at the outbreak of war, under the command of Sir John French. The German 1st Army, commanded by General von Kluck, had not expected to meet any British troops at Mons when his troops arrived there on 23 August. His shock was even greater when the BEF revealed the high quality of their marksmanship by killing thousands of Germans during their early uncoordinated assaults. The Germans claimed that the British were using massed machine guns, but it was merely the concentrated fire of highly trained troops, using Lee Enfield Mk 4 rifles. At Mons, Le Cateau, the Marne and First Ypres, the BEF fought the Germans to a standstill, suffering 95,000 casualties by the end of 1914 – almost the entire BEF force that had gone to France in August.

The Battle of Sedan 1940

Sedan

French
Commanders: General Huntzinger (2nd Army) and General Corap (9th Army)
Numbers: 300,000 men: 22 divisions

German
Commanders: Field Marshal Gerd von Runstedt (Army Group A) and General von Kleist (Panzer Group) with XLI Panzer Corps under General Reinhardt, XIX Panzer Corps under General Guderian.
Numbers: 500,000 men: 45 divisions

The dreadful casualties suffered by France on the Western Front between 1914 and 1918, and the successful defence of the Verdun fortresses in 1916, were twin influences on French military strategy in the inter-war period. In any future war with Germany, France could not afford to squander the lives of her young men in fruitless assaults against strongly defended positions. Verdun had shown the way: in modern warfare the defender had all the advantages. If France were to ring her frontiers with Verdun-like fortifications, the Germans could fling themselves onto its concrete bastions till kingdom come. But the French had drawn the wrong conclusions from the fighting on the Western Front in 1918; it was if the tank had never been invented. The Germans, on the other hand, had learned the lessons of their defeat very well, and during the 1930s German tank specialist Heinz Guderian, inspired by English disciples of mobile warfare like Basil Liddell Hart and Major-General J.F. Fuller, was developing the very blitzkrieg tactics that would win the battle of Sedan for Germany in 1940.

The monumental strength of the Maginot Line – a line of apparently impregnable fortifications constructed after 1931 from the Swiss frontier to Luxembourg – made France complacent. To the French High Command its existence left the Germans no option but to re-run the Schlieffen Plan of 1914. The Germans would then be stopped

in Belgium, along a line running from Antwerp to the River Meuse, by the cream of the French army – 30 divisions, including 2 of the 3 new armoured divisions, 5 of the 7 motorized divisions and all 3 light mechanized divisions. When warned of German blitzkrieg tactics used in Poland, French commander-in-chief General Maurice Gamelin refused to listen, saying 'We are not Poles, it could not happen here.'

What is so surprising is that Gamelin refused to see what everyone else could see so clearly, that the centre of the French line, around Sedan, was shockingly fragile. The weakest elements in the entire French front, Corap's 9th Army and Huntziger's 2nd Army, would be left to hold the line along the Meuse, from where the river runs through the Ardennes, south of Namur, to Sedan and then

Heinz Guderian, pioneer of blitzkrieg tactics and commander of the three Panzer divisions aiming for the River Meuse south of Sedan. PN

to the Maginot Line. For more than a hundred miles of the Ardennes, the line was held by just 4 light cavalry divisions, some still equipped with horses, and 10 mediocre infantry divisions, behind whom there were no reserves at all. And facing them, across the Meuse, was Field Marshal Karl von Rundstedt with 45 infantry divisions and 10 Panzer armoured divisions.

Defending Sedan itself were just 3 'B' divisions: the 55th, 71st and 53rd, of whom one officer commented, 'Nonchalance was general; it was accompanied by the feeling that France could not be beaten, that Germany would be beaten without battle . . . the men are flabby and heavy . . . the training is mediocre.' The 55th had only 20 regular officers out of 450, while the 71st, from Paris, was of very poor quality, ill-disciplined, and feebly led by the ailing General Baudet. On 10 May 1940 over 7000 of its men were missing through illness or on leave.

By May 1940 French military intelligence, the Deuxième Bureau, had built up a picture of German intentions that was markedly different from that of the commander-in-chief. They had monitored a growing interest on the part of German intelligence in road conditions along the Sedan-Abbeville axis, which could only presage heavy military commitment to that area. Moreover, the Bureau's spies had managed to locate all the German Panzer divisions and the three motorized divisions, and all indications pointed to the Ardennes as their target. From Swiss sources the French learned of the construction of eight military bridges across the Rhine between Bonn and Bingen, again indicating that the spearhead of the German attack was not intended either in the south against the Maginot Line or in the north against Belgium. The French military attaché in Berne even informed Gamelin that he had strong evidence to suggest a German strike at Sedan, beginning some time between 8 and 10 May. And yet with all this accumulation of evidence suggesting Sedan, Gamelin refused to alter his view that the main German strike would come in Belgium.

When the Germans began their attack on 10 May 1940 the British Expeditionary Force under Lord Gort along with the French 7th and 1st Armies (under Giraud and Blanchard respectively) advanced into Belgium to counter what they believed was the main German thrust by Field Marshal von Bock's Army Group 'B'. To the French it was like a replay of 1914; the Germans seemed to be relying on the Schlieffen Plan again. But they were wrong – von Bock was merely wielding 'the matador's cloak'.

In the forested hills of the Ardennes, considered impassable by Gamelin, the Germans had concentrated Army Group 'A', a force spearheaded by General von Kleist's Panzer Group of seven armoured divisions, which would cut a swathe through the weak French divisions between Namur and Sedan. Von Kleist's command was divided into three attack units: Hoth's 5th and 7th Armoured Divisions striking between Namur and Dinant; Reinhardt's 6th and 8th towards Monthermé; and in the south Guderian's 1st, 2nd and 10th divisions heading for the River Meuse south of Sedan. The Ardennes should have been easy to defend, with many gorges and small villages that could have provided cover for determined troops to fight 'rearguard actions', yet in the event French resistance was minimal.

As the heavy German columns moved towards the French border on 10 May they presented a perfect target for air attack. Admittedly overhead was the reassuring presence of the Luftwaffe, but such dense concentrations of armoured vehicles – Guderian's advanced units alone had 10,000 – without room to manoeuvre on the narrow roads, should have provided easy targets for Allied bombers. Yet through administrative muddle on 10 and 11 May, the mass of Allied air strength was used in the north to support the French armies in Belgium, leaving only 37 planes in support of the 2nd and 9th Armies around Sedan. Even then the few British and French pilots who were committed to the Ardennes were ordered to avoid bombing built-up areas, placing an impossible burden on pilots already heavily outnumbered in the air.

By the morning of the 11th it had at last dawned on the French High Command that the Germans were striking at Sedan, so they belatedly ordered up the 2nd and 3rd Armoured, 3rd Motorized and 14th, 36th and 87th Infantry Divisions to cover the

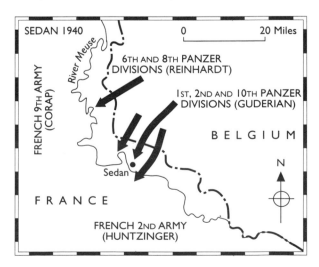

183

threatened sector. But French time schedules were those of an earlier war, and they still believed that the Germans would not attempt a crossing of the Meuse until they had brought up their heavy guns to support their tanks. According to the French this should take four to six days. But the devastating use of the Stuka dive bombers was making artillery support redundant.

By 12 May Guderian's armoured divisions had reached Sedan and were pushing on towards the Meuse. The Germans could hardly believe their luck; progress was far ahead of schedule. The German armour had been instructed by von Kleist 'not to rest or relax; to move forward night and day, looking neither left nor right, always on the alert; the group must exploit its initial surprise and the enemy's confusion; take him everywhere unawares and have only one aim in mind: to get through'.

German soldiers paddle a rubber dinghy along a river during the invasion of France. PN

Guderian needed no such encouragement and plunged ahead, ordering his three divisions to cross the Meuse between Donchery and Sedan. By the evening his troops were on the banks of the river.

Under Luftwaffe cover, German sappers began crossing the deep, wide and fast-flowing river in rubber dinghies, while the bridges on the canal alongside the river were captured intact. By the morning of 13 May the situation had become desperate for the French, with the 1st Panzer Division at Chemery three miles behind the French lines and the 2nd and 10th Panzers on the Meuse. Yet so far only German infantry were across the river and the German armoured divisions were in positions that could be counter-attacked from the flanks. But French morale was breaking and several units were panicking, particularly the gunners, who had hitherto held such a high position of respect in the French army.

Guderian had got the bit between his teeth and was not going to stop for anyone. Short of artillery, he substituted the far more effective and infinitely more mobile Stuka dive bombers to pound the areas in advance of his tanks. The psychological effect of the Stukas, with their ear-splitting siren and their near-vertical descent, shattered French morale. While Guderian's engineers assembled pontoons to get the tanks across the river, assault troops overran French pillboxes, finding resistance lighter than expected. By the evening of 13 May the Germans had stabilized their crossing points and a bridgehead three miles wide and several miles deep had been secured. The French were in disorderly retreat, with a massive hole punched in their line between the 9th and 2nd Armies.

The moment had come for a major French counter-attack. But where were the much vaunted French armoured divisions? Their failure in the first few hours after the crossing of the Meuse was to prove decisive to the outcome of the entire campaign. The tank was the central weapon in the defeat of France in 1940 and it is often assumed that the Germans owed the ease of their victory to an overwhelming superiority in modern armaments, tanks, anti-tank guns and aircraft. But this was not so. In May 1940 the French had more tanks, and more powerful tanks at that, on the northeastern frontier than the Germans. The French commanders simply misused equipment in many respects superior to that of their enemy.

To the Germans, the Panzer division was a sword, sharp as well as heavy, 'to be used to slice through the enemy front and turn a tactical success into strategic victory'. The Polish campaign had shown it enjoying freedom of movement, with

TANKS AT SEDAN MAY 1940

FRENCH

Type	Weight	Crew	Armament	Armour	Speed
Char. B	31 tons	4	1 x 75 mm, 1 x 45 mm, 2 MGs	60 mm	17 mph

GERMAN

Type	Weight	Crew	Armament	Armour	Speed
PzKw III	22 tons	5	1 x 50 mm, 2 MGs	60 mm	30 mph
PzKw IV	23 tons	5	1 x 75 mm, 2 MGs	65 mm	25 mph

other units subordinated to it. When the situation demanded it, several Panzer divisions would be grouped together into an armoured corps of immense striking capacity. Against this, France's commanders had no real doctrine of armoured warfare, using tanks as an auxiliary of the infantry and as a mobile force to plug gaps in their continuous line of defence.

The occupation of Czechoslovakia in 1938–9 had brought Germany control not only of the Skoda works in Bohemia but also of a large number of Czech army tanks. Yet even with these, German armoured strength was outnumbered by the French, and in the Char. B tank France had the strongest armoured vehicle on either side. Viewed simply in terms of numbers and tonnage, the Germans were running a considerable risk in taking the offensive against an enemy with such armoured strength. However, the advantage of surprise lay with them, and the French doctrine of a continuous front enabled the Germans to achieve local supremacy in armour, always seeming to the French defenders to be advancing in overwhelming numbers and strength.

The French armoured divisions were the strongest units on the battlefield on 10 May 1940, yet the fate of just one of them illustrates how they were wasted. The 3rd Armoured Division, under General Brocard, had two battalions of Hotchkiss H-39 tanks and, although fewer in number than the 10th Panzer Division, it had greater strength than the German unit, half of whose tanks were light Mark Is and Mark IIs, not intended for tank-to-tank combat. Unlike some units in the French army, morale was high amongst the 3rd Armoured Division, though it had not been formed long and had only started divisional training on 1 May. It was in training at Rheims when it received its orders to move on 12 May, and had some 40 miles to cover through areas encumbered with refugees, pushing their possessions on carts or riding in horse-drawn wagons. Its journey was full of problems, caused by a lack of engineers to repair the tanks and sappers

to clear the way for them, while the heavy 'B' tanks had difficulty crossing the River Aisne. At one point the crush of refugees was so great that the tanks had to force their way through by crushing cars and wagons that obstructed their way. The journey through a country filled with desperate refugees and deserters was not an experience to boost morale. As the reinforcements advanced they heard wild tales from the fugitives of masses of tanks pursuing them, exaggerated by fear in both size and quantity. Nevertheless, at dawn on 14 May, 'full of spirit and eager to have a go at the enemy', the 3rd Armoured Division reached Stonne, and Brocard reported to General Flavigny, now commanding the new XXI Corps.

Brocard informed Flavigny that in view of its 30-mile night march his division would not be ready to go into action for some 10 hours. Flavigny insisted that an attack should be launched at 1100 hours, but so slow was Brocard's preparation, particularly the refuelling of the tanks, that his division was not deployed until nearly 1600 hours. However, Flavigny was already having second thoughts. He had not been impressed by what he had seen of Brocard's division, and doubted its combat readiness. As an old tank commander himself, with World War I experience, his mind was already turning to thoughts of defending the second line and restoring the continuous front. Thirty minutes before the division was due to attack, Flavigny came to a decision that was to have a marked effect on the future fortunes of France. He ordered the 3rd Armoured Division to abandon its counter-attack instruction and disperse itself defensively along a 12-mile front, from Omont to Stonne, to cover all tracks or possible points of penetration and form 'corks', consisting of one 'B' heavy tank with two Hotchkiss H-39s. This use of tanks in 'penny packets', as part of a static defence, was a violation of everything the modern tank stood for. Colonel Le Goyet has pointed out that once consolidation became the French aim there was 'a line, a few tanks, but no 3rd

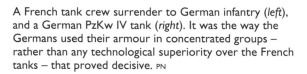

A French tank crew surrender to German infantry (left), and a German PzKw IV tank (right). It was the way the Germans used their armour in concentrated groups – rather than any technological superiority over the French tanks – that proved decisive. PN

Armoured Division. The steel lance was buried for ever, and so was the counter-attack' – and so was France.

On 14 May German pontoon bridges over the Meuse were attacked by British and French planes, though only three were damaged and these quickly repaired. It was too late. From Dinant in the north to Sedan in the south Corap's 9th Army had collapsed under the weight of von Kleist's blitzkrieg attack. Guderian had now reached open country behind the French lines, and as he drove westwards his only companions were fleeing French civilians. In four days he reached the Channel coast. The battle of Sedan was over; the outcome of the battle of France was now a forgone conclusion.

The French defeat was the result of many factors, not least of which was a willingness to allow the Germans to dictate how the battle should be fought. The Germans played to their strengths and the French let them. The German commanders could hardly believe their luck; everything that had been planned was working not only to schedule but often considerably ahead of it. With Guderian leading the assault on Sedan in person, there was never any question of 'reining back' or 'stopping to consolidate' – it was speed and power all the way, allowing the panzers to surprise and overwhelm the French defenders by the unexpected rate of their advance. Guderian took risks that would have been unthinkable in any earlier era, but he was justified by the results. His combination of tanks and aircraft numbed the French defenders, sapped their morale, and finally broke their spirit.

The fall of France after the battle of Sedan followed as night follows day. It was more than a military defeat, it was a shattering blow to the spirit of a nation. In some ways it was the final act in a drama that had started 300 years before on the field of Rocroi. The French army – the army of Condé and Turenne, of Saxe and of Napoleon – had succumbed with scarcely a struggle. France's status as a European power had crumbled; her voice in world affairs was stilled. The mantle of European salvation had passed briefly to Britain, before being taken up by the United States and the Soviet Union – the superpowers of 1945.

The Battle of Britain 1940

Britain

British
Commander: Air Chief Marshal Sir Hugh Dowding
Numbers: 1100 planes; 55 squadrons giving effective strength of 666 planes, 80% Hurricanes and Spitfires

German
Commander: Reichsmarschall Hermann Göring
Numbers: 3 Airfleets amounting to 800 single-seat fighters, 300 heavy fighters, 300 Stuka dive bombers, 1000 long-range bombers

After the fall of France in June 1940 Hitler had expected Britain to sue for peace. Neither he nor his military planners had given serious thought to continuing the war in the West, and Hitler himself was already preoccupied with the idea of an attack on the Soviet Union. But Britain did not surrender and few even entertained the thought of a negotiated peace. In fact the whole British attitude puzzled and perplexed the Führer. Quotes like the following were typical of Britain's reaction to the collapse of France:

Personally I feel happier now that we have no allies to be polite to and to pamper – King George VI

Anyhow, sir, we're in the Final, and it's to be played on the Home Ground - The commissionaire at the United Services Club

Thank God we're alone now – Air Chief Marshal Dowding

Inspired by Churchillian rhetoric the British people were displaying what Basil Liddell Hart has called their 'sublime stupidity'. But General Alan Brooke was not impressed by mere rhetoric:

The more I see of conditions at home, the more bewildered I am as to what has been going on in this country since the war started. It is now ten months since the war started and yet the shortage of trained men and equipment is appalling.

By the beginning of July Hitler was having to face the unpleasant prospect of planning a crossing of the English Channel from scratch. The elimination of the French navy at Mers-el-Kebir on 3 July had shocked the Germans by its decisive and ruthless demonstration of British sea power. Up to now Hitler had believed Britain's commitment to the war was only half-hearted; now he knew he was in for a fight. His response, though bold, showed signs of the hysteria or 'impulsive wilfulness' that was to become a feature of his strategic thinking from this time onwards. On 16 July he announced the existence of a plan to invade England – Operation Sealion:

As England, despite her hopeless military situation, still shows no sign of willingness to come to terms, I have decided to prepare, and if necessary to carry out, a landing operation against her.

The aim of this operation is to eliminate the English motherland as a base from which war against Germany can be continued and, if necessary, to occupy it completely.

While Field Marshal von Brauschitsch moved 13 elite Wehrmacht divisions to the Channel coast, and fleets of flat bottomed boats and barges were assembled, both army and navy experts confronted the problem of crossing the narrow strip of the English Channel in the face of the enormous threat of the Royal Navy. The Germans believed they would need 39 divisions to complete the conquest of Britain, and that by the third day 260,000 men, 40,000 vehicles and 60,000 horses would need to be ashore on the coasts of Kent and Sussex. But the spectre of Britain's 800 torpedo boats and light craft breaking into the crowded troop convoys was one that caused the planners nightmares. As one German expert put it, 'The German invasion craft were certain to suffer heavy losses if these small, fast English warships got in amongst them [the invasion barges] in half-light or at night.' There was simply no chance of a successful invasion unless the Royal Navy could be kept well away from the crossing points, and this would have to be done by the Luftwaffe. And before the German air force could go over to the job of attacking British shipping, air supremacy had to be achieved. The first task was to destroy the RAF, and Reichmarshal Göring promised to achieve this in just four weeks – an estimate based on wishful thinking and poor intelligence. On the other hand, the head of RAF Fighter Command, Air Chief Marshal Hugh Dowding, saw his task very clearly:

Mine was the purely defensive role of trying to stop the possibility of an invasion, and thus give this country a breathing spell . . . It was Germany's objective to win the war by invasion, and it was my job to prevent an invasion taking place.

Figures for the comparative strengths of the Luftwaffe and the RAF at the start of the battle of Britain are notoriously difficult to give, as no two experts will ever agree. Suffice it to say that throughout the attritional fighting in August and September both sides were building new planes as

Hurricane fighter pilots resting between combat engagements. PN

fast as they could and replacing lost planes; they were also – with greater difficulty – replacing lost pilots and aircrew. At its strongest the RAF fielded 55 squadrons, and – at any one time – could put 666 aircraft into the air, out of a total strength of some 1100 planes. Eighty per cent of Dowding's fighters were Hurricanes and Spitfires, the only British fighters that could face the best German plane, the Me. 109; the RAF's Blenheims, Defiants and Gladiators could only be used in a secondary capacity. On the German side, the three air fleets of the Luftwaffe fielded about 800 single-seat fighters and 300 heavy fighters, as well as 1000 long-range bombers and 300 Stuka dive bombers. Plane for plane the Germans had the advantage, with the excellent Me. Bf109E outperforming the Spitfire and the slower Hurricane; but the quality of RAF pilots, drawn from 14 countries including Nazi-occupied Poland and Czechoslovakia, was supreme. However, where the Germans suffered most was in

their underestimation of RAF strength, and in their failure to realize the crucial role of British radar.

By 1940 radar had become a decisive arm of air defence, allowing the defenders to have enough warning of an approaching attack and its direction to allow their fighters to get airborne in time to meet the intruders. Once the enemy came in view the Royal Observer Corps came into play and German pilots were astounded to hear the air waves 'full of English voices' giving precise positions of the German planes. It was part of a far more sophisticated air-defence system than they had themselves, and its heart was Hugh Dowding's Operations Room in Bentley Priory, at Stanmore in Middlesex.

The battle began on 10 July with German raids on British convoys in the Channel and on other naval targets, but the Germans were never able to achieve local air superiority, and their losses were always much higher than those of the British. The latter were often able to rescue pilots from their lost planes, whereas the German aircrew from destroyed planes were always either killed or captured.

On 1 August 1940 Hitler gave instructions for what was to be known as *Adler Tag* – Eagle Day – the start of the major air offensive:

The Luftwaffe will use all the forces at its disposal to destroy the British air force as quickly as possible . . . August 5th is the first day on which this intensified air war may begin, but the exact date is to be left to the Luftwaffe and will depend on how soon its preparations are complete, and on the weather situation.

Eventually bad weather postponed Eagle Day to 13 August. Yet on 12 August the Germans had scored a success against the British radar defence system, a success which should have pointed the way forward for them: an attack on the Isle of Wight radar station at Ventnor put the unit out of action for weeks. Ironically, Göring had just reached the conclusion that such raids were a waste of time, and so Britain's radar was saved. On 13–14 August the Germans flew 1485 missions, losing 45 aircraft to the RAF's 13 – hardly a promising start for the Luftwaffe. At this time Göring was estimating RAF strength at just 300 serviceable fighters, whereas Dowding had 700. On 15 August the Germans flew 1786 sorties in an attempt to crush Fighter Command once and for all, hitting airfields and communications sources, but their losses of 76 aircraft – exaggerated by a jubilant RAF to 180 – was their largest loss of any day during the entire battle. Göring was losing so many senior air crew that he ordered that no more than one officer should fly in any plane. The fighting on 18 August was seen by many as the decisive day in the battle.

KEY FIGHTERS USED IN THE BATTLE OF BRITAIN

German Messerschmitt Bf109E-3 fighter

Engine: 1 Daimler-Benz DB 601 Aa 12-cylinder V inline, 1175 hp
Armament: 2 x 20 mm MG FF cannon in wings, 2 x 7.9 mm machine guns in fuselage
Max speed: 348 mph at 14,000 ft
Climb rate: 7 min 45 sec to 20,000 ft
Ceiling: 35,000 ft
Range: 410 miles

British Hawker Hurricane I fighter

Engine: 1 Rolls-Royce Merlin III 12-cylinder V inline, 1030 hp
Armament: 8 x .303 in Browning machine guns
Max speed: 324 mph at 16,000 ft
Climb rate: 8 min 30 sec to 20,000 ft
Ceiling: 34,200 ft
Range: 505 miles

British Vickers Supermarine Spitfire 1A fighter

Engine: 1 Rolls-Royce Merlin III 12-cylinder V inline, 1030 hp
Armament: 8 x .303-in Browning machine guns
Max speed: 365 mph at 19,000 ft
Climb rate: 9 min 24 sec to 20,000 ft
Ceiling: 34,000 ft
Range: 575 miles

Historian Alfred Price considers this the 'real "Battle of Britain" day':

The Luftwaffe had 100 aircraft put out of action, 69 of them wrecked or damaged beyond repair. Fighter Command had 73 fighters put out of action, 39 of them wrecked or damaged beyond repair . . . Never before during the battle, nor afterwards, would the two sides suffer such heavy material losses during a single day.

Göring now switched his single-seat fighters to the command of Kesselring's Luftflotte 2 in northeast France. Because of the short range of the German fighters Göring had concluded that he should concentrate the fight over the southern English counties, destroying RAF airfields where possible. The fighting was intense and dogfights took place all across the skies of Kent, Sussex and Surrey. In the thick of the fight an observer once recorded 14 parachutes in the air at the same time. RAF pilot Richard Hillary described his experiences in the heat of action:

We ran into them at eighteen thousand feet, twenty yellow-nosed Messerschmitt 109s, about five hundred

A German Messerschmitt 109 fighter shot down on the southeast coast of England. PN

feet above us. Our Squadron strength was eight and as they came down on us we went into line astern and turned head onto them. Brian Carbury, who was leading the section, dropped the nose of his machine, and I could almost feel the leading Nazi pilot push forward on his stick to bring his guns to bear. At the same moment Brian hauled hard back on his control stick and led us over them in a steep climbing turn to the left. In two vital seconds they lost their advantage. I saw Brian let go a burst of fire at the leading plane, saw the pilot put his machine into a half roll, and knew that he was mine. Automatically, I kicked the rudder to the left to get him at right angles, turned the gun-button to 'Fire' and let go a four-second burst with full deflection. He came right through my sights and I saw the tracer from all eight guns thud home. For a second he seemed to hang motionless; then a jet of red flame shot upwards and he spun out of sight.

In his search for a quick victory to allow Operation Sealion to go ahead Göring squandered German successes against the airfields by shifting to a target that he believed the British would commit everything to defend: London. The background to this decisive and – from Germany's point of view

– fatal decision was that on 25 August British bombers had attacked Berlin. Although they had caused minimal damage, the blow to German prestige was enormous. How could the German people believe that the British were on the point of surrender if their bombers were in the sky over the German capital? In retaliation, Hitler ordered that London should be given the same treatment as Warsaw and Rotterdam. The shift in German bombing to London was the decisive moment of the battle of Britain. As time was to show – in 1943 and 1944 over Germany – victory in war could not be won by attacking urban areas in an attempt to lower civilian morale.

The four weeks between 15 August and 15 September saw the height of the attritional battle. In this period the RAF lost 493 planes with only 201 aircrew killed; the Germans lost 862 planes but with 1132 aircrew killed. This haemorrhaging of trained and experienced pilots and crew could not be sustained indefinitely.

Daylight raids on London were launched regularly in early September, but though they caused much damage and heavy civilian casualties, they did nothing to reduce Britain's war potential. The Blitz had begun – but as one commentator observed, the martyrdom of London was to save the whole country:

The attraction of London was the German Air Force's undoing. Like an indestructible sponge it absorbed punishment and diverted what might have been the death blow from the sorely tried organism of defence.

On 10 September Hitler decided to postpone Operation Sealion for seven days as no victory in the air was in sight. On 15 September, with just two days to go before the deadline, Kesselring launched a heavy series of raids, but in intense fighting he suffered losses of over 60 planes. That day – eventually chosen as 'Battle of Britain' day – was not perhaps as decisive as 15 August, yet it was enough to convince Hitler that the air war over Britain could not now be won. RAF bombers had reinforced that conclusion by raiding the German invasion ports and destroying 200 of the landing craft. By now Hitler had lost all faith in Göring's air offensive and postponed Operation Sealion again – this time indefinitely.

The Luftwaffe continued to strike London for 23 consecutive days in daylight, but their casualties were becoming prohibitive. By October they had lost 1733 planes to an RAF figure of 915, and it was clear that the air war had been lost. British factories were producing aircraft at a faster rate than the Germans, and though it was the courage of the pilots that actually achieved victory in the air, the battle of Britain was a triumph for thousands of land-based personnel: air controllers, radar operators, engineers, ground crew and factory workers. If Churchill overlooked this when he said 'Never in the field of human conflict has so much been owed by so many to so few', he was only reflecting the public view that, as in 1914–18, the British flyers were the heroes, the 'knights of the sky'.

The Germans had lost the battle of Britain and, in the eyes of some Germans, the consequences for Germany were already fatal. General Werner Kreipe claimed:

Though the air battles over England were perhaps a triumph of skill and bravery so far as the German air crews were concerned, from the strategic point of view it was a failure, and contributed to our ultimate defeat. The decision to fight it marks a turning point in the history of the Second World War. The German Air Force . . . was bled almost to death, and suffered losses that could never again be made good throughout the course of the war.

Germany had suffered a decisive defeat. For the German historian Klee,

The invasion and subjugation of Britain was made to depend on victory in that battle and its outcome therefore materially influenced both the further course and the fate of the war as a whole.

A German victory in the battle of Britain, even if not followed by an invasion of England, must have brought Britain to her knees in spite of Churchill's resolve to carry on the war from Canada. If the Royal Navy had been neutralized, the possibility of any future American involvement in the war would have been unlikely. And without British and American aid, it is doubtful if the Soviet Union could have survived an attack from what would have been a virtual 'United Europe' under German control.

With an undefeated Britain at his back and an unrepentantly pro-British United States in the wings, Hitler turned his attention to his favourite policy of war with the Soviet Union. By accepting the certainty of a war on two fronts Hitler was flying in the face of traditional German policy. In the event, his failure to achieve victory over Britain in 1940, or a negotiated settlement with pro-Nazi elements there, was to prove ultimately fatal for the Third Reich.

The Battle of Midway 1942

Midway

American and Japanese Ships at Midway

Force	Battleships	Large Carriers	Small Carriers	Cruisers	Destroyers
Japanese Main Fleet (Yamamoto)	7	-	1	3	21
Carrier Strike Force (Nagumo)	2	4	-	3	12
Invasion Force (Kondo)	2	-	1	10	20
Total Japanese Strength	**11**	**4**	**2**	**16**	**53**
American TF 16 (Spruance)	-	2	-	6	11
American TF 17 (Fletcher)	-	1	-	2	6
Total US Strength	**-**	**3**	**-**	**8**	**17**

The battle of Midway was the first naval encounter in which the combatant ships never saw each other. It marked the emergence of the aircraft carrier as the new capital ship in naval warfare, rendering the battleship – even the super-battleships built by Japan – obsolete and helpless in the face of carrier-based air attack. The American victory, over a far more powerful Japanese fleet, marked a watershed in the history of the Second World War. Before Midway Japan had enjoyed uninterrupted success, but afterwards it became only a matter of time before the industrial potential of the United States equipped her fighting men with overwhelming material advantages. The qualitative advantage the Japanese enjoyed at the start of the war in men, ships and planes was also destroyed at Midway. And after Midway the Japanese could never again endanger the American naval base at Hawaii or threaten to bring the war to the west coast of the United States.

Yet for five minutes on 4 June 1942 the fate of nations hung in the balance. At 10.25 on that morning Admiral Chuichi Nagumo on the bridge of the Japanese carrier *Akagi* turned his ship into the wind prior to launching a massed attack on the three

American carriers of Admirals Fletcher and Spruance, a raid that could have virtually eradicated American naval power in the Pacific and decisively shifted the power balance between Japan and the United States for years to come. Yet within those five minutes the Japanese were to taste total defeat. Nemesis fell from the skies in the shape of Douglas SBD Dauntless dive bombers from *Enterprise* and *Yorktown*, which destroyed three of Nagumo's carriers. If ever there was a 'close-run thing' it was the battle of Midway.

After Japan's devastating attack on Pearl Harbor on 7 December 1941, American public opinion pressed for retaliation against Japanese cities. In April 1942 the carriers *Enterprise* and *Hornet* launched a daring strike by 16 B-25s against Tokyo known as the 'Doolittle Raid'. Damage to Tokyo was slight, but the Americans had shown that they could hit the Japanese homeland; Japan's military leaders, particularly Admiral Isoruko Yamamoto, felt humiliated by their failure to protect the emperor. Japan had proved vulnerable to a carrier-based attack from the northern Pacific – between Hawaii and the Aleutians – and the Japanese determined to fill this gap in their defences. Thus, although Japanese successes in the early months of the war held out the prospect of a triumphal procession through Southeast Asia as well as Australasia and Oceania, this would have to wait until the threat to the homeland was removed.

Admiral Yamamoto, who had master-minded the Pearl Harbor raid, had been far from satisfied with the outcome. Parts of the American Pacific Fleet had escaped, notably the aircraft carriers, and while these remained afloat they posed a real threat to Japan's widespread conquests. Yamamoto looked for a way of drawing them to destruction in a decisive battle, and chose the coral atoll of Midway, 1000 miles northwest of Hawaii, as a suitable killing ground. He reasoned that the Americans would risk their carriers to defend their base on Midway. At first, Yamamoto's plan was rejected by the Japanese High Command, but after the Doolittle Raid everyone agreed that the American carriers must be sunk, whatever the cost.

However, in spite of his supremacy in both the quality and quantity of his ships, Yamamoto was labouring under two considerable handicaps. Firstly, although the Japanese were not aware of this, the Americans had broken their codes and were able to identify fairly closely what the enemy was planning.

Secondly, Japanese naval strategy was so subtle that in its efforts to confuse the enemy it often ended up by confusing itself. For the Midway operation, Yamamoto divided his massive fleet – consisting of 11 battleships (including his flagship, the giant *Yamato*), 5 carriers, 12 cruisers, 43 destroyers, 10 submarines and a host of transports and other craft – into five groups, operating over 2000 miles of sea. Thus, while the main group would support a landing on Midway, the initial strike, a feint to deceive the Americans, would be an attack on Dutch Harbor in the Aleutians. The Japanese plan suffered from the defect that it depended entirely on the Americans doing what the Japanese expected them to do. If the Americans did something different then the plan would fail. As it happened, by breaking the Japanese codes, the Americans were able to position their carriers near Midway un-

The carrier *Yorktown* after receiving three hits from Japanese Val dive bombers. Shortly afterwards she received two strikes from Kate torpedo bombers, and finally succumbed to a third attack by the Japanese submarine I-168. PN

known to the Japanese. They could also use their radar (which the Japanese did not have) to give early warning of air attack and use the island of Midway as an 'unsinkable aircraft carrier' from which to launch attacks on the Japanese ships. All of these factors would weigh against Yamamoto when the time came. Against this, however, the Japanese had better planes, better torpedoes, more ships and higher morale. The outcome would depend on the unexpected – and luck.

The first unexpected event concerned the American carrier *Yorktown*, severely damaged the month before at the battle of the Coral Sea. It seemed impossible that the *Yorktown* could be ready to fight again for months, yet a team of 1400 dockworkers at Pearl Harbor worked continuously for 48 hours and she was made battle-ready, becoming the flagship of Task Force 17 with Admiral Frank Fletcher aboard. The two other American carriers, *Enterprise* and *Hornet*, under Admiral Raymond

Spruance, made up Task Force 16, and the two groups rendezvoused at the appropriately named 'Point Luck' northeast of Midway.

On 4 June Nagumo's four carriers, his flagship *Akagi*, along with *Kaga*, *Hiryu* and *Soryu*, ignorant of the fact that the Americans were expecting them, approached Midway from the northwest. Nagumo launched a strike by 108 aircraft from the four carriers to soften up Midway's ground installations and airfield prior to an invasion, keeping back a similar force in case American ships should try to intervene. The Japanese submarine I-168 witnessed the raid, its captain reporting that 'the island turned into a mass of flames, with exploding fuel tanks and military buildings'. The aged and outclassed American fighters were overwhelmed by the Japanese Zero fighters, which shot down 17 Buffaloes and Wildcats. The raid on Midway had succeeded in causing widespread destruction, but it had failed to put the runway out of action. The attack leader, Lieutenant Tomonaga – deputizing for the brilliant Commander Mitsuo Fuschida, who was recovering from appendicitis aboard the flagship – radioed to Nagumo on the *Akagi* that a second attack would be necessary. At that moment the Japanese carriers were themselves under attack by bombers from Midway, but these failed to register a single hit and many were shot down by the protective screen of Zero fighters. It seemed that everything was going Nagumo's way. But at this point he made a decision that was to cost him the battle. His second-strike aircraft had been equipped with torpedoes for use at sea against enemy ships. But Tomonaga's message that another attack would be needed on Midway meant that these planes would have to be re-equipped with bombs – and this would take precious time. Nevertheless, Nagumo issued the order to replace the torpedoes with bombs.

While his crews began the arduous job of rearming the planes Nagumo ordered air patrols to sweep to the east of Midway, looking for American ships. A plane from the cruiser *Tone* reported seeing 10 ships – presumably American – but no carriers. This was a surprise – but if there were no American carriers in the vicinity it need not be too serious. To add to his problems Nagumo was now faced with the problem of taking aboard the first-strike planes returning from Midway. In the rush to rearm the second wave, bombs and torpedoes were carelessly left lying around the decks of the carriers, posing a potential danger if they should be attacked. Further reports from the *Tone's* spotter plane now revealed that contrary to earlier information there was an American carrier in the vicinity, presumably *Yorktown*. Nagumo now changed his mind again, ordering his

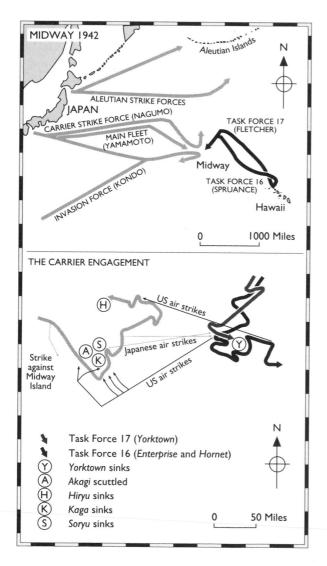

DECISIVE AIRCRAFT AT THE BATTLE OF MIDWAY

Douglas SBD Dauntless Dive Bomber

Engine: 1 Wright R-1820 Radial, 1200 hp
Armament: 2 x .5 in and 2 x .3 in machine guns + 1000 lb bomb load
Max speed: 252 mph at 13,800 ft
Climb rate: 1700 ft per minute
Ceiling: 24,300 ft
Range: 1115 miles at full bomb load

Mitsubishi A6M Zero Fighter

Engine: 1 Nakajima Sakae 21 Radial, 1,130 hp
Armament: 2 x 20 mm cannon, 2 x 7.7 mm machine guns
Max speed: 351 mph at 19,685 feet
Climb rate: 4500 ft per minute
Ceiling: 35,100 ft
Range: 1000 miles

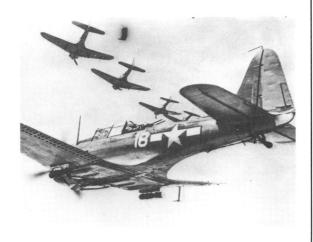

A flight of Douglas Dauntless dive bombers. HDC

ground crews to replace the bombs with torpedoes, in order to attack the ships sighted by the air patrol. More time was wasted. The attack could not now take place until 10.30 a.m.

The unsuccessful raids by the land-based aircraft from Midway had at least given Fletcher and Spruance a firm fix on Nagumo's carriers, and they proceeded to prepare their own air strikes. But things were no easier for the Americans. Nagumo had changed course and the bombers and fighters launched from *Hornet* failed to locate the Japanese carriers at all, many having to refuel on Midway and others ditching in the sea after running out of fuel. Only *Hornet*'s torpedo bombers led by Lieutenant-Commander John Waldron found their target, and these made a brave but unsuccessful attack, with all 15 being shot down by Japanese Zeros and anti-aircaft fire. The only survivor of the 30 aircrew was Ensign George Gay. Gay had an amazing escape: swimming free of his crashed plane he hid under a rubber seat cushion, from where he had a ringside view of the next attack. He was picked up the next day by a Catalina flying boat. *Enterprise*'s torpedo bombers attacked next and met the same fate as those from *Hornet*. That morning only half of the American planes launched from the carriers reached the target, and of them only 7 returned intact. As the Zero pilots returned triumphantly to their carriers to refuel they were applauded by their aircrews. The battle was going well for Nagumo: the Americans had not scored a single hit. For many Japanese pilots the greatest danger now was hubris.

But the massacre of the American fighters and torpedo bombers had not been in vain. They had drawn the deadly Zero fighters down to sea level, allowing *Enterprise*'s dive bombers under Lieutenant-Commander Wade McClusky and a similar group from *Yorktown* to make an unobserved approach at high altitude. On the *Akagi* feverish activity had continued, even during the attacks of the American torpedo bombers, to prepare their own planes for a retaliatory strike. Plane after plane had been brought up from below and arranged on the flightdeck. Engines were running and a triumphant Nagumo ordered his flagship to turn into the wind to allow his planes to take off. Suddenly *Akagi*'s lookouts cried out the chilling words 'Dive bombers!'

McClusky had been lucky. His flight of 30 Douglas Dauntless dive bombers had not located the Japanese carriers at the expected point and were running short of fuel. At 10.00 a.m. he ordered a change of direction to the northwest and suddenly noticed a destroyer heading in that direction at high speed. It was the *Arashi*, which had been hunting for the American submarine *Nautilus*. Having failed to make contact it was now speeding to catch up with the rest of the fleet. Confident he was flying in the right direction now, and knowing that he had no chance of getting back to his home carrier with his fuel tanks almost empty, McClusky decided to go for broke. Sighting the four carriers ahead, with their fighter cover far below finishing off the American torpedo planes, he ordered his group to attack.

From out of the clouds McClusky's dive bomb-

A Japanese heavy cruiser of the Mogami class lists heavily after being hit by US aircraft. A torpedo hangs useless from the port side, while steam and smoke rise from the wreckage. HDC

ers arrowed down towards the Japanese ships. First three bombs crashed into the *Akagi*, burrowing through the deck into the hangars below and igniting the bombs and torpedoes there. The first bomb twisted the midship elevator like 'molten glass' and planes were sent spinning like flaming Catherine wheels. Soon thick black smoke was filling the companionways, forcing everyone out into the open. Commander Fuschida – who had led the airstrike on Pearl Harbor – tried to jump 10 feet to the flight deck, but in his weakened condition only succeeded in breaking both ankles. Strapped onto a bamboo stretcher he was transferred to a waiting destroyer. The officers on the bridge were helpless to stem the terrible fires that raged below decks, and only after great pressure was Nagumo persuaded to abandon his flagship and transfer to the cruiser *Nagara* by climbing out of a window on the bridge and clambering down a smouldering rope into a waiting boat. As the official portrait of the emperor was transferred with him, Nagumo could see disaster all around him. Four bombs in succession had sealed *Kaga*'s fate, while a little way off *Soryu* was pumping smoke into the air in great billows. Her popular captain, Yanagimoto, was determined to go down with his ship. His crew even sent Chief Petty Officer Abe, a champion wrestler, to force the captain to come with him if necessary, but at the last moment his resolve failed as he saw Yanagimoto, sword in hand and silhouetted against the flaming cabin, singing the national anthem and preparing himself for death.

Only the *Hiryu*, fortunate to be 10 miles to the north of the other carriers, had escaped the catastrophe, and on her rested the responsibility of striking back at the American carriers. Admiral Yamaguchi, aboard the *Hiryu*, immediately launched a strike of 58 planes, including 36 Val dive bombers and 10 Kate torpedo bombers, with fighter escort. Twenty miles west of the carrier, *Yorktown*'s fighters met the incoming Japanese bombers, shooting down 11 of them, but the rest got through. Told that an attack was coming, Admiral Fletcher briefly looked up from his charts to tell a worried aide, 'Well, I've got on my tin hat. I can't do anything else now.' The Vals flew on through the anti-aircaft fire from the carriers and her supporting cruisers and achieved three hits. These set *Yorktown* ablaze, virtually stopping her in the water. In the moments before the bombs hit, one Wildcat fighter pilot took off from *Yorktown*'s heaving decks, shot down a passing Val, was hit in turn by a Zero, bailed out, landed in the sea and was rescued by a destroyer, having been in the air for less than sixty seconds. Before the wave of Kate torpedo bombers hit, the carrier's support ships fired their guns into the sea across the planes' path, creating a wall of spray to conceal the crippled flat-top. But their efforts were in vain. The Kates scored two torpedo strikes and the carrier took on a severe list. There was no alternative now but to abandon ship. But in this game of tit-for-tat Spruance was already preparing a new strike from *Enterprise* to take care of the remaining Japanese carrier. Soon the *Hiryu* had been found and overwhelmed by American dive bombers. It took some time for the Japanese carriers to sink, with the US submarine *Nautilus*

surfacing to torpedo the stricken *Soryu* and finish her off. The four carriers took with them to the bottom over 2200 of their crewmen, along with some 250 planes. The *Yorktown* in turn succumbed to a torpedo attack from the Japanese submarine I-168.

It was a brilliant victory for the Americans, a product of guts and clear direction. For the Japanese it had been a thoroughly ragged display by everyone from Yamamoto and Nagumo at the top right down to *Tone*'s spotter pilot, belying their navy's reputation for professionalism. The Japanese paid for their over-confidence with a shattering defeat. The loss of the four carriers, their planes and their experienced aircrews could not be made up for a very long time – if ever. Yamamoto's battleships – whatever their size – counted for little in this new kind of warfare. Without air cover they proved to be helpless against massed air attacks from American carriers, which would be produced by American shipyards at a rate that the Japanese could not possibly match. Spruance and his pilots had won America the breathing space she needed to turn her massive industries to the task of producing war materials. There were still Japanese victories to come, but after Midway defeat for Japan was only a matter of time.

The Battles of El Alamein 1942

El Alamein

British

Commander:	Lieutenant-General Bernard Montgomery
Numbers:	200,000 men and 1000 tanks, mainly Grant and Sherman. 9 infantry and 3 armoured divisions

German

Commander:	General von Stumme (later General Erwin Rommel)
Strength:	96,000 German and Italian troops, with 500 German and Italian tanks

On 28 June 1942 the British armies in North Africa stood on the brink of total defeat. In the words of General Sir Alan Brooke, 'The Middle East situation is about as unhealthy as it can be, and I do not very well see how it can end.' General Erwin Rommel's Afrika Korps had just taken Tobruk and driven the British 8th Army back 750 miles from the frontiers of Libya to a line not two hours drive from Alexandria and the Nile Delta. In Cairo a pall of smoke rose from the British Embassy as records and secret documents were burned. In Alexandria Barclays Bank paid out one million pounds in a single day as customers panicked and fled, their cars clogging the roads to the east. Britain was facing a defeat that would rank with the most disastrous in her history, with the certain loss of Egypt and her vast military base there, as well as the Suez Canal, her lifeline to the east. But more than that, in the context of the war itself, the consequences for the Allies of a British collapse would have been to allow a refuelled and resupplied Rommel to drive on to occupy the Middle East with its tremendous oil resources, and to link up with German forces which were on the point of taking Rostov, and pushing south into the Caucasus, undermining the Soviet Union's southern front. Command of the Red Sea would have enabled Italian and German warships and submarines to threaten Allied links with the Far East and open up the possibility of Germany 'joining hands' with the Japanese in the Indian

Ocean. Nor was this simply a 'Domesday scenario' from some demented war-gamer. It was a part of Hitler's long-term strategical plan, and if Rommel could drive the British from their hastily erected defences at El Alamein there was nothing left to prevent him achieving it.

The British 8th Army commanded by General Sir Claude Auchinleck were dug in on the 40-mile-wide 'Alamein Line' stretching from the coastal village of El Alamein to the Qattara Depression, just 60 miles west of the Nile. To the British soldiers at Alamein there was no defensive line, just open, seemingly limitless desert, but Auchinleck was with them, sharing their hardships and their rations. It was an inhospitable place, as General Bayerlein of the Afrika Korps describes:

A stony, waterless desert where bleak outcrops of dry

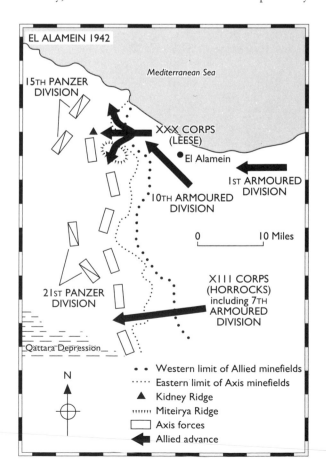

EL ALAMEIN 1942

Mediterranean Sea

15TH PANZER DIVISION

XXX CORPS (LEESE)

El Alamein

1ST ARMOURED DIVISION

10TH ARMOURED DIVISION

0   10 Miles

XIII CORPS (HORROCKS) including 7TH ARMOURED DIVISION

21ST PANZER DIVISION

Qattara Depression

N

• • Western limit of Allied minefields
····· Eastern limit of Axis minefields
▲ Kidney Ridge
""""" Miteirya Ridge
▢ Axis forces
◀ Allied advance

198

rock alternated with stretches of sand sparsely clotted with camel scrub beneath the pitiless African sun – such was the Alamein front in July of 1942. Lying between the rocky hillock of Tel el Eisa on the Mediterranean coast and the 600-foot pyramid of Qaret el Himeimat near the edge of the Qattara Depression, it was the one position in the whole of the Western Desert which could not be outflanked.

Yet here the British 'Desert Rats' turned on Rommel's Afrika Korps, and in prolonged fighting during July 1942 inflicted a decisive check on the German advance. Although British casualties were heavier than Rommel's, there can be no doubt that if there was a single turning point in the whole Desert War it was here, in this vital but unheralded 'grapple' that saved Egypt. Auchinleck had absorbed punishment from a reinforced Afrika Korps and had 'wasted' Rommel's enormous materiel gains from his capture of Tobruk. The Afrika Korps that Montgomery would later face had had its wings clipped. But Churchill, for one, refused to see it that way. He wanted a new commander and appointed General Harold Alexander to replace Auchinleck as overall Middle Eastern commander and Lieutenant-General Bernard Law Montgomery to lead the 8th Army in place of General Ritchie. Montgomery's orders were simple: 'Go down to the desert and defeat Rommel.' General Montgomery was not Churchill's original choice to succeed Ritchie, but when General 'Strafer' Gott was killed in a plane crash, 'Monty' got the job on Alexander's recommendation.

The Germans had no intention of letting the new man settle in. On 31 August Rommel attacked the 8th Army around the Alam Halfa Ridge, but in a hardfought, drawn battle the German offensive was held. Rommel's health now collapsed and he was taken to Austria for treatment, leaving the ailing General Georg von Stumme in charge of German forces. Montgomery meanwhile set about stamping his authority on the 8th Army. He brought his own peculiar sense of humour to the task, telling both officers and men that they would soon 'knock the enemy for six, right out of Africa', and that their job was to kill Germans, 'even the padres – one per weekday and two on Sundays'. But his humour was measured; he could also be prickly and dictatorial. Of him it was said, 'In defeat, indomitable; in victory, insufferable.' He was helped by the sort of massive reinforcement in men and materiel for which Auchinleck would have given his eye-teeth.

By October, the 8th Army stood at 9 infantry and 3 armoured divisions, totalling 200,000 men, with over 1100 tanks – including American Grants and Shermans with 75 mm guns, a match for the Panzer

Australian infantry advance through the smoke at El Alamein. IPA

Mark IV tank – and strong artillery, which Montgomery was going to use as if preparing for one of Haig's vast World War One setpieces. Against this von Stumme could oppose about 96,000 men – half German and half Italian units with a stiffening of German NCOs – as well as 500 tanks, of which only half were German and the rest relatively weak Italian models. On paper, everything favoured Montgomery, who had a 2-to-1 advantage in men and 3-to-1 in materiel, as well as air supremacy.

On the night of 23 October 1942 the first stage of Montgomery's plan – Operation Lightfoot – began with a powerful bombardment from 900 heavy and medium guns, taking the enemy completely by surprise. The British gunners were soon deafened by the roar of their own pieces, their thick gloves burned away by the heat of the barrels. Rommel was convalescing in Austria at the time and the unfortunate von Stumme – rushing to the front and ambushed by an Australian patrol – succumbed to a heart attack.

Under cover of the artillery two British infantry strikes were made: in the north four divisions of Leese's XXX Corps struck along the coast from El Alamein to tear corridors through enemy minefields towards Kidney Ridge and over the Miteirya Ridge, opening the way for Gatehouse's 10th Armoured Division from Lumsden's X Corps; further south, Horrocks's XIII Corps made two thrusts: one east of Jebel Kalakh and the other towards Himeimat. This southern thrust was designed to mislead the Germans into thinking it was the main strike and to persuade them to commit part of their armour away from the main thrust in the north. Captain Grant Murray described the advance in the darkness:

Line upon line of steel-helmeted figures, with rifles at the high port, bayonets catching in the moonlight . . . gave us the thumbs-up sign. We watched them plod on towards the enemy lines, which were by this time shrouded in smoke.

Afrika Korps artillery in action in North Africa. PN

Everywhere the British troops were held up by the depth of Rommel's minefields – his 'Devil's gardens' of 500,000 anti-tank and anti-personnel mines – which were up to five miles deep. And the German artillery, notably their 88mm guns, took a heavy toll of the British armour. Major John Larkin saw 27 British tanks 'go up in sheets of flame one by one, just as if someone had lit the candles on a birthday cake'. By 25 October Rommel had reluctantly returned from Austria to take command of his Afrika Korps, admitting 'there are no more laurels to be earned in Africa'. Short of tanks and fuel and subject to constant bombing and strafing from the RAF, the best he could hope for was to hold the British in a clinch. But in this kind of attritional struggle he knew he must lose in the long run.

On 31 October, Montgomery, undeterred by his lack of progress so far, launched the second phase of the operation, code-named 'Supercharge', directed towards Tel el Aqqaqir. The attack overran the Italian Trento Division and punched holes in the German defences, allowing British armour to break out into open desert behind the German lines. In Montgomery's words,

A real hard and very bloody fight has gone on now for eight days. It has been a terrific party and a complete slogging match, made all the more difficult in that the whole area is just one enormous minefield . . . I have managed to keep the initiative throughout, and so far

Rommel has had to dance entirely to my tune; his counter-attacks and thrusts have been handled without difficulty up to date. I think he is now ripe for the hard blow which may topple him off his perch. It is going in tonight and I am putting in everything I can into it . . . If we succeed it will be the end of Rommel's army.

Rommel, now with just 35 tanks operational and most of his vehicles short of fuel, was faced with complete disaster. Rejecting Hitler's directive to 'stand and die' he ordered a general withdrawal on the night of 4–5 November, abandoning most of his Italian troops. What began as a strategic withdrawal to regroup eventually became a full retreat for nearly 1500 miles, as the 8th Army raced the Afrika Korps all the way back to Tunisia.

Four of Germany's best divisions and eight Italian ones had been destroyed in the battle, and the Axis troops had suffered 20,000 battle casualties, with a further 30,000 prisoners. Almost the entire Axis tank strength had been eliminated, along with 1000 guns. The 8th Army had suffered heavy

British Crusader tanks pressing westwards, helping to turn Rommel's strategic withdrawal into a full retreat. PN

losses themselves: 13,500 battle casualties, 500 tanks and over 100 guns, for the battle had been fought with unprecedented ferocity, the British knowing that defeat would have cost them Egypt and the Suez Canal. When news of Montgomery's victory reached Britain, Churchill ordered the church bells to be rung – not as they once would have been, to signal invasion – but to celebrate Britain's greatest victory of the war. In Churchill's words, 'Before Alamein we never had a victory. After Alamein we never had a defeat.' Churchill was unfair, as usual, in his generalization. Without Auchinleck's defensive victory at the first battle of El Alamein there would have been no second battle of El Alamein to give Montgomery his greatest triumph.

The Battle of Stalingrad 1942–1943

Operation Barbarossa – the German invasion of the Soviet Union in June 1941 – had begun so well for the Wehrmacht that it seemed as if the Führer's description of Russia as a rotten structure only waiting for someone to kick in the door before it collapsed had been right. German troops advanced hundreds of miles, and Soviet prisoners were rounded up in their millions. But the sheer size of Russia, the dreadful winter of 1941 and stiffening Soviet resistance all contributed to a slowing of progress and a need to reassess strategy.

Hitler's plans for the Eastern Front in 1942 involved an offensive in the south, between the Black Sea and the Caspian, followed by a drive into the oilfields of the Caucasus. Whether this was the first step in an even greater campaign that would take in Persia, Iraq and the British oilfields of the Middle East, before linking up with Rommel's Afrika Korps as they drove into Egypt, we cannot be sure. Suffice it to say that Germany's oil requirements in 1942 were massive and it was imperative for Hitler to find alternative sources.

In June 1942 General Halder criticized Hitler's grand strategy, warning him that the Soviets had assembled massive forces to the east of the Caucasus and would counter-attack any German pressure in that area. He also warned the Führer that Soviet tank production was at that moment outstripping German by 1500 a month to 600. Hitler exploded, sacking Halder with the words, 'Spare me this idiotic nonsense. The Russians are finished. In four

week's time they will collapse' – ominous words, which would return to haunt him.

On the southern front Hitler planned to use Army Group B, commanded by General von Weichs, to take up defensive positions along the River Don, as well as capturing the city of Stalingrad (modern Volgograd) – a vital industrial and communications centre – while Army Group A, under Field Marshal List, was to drive into the Caucasus towards the oilfields at Tiflis, Batu and Bakum. The problem was that Army Group B was far too weak to defend Group A's flank and capture Stalingrad. Of the seven armies in Group B, only two were frontline German units, and four were weak Romanian, Italian or Hungarian armies. To make matters worse, Hitler's own attempt to control events personally had led to the resignation or dismissal of able men like Rundstedt, Bock and Halder, and their replacement by weaker and more compliant officers.

On 22 June Army Group B began its assault on Stalingrad, the task of taking the city falling to the crack German 6th Army, commanded by General

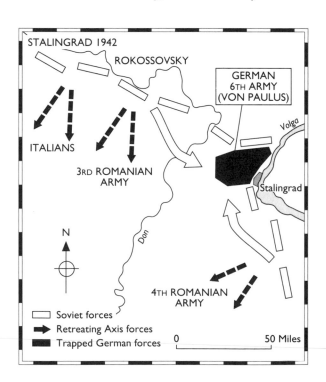

STALINGRAD 1942
ROKOSSOVSKY
GERMAN 6TH ARMY (VON PAULUS)
Volgo
ITALIANS
3RD ROMANIAN ARMY
Stalingrad
N
Don
4TH ROMANIAN ARMY
□ Soviet forces
■▶ Retreating Axis forces
■ Trapped German forces
0   50 Miles

Friederich von Paulus, and the 4th Panzer Army, temporarily under the same command. It took two months of heavy fighting before the 6th Army entered the suburbs. The Soviets had entrusted the defence of Stalingrad to a three-man military council, including General Yeremenko and future Soviet leader Nikita Khrushchev. They had evacuated all 'useless mouths' – old people, women and children – and turned the city into a fortress. When the German bombardment became too heavy, factory workers left their lathes and machines and joined General Chuikov's Red Army soldiers in intense house-to-house fighting against the Germans. By 22 September von Paulus had occupied the centre of the city and the right bank of the River Volga – but Soviet resistance was stiffening all the time, and even in the most difficult conditions the Stalingrad tank factories kept working. Heavy bombing by the Luftwaffe had destroyed so many buildings in the city that the Germans found their progress held up by fallen masonry, in which the Soviet defenders lived and fought with a remarkable tenacity. Tanks became useless in this rubble, and the fighting was often hand-to-hand, using rifles, bayonets and even knives. Progress slowed to a crawl and casualties mounted as every house had to be taken from the Soviet defenders. Soviet general Talensky described the fighting:

During the first stage our losses were, of course, very heavy indeed. And yet the people who survived acquired a tremendous experience in the technique of house to-house fighting. Two or three men of such experience could be worth a whole platoon. They knew every drainpipe, every manhole, every shell hole and crater in and around their particular building, they knew every brick that could serve as shelter. Among piles of rubble, which no tank could penetrate, a man would sit there, inside his manhole or crater, or hole in the floor, and, looking through his simple periscope, he would turn on his tommy-gun the moment he saw any German within firing distance. Seldom anything less than a direct hit could knock him out.

A German soldier wrote:

Imagine Stalingrad – 80 days and nights of hand-to-hand struggles. The streets are no longer measured in metres but in corpses. Stalingrad is no longer a town. By day it is an enormous cloud of burning, blinding smoke. It is a vast furnace lit by the reflection of the flames.

Meanwhile, the Soviet commander, Marshal Timoshenko, had been sacked by Stalin and replaced by Marshal Zhukov, who, with artillery general Voronov and airforce chief Koikov, was planning a huge counter-attack. South of Stalingrad

The Stalingrad department store in whose basement von Paulus set up the HQ of the German 6th Army. AKG

a million Soviet troops with 900 new T-34 tanks were preparing to strike at the weak points in Army Group B. On 19 November the Soviets under General Rokossovsky attacked the Romanian 3rd and 4th Armies, cracking each of them and driving the poorly trained Romanian troops back in disorder. Immediately von Paulus with the German 6th Army was isolated – and indeed surrounded – with no support on either flank. In a matter of days 300,000 German and other Axis troops were trapped in the city. General von Weichs decided that he had no option but to pull von Paulus out from the trap that Stalingrad had clearly become. But the Führer intervened to prevent him. Hitler had been convinced by an idle boast from Göring that the Luftwaffe could keep von Paulus supplied with 500 tons of supplies each day and that there was no need to pull him out. Grasping at straws, Hitler ordered one of his best commanders, Manstein, to try to rescue the 6th Army in Stalingrad. Manstein had little faith in Göring's boasts, justifiably as it turned out, for over the next 11 days no more than 150 tons – and usually much less than that – was dropped daily into von Paulus's lines by the Luftwaffe. Manstein was convinced that the 6th Army must be evacuated, otherwise it would be lost in the ruins of Stalingrad. Instructing von Paulus to be ready to make a sortie towards him, Manstein began 'Operation Winterblitz', striking towards Stalingrad from the north with his Army Group Don, followed by an immense column of supply vehicles, with heavy lifting gear and bulldozers to rescue von Paulus's guns. But von Paulus stubbornly insisted that he had an order from the Führer to hold his position and refused to assist Manstein's rescue bid. At one stage Hoth's 4th Panzer Army was a mere 30 miles from the 6th Army's lines, and the trapped German soldiers could see the flares in the night sky fired by their comrades. While von Paulus mulishly clung to the notion that a break-out was impossible, his troops were starving and freezing to death. As one German soldier wrote:

Until Christmas 1942 the daily bread ration for every man was 100 grammes. After Christmas the ration was reduced to 50 grammes per head. Later on only those in the forward line received 50 grammes per day. No bread

was issued to men in regimental headquarters and upwards. The others were given watery soup, which we tried to improve by making use of bones from horses we dug up.

Weather conditions were appalling:

Completely cut off, the men in field grey just slouched on, invariably filthy and invariably louse-ridden, their weary shoulders sagging, from one defence position to another . . . And whenever any individual could do no more, when even the onward driving lash of fear ceased to have meaning, then like an engine which has used its last drop of fuel, the debilitated body ran down and came to a standstill. Soon a kindly drift of snow covered the object and only the toe of a jackboot or an arm frozen to stone could remind you that what was now an elongated white hummock had quite recently been a human being.

When Manstein contacted Hitler and asked him to order von Paulus to comply, the Führer refused, congratulating the 6th Army commander on his tenacious defence. Matters took a turn for the worse on 20 December when the Soviets poured out from a thick, icy fog and completely overran the 8th Italian Army. Manstein rushed to reinforce the German lines, but all the time his own forces were

---

Soviet infantrymen shelter behind fallen masonry in the devastated city. ME

diminishing. He believed that the last possible date for a withdrawal by the 6th Army was the end of December. He was right. In the words of General Mellenthin:

It was often asked, 'Is there nobody to tell Paulus the truth?' To which the answer was, 'Before 24 December there was no need, since there was still a hope that 6th Army might break out. After 24 December there was no point, for what is the purpose in telling a man condemned to death that he must surely die ?'

In the first few days of January 1943, the Soviets captured the two German airstrips in Stalingrad and split the defending troops into two groups. Without any landing facilities all supplies had to be dropped by parachute, and most fell into Soviet hands. It was only a matter of time now before the 6th Army was overrun: 30,000 of its men were receiving medical attention and, it is estimated, up to 18,000 more were lying injured and untended in the rubble of the city. On 30 January the Soviets occupied the centre of the city and began to mop up the last vestiges of German resistance. Hitler had radioed von Paulus that there must be no surrender:

Surrender is forbidden. 6th Army will hold their positions to the last man and the last round and by their heroic endurance will make an unforgettable contribution towards the establishment of a defensive front and the salvation of the Western world.

This was all very well in the comfort of Berlin, but in the hell that Stalingrad had become it was the final straw. A nerve-racked von Paulus – recently promoted Field Marshal on the grounds that no German of that rank had ever capitulated – surrendered on 31 January. What was left of the 6th Army – 90,000 men – marched off into captivity, few ever to return to Germany. Along with them the Soviets captured 60,000 vehicles, 1500 tanks and 6000 artillery pieces. It was a shattering defeat for Germany, and a personal humiliation for the Führer. In the final stages of the fighting Stalingrad had claimed the lives of 147,000 German soldiers.

Germany's defeat at Stalingrad was the turning point of the war on the Eastern Front – indeed of the entire Second World War. Hitler had expected to be able to win an easy victory over the Soviet Union, but had seriously underestimated the capacity of the Soviet state to absorb punishment and to fight back. Before Stalingrad the Germans had been confident, measuring advances in hundreds of miles and prisoners in millions, but afterwards the Eastern Front began to absorb the full resources of the Third Reich just to hold back the teeming Soviet hordes, whose new tanks and planes outperformed

Von Paulus and his adjutants – together with 90,000 German troops – surrender to the Soviets, 31 January 1943. AKG

their German counterparts. From Stalingrad the Soviet people drew inspiration, and in the next 30 months the tide of war carried Communism inexorably westwards, until it covered the Balkans and much of Central Europe. Stalingrad began a process that was to make the Soviet Union one of the world's superpowers, impose an 'iron curtain' on Europe, and plunge the world into the uncertainties of a Cold War.

The Battle of Dien Bien Phu 1954

> **Dien Bien Phu**
>
> **French**
> Commander: General Navarre, General Cogny and Colonel de Castries
> Numbers: 10,000 men (20 battalions of infantry, including Foreign Legion)
>
> **Vietminh**
> Commander: General Giap
> Strength: 50,000 men (5 divisions), with 190 guns

After the defeat of France in June 1940 and the subsequent collapse of her colonial empire in the East, nationalist movements in French Indo-China fought against the Japanese troops of occupation, hoping that at the end of the war they would win their independence. But when Japanese troops surrendered in 1945 the French demonstrated their intention to reoccupy their former colonies. In Vietnam they were stoutly resisted by the Vietminh, a Communist-led nationalist movement headed by a former London pastry cook named Ho Chi Minh. On 2 September 1945 Ho proclaimed the Democratic Republic of Vietnam, which the French refused to recognize. From their strongholds in the extreme north of the country, along the Chinese borders, Ho's guerrillas under the command of ex-history teacher Vo Nguyen Giap – whose wife had died in a French prison – attacked French troops arriving in southern Vietnam. For the next eight years a bitter war raged through Vietnam. Even with the support of the United States the French were not able to defeat the Vietminh, and by the time General Henri Eugène Navarre took command of French forces in Vietnam, most people in France were thoroughly sickened by the cost in lives and money that the war had imposed.

By 1953 the strategic position in the Far East had changed. With Stalin now dead, the Soviets were trying to establish better relations with the West and saw a settlement of the Korean and Indo-Chinese wars as a way of achieving this. Now that the war in Korea was over, Communist China was in a position to send supplies to the Vietminh on a much larger scale. Both these factors were pushing France in the direction of a settlement of the Indo-China situation. The French government made it clear to Navarre that they were looking for a way out of the war and did not expect him to win great victories. Even with a total force of 517,000 men – 369,000 of whom were Vietnamese – Navarre could not hope to pin down his elusive enemy for long enough to inflict a decisive defeat on the Communists.

Navarre had convinced himself that control of the air would enable him to place a large French force in a forward base and keep them supplied with food and munitions, even during a siege by the Vietminh. He hoped that such a force would persuade General Giap to abandon his guerrilla tactics and concentrate a large force around the base, which would give the French the chance to use their tanks to inflict a decisive defeat on them. Navarre selected a village named Dien Bien Phu, some 200 miles to the west of Hanoi, right on the border with Laos. The village was situated in a long, narrow valley, overlooked by mountains and surrounded by thick undergrowth. Not only would the garrison at Dien Bien Phu act as a lure to Giap's guerrillas, but it would also deter the Communists from entering the kingdom of Laos. It was a gamble, and when Navarre informed the French government of his plan their acceptance involved a *volte-face* from the instructions they had originally given him. They had not been looking for a victory, but now they were agreeing to let their commander gamble with the lives of 13,000 French soldiers, not to mention billions of francs and national prestige.

On 20 November 1953 French, African and Vietnamese paratroopers landed around Dien Bien Phu and, after a stiff fight with a nearby guerrilla force, succeeded in taking possession of the valley. Soon an airstrip had been built and thousands of French troops were ferried in, along with tanks, heavy artillery and equipment to erect a series of powerful blockhouses. But the French air capacity was being stretched to its limit, and only a tenth of the supplies necessary to build and maintain the camp were brought in on time. The French preparations went on in full view of the Vietminh, who occupied the surrounding high ground. When he heard what was happening General Giap could hardly believe his luck. Such folly was inconceivable – it must be a trap. In fact it was, but it was the French who were going to be trapped. Giap decided to take up the French challenge and ordered three divisions – the 308th Infantry, 312th Infantry and 351st Heavy Weapons – to begin marching towards Dien Bien Phu. Two other divisions, even closer to the French base, could be there in days. Navarre was matching about 10,000 French troops against nearly 50,000 Vietminh because his personal arrogance convinced him that Giap could not assemble more than 20,000 men and that these would be of poor quality and badly supplied. A Vietminh soldier – Cao Xuan Nghia – described just how it was done:

We had to cross mountains and jungles, marching at night and sleeping by day to avoid enemy bombing. We sometimes slept in foxholes, or just by the trail. We each carried a rifle, ammunition and hand grenades, and our packs contained a blanket, a mosquito net, and a change of clothes. We each had a week's supply of rice, which was refilled at depots along the way. We ate greens and bamboo shoots that we picked in the jungle, and

occasionally villagers would give us a bit of meat. I'd been in the Vietminh for nine years by then, and I was accustomed to it.

Using vast numbers of peasants with Peugeot bicycles – purchased from pre-war French shops and capable of carrying 500 pounds in weight – as well as every kind of wheeled, human or animal transport, Giap kept his front-line troops supplied.

In December Navarre and General Cogny – Navarre's bull-like commander in northern Vietnam – chose the man they wanted to command Dien Bien Phu: Colonel Christian de Castries. De Castries was a dashing tank commander, an aristocrat and world champion horseman, more suited to the warfare of an earlier age. As an exponent of aggressive and mobile warfare he was a curious choice for a task involving tenacity and bulldog defence. Navarre spent Christmas with the troops in the base at Dien Bien Phu and supervised the building work that was going on all round. The French were in high spirits, spoiling for a fight and convinced, like their commander, that the Vietminh offered no real threat. Yet Navarre was not being honest with his men. Even at that moment two Vietminh divisions had occupied the high ground

VO NGUYEN GIAP

Originally a schoolteacher in Vietnam, Giap became a revolutionary and was forced to flee to China. He was trained there by Mao's Communist Red Army and learned the futility of pursuing conventional forms of warfare against trained opponents. Instead he learned infiltration techniques, and these were to stand him in good stead when he returned to Vietnam to fight against the Japanese army of occupation. In 1945, acting on the orders of Ho Chi Minh, Giap organized a national resistance army and took it into the mountains along the Chinese border. After the victory of the Communists in China in 1949 he received help from the Chinese to launch attacks on French garrisons. Although defeated in the Red River region in 1951, he showed resilience and patience, organizing small, mobile guerrilla units. In 1954 his Vietminh troops inflicted a heavy defeat on the French at Dien Bien Phu, a defeat from which France did not recover. With the creation of Communist North Vietnam Giap became minister of defence in Ho Chi Minh's government and directed his country's strategy in the protracted war against Vietnam and its American allies, culminating in total victory in 1975.

Giap and his general staff during the Indo-China War. AKG

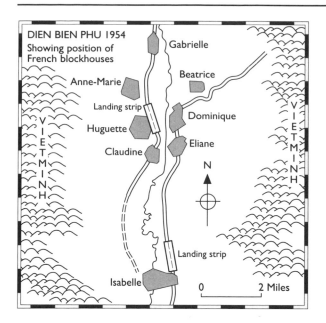

DIEN BIEN PHU 1954
Showing position of
French blockhouses

Gabrielle

Anne-Marie

Beatrice

Landing strip

Dominique

Huguette

Eliane

Claudine

N

VIETMINH

VIETMINH

Landing strip

Isabelle

0   2 Miles

surrounding the valley, and the only way into and out of the base was by air. In the wet, foggy conditions of that area the French air force was unable to strike effectively at the newly arrived Communists, and they were given time to dig in. Had the French been aware of the ant-like columns of human porters carrying and dragging heavy guns through the jungle, they would not have enjoyed the carol singing by their German comrades in the Foreign Legion. 'Stille Nacht' it might be, but it was not going to stay that way for long.

Navarre had become depressed by the size of the Communist effort. He had underestimated Giap, and began to consider ways of evacuating the troops from Dien Bien Phu. But they were now completely surrounded and it would need an enormous effort by the air force to get them out. Even the tanks that Navarre had seen as a decisive weapon in the defence of the base were now seen to be useless. The terrain, which had looked so suitable on faulty French maps, turned out to be heavily covered in bush, which entangled the armoured vehicles and rendered them useless. The problem was compounded by the rains, which, when they came, made the ground so soft that the tanks became bogged down and inoperable.

By January 1954 Giap's full strength had arrived and had taken up position in the jungle and on the hills surrounding the French base. While they entrenched themselves Giap spent 10 days studying the French position for weaknesses. He was not going to play into the enemy's hands by wasting lives in 'human-wave' attacks. He had a well-established supply line spreading back 70 miles to Tuan Giao and, contrary to French expectations, he

could keep his troops in action for months. The French defenders, on the other hand, were entirely dependent on air drops, and in poor flying conditions loads would either be lost or returned to base if visibility was too bad. Time was on Giap's side, and so he decided to wait. During the foggy, damp weather of February and March, he let the elements work for him to lower French morale. The French were frustrated: they had expected the Vietminh to attack at once and walk straight into their assembled heavy artillery, particularly their twenty 105 mm howitzers. French views of Vietminh artillery are illustrated by this comment of Navarre's: 'They must have a gun or two but most of the time the shells don't even explode. It's a farce.' But Giap had learned from his mistakes earlier in the war. He had obtained from the Soviet Union over forty 105 mm guns and was taking his time in digging them into the hillsides. Giap had a further 150 lighter artillery pieces, though the French liked to ridicule the Communist gunners as incompetent.

As days passed, and Giap still did not attack, Navarre became more depressed. In his heart he knew that the defenders of Dien Bien Phu were doomed, and yet he dared not admit it publicly. In Geneva talks were going on to end the Korean and Indo-Chinese wars, and yet the most decisive battle of either war was about to be fought before peace could be restored diplomatically. Afraid that a peace settlement might rob him of his victory at the eleventh hour, Giap ordered the attack on Dien Bien Phu to begin on 13 March.

Colonel de Castries had prior knowledge of the Vietminh attack, which he gained from Communist prisoners taken on 13 March. At 5.00 p.m. he retired to his bunker to keep in touch with Cogny in Hanoi and with his own commanders spread around the base. As he did so he could hear the sound of artillery fire and the fierce staccato of machine guns and automatic weapons. The onset of the Communist artillery was overwhelming and the French were shocked to find themselves outgunned right from the start. The arrogant one-armed artillery commander, Charles Piroth, had airily boasted to Navarre that 'no Vietminh cannon will be able to fire three rounds before being destroyed by my artillery'. Such talk had been easy. But now Piroth was humbled by his failure to match the Vietminh gunners. Later he was to pull the pin on a hand grenade and kill himself in his quarters.

Chaos reigned and many French telephone wires – carelessly laid in the open and above ground – were immediately cut by the impact of Communist shells. But the Vietminh infantry attack was in its turn being cut to pieces by the concentrated French fire; hundreds of fanatical peasant-soldiers stormed into the teeth of a torrent of rifle and machine-gun fire, blocking the firing slits of French bunkers with their bodies and leaping onto barbed wire entanglements so that their comrades could pass over their bodies. Strongpoint Beatrice, with a garrison of 750 men, was overrun and only 194 French soldiers survived the struggle.

On 28 March a French aeroplane trying to evacuate the wounded was destroyed on the ground. One of its survivors – Nurse Lieutenant Geneviève de Galard-Terraube – became an unwitting member of the garrison of the doomed base and stayed there for the next six weeks helping an overworked medical staff deal with the hundreds of battle casualties. She was later decorated with the Legion of Honour.

News of the plight of Dien Bien Phu spread throughout Vietnam and inspired many French volunteers – like Texans flooding to the Alamo in 1831 – to go to the base to fight alongside their doomed comrades. French paratroopers – some of the toughest fighters in the world – led by the legendary Lieutenant-Colonel Marcel Bigeard, risked their lives by dropping at night within the French-held areas of the base. They stiffened the resistance but could not turn the tide. Each day the Vietminh closed in, sometimes by undermining French positions, sometimes by digging trenches forward until

they were so close to the defenders they could almost shake hands, but often by sheer hand-to-hand fighting. The heavy rain continued to hamper the French airforce, which was forced to fly low and consequently suffered heavy casualties: 62 planes shot down and a further 167 badly damaged.

The French defenders – like their distant commanders in Hanoi and Saigon – knew they were doomed unless a major rescue bid could be launched. As one man put it – recalling the words of one of his predecessors at Sedan in 1870 – they were in a chamber pot and the enemy was unbuttoning his trousers. But France no longer had the will – or the resources – to do any more for her soldiers. All eyes turned to the United States, the one power that might have been able to rescue the defenders of Dien Bien Phu. Many Americans were prepared to support anyone who was fighting Communism, but the current Geneva talks made it difficult to risk antagonizing the Soviet Union and China, and possibly escalating the struggle into a full-blown Far Eastern war. American president Eisenhower approached Britain and asked prime

Vietminh troops celebrate their victory on the wreckage of a French B-26, 7 May 1954. AKG

minister Churchill if he was willing to undertake joint action to help France. However, the British had no wish to be drawn into France's colonial problems and were reluctant to jeopardize the peace process at Geneva. Rebuffed, the Americans reluctantly concluded that they could not unilaterally interfere to help the French. A plan for using atomic bombs had even been considered, but finally the Americans decided that 'it was the wrong war at the wrong time'.

All that was left was suffering – and honour. Half the French garrison was dead or wounded; food and ammunition were in short supply. Whether their morale would have been lifted if the French had seen how the Communist soldiers suffered is uncertain. In the battle so far the Vietminh had suffered terrible casualties: 7900 killed and over 15,000 wounded. Few seriously injured men received medical treatment and some of the scenes in the Vietminh lines resembled the muddy horrors of the Somme or Passchendaele. But the Vietnamese knew that they were winning – and this lifted morale. On 1 May Giap ordered an all-out attack, and soon the French defenders were hemmed into an area just a quarter of a mile square. At 5.30 p.m. Navarre ordered de Castries to cease firing. The French had no intention of surrendering – there must be no white flags – but lives would be saved if they simply stopped fighting. Colonel – now General – de Castries put on a clean uniform, with a chestful of decorations, and stood silently as Vietminh soldiers burst into his office. As he was marched out under guard he could see that the Tricolour had been pulled down and replaced by the red flag of the Democratic Republic of Vietnam. Like shrouds, 80,000 French parachutes lay discarded right across the narrow, muddy valley.

The French defeat at Dien Bien Phu in 1954 was a result of military arrogance on the part of French commanders. An American adviser had told the French, 'The Vietminh have no vehicles and no aeroplanes. How can they be mobile?' Such contempt for an Asian enemy was typical of the ethnocentrism of commanders schooled in the colleges of Western Europe and America, rather than the hard school of guerrilla warfare in the jungles of Indo-China.

The battle of Dien Bien Phu brought an end to French rule in Vietnam and led to the establishment of two states, a Communist north and an American-sponsored south, divided at the 17th parallel. But the Communists never accepted the division of the country and guerrillas – named Viet Cong – began infiltrating the south of the country in an attempt to subvert the government of South Vietnam. In 1961 the United States became actively involved in sending arms and military advisers to help the South Vietnamese in their struggle against the North. By the mid-1960s America had committed herself to the defence of the South and a full-blown war had begun in Vietnam, which only ended with the fall of Saigon to the Communists and the evacuation of the last American advisers in 1975.

The Six Day War: Israeli Airstrike 5 June 1967

Six Day War

Israeli
Defence minister:	Moshe Dayan
Army:	264,000 troops
Tanks:	800
Airforce:	300 combat planes

Egypt
Commander:	President Nasser
Army:	240,000 troops
Tanks:	1200
Airforce:	500 combat planes

Syria, Jordan, Lebanon and Iraq
Armies:	307,000 troops
Tanks:	1304 tanks
Airforce:	457 combat planes

The creation of the state of Israel in 1948 introduced a new and controversial factor in the tortured politics of the Middle East. Israel had no secure frontiers and before 1967 felt constantly threatened by neighbouring Arab states committed to her destruction. Settlements in the northern part of the country were overlooked by Syrian troops and artillery on the Golan Heights, while in the southern frontier areas like the Gaza Strip and Sinai there was a constant threat of cross-border raids by fedayeen guerrillas. The central regions of Israel were also endangered by the West Bank territory of Jordan, which virtually split the country in half and could be used by guerrillas to raid densely populated areas. Even Jerusalem – which the Israelis regarded as their historical capital – was split, with Jordan holding the eastern part. And above all, President Nasser of Egypt kept the Suez Canal closed to Israeli shipping, which could only use the Red Sea port of Eilat – on the Gulf of Aqaba – for trade with the outside world. And if Nasser should choose to close the Strait of Tiran (giving access to the Gulf) to Israeli ships, Israel's lifeline to the rest of the world would be cut.

Since the Suez War of 1956 United Nations troops had patrolled the Sinai frontier to reduce the danger of clashes between Egyptian and Israeli troops. This had not reassured the Israelis, who looked to the United States and France to keep them supplied with the latest weaponry to maintain their military advantage over their Arab enemies. In his turn Nasser had been receiving long- and medium-range bombers from the Soviet Union, with which he hoped to be able to strike at Israeli

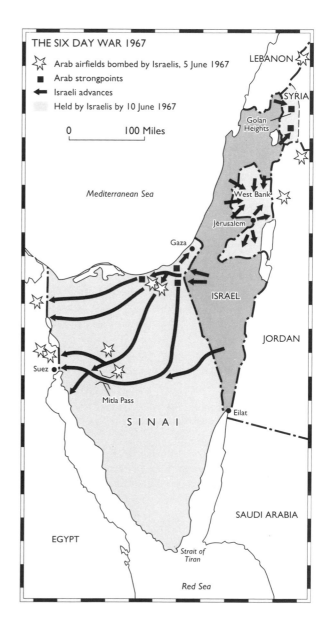

THE SIX DAY WAR 1967

☆ Arab airfields bombed by Israelis, 5 June 1967
■ Arab strongpoints
← Israeli advances
░ Held by Israelis by 10 June 1967

0 _____ 100 Miles

cities like Tel Aviv and Haifa, only 30 minutes' or
less flying time away. With the ever-present danger
of an Arab attack, Israel assumed the right to
retaliate – in advance. The concept of the pre-
emptive strike was important to Israeli military
leaders, and when in 1967 Nasser began to raise the
temperature, ordering UN troops to leave the Sinai
border and even closing the Strait of Tiran to Israeli
ships, Israeli defence minister Moshe Dayan was
convinced the time had come for a pre-emptive
strike.

Israel was facing the greatest threat to her
existence since 1948, with the possibility of attacks
on three fronts: from Egypt in Sinai, from Jordan
in the West Bank and from the Syrians in the Golan
Heights. Heavily outnumbered, Dayan knew that he
could not allow the Arabs to make the first move.
At 7.45 a.m. on 5 June, and for the next three hours,
Israel launched the first decisive aerial 'blitzkrieg' in
history, attacking dozens of airfields in Egypt, Syria,
Jordan and Iraq and destroying over 400 Arab
planes on the ground for the loss of just 26 of her
own.

Ten major Egyptian bases were hit by Israeli
Mirage and Mystère jets flying in low under Arab
radar screens, and by the time the Cairo West
control tower was broadcasting 'We are being

attacked . . . we are being attacked . . .', dozens of
Egyptian planes were already smoking wrecks. The
first wave of jets had pitted the runways to prevent
any interceptors getting into the air, while subsequent waves strafed the maintenance works and
control towers. At Cairo West 30 Tupolev Tu-16
bombers – which the Israelis particularly feared –
were picked off one by one, with their fuel tanks
exploding and pumping black smoke into the air. At
Cairo International, dozens of MiG-21 fighters –
the USSR's best at that time – were lined up as if
for action. But the Israelis fired their cannons into
the fuel tanks and the MiGs exploded, two or three
at a time. In Sinai, each Egyptian airfield was
attacked virtually simultaneously, and squadrons of
MiGs, sometimes the older 17s, were destroyed. At
Abn Sueir four MiGs got into the air but were shot
down in one of the few dogfights of the day. At Ras
Banas the Israelis destroyed more Soviet bombers
– Ilyushin Il-28s this time.

Some of the Israeli jets had returned for refuelling and were making second strikes before the enemy knew what had hit them. At Jebel Libni three unlucky Egyptians were caught taxiing on the runways and died in the flaming wrecks of their planes. At Bir Gifgafa one of the USSR's latest helicopters – the huge Mi-6 – was caught hovering above the ground with a full cargo. Two Mystères shot it out of the air and it crashed in flames onto some Il-16 bombers, causing a huge fireball.

While the Egyptian air force was being wiped out, the Israelis quickly turned their attention to the lesser – yet still potent – threat from other Arab air forces. Jordan's small airforce of MiGs, Hunters and Il-14 bombers was destroyed in minutes, while in Syria 57 planes were destroyed on the ground.

This brilliantly coordinated strike won the war for Israel in a matter of hours. With total air superiority Moshe Dayan was now able to carry out ground operations to achieve the territorial targets Israel was aiming for. In Sinai, Israeli armour overran Egyptian positions and the retreating Arab columns of tanks and vehicles were trapped and destroyed in the Mitla Pass by Israeli planes. In a matter of six days Israel took the Gaza Strip, reached the Suez Canal, and re-opened the Strait of Tiran. East Jerusalem was seized from the Jordanians, as well as the whole West Bank territory. In the north the Golan Heights were occupied after a stiff fight with the Syrians. The map of the Middle East had been changed within a week. The Arabs – notably Egypt – had suffered a stupefying defeat. Soviet planes and tanks were so much scrap and Egypt had lost control of the entire Sinai Peninsula.

Israel had gained all the frontiers she had wanted and had achieved total military superiority in the area. Overnight she had become the dominant power in the region.

But the airstrike of 5 June 1967 was decisive less in the victory that it brought Israel than in the problems it created. Israel had won the 'Six Day War' so decisively that the Arabs felt humiliated. They would never accept Israel as a neighbour now that she had conquered so much Arab territory and created so many refugees. The Palestinian problem, which had started with the creation of the state of Israel, now snowballed, and all Israel's neighbours felt embittered by her actions. Since 1948 hundreds of thousands of Arab people had lost their homes in Israel, and been forced to live in camps in Sinai, Gaza and the West Bank. Now even these camps had been taken and once more the refugees were forced to flee to neighbouring Arab states in search of somewhere to live.

Now that the Israelis had something with which to bargain – Arab land – they had an opportunity to negotiate with their neighbours to win a peaceful future. However, many Israelis – inspired by their military successes – refused to return land that they saw as part of *Eretz Israel* – their biblical land. They encouraged Jews from Africa and the Soviet Union to settle in these newly won territories, particularly the West Bank, so that the land would cease to be Arab and become Jewish. The problems of the Middle East, rather than being solved by Israel's pre-emptive strike, were made many times worse, creating a legacy of bitterness that has continued to ferment for a whole generation with little hope of a solution.

The Second Gulf War 1991

The Second Gulf War

Iraq

Commander:	President Saddam Hussein
Aircraft:	1050 (649 combat fighters including 30 MiG-29s, 32 MiG-25s, 90 MiG-23s, 155 MiG-21s)
Ground Troops:	260,000 (originally estimated at 540,000)
Tanks:	under 2000 (mainly T-72s; originally estimated at 4000 tanks)

Coalition

Commanders:	General Colin Powell, General Norman Schwarzkopf
Aircraft:	1820 combat aircraft (1376 American, 175 Saudi, 69 British, 42 French)
Main Types:	110 A-6E, 144 A-10, 100 F-14, 120 F-15C, 261 F-16, 190 F/A-18, 103 Tornado
Ground Strength:	

	Men	Tanks
Afghanistan	300	
Bahrein	3500	
Bangladesh	2000	
Czechoslovakia	520	
Egypt	40,000	400
France	13,500	110
Kuwait	7000	
Morocco	2000	
Oman	2500	24
Niger	400	
Pakistan	10,000	
Qatar	4000	24
Saudi Arabia	95,000	550
Senegal	500	
Syria	20,000	
UAE	4000	
United Kingdom	35,000	210
USA	532,000	2000

Naval strength (major units): 8 aircraft carriers, 2 battleships, 20 cruisers, 20 destroyers, 5 submarines

Victory in battle can be decisive or otherwise depending on what use is made of it. At Cannae in 216 BC, Hannibal achieved a total victory over the Romans, but, ignoring the advice of his generals, he did not advance to take Rome itself; as a result the war dragged on for another 14 years until his final defeat at Zama. Operations Desert Storm and Desert Sabre during the Gulf War in January and February 1991 comprise the most one-sided military encounters in recorded history. If ever a victory was decisive this one was, and yet to call it so may be very misleading. If judged in terms of the US-led Coalition's achievement of the UN's aim of removing the Iraqis from Kuwait, then it was completely successful. However, if it is seen in terms of the unstated aims of the Coalition forces – notably the United States and Britain – to weaken Iraq's military potential, destroy her nuclear capacity and overthrow the regime of Saddam Hussein, then it clearly failed.

Saddam Hussein was not always an enemy in the eyes of the Americans. As an opponent of the unstable, fundamentalist state of Iran in the First Gulf War he was regarded as a useful tool of the United States between 1979 and 1988, and became a recipient of American and European aid. Although a brutal dictator and a mass killer, even of his own people, he was seen as a stabilizing force in an area of great strategic importance for the West. Even as late as February 1990, an American diplomat told Saddam, 'You are a force for moderation in the region and the United States wishes to broaden her relations with Iraq.' In fact, Saddam was confident that the United States would not oppose his occupation of Kuwait when it came, and quoted the American ambassador in Baghdad as saying that her country had 'no opinion on Arab–Arab conflicts, like your border disagreement with Kuwait'. Saddam Hussein found it easy to bluff the Americans. They felt he was their 'creature' and failed to take seriously the numerous intelligence warnings in the summer of 1990 of the build-up of Iraqi forces on the border of Kuwait. When the invasion came – on 1 August 1990 – it was a bombshell to President George Bush's administration. Bush felt betrayed. And now he faced an additional worry. Would Saddam Hussein stop at Kuwait or would he order his tanks into Saudi Arabia to make himself master of the world's richest oilfields? Part of Saddam's strategy was based on the theory that the Western powers, notably the USA, would not use force to evict him from Kuwait because they would be unwilling to suffer the 10,000 casualties that he was convinced he could inflict on them in a war to liberate the sheikhdom.

Saddam had given a lot of thought to Western psychology. As well as believing the USA would not accept high casualties, he also believed that he could use the threat of chemical and biological weapons to be delivered by his Scud missiles against Israel as a form of blackmail. In addition, since the war with Iran, he had spent so much money on state-of-the-art defences against air attack, including bunkers so strong and sophisticated that they could resist even the latest American technology, that he felt confident in outfacing Western threats in the UN. Nor was he slow to exploit Western intelligence failures. He encouraged the West to overestimate his military potential – one US report stated 'Iraq is superb on the defense' – so that by the UN deadline of 15 January, by which time he was supposed to have evacuated Kuwait, the Americans believed he had 540,000 men dug into a formidable line of defences on the Kuwait-Saudi border. In fact he scarcely had more than 260,000.

But when the Americans and their allies called Saddam's bluff by launching Operation Desert Storm, the Iraqi dictator was revealed for what he was, a posturing bully. The fury of the air campaign was beyond anyone's experience. In the space of a few days the Coalition revealed an array of technological marvels that were light years beyond anything that Saddam Hussein could imagine, and compared to which his Scud missiles were like slingshots. The best of the Iraqi airforce took sanctuary in Iran, while the first two MiG-29s that took off to engage American F-15Es only succeeded in shooting each other down by mistake. B-52s from European bases pounded his nuclear, chemical and biological weapons plants, while Tomahawk cruise missiles from American battleships in the waters off Kuwait picked out targets in Baghdad with the skill of a cat burglar. Day and night for over five weeks the devastation of Iraq continued. After military installations and communications networks had been destroyed, the bombers turned their attention to softening up Iraqi ground troops, particularly the Republican Guard with their Soviet T-72 tanks.

Saddam's own strategy baffled military experts. He did not use his airforce at all and abandoned his ground troops to an unbelievable pounding. Apart from one sideshow – the raid on Khafji – undertaken on the initiative of one of his best generals,

Saddam Hussein as heroic warrior; from a mural at Basra. PN

Qatari troops in Khafji, 1 February 1991, during the Iraqi
raid on the Saudi border town. GAMMA

his ground troops simply stayed in their bunkers
and took a drubbing. His random use of Scud
missiles was a political rather than a military tactic.
By targeting Israel he was hoping to force the
Israelis to retaliate against Iraq, which might have
broken the Coalition against him, by persuading
Arab states like Egypt and Syria to withdraw rather
than support the Zionists. But the ploy failed,
notably through the undercover work of the British
SAS, who neutralized many of the launch sites in the
Iraqi desert. General Schwarzkopf, the Coalition
commander-in-chief, later thanked the undercover
operatives 'for keeping Israel out of the war'.

But Saddam's track record as an international
criminal and a mass murderer gave him a political
advantage over democratic leaders like George
Bush, John Major and François Mitterrand. They
believed that Saddam was quite capable of committing a great crime, with chemical weapons or germ
warfare. His destruction of the Kuwaiti oilwells and
his release of oil into the Gulf show that they were
not wrong. Yet Saddam did not use the terror
weapons that he had used on his own Kurdish

people because he feared that he would be toppled
from power and put on trial by the Allies if he did.
However, the threat was a more potent weapon
than the use would have been. At the outset of the
conflict Mrs Thatcher had pressed for Saddam to
be tried by an international court as a war criminal,
but after her replacement by John Major the
question of trying Saddam Hussein was heard far
less often. In any case, the Americans were uneasy
on the question. They wanted to see him toppled
from power – even preferably killed – but they were
not prepared to make it a war aim. It was a weakness
of a democracy at war that it could not play by the
same rules as a brutal dictatorship.

Even after five weeks of Desert Storm, Coalition
intelligence continued to exaggerate the threat
posed by Iraq's ground forces. Even if less tanks
had been destroyed than Allied pilots claimed, it was
the morale of the Iraqi soldiers that had cracked.
Desertions were taking place on an incredible scale.
Many Iraqis were selling their Kalashnikov rifles in
Kuwait City to get their bus fare home. Raw recruits
had been put through a bombing experience
unparalleled in military history. One soldier who
fled to Basra remembered what it had been like:

Many were deaf from the bombing and there were
dozens with burns and appalling injuries. We saw many

dead and dying. Some of them had been injured as they fled across the minefields.

The Allies had no way of assessing how far Iraqi morale had fallen, and were not prepared to take any chances. Yet the Iraqi frontline troops were receiving no food or water. One platoon was only saved from dying of thirst by the heavy rain that fell. The Republican Guard units still showed skill in concealment, even if their fighting spirit was low. They often used inflatable dummy tanks – bought from Britain – to confuse the Allied flyers. One British pilot had the embarrassment of claiming the destruction of 13 tanks only to discover that he had shot up British fakes that had been used for training back home.

General Norman Schwarzkopf planned the ground offensive – Desert Sabre – on the basis of the intelligence reports he was continually fed. From these he believed that the Iraqi ground defences were still formidable and that the Republican Guard offered a potent threat. To keep the Iraqis guessing he maintained a substantial force of marines – some 17,000 – at sea off the coast of Kuwait, convincing Iraqi generals that there would be an amphibious landing by the Americans to retake Kuwait City. But this was never a real option if keeping casualties to a minimum was the aim: the seaward approaches to Kuwait had been heavily mined, and the British minesweepers could not have guaranteed a safe passage for the landing craft. Saddam was also hoping that the American marines, with the Saudis, Egyptians and Syrians, would make a frontal assault on his strong defences – barbed wire, oil-filled trenches and minefields, supported by tanks strongly dug in – all along the Saudi border with Kuwait. Schwarzkopf was preparing just such a strike, but intended as a feint, for his main strategy was to deliver a left hook by the mass of American, British and French armour from positions hundreds of miles to the west of Kuwait. The French units and the US 82nd Airborne Division were ordered to head deep into Iraq across the desert as far as Samawah to cut the road to Baghdad, and cut off the Iraqi line of retreat. US 101st Airborne and 24th Mechanized were targeted on Nasiriya on the Euphrates, swinging round to take Basra, Iraq's second city. The massive US 7th Corps with the British 1st Armoured Division – the 'Desert Rats' – were given the job of taking on the Republican Guard – the supposed elite of the Iraqi army – in northern Kuwait and south of Basra. Iraq's complete lack of air intelligence meant that this vast manoeuvre – a southpaw Schlieffen Plan – was able to take place without the Iraqis knowing a thing about it. Even the Soviets – with their spy satellites – kept faith with the Coalition and revealed nothing to Saddam Hussein.

When the assault began, on 23 February, the Americans' main fear was heavy casualties: they had 17,000 body-bags in Saudi Arabia, but were hoping to get away with less. In the event, casualties were fewer than on many NATO manoeuvres. When the US commander of the 101st Airborne reported to Schwarzkopf that he had reached the Euphrates valley, 'Stormin' Norman' was delighted, but hesitantly asked what the casualties had been. 'One report of one wounded soldier, sir,' was the reply.

Such was the intensity of the Coalition firepower that only the Republican Guard offered much resistance, and most of the Iraqi ground troops did everything they could to surrender, waving white flags, white towels and even underpants. One group had already built a POW camp in the desert, complete with wire, and were sitting inside it as the Allies approached. A lone British corporal, driving a tractor, accepted the surrender of 100 Iraqi

SMART WEAPONS

The Gulf War gave the United States and other NATO countries such as Britain and France the opportunity to demonstrate – for the first time in military history – high-technology weapons that seemed to have a mind of their own, capable as they were of hitting specific targets at great range. One of the most important of these 'smart weapons' was the BGM-109 Tomahawk cruise missile, originally designed to carry nuclear weapons but, in the Gulf, equipped with a 500 kg high-explosive warhead. During the war these TERCOM-guided (terrain contour matching) missiles were fired from the American battleships *Wisconsin* and *Missouri* and were targeted on sites deep inside Iraq and frequently in Baghdad itself. The Tomahawk missile is incredibly accurate – to within 10 yards after a 1,500-mile flight – and once launched it will follow an irregular flight pattern (based on 25 possible routes) to confuse enemy air defences. By using terrain contour matching the missile's computer is able to compare the terrain over which it is flying with its pre-launch programme and thereby correct its flight path. Once its sensors report that it has reached its target position it explodes. Pictures from the video cameras onboard showed time after time that the Tomahawk was striking buildings in Baghdad or even selected parts of buildings within inches of its pre-flight target.

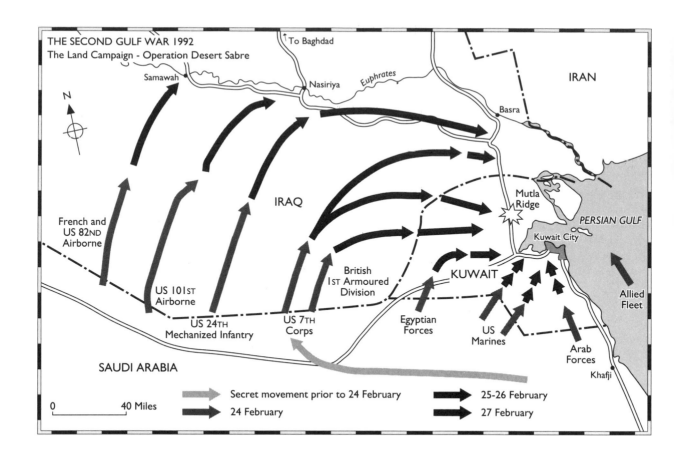

THE SECOND GULF WAR 1992
The Land Campaign - Operation Desert Sabre

To Baghdad

IRAN

Samawah

Nasiriya

Euphrates

Basra

IRAQ

Mutla Ridge

PERSIAN GULF

Kuwait City

French and US 82ND Airborne

US 101ST Airborne

US 24TH Mechanized Infantry

US 7TH Corps

British 1ST Armoured Division

KUWAIT

Egyptian Forces

US Marines

Allied Fleet

Arab Forces

SAUDI ARABIA

Khafji

0   40 Miles

Secret movement prior to 24 February

24 February

25-26 February

27 February

---

soldiers, forcing them to lie down in the sand by firing a shot over their heads – he received the Military Medal for his courage. On the Kuwait frontier, Iraqi troops came out to welcome the Americans and point out the minefields to them. But for every farce there was a tragedy. One officer reported the effect of Coalition bombing on one group of Iraqi soldiers:

Their whole world had been destroyed. The overpressure was so incredible. There was blood coming from their eyes and mouths. They had no will to do anything, their legs wouldn't work, they were paralysed. We'd see groups of soldiers who were aimless, ambling around, and you'd shout at them, but you wouldn't get through.

Where the M1A1 and Challenger tanks met the Soviet T-72s the result was always the same. The Iraqi tank crews were too slow or too inaccurate and the American depleted-uranium shells just 'melted them down'. These were not battles, they were massacres. Challengers picked off the old Soviet T-55s as if they were shooting clay pigeons. One American unit knocked out 50 Iraqi tanks in just 10 minutes.

On 25 February Saddam Hussein bowed to the inevitable and ordered a general withdrawal from

Kuwait. But this was easier said than done. Iraqi frontline troops – reservists and conscripts mainly – had no chance of getting through their own minefields and avoiding the massive Coalition forces, and so perhaps 100,000 of them surrendered. The Republican Guard, on the other hand, had been held far enough back to make escape possible. It was the troops occupying Kuwait City who suffered the worst disaster. Fleeing in every motorized vehicle imaginable – cars, buses, taxis, lorries, earthmovers, even fire engines – this occupying army was trapped on the Mutla Ridge and bombed by American planes for eight hours. Overhead American planes were stacked up, circling like airliners waiting for clearance to land at an airport. Some of the American pilots felt real hatred for their victims, the men who had raped, pillaged, tortured and murdered the peaceful inhabitants of a once-rich city. As one said, 'If I could have killed every Iraqi in Kuwait City, I would have.' Hundreds – perhaps thousands of vehicles – were destroyed with their passengers, but there was no pity for the Iraqis, who were, according to another pilot, 'The worst people on the face of the earth.'

Militarily the war had been a picnic, a 'no-contest walkover' in the words of one expert. But politically it had been a nightmare. The main problem was when to stop. For President Bush, General Colin Powell and Norman Schwarzkopf 'the sooner the better' seemed to be the motto – before anything could go wrong. They had avoided heavy casualties so far, so why go on and risk them in confrontation with a beaten and desperate Republican Guard? But not all America's Coalition partners agreed. The strongest voices raised against the 100-hours' deadline were those of the British. If the purpose of the war had been to clear the Iraqis out of Kuwait then the war should end now that that target had been achieved. However, Saddam Hussein still ruled in Baghdad and he still possessed substantial forces. It had been the threat of Iraqi militarism that had united the Coalition, even more than a commitment to free Kuwait. Prime Minister John Major appealed to Bush 'to go on a little bit longer and tie it all up'. But the Americans were too happy with their victory to question whether it was the decisive one that could have been achieved within the next 48 hours.

To the Americans Saddam Hussein was finished. No one could survive the humiliation he had suffered; surely his people would overthrow him? Having overestimated his military potential before the war they were now making the opposite error of underestimating his capacity to survive. Saddam

had not committed his Revolutionary Guard to a fight to the finish with the Americans precisely because he was thinking ahead, to how he would stay in power after the war. Four divisions had been stationed around Takrit, ready to come to his aid in Baghdad if needed. Without the Republican Guard he could not have survived the Shi'ite rising in the south and the Kurdish uprising in the north. The ruthless suppression of his own people was something at which Saddam excelled.

Had President Bush blundered when he suggested that the Iraqis 'take matters into their own hands' and overthrow Saddam, who, he declared, was 'worse than Hitler'? Had he given the Kurds reason to think he would support them in their rising? They clearly thought so, but then they were not students of American politics. Bush was a winner and wanted to stay that way. In spite of John Major's desire to finish the job and destroy Saddam, the Americans had their own reasons for wanting to see him survive, or if not him personally, then at

French troops with a Mistral rocket launcher. With the US 82nd Airborne, the French made up the westernmost thrust of Operation Desert Sabre, directed at the town of Samawah on the Euphrates. GAMMA

MAIN BATTLE TANKS OF OPERATION DESERT SABRE

M1 Abrams

Crew: 4
Speed: 45 mph
Armament: 1 x 120 mm gun; 1 x 50 mm calibre MG; 1 x 7.62 mm MG

The M1 is equipped with state-of-the-art Chobham armour, making it impervious to attack by enemy anti-tank missiles. It is fast, mobile and heavily armoured. The M1A1 has depleted uranium in its armour, doubling its protection, and making the Abrams the best tank in the world.

Challenger

Crew: 4
Speed: 35 mph
Armament: 1 x 120 mm gun; 2 x 7.62 mm MG

Like the M1 equipped with Chobham armour and the 120 mm gun, the Challenger is a powerful tank, although its reputation in NATO was not high due to its poor fire-control system. For the Gulf War its armour was increased to face the Iraqi anti-tank missiles and the T-72 tank.

T-72

Crew: 3
Speed: 37 mph
Armament: 1 x 125 mm gun; 1 x 12.7 mm MG; 1 x 7.62 mm MG.

The latest type of Soviet tank, dating from the late 1960s, was employed by the best of the Iraqi units but was no match for the Abrams or the Challenger. Its main gun has a shorter range and its armour (250 mm thick) is only half as strong as that of its rivals.

least someone like him: a military dictator of the Sunni sect, who would maintain Iraq's borders, resist pressure from Syria, Turkey and the Kurds to destabilize Iraq, and prevent the spread of Iranian Shi'ite fundamentalism.

If Desert Sabre was not decisive it was because the Americans did not want it to be. American tanks sat and watched the Hammurabi Division of the Republican Guard make its way back to Baghdad with 800 modern tanks and 800 guns, enough to rout any popular rising but also enough to discourage predatory neighbours from further interference in Iraqi affairs. With a force like that Saddam Hussein could sleep easily in his bed. After all, he had faced up to the world's greatest power and survived. Certainly his people had suffered – possibly 8000–15,000 Iraqi soldiers and 45,000 civilians had died – but then when had Saddam Hussein worried about what happened to his own people? The important thing was he had survived. He had lost a battle but he might still win the war. In the words of one Omani minister, 'In the moment of triumph, when the Americans could have imposed a little bit of their new world order here in Arabia, they didn't. What happened? They got cold feet.'

Index